LEADERS
OF THE
MEXICAN
AMERICAN
GENERATION

LEADERS
OF THE
MEXICAN
AMERICAN
GENERATION

Biographical Essays

edited by

ANTHONY QUIROZ

foreword by
Arnoldo De León

UNIVERSITY PRESS OF COLORADO
Boulder

Published by University Press of Colorado
5589 Arapahoe Avenue, Suite 206C
Boulder, Colorado 80303

 The University Press of Colorado is a proud member of
Association of American University Presses.

The University Press of Colorado is a cooperative publishing enterprise supported, in part,
by Adams State University, Colorado State University, Fort Lewis College, Metropolitan State
University of Denver, Regis University, University of Colorado, University of Northern Colorado,
Utah State University, and Western State Colorado University.

∞ This paper meets the requirements of the ANSI / NISO Z39.48–1992 (Permanence of Paper).

ISBN: 978-1-60732-336-5 (cloth)
ISBN: 978-1-60732-525-3 (paperback)
ISBN: 978-1-60732-337-2 (ebook)

Chapter 2 was previously published as "Alice Dickerson Montemayor: Feminism and Mexican
American Politics in the 1930s," in *Writing on the Range: Race, Class, and Culture in the Women's West*,
edited by Susan Armitage and Elizabeth Jameson (Norman: University of Oklahoma Press, 1997),
435–56. Chapter 4 was previously published as "Jovita González Mireles: A Sense of History and
Homeland," in *Latina Legacies: Identity, Biography, Community*, edited by Vicki L. Ruiz and Virginia
Sánchez Korrol (Oxford: Oxford University Press, 2005), 158–74. Chapter 5 was previously pub-
lished as "Of Poetics and Politics: The Border Journeys of Luisa Moreno," in *Women's Labor in the
Global Economy: Speaking in Multiple Voices*, edited by Sharon Harley (New Brunswick, NJ: Rutgers
University Press, 2007), 28–45. All are reprinted with permission.

Library of Congress Cataloging-in-Publication Data
Quiroz, Anthony, 1958–
  Leaders of the Mexican American generation : biographical essays / Anthony Quiroz.
    pages cm
  ISBN 978-1-60732-336-5 (cloth) — ISBN 978-1-60732-525-3 (pbk) — ISBN 978-1-60732-337-2 (ebook)
  1. Mexican Americans—Politics and government—20th century. 2. Mexican Americans—
Biography. 3. Mexican Americans—Civil rights—History—20th century. 4. Southwest, New—
Race relations—History—20th century. 5. Intellectuals—United States—Biography. 6. Social
reformers—United States—Biography. 7. Political activists—United States—Biography. I. Title.
  E184.M5Q58 2014
  973'.046872—dc23

                    2014024524

Cover photographs (clockwise from top left): Jovita González; José de la Luz Sáenz; Luisa Moreno;
John J. Herrera; Ernesto Galarza; Vicente and Maria Ximenes; Alice Dickerson Montemayor; Gus García

Contents

Intellectuals and Ethnic Consciousness

Legal, Political, and Labor Activists

Foreword

When I first entered the history profession some four decades ago, the most pressing question in Chicano history was did Mexican Americans have a history? According to the extant social science literature of the period, then under a scathing assault by Octavio Romano, professor of anthropology at the University of California, Berkeley (and others), they did not. Sociologists, anthropologists, educators, and psychologists, as an academic community, contended that due to deficient cultural values, Mexican Americans had seldom been movers in history.

Over the span of my teaching career, the historiographic outpouring in Mexican American history has been such that no rational person would today entertain such an inane question. Currently, those who research and write Mexican American history, like their counterparts in the larger profession, concern themselves with matters of gender, demography, identity formation, cultural change, and the like. They engage in discourses surrounding whiteness studies or comparative history or debate the value of new interpretative propositions and insightful analytical techniques or deliberate the meaning of nuance in history, to name only a few points of interest. In studying newer subjects and utilizing innovative methods in research and writing, the cadre of Mexican American historians in Texas has succeeded to the extent that today Tejano scholarship is recognized not only as reflecting the best work being done in Texas history but as leading the way in interpreting the state's past.

Despite historiographic progress, some old topics remain intriguing. Several reasons may explain this enduring interest: perhaps research on them never fully ended, perhaps their significance in history remains relevant today, or maybe the subject continues to elicit debate as to its place in the larger narrative. This is the case with the cohort generally labeled the "Mexican American generation"—the subject of this collection.

Numerous questions still surround this topic. Was there really a Mexican American generation? Most historians allow that a corps of Mexican American leaders, from around the 1930s to the early 1960s, did pursue a civil rights agenda that called for integration and accommodation and who did sincerely believe in the possibility of achieving the American promise. But did not similar sentiments prevail in Mexican American *colonias* before the 1930s, perhaps even in the nineteenth century? Recent publications find the wellspring for the Mexican American generation (at least in Texas) in events such as the Plan de Diego (1915), the Mexican Revolution (1910–1920), and World War I (1914–1919). In other words, progressive thinking somewhat akin to that manifest by the 1930s existed before the Depression decade. Were the spokespersons of the 1950s, on the other hand, transitional figures who set the stage for the Hispanic generation (post-1980), which advocates centrist politics and Americanization? Asked another way, were participants in the Mexican American generation that unique in the platform they advanced, and does their story confine itself to those three decades?

Also, some would ask if the generational paradigm is nothing more than an academic construct, a tool useful to historians who like history divided neatly into readily manageable eras with identifiable features. In *Historia: The Literary Making of Chicana and Chicano History* (College Station: Texas A&M University Press, 2001), Louis Gerard Mendoza maintains that the model does not mirror reality for it fails to capture the experiences of all segments of the Mexican American population. Because historical monographs on the Mexican American generation focus on the middle class, on professionals, and on the ideology of males (who are in the forefront of executing political strategies), they do not—unlike the creative literature of the 1930s through the 1960s—acknowledge the presence of women, the working class, grass-roots leaders, and other subaltern constituencies whose experiences differ starkly from those of their more privileged contemporaries. If these latter elements are considered, the concept of the Mexican American generation becomes untenable.

Others wonder if the Mexican American generation was genuinely significant. Outside of Texas, this generation appears not to have the same appeal as ethnicity, sexuality, urbanization, religion, education, literary expression, and historical memory. As today's younger scholars investigate these topics or undertake explorations of new areas in Mexican American history—transnational influences, globalization, and the browning of America come to mind—they tend to consider the Mexican American generation as a subject belonging to an earlier historiographic age—or put another way, they diminish its historic importance.

In today's flourishing scholarship, with its fascinating options for studying history, some would expectedly raise questions about the best analytical mode to use in investigating the topic. Are some of the new concepts—interdisciplinary frameworks, postmodernism, modernization theory, the world-systems model, and related perspectives—useful in interpreting the subject? Is a gendered analysis or a gendered discourse essential? Does the traditional narrative avenue work best? What of the biographical method?

This collection offers answers to many of these questions, among them the one concerning the actual existence of a Mexican American generation. The weight of the collection adduces the fact that during this time period a circle of prominent men and women, by their leadership, civic involvement, and proactive stances, constituted a generational cohort. Then, of course, their successors (those of the Chicano generation, 1960s to 1970s) recognized their presence in history; for militants, however, members of the Mexican American generation had gone about trying to improve conditions for *la raza* in a foolish way. They had been too much the accommodationists, too trusting of mainstream politicians, and too confident that the system would respond to Mexican American needs.

Other factors aside from leadership characteristics mark the Mexican American generation as being a force in history (and not the concoction of academicians). While the creative literature may not depict characters such as those associated with the Mexican American generation, other indicators do confirm the peculiarities of the age. Certainly during and after World War II, Mexican American communities throughout the country became distinct from those of previous generations. Young Mexican Americans from different strata became increasingly educated and bilingual. Their comportment reflected biculturation, as witnessed in their outlook toward citizenship, patriotic duty, and lifestyle as well as their discipline and cultural tastes. They endorsed the agenda for better schooling, social integration, and voting rights as necessary to fulfill their aspirations as Mexican Americans. The leaders of the Mexican American generation embodied these attitudes.

This collection also answers questions about significance. Certainly the Mexican American generation improved the Mexican American condition. Admittedly, its leadership had not overturned the old social order (as noted above, such was the criticism of 1960s and 1970s militants), but they had made inroads toward that end. Because of their efforts, Mexican Americans could no longer be excluded from jury duty, nor could school districts legally segregate Mexican American students. Their protests against segregation toppled Jim Crow for Mexican Americans by the 1960s, and their struggle for voter rights helped in the demise of the poll tax and other voting restrictions. Involvement in the Viva Kennedy clubs brought Mexican American issues to national attention after 1960. Mexican American leaders gained momentum in seeing that Mexican American labor organizing was integrated into the larger US labor movement.

The collection further suggests at least one analytical path to studying the Mexican American generation: that of biography. This approach (at least for the moment) appears a practical option for settling the argument as to whether there lived from the 1930s through the 1960s a group of individuals with common backgrounds and goals who collectively fit the designation of the "Mexican American generation." Several articles included herein detail the mutual characteristics of these figures (both women and men) as well as their shared vision of America. The biographical venue also allows leaders from different parts of the country to receive deserved recognition.

Leaders of the Mexican American Generation: Biographical Essays, then, represents more than a chronicle of personalities who left a mark in Mexican American history. At the very least, the collection hints that there must be historical actors in other time periods (aside from the 1930–1960 epoch) that deserve individual scholarly treatment. It indicates that commitment to beliefs does not restrict itself to any one state in the union; women and men from Arizona and New Mexico displayed valor in staring down injustices the same as their counterparts in the more populated states of Texas and California. Then, of course, it acts to silence those who once said Mexican Americans had no history.

Arnoldo De León, Angelo State University

Preface

The American GI Forum (AGIF) celebrated its sixtieth anniversary in March 2008 at its executive board meeting in Corpus Christi, Texas, and again in September at its general meeting, also in Corpus Christi. I had the unique privilege of organizing a day-and-a-half symposium of scholars who had written on the history of the AGIF as part of the March meeting. Born of the discrimination of the early twentieth century, the group's founding members marked a new direction in an ongoing struggle for equality in the United States of America. Building upon a growing sense of patriotism and belonging, AGIF members, both singly and in partnership with other groups such as the League of United Latin American Citizens (LULAC), began a renewed effort to ensconce their people in society, promote education for Mexican American youth, end jury discrimination, gain representation on draft boards, and otherwise integrate themselves as contributing and equal members of American society. These actors wanted to claim their rightful place as first-class citizens on all fronts.

The panel of scholars gave back to the forum members their understanding of the group's history. I was struck by the Forumeers' animated spirit in engaging the speakers during that interchange. Agreeing with some of the speakers' points and contesting others, I was impressed by the depths of the seriousness of the approximately fifty or so executive board members who attended our sessions. They made the panelists and me keenly aware of the significance of the history we all write. Sometimes scholars get so wrapped up in speaking to each other that we overlook the importance of historical actors themselves. This audience did not let that happen. Questioning our interpretations and asking questions in order to clarify our facts, they kept us honest and helped us hone our own understandings of their past.

Prior to the symposium I had been toying with the idea of putting together a collection of biographical essays featuring key leaders of what some Mexican American scholars refer to as the Mexican American Generation—a period bounded by the years from 1920 to 1965. My experience at the symposium convinced me to pursue this project. I asked all of the panel members to contribute to a collection of such pieces. Some agreed and appear here (Michelle Hall Kells, Carl Allsup, Tom Kreneck, Pat Carroll, and myself). Others had too many other prior commitments and, unfortunately, could not take part. I then embarked on a long process of seeking other contributors. Cold calling some folks and asking contributors for leads to others, I sought to gather a group of research that would showcase the contributions and significance of this generation of Mexican American activists, all of whom deserved to have their stories told.

In conducting this search I looked for works on the obvious key players of this period: J. Luz Sáenz, Alonso S. Perales, Alice Dickerson Montemayor, Jovita González Mireles, Luisa Moreno, Félix Longoria, Héctor P. García, attorney Gus García (no relation to Hector), Vicente Ximenes, Eduardo Roybal, John J. Herrera, Ralph Estrada, and Ernesto Galarza. While by no means comprehensive, this is a respectable list of contributors to the ideals and actions of this generation. Their arguments, their worldviews, and their actions all shaped the character and identity of this generation. Whether arguing in court, writing, producing reports for governmental agencies, organizing workers, holding public office, forming new associations, or otherwise resisting the status quo, these individuals identified both the core values and the foci of the generation while also demonstrating its diversity.

I would like to thank all the authors for their contributions to this collection. I would also like to thank my editor at the University Press of Colorado, Darrin Pratt, and his wonderful staff, especially Jessica d'Arbonne, Laura Furney, and Diane Bush. Also helpful in conceptualizing this anthology were Linda Kerber, Arnoldo De León, Carlos Blanton, and David Blanke as well as the anonymous readers for UPC. All of their comments on this manuscript made it vastly better. I owe a debt to the fine staff at the Houston Metropolitan Research Center and to Michael Rowell, Ceil Venable, and especially Grace Charles of the Special Collections and Archives at the Mary and Jeff Bell Library at Texas A&M University–Corpus Christi for their assistance. I would also like to thank my colleagues at Texas A&M University–Corpus Christi for being so patient with a part-time chair as I put the finishing touches on this work. As importantly, I would like to thank the contributors for their dedication and patience to this project even when it appeared as if the project might not be able to be completed—for reasons they understand. I would also like to thank Erin Cofer, a bright, talented graduate student in our program, for all her editorial and typographical help. Finally, I would like to thank my loving wife for putting up with my crankiness as this work wound down to completion. She is truly an angel on earth.

LEADERS

OF THE

MEXICAN
AMERICAN
GENERATION

Introduction

ANTHONY QUIROZ

The serious, scholarly study of Mexican American history is a relatively recent development. Begun by a handful of researchers in the 1920s, the field grew slowly through the 1950s and expanded rapidly after the 1960s to the present. Through their research, scholars of the Mexican American historical experience have both contributed to our understandings of historical processes and discovered new directions for historical inquiry. Their findings have shed light on the broader sweeps of American history by showing the symbiotic relationship between Mexican Americans and the rest of the country. Mexican Americans were generally ignored, marginalized, and disrespected in the traditional canon of American history until the late twentieth century. But as their numbers grew, so too did the number of scholars interested in studying them. Mexican Americans have now become more firmly entrenched in scholarly discussions about historical issues such as race and ethnicity, gender relationships, class, politics, education, economics, culture, and in an ongoing negotiation of the meaning of *American*. This book contributes to that growing body of literature by providing students

DOI: 10.5876/9781607323372.c000

of Mexican American history with a compilation of biographies of key Mexican Americans active from about 1920 through the 1960s. The purpose of this work is to offer readers a concise biographical overview of some of the actors who made Mexican American history during this period and to cast them in the context of their times in order to shed light on the historical significance of their contributions.

The folks who became socially active during this period inherited a social climate of hostility based on deeply rooted, pervasive racism. Anti-Mexican sentiments were born in the nineteenth century—first in Texas in the aftermath of the Texas Revolution against the Mexican government in 1835–1836 and across the entire American Southwest after the end of the Mexican-American War in 1848. Gradually dispossessed of their land, Mexican-descent farmers and ranchers experienced downward mobility throughout the nineteenth and early twentieth centuries. Poor *trabajadores* (workers) remained mired in an economic system that disallowed opportunities for upward mobility. Anglo employers saw them as lazy, incompetent, and dishonest, and they relegated these laborers to low-wage, low-skill manual jobs. Those with agricultural skills could find work on farms and ranches. With the loss of land and opportunity came a degraded social and political status. Mexican Americans had been successfully relegated to second-class citizenship by 1900.[1]

Immigration from Mexico remained slow but increased somewhat during the late nineteenth and early twentieth centuries due to the increasing resentment of the Porfiriato. The reign of Porfirio Diaz, the powerful president of Mexico from the 1880s through the Mexican Revolution that began in 1910, was marked by increased investment in Mexico by Europeans and Americans and an improved economy. But these successes came at a steep cost. Peasant farmers were displaced from their traditional lands and the economic prosperity was not equally distributed. The rich became wealthier while the poor and middling sorts declined financially. The revolution (which ended in 1921) and its aftermath sent over 1 million immigrants to the United States between 1910 and 1930. These immigrants came from all socioeconomic classes, although most were peasants. Mexicans who crossed over during these decades originally imagined that they would return to Mexico once the social unrest died down. The poor took low-paying jobs in cities and the countryside. Many middle-class émigrés opened their own businesses. Over time, many immigrants decided to stay, thereby boosting the numbers of the Mexican-descent population. Through subsequent decades, they and their children adhered increasingly to a developing identity as Mexican Americans.[2]

Both internal and external forces shaped this new self-image. Internally, some Mexican Americans had been promoting an Americanized identity as early as the late 1800s. Ana Martinez-Catsam has shown how Pablo Cruz used the Spanish-language newspaper in San Antonio, *El Regidor*, to both criticize the Porfiriato and promote a stronger sense of American citizenship around the turn of the century.[3] The same period saw the small but steady growth of a middle class comprised of shop owners (barbers, shoe repairman, neighborhood shopkeepers, and the like) and educators. Members of this segment of the population began to see their interests as resting on the northern side of the Rio Grande rather than on the southern side. As such, they gradually developed a sense of belonging in the United States and a desire to gain access to the American dream as full citizens.

The Mexican American worldview was reinforced by the experiences of World War I, the Great Depression, and World War II. By virtue of the draft and voluntary military service, Mexican Americans were, for the first time in American history, officially included on a large scale in a truly American project: making the world safe for democracy. Once the war ended, these veterans and their friends and family members believed that they had all earned the right to equal access to education, employment, and public places such as restaurants, beaches, and movie theaters. But the unrelenting pressure of discrimination crushed these hopes. Nothing changed for the mass of Mexican Americans in the post–World War I years. Indeed, the Great Depression witnessed the mass deportation of up to a half million Mexicans and Mexican Americans to Mexico. Seen as a drain on the limited welfare system and as competition for a decreasing number of jobs, Mexicans either voluntarily returned to Mexico or were rounded up in sweeps in several US cities between 1929 and 1939. Unfortunately, some of the people sent "back" were American citizens. Some were children born here who were legal citizens by birthright, and others were adults who were either born here or who had gained citizenship. But in the zeal to rid the nation of unwanted burdens, such differences went unnoticed. The bombing of Pearl Harbor on December 7, 1941, brought the United States into World War II. A quarter million to a half million Mexican Americans served in World War II. As such, they met other individuals from other parts of the country where Mexicans faced far less discrimination. They gained new skills, traveled the nation and the world, and returned home after the war as changed men. But, yet again, home had not changed in their absence. Their children could still not attend Anglo schools. Restaurants displayed signs that read "No Mexicans" or worse. In many places they were disallowed to serve on juries.[4]

Several civil rights organizations emerged out of these decades of social ferment. The League of United Latin American Citizens (LULAC) was created in Corpus Christi, Texas, in 1929. Members of LULAC—an amalgam of the League of Latin-American Citizens, the Order of Knights of America, and the Order of Sons of America—were inspired by the Mexican American community's efforts to defend freedom in the Great War. Originating in and led by the developing middle class, LULAC challenged various types of segregation and employment discrimination. But the Great Depression severely cut into its abilities to wage war on social injustice. After World War II, however, LULAC regained its pre-Depression momentum and found a new ally in the American GI Forum (AGIF), created by Dr. Héctor P. García in Corpus Christi, in 1948. Originally conceived as a veteran's rights group, the AGIF was quickly drawn into civil rights activities, a role that came to define them throughout the next several decades. At the same time and after, other groups, such as the Community Service Organization, were forming in California. These types of organizations filed successful lawsuits against segregated school districts, brought an end to jury discrimination, and promoted education at all levels (elementary through graduate school). They expressed through their publications (such as the AGIF's monthly organ, *The Forumeer*) an identity as equal citizens deserving of the same rights and responsibilities as Anglo citizens. Not all activists belonged to organizations such as LULAC or the AGIF. Others were writers, teachers, academicians, and attorneys. All of them struggled to bring about an end to a multitiered society comprised of gradations of citizenship based on racial and ethnic definitions.[5]

The desire to attain citizenship was at the heart of their efforts. Officially, citizenship can be understood from a governmental perspective. One is a citizen of the United States by birthright or through naturalization. Citizenship carries rights and responsibilities such as voting, having to obey the laws, and submitting to selective service and jury duty. But citizenship's meaning runs far deeper in the social and cultural layers of society. Natalia Molina shows how citizenship was legally defined in literal black-and-white terms in the 1920s and 1930s; to be allowed citizenship, one had to fit one of those two racial categories. Such thinking denied citizenship to outside groups, including Asians and Asian Indians. Mexicans, however, proved a thorny lot. Anti-immigration forces argued that they were clearly African or Indian or a mixture and therefore did not qualify to be called Americans. Even though the nation embraced strong anti-immigrant attitudes, their desire to prevent Mexicans from gaining citizenship was trumped in Texas in the 1920s by the larger "need to preserve diplomatic and trade relations with Mexico, as well as the State Department's commitment to protecting American-owned oil properties there." As I argued in *Claiming Citizenship: Mexican Americans in Victoria, Texas*, citizenship also was defined by the acceptance of specific values (Christianity, family, patriotism), practices (political participation), traits (responsibility, loyalty), and beliefs (superiority of capitalism, dangers of socialism). The acceptance of these sensibilities did not mean a desire to abandon one's Mexican heritage. Rather, it reflected a desire to create a complicated bicultural identity. This vision of citizenship dominated the Mexican American community throughout the 1940s and 1950s.

Struggles for equality continued through the 1960s and 1970s. Despite the gains made in the previous decades, social unrest, largely driven by the Vietnam War, marked the 1960s and 1970s. Mexican Americans found themselves caught up in a national whirlwind of agitation from African Americans, women, Native Americans, gays, and young people. While they benefited from passage of the Civil Rights Act of 1964 and the Voting Rights Act of 1965, Mexican-descent Americans still faced social, economic, and political discrimination. Although life had improved by the end of the twentieth century, Mexican Americans had not yet achieved full equality as equal citizens while poverty, crime, and other problems continued to plague portions of the community. This wide swath of Mexican American history, as just described, is long and complex. For it to make sense, it must be dissected.

Historians periodize. We examine wide sweeps of history and identify periods that offer explanatory insight into the human condition. We may speak of decades or centuries, but these are artificial structures imposed on human action. By focusing on the ways in which people think and act, scholars can more substantively discover meaningful patterns of behavior. In the preface to the third edition of *Mexican Americans in Texas: A Brief History*, Arnoldo De León notes that researchers of Chicano history take different positions on the matter of periodization. Mainstream writers who researched and published works prior to the appearance of Mexican American history in the early 1970s focused primarily on colonial Spain and early Mexican history. They tended to believe that Spanish-Mexicans had a history only until the Spanish or Mexican eras ended in the borderlands (1821 or 1848, respectively) and then ceased being actors. De León notes further that generally, historians have differed on what specific date denotes the beginning of "Mexican American history." One school argues that Mexican American history began in 1848 with the signing of the Treaty of Guadalupe Hidalgo, which ceded the American Southwest to the United States following the Mexican-American War—that event transformed Mexicans into American citizens. A subset within this group argues for 1836 as the start of Mexican American history because of the successful Texas Revolution against Mexico. For another set of scholars, Mexican American history has its origins toward the end of the nineteenth or early in the twentieth century, when increased immigration from Mexico gave rise to a large presence of Mexican Americans in the United States. To this school, immigration, class, and conflict with corporate America now became the most salient identifiers of Mexican American history. De León explains that a third body of researchers posits that Mexican American history is part of a continuum dating back to the colonial Spanish period. These authors stress a connection of events from the time of the Spanish arrival in the borderlands to the present.[6] By studying this long period of time, historians address the shortcomings of researchers who wrote and published prior to 1970, demonstrating that Mexican Americans had a distinct historical experience, apart from Anglos who were late arrivals in the borderlands. And while we cannot technically discuss Mexican Americans until after 1848, the people, the culture, and the traditions that define Mexican Americans trace back to the *mestizaje*.

In line with this train of thought, Juan Gómez-Quiñones lays out the following structure: "1600–1800, settlement; 1800–1830 florescence; 1830–1848 conflict; 1848–1875 resistance; 1875–1900, subordination." The twentieth century falls into the second part and is organized as 1900–1920, a period of emigration and urbanization, and 1920–1941, a time marked by "intense repression, and major labor and political organizing." He sees the World War II era as an interregnum, but the era from 1945 to 1965 witnessed a Mexican American population that sought inclusion through compromise. The Chicano movement marked the years from 1965 to 1971.[7]

Regardless of the varying views of the historical origins of a Mexican American people, historians have tended to follow a general periodization somewhat akin to the one laid out by Manuel G. Gonzales and Cynthia M. Gonzales in their book *En Aquel Entonces: Readings in Mexican-American History*. The authors explain Mexican American history in terms of the creation of a Mexican American people (1598–1846); racial tensions (1846–1900); migration and labor (1900–1940); the emergence of a middle class (1940–1965); and the Chicano movement and after (1965–2000).[8] Theirs is an identity-driven model.

This anthology, however, speaks to a generational periodization of twentieth-century Mexican American history. Many scholars have employed this model, which identifies (with some variation) the following basic structure: 1848–1900, conquered generation; 1900–1930, immigrant generation; 1930–1960, Mexican American generation; 1960–1980, Chicano generation; 1980 to the present, Hispanic generation. All the actors in this anthology were active during a period that has been designated as the Mexican American generation.

When studying Mexican American history, the analytical tool called a generational model offers scholars valuable interpretive insights. Rodolfo Alvarez first proposed the idea of applying a generational periodization to organize Mexican American history in 1973 in "The Psycho-Historical and Socioeconomic Development of the Chicano Community in the United States." Alvarez defines a *generation* as "a critical number of persons, in a broad but delimited age group, [that] had more or less the same socialization experiences because they lived at a particular time under more or less the same constraints imposed by a dominant United States society." Alvarez argues that Mexican Americans' history could be traced via four generations. First came the creation generation, which began in Texas in 1836 but spread to the rest of the Southwest with the end of the Mexican-American War and lasted until the turn of the century. The migrant generation occurred "after 1900 and before World War II." The Mexican American generation was defined largely by the experience of World War II, beginning "somewhere around the time of the Second World War, and increasing in importance up to the war in Vietnam." Alvarez dates the Chicano generation as occurring from the late 1960s through publication of his essay. For Alvarez, each generation was defined by a shared experience as defined by psychohistorical and socioeconomic factors as well as common responses to those conditions.[9]

In his 1987 book, *Mexican Americans: Leadership, Ideology, and Identity, 1930–1960*, Mario T. García built upon Alvarez's construct by drawing from a broad array of sources to further argue for the interpretive value of a generational approach to historical study. Although the general outline of the generations is similar to that of Alvarez, García's formulation is driven not by psychohistorical factors so much as similar political, social, and economic environments that led to the creation of specific self-definitions. García explains that generational periods are "specific to a certain period which trigger a particular political response or responses by a collection of individuals who come of political age during this time." He asserts that a political generation is not simply a result of history; it also becomes an active agent shaping the direction of history.[10]

This work is founded on the premise that García's concept is still sound, on two fronts in particular. First, each distinct generation existed in a discrete social, cultural, and political environment. Each generation also came to represent a specific identity that expressed its definition of citizenship within the context of that milieu. But García does not imply that these temporal boundaries are concrete. This generation was built on the experiences of those that preceded it, just as it set the stage for events that followed. As discussed earlier in this introduction, the intellectual roots of the Mexican American generation were planted in the late nineteenth century. The labor activism of this era predated the class consciousness of the Chicano movement.

Second, García emphasizes the need to understand the complexity of this generation. Contrary to later scholarly critics of this period's activists, García shows that leaders came from multiple backgrounds and had varying agendas. David G. Gutiérrez, in his 1993 essay "Significant to Whom? Mexican Americans and the History of the American West," demonstrates that the oppression of previous generations informed and inspired writers of the Mexican American generation. Gutiérrez notes that the American story of westward movement was couched in terms of Mexican weakness and inferiority, which justified American expansion and subsequent discrimination. Further justification for the marginalization of Mexicans was the prevalence of stereotypes that homogenized Mexicans in negative terms—and Anglo-Americans in positive ones. But through their scholarship, individuals such as Ernesto Galarza, Jovita González, George I. Sánchez, and Arthur Campa, among others, proved that people of Mexican descent were no more homogeneous than any other group of people. This was a significant discovery on the road to combatting racism based on commonly accepted stereotypes.[11]

Informed by that argument, this collection applies a similarly malleable definition of *generation*. Yes, this cohort involved members of organizations such as LULAC, which was generally led by the middle class, or the AGIF, whose members hailed mostly from the working class. Yet both organizations made claims to equality based on patriotism and fealty to the nation's history as well as to its political and economic systems. At the same time, the efforts of labor activists such as Ernesto Galarza and Luisa Moreno targeted workers' immediate material needs rather than ideological struggles over definitions of citizenship. What unites this diverse array of people is a commitment to securing improved living and working conditions for Mexicans and Mexican Americans. Their ideas and actions marked the onset of a civil rights struggle that continues to the present.

As such, the Mexican American generation provides the first key to understanding the intellectual and civic transformation of a people who initially considered themselves primarily Mexican to those who now created a bicultural identity and saw themselves increasingly as Americans of Mexican descent. The emergence of this new vision shaped the course of Mexican American actions to the present day. Throughout subsequent decades, the Chicano movement and now the Hispanic generation have remained true in some measure to the basic ideals laid out by this group. To be sure, the Chicano movement fueled an increase in production of new forms of art, music, scholarship, and activism. But throughout the decades, Mexican Americans have continued to act through labor organizations and political activism, much as was done during the period under study in this work. Actions of the Hispanic generation have further contributed to our political empowerment and led to the increased presence of Mexican Americans (and Latinos in general) in the popular culture through an increased presence in sports, film, music, business, education, and politics. And although the Mexican American community has become more diverse over time, many of the values, practices, traits, and beliefs that defined citizenship for this generation remain relevant. One useful way to learn about the importance of this generation is through studying biographies of its leaders.

Biography has held a warm place in the public's heart as a form of historical production. History buffs are often fanatical about collecting biographies of important politicians or military figures. Public and school libraries house voluminous collections of lively stories of past lives and their excitement, drama, and contributions to social progress. Nonprofessional historians, who generally tended to write uncritical hagiographies that enforced lessons about patriotism, religiosity, hard work, or other values, frequently produced these works. Even when written by academic historians, biographies sometimes focused too narrowly on their subjects to the detriment of deeper historical analysis. And so, as David Nasaw laments in his introduction to the *American Historical Review*'s "*AHR* Roundtable: Historians and Biography," "Biography remains the profession's unloved stepchild, occasionally but grudgingly let in the door, more often shut outside with the riffraff."[12]

But Lois Banner notes in her contribution to this same roundtable, "At its best, biography like history, is based on archival research, interweaves historical categories and methodologies, reflects current political and theoretical concerns and raises complex issues of truth and proof."[13] A truly well-written biography is steeped in rigorous research and holds itself to the same demands of truth claims as traditional analytical history. Indeed, she demonstrates how in the process of writing a comparative biography of Ruth Benedict and Margaret Mead (two twentieth-century anthropologists who were also friends and lovers), she had to become adept with the fields of

intellectual history, the history of the professions, and the history of the concepts of race and racism. To write about Benedict's upbringing, I had to learn about the history of the Baptist Church. To write about Mead's religious beliefs, I had to learn about the Episcopal Church. To understand their anthropological fieldwork, I had to study the Pueblo Indians and the tribal indigenous people in Samoa and New Guinea. To elucidate Mead and Benedict's individual selves, sexually different from the norm, I had to investigate the history of lesbianism and bisexuality and to master "queer theory." Then I had to read and analyze the 50,000 letters, documents, and other written materials about their lives in the Margaret Mead Papers at the Library of Congress, and figure out how to intertwine the story of their individual lives with the times in which they lived.[14]

Thus, one can easily see that a conscientious, serious work of scholarly biography can do more than tell interesting stories about people's lives. It can help explain the nature of social relationships and the interplay between individuals and their environments. Just as broad topics such as "the presidency" or "the Chicano movement" and narrower ones such as "community studies" offer their own specific types of historical insights, so too can biography bring its own kind of light to our understandings of the past.

Students of Mexican American topics, like other historians, largely ignored the genre of biography. An early biographical work came about when Americo Paredes published *With His Pistol in His Hand: A Border Ballad and its Hero* in 1958.[15] This seminal work not only began the process of unraveling the imagined mythology surrounding the Texas Rangers, it also focused on the role of a South Texas rancher who suddenly became an outlaw because of a misunderstanding between him and local law enforcement agents. The story of Gregorio Cortez is telling because it gets at the nature of relations between Anglos and Mexicans in Texas in early twentieth-century Texas. And it does so in a critical way that challenges much of the mystique surrounding Texas and western history. Paredes's work, while influential in its own right, did not ignite a blaze of biographical studies. In 1973 Juan Gómez-Quiñones published *Sembradores: Ricardo Flores Magón y el Partido Liberal Mexicano: A Eulogy and Critique.*[16] Biography as a central focus remained marginal until the next decade.

The field has seen an increase in biographical publications since the late 1980s. Perhaps one of the most prolific producers of individual biographies or collections of individual papers has been Mario T. García, who has produced no less than eight book-length works of individual biographies, collections of biographies, edited memoirs, and autobiographies as well as paper collections.[17] García's body of work sustains the argument that biography can serve as a valuable method of historical study by locating the subject squarely in the context of the times. As noted above, García's book on the Mexican American generation strongly influenced this work. Apart from García's impressive body of work, a short list of just some of the other book-length biographies produced since 1990 includes *César Chávez: A Triumph of Spirit* by Richard Griswold del Castillo and Richard A. Garcia (1995); Thomas H. Kreneck's work on Houston entrepreneur and LULAC leader Felix Tijerina (2001); Ignacio M. García's *Héctor P. García: In Relentless Pursuit of Justice* (2002); and Elliott Young's *Catarino Garza's Revolution on the Texas-Mexico Border* (2004).[18]

Apart from full-length biographies, scholars have produced shorter works that have appeared in various types of collections. In her latest work, *No*

Mexicans, Women, or Dogs Allowed: The Rise of the Mexican American Civil Rights Movement (2009), Cynthia E. Orozco offers a chapter dedicated to brief overviews of the lives of LULAC's founders. Biographies of Mexican Americans have also appeared in anthologies centered on women's history, such as Vicki L. Ruiz and Virginia Sánchez Korrol's *Latina Legacies: Identity, Biography, and Community* (2005). Others, like collections by Donald E. Chipman and Harriett Denise Joseph on important figures in Spanish Texas and by Jesús F. de la Tejas on biographies of key Tejano leaders from the nineteenth century, have focused on time periods, albeit not generationally defined ones. And Teresa Palomo Acosta and Ruthe Winegarten have provided biographical insights for a range of Tejanas over a span of 300 years.[19]

This collection is designed to fit into this last type of biography: the anthology. In an attempt to make itself as beneficial for as wide a range of readers as possible, this book presents a core of the era's leaders in order to share their ideas and contributions—all under one cover. One goal of the book, then, is to offer students a rich collection of historical biographies that will enlighten and enliven their understandings of Mexican American history.

The contributors to this anthology examine the lives of thirteen individuals and the conditions they faced as well as their reactions to their environment. By understanding the subjects' thoughts and actions, readers will gain richer insights into the key issues and conflicts of the day and the ways in which American society and Mexican culture helped create the Mexican American experience between 1920 and 1960—the Mexican American generation. By keeping entries relatively short and accessible, this book is designed primarily as an educational tool in the classroom as well as for the enjoyment of the general public.

A wide range of actors appear in this volume: men and women, professional and nonprofessional, the publicly visible and those less so. All of these individuals contributed to the idealization of the Mexican American generation. They identified and expressed an identity as Mexican Americans that shaped and was shaped by their experience. The reader will also notice that people highlighted in this work come from California, Arizona, New Mexico, and Texas. This fact demonstrates that the majority of the Mexican American population was concentrated in the American Southwest during these years and that the leadership of that generation drew primarily from this area, particularly California and Texas. Further, the two major civil rights organizations of the time, LULAC and the AGIF, were created in Texas and spread across the nation over time, moving through the Southwest first.

Readers will also notice a bit of overlap across the various essays. José de la Luz Sáenz (a founder of LULAC) and Dr. Héctor P. García (founder of the AGIF) both appear in this collection and are referred to in other essays in this collection. Some of the attorneys featured herein, such as Gustavo "Gus" L. García and John J. Herrera, often worked for one or the other of these organizations. The interactions between these individuals and others who do not appear in this collection speak to the web of connections between this generation's activists and their determination to fight social injustice.

Readers should be aware that due to the variety of authors in this collection, many synonyms for "Mexican American" are used throughout these essays. Hence, Emilio Zamora refers to a "Mexican" struggle for civil rights, in keeping with the language use at the time. In another essay, María Eugenia Cotera uses the phrase "Texas Mexicans." Other authors use other choices, but the topic is always focused on Mexican Americans.

The essays in this book are presented in two parts. Part 1 focuses on the ways in which a Mexican American identity was being formed during this time period. Emilio Zamora opens this segment of the book by discussing José de la Luz Sáenz, who stood as an icon of this generation. Cofounder of LULAC, author of *Los méxico-americanos en La Gran Guerra y su contingente en pro de la democracia, la humanidad y la justicia* (1933) (the first work to openly acknowledge the role of Mexican Americans in World War I), as well as a contributor to discussions and debates over the place of Mexican Americans in American society, Sáenz contributed solidly to the cause of Mexican American civil rights, helped shape the generation's political and social agendas, and informed its goals and ideas. Throughout his life, Sáenz used his ideas and his writing to insert the Mexican American experience into the broader narrative of American history. Zamora helps us understand Sáenz by examining his writings and the factors that influenced the development of his ideology. Thus, we see more deeply into the heart and soul of this visionary leader who played a central role in the early struggle for Mexican American civil rights during this generation.

Cynthia E. Orozco offers a biographical interpretation of LULAC organizer and activist Alice Dickerson Montemayor. Countering traditional notions about the marginal nature of women in the formative years of

LULAC, Orozco demonstrates that many women participants were not married; many were single or lesbian. She further shows how, despite sexuality or marital status, all women involved in the organization sought their own course for social change. And while historians have noted a separation of ideology between the Mexican American generation and the subsequent Chicano generation, Orozco points out that the efforts of people such as Montemayor set the stage for increased levels of women's activism that came later in the 1960s and 1970s. Montemayor introduced progressive ideas to LULAC, decrying women's oppression decades before the Chicana feminist movement. She questioned the myth of male superiority and argued that women were as competent as men, if not superior. She identified machismo in action and fought to eradicate it through informed feminist reasoning. While she exhibited a feminist consciousness, she also embodied a female consciousness in her concern for children and family.

Richard A. Garcia argues that Alonso S. Perales was a major contributor to the ideals of the Mexican American generation. As a founding member of LULAC, Perales constantly struggled with questions of his identity as a Mexican and an American. At the heart of this belief system was his embrace of the concept of America as a society that held the promise of equality. Some historians have upbraided this generation for focusing on economic success and social status, frequently at the expense of their working-class compatriots. But Perales's close personal friend and LULAC organizer Adela Sloss-Vento noted, "The unity of Americans of Mexican descent was the dream of attorney Perales; [he was a] man of high morals, ethics and principles, who did not like to compromise his principles for material gain." Perales later wrote to Sloss-Vento, "My only purpose in forming the said organization [LULAC] . . . [was] to bring about the rapid intellectual, social and political evolution of Americans of Mexican descent, to promote the social welfare of all Latin people residing in Texas and to produce the highest type of American citizen." Thus, the very words of Perales himself counter such criticisms and indicate a dedication to the uplift of the Mexican American people as a group, not just a certain segment. Emphasizing Perales's dedication to the concept of pragmatic-realism, Garcia demonstrates the ways in which Perales developed a carefully constructed worldview that desired to marry the promise of American society with the needs and interests of his people.

Jovita González Mireles is well known to scholars of Mexican American history, literature, and culture as a teacher and a writer, but she is virtually unknown beyond these boundaries. And readers may be surprised to learn that this woman published six books during her lifetime. In her contribution, María Eugenia Cotera touches on these works but more strongly emphasizes González's literary contributions as a folklorist who worked closely with J. Frank Dobie of the University of Texas. Motivated by a desire to recapture Mexican American history and culture, she emphasized commonalities across ethnic boundaries and believed that only by understanding each other could Anglos and Mexican Americans attain some form of progress. In doing so, González was influenced by the intersections of race and gender. And while some critics have branded her writings and pedagogy as reductive and assimilationist, Cotera convincingly posits that, in fact, González sought to preserve memories of the Mexican American experience of her own time and thereby promote her own individual perspective.

Vicki L. Ruiz provides an intriguing look at the interaction of a historian with her subject by sharing the life story of Luisa Moreno, a Guatemalan-born labor activist who, as a Latina, worked toward improving life for workers, including Mexican Americans. Based on numerous sources, including her own personal interviews with Moreno, Ruiz provides an intimate glimpse into Moreno's world. Moreno worked with numerous labor organizations from Florida to California. Throughout her years of activism, she led an intriguing life until she left the country voluntarily. Although Mario T. García also dedicates a chapter of his book *Mexican Americans* to Moreno, Ruiz's essay targets the complexity of her life as a daughter and a woman along with her involvement in the labor movement. By artfully tracing the twists and turns in Moreno's life story, Ruiz deftly demonstrates how historians can engage in a fruitful, sensitive relationship with their historical subjects.

Félix Longoria was a Mexican American who died defending his nation in the Philippines toward the end of World War II. Upon return of his remains to Three Rivers, Texas, in January 1949, his widow was denied services at Rice Funeral Home, the only such facility in the small town. Drawing from his monograph on this incident, Patrick J. Carroll discusses a key moment in the struggle for Mexican American civil rights. South Texas had long been defined by racial and ethnic segregation in life and death (as cemeteries were often segregated). Carroll shows the ways in which this event sparked a new national consciousness about Mexican Americans and their desires for social justice. Contacted by the sister of Longoria's widow, Dr. Héctor P. García quickly informed the media and elected officials, including the newly elected senator from Texas, Lyndon B. Johnson, about this injustice. An American hero who made the ultimate sacrifice for his country, Longoria suffered—even in death—from the racist attitudes that had so long defined relations between Anglos and Mexicans in South Texas. This episode, according to Carroll, served as a catalyst, spurring the post-1945 Mexican American civil rights movement. After negative national attention was drawn to the backward worldviews of Anglo South Texas, Senator Johnson arranged for Longoria's burial at Arlington National Cemetery. This event is significant because it shows the ways in which Americans around the nation considered Mexican Americans as true citizens, and it placed both Dr. García and the American GI Forum into national prominence as civil rights leaders. Thus, Longoria's story is salient to this collection because the circumstances surrounding his burial sparked a regeneration of civil rights struggles.

The second part of the book looks at the ways in which different people acted on the ideas developed by this first set of subjects. Apart from Longoria himself, Dr. Héctor P. García figures prominently in the story of the battle over Longoria's funeral arrangements. Carl Allsup adds to this story in his study of the life and significance of García. Immigrating to the United States during the Mexican Revolution, later attending medical school at the University of Texas, and subsequently joining the Army during World War II, García established a practice in Corpus Christi after the war. In response to complaints by the veterans he treated, García formed the American GI Forum in 1948. Thus, he helped pave the way for a renewed civil rights battle by Mexican Americans as equal American citizens. In many ways García stands as a giant of this generation. Laying out a patriotic definition of resistance (a loyal opposition), he influenced the course of the post–World War II civil rights struggle and placed the American GI Forum in the center of lawsuits to integrate schools and jury panels, the creation of Viva Kennedy clubs, and immigration policy. All these activities, according to Allsup, made García a "giant of the twentieth century."

Crucial to the legal fights waged by García, the AGIF, and LULAC were attorneys like Gus García. Graduating at the top of his high school class, he was allowed entrance at the University of Texas for his bachelor's degree. He entered the university's law program in 1936, at which point he became friends with numerous luminaries, such as future Texas Governors John Connally and Allan Shivers. As a champion of Mexican American rights, García put his brilliant eloquence to work in a range of cases, including the landmark educational desegregation case, *Delgado v. Bastrop ISD* (1948), and the very significant jury discrimination case, *Hernández v. State of Texas* (1954). The *Delgado* decision ended legally segregated schooling for Mexican American students in Bastrop and the surrounding school districts. The *Hernández* case successfully challenged traditional practices in Jackson County of excluding Mexican Americans and other nonwhites from serving on juries. This victory succeeded on many levels. García was the first Mexican American to argue before the US Supreme Court, and the case became a significant victory for Mexican American civil rights as it allowed for jury service around the nation, not just in one location. García, as much as anyone, helped cultivate a legal framework for inclusion of Mexican Americans in public schools and on juries.

Thomas H. Kreneck shares his own personal insights into the "fabulous" life of John J. Herrera. Kreneck, like Ruiz, also knew his subject. He oversaw the acquisition of the John J. Herrera Papers by the Houston Metropolitan Research Center and interviewed him formally several times. Little known outside of historical and political circles, Kreneck shows Herrara to be a key figure in the promotion of the Mexican American agenda at mid-century. Herrera was the third attorney in the trio that argued the *Hernández* case before the Supreme Court in 1954. Herrera also helped arrange a talk by President John F. Kennedy to a LULAC audience at the Rice Hotel in Houston the night before Kennedy's assassination. Both acts indicate the ways in which this generation of activists tied the Mexican American community more closely to American society and the trajectory of American history. In many ways, Herrera represents the experience of members of his generation. For reasons explained in the essay, Herrera grew up poor and worked several full-time jobs while attending law school at night. Most people would have given up such a seemingly unattainable goal. But Herrera persevered, eventually earning his law degree. He went on to become a leading voice for the Mexican American population. So involved was Herrera with LULAC that he became known as "Mr. LULAC."

As a rhetorician, Michelle Hall Kells brings her own unique perspective to our study of the Mexican American generation as she shares her understanding of the construction and use of rhetoric. In her examination of Vicente Ximenes, Kells argues that for a social movement to have a substantive, lasting impact it must become enmeshed with the political system and the administrative units that enforce the law. By engaging in nonthreatening, yet clearly articulated, rhetoric favoring the inclusion of Mexican Americans as equal citizens, Ximenes shaped and enforced policy in a number of government positions in the Johnson administration. Kells presents a political biography of Ximenes, followed by an examination of the role he played as chair of the Cabinet Committee Hearings on Mexican American Affairs, held in 1967 in El Paso. Identifying the pillars of Ximenes's rhetorical strategies, Kells demonstrates the ways in which he helped spur the Mexican American community to action. She argues that the 1967 hearings were crucial to the emergence of the Chicano movement. (Julie Leininger Pycior addresses a different perspective on these hearings in chapter 12.) Kells is also sensitive to the pressures of the Cold War on civil rights activists branded as subversives for criticizing the social and political status quo. It was not uncommon in the 1940s–1980s for civil rights opponents to level charges of radicalism at African American and Mexican American activists. Hence, Ximenes, as an AGIF organizer, countered such attacks by holding meetings at a Catholic church to maintain a respectable, God-fearing, patriotic appearance. Kells posits that Ximenes "represents one of the few civil rights leaders who functioned as an activist, agitator, and mobilizer as well as operated as a national-level government representative, administrator, and policy-maker." In her opinion, these widespread actions helped move members of the Mexican American generation forward in their pursuit of citizenship in the United States.

Laura K. Muñoz reminds us that key civil rights struggles of this period were also fought in Arizona. Attorney Ralph Estrada, Muñoz argues, was a key figure in the Mexican American civil rights movement. Estrada came from a lower middle-class background. His father owned Estrada Brothers Grocery, a small store in Tempe. A three-sport letterman in baseball, basketball, and football, Estrada took that level of determination to heart as a lawyer, fighting the cases *Gonzales v. Sheely* and *Ortiz v. Jack* in 1951. Estrada's victory in the *Gonzales* case only applied to one school district in Arizona, yet it set the stage for the more important *Ortiz* case that same year in which segregated schooling across the state was found unconstitutional. Beyond his legal endeavors, Estrada also acted as attorney and president of the Alianza

Hispano-Americana. Further, like many other members of his generation, Estrada supported the Viva Kennedy clubs, helping to elect the nation's first Catholic president. Because of his assistance to Kennedy, Estrada was later sent to Nicaragua for two years as a representative of the US Agency for International Development.

Julie Leininger Pycior traces the life and contributions of Ernesto Galarza. Active in labor organizing into the 1960s, Galarza's experience predated the Chicano movement, going back to the 1940s. Born in the Sierra Madre de Nayarit, Galarza's family, persecuted by the Porfirio Díaz regime, fled to the United States, living in Arizona and then settling in Sacramento, California. One interesting difference about Galarza's early education in Sacramento was his good fortune in having teachers who encouraged him to use the Spanish language and learn more about his heritage; this was a very uncommon experience in the early twentieth century, a period marked by segregated schools for whites, blacks, and Mexican Americans. Galarza grew up poor. His older brothers did not attend school because they had to work. Ultimately, in contrast to most Mexican Americans of this period, Galarza earned a doctoral degree in 1944 from Columbia University, writing his dissertation on public policy. Throughout his life, he fought for the poor and dispossessed. Critical of business interests and governmental foot-dragging, Galarza battled overwhelming odds to protect the rights of workers and immigrants. At a 1967 conference on Mexican American civil rights in El Paso, Galarza and others pushed the needs of farmworkers, recognition of land rights under the Treaty of Guadalupe Hidalgo, and an end to the Vietnam War. He later was instrumental in the formation of the Mexican American Legal Defense and Educational Fund and the National Council of La Raza. Defending poor and dispossessed Mexican Americans while promoting the need for education, Galarza famously argued that "Vale más la revolución que viene que la que se fue" (The revolution that is coming is more important than the one that passed).

Lastly, Kenneth C. Burt's chapter sheds new light on the political career of Edward R. Roybal of Los Angeles. Burt describes Roybal as being born to a working-class family with deep roots in American soil (four hundred years) and who served in the military during World War II. As with many veterans, he returned to the United States ready to make significant changes in conditions for Mexican Americans. And while Burt allows that

Roybal is perhaps best known for being the first Mexican American elected to a city council since 1881 and for his twenty years of service in the US House of Representatives, another key aspect of his legacy often gets overlooked. Scholars have not duly noted that what kept Roybal successful through those years was his ability to lead through coalition building. Burt notes how Roybal won election to the Los Angeles City Council in 1949. He put together a progressive coalition of left-leaning groups such as Mexican Americans, African Americans, Jews, other immigrant groups, and organized labor. Roybal cut his political teeth by helping organize the Community Service Organization and the Mexican American Political Association. Later he founded the Congressional Hispanic Caucus and the National Association of Latino Elected and Appointed Officials. The essay shows the depths of Roybal's dedication to his people and the ways in which he represented this generation. It also shows that Mexican Americans did not act alone. As in this case, they often sought to work with other similarly oppressed groups. According to Burt, Roybal's coalition-building skills anticipated the later election of Antonio Villaraigosa as mayor of Los Angeles. As Burt puts it, "the Roybal model of coalition politics has proved to have enduring value in an increasingly multicultural society."

Here readers will see how these actors entered a world not of their own choosing, one that shaped and attempted to limit their life choices. They resisted such impositions and developed an ideology steeped in concepts of equality, as defined in the nation's governing principles and documents, using the limited tools at their disposal. Their thoughts and actions, then, reinforce the words of Karl Marx in *The German Ideology* (1845), "circumstances make men just as much as men make circumstances." These men and women reconfigured their environment in ways that secured a somewhat brighter future for future generations, an environment that has been both edified and challenged in recent years.

Notes

1. See Arnoldo De León, *They Called Them Greasers: Anglo Attitudes toward Mexicans in Texas, 1821–1900* (Austin: University of Texas Press, 1983), for a detailed discussion of ethnic relationships and the history of the development of negative stereotypes.

2. For more information on the Porfiriato and its effects on immigration to the United States, see Rodolfo Acuña, *Occupied America: A History of Chicanos* (Boston: Longman, 2011); and Michael C. Meyer, William L. Sherman, and Susan M. Deeds, *The Course of Mexican History* (New York: Oxford University Press, 1999).

3. Ana Martinez-Catsam, "Frontier of Dissent: *El Regidor*, the Regime of Porfirio Díaz, and the Transborder Community," *Southwestern Historical Quarterly* 112 (April 2009): 389–408.

4. Ignacio M. García, *White But Not Equal: Mexican Americans, Jury Discrimination, and the Supreme Court* (Tucson: University of Arizona Press, 2009); and Matt S. Meier and Feliciano Ribera, *Mexican Americans / American Mexicans: From Conquistadors to Chicanos*, rev. ed. (1972; repr., New York: Hill and Wang, 1994).

5. Benjamin Marquez, *LULAC: The Evolution of a Mexican American Political Organization* (Austin: University of Texas Press, 1993); Henry A. J. Ramos, *A People Forgotten, a Dream Pursued: The History of the American G.I. Forum, 1948–1972*, 2nd ed. (1982; repr., Austin: University of Texas Press, 1983); Carl Allsup, *The American GI Forum: Origins and Evolution* (Austin: Center for Mexican American Studies, University of Texas at Austin, 1982); Craig A. Kaplowitz, *LULAC, Mexican Americans, and National Policy* (College Station: Texas A&M University Press, 2005); and Cynthia E. Orozco, *No Mexicans, Women, or Dogs Allowed: The Rise of the Mexican American Civil Rights Movement* (Austin: University of Texas Press, 2009).

6. Arnoldo De León, *Mexican Americans in Texas: A Brief History*, 2nd ed. (Wheeling, IL: Harlan Davidson, 1999), 1–3.

7. Juan Gómez-Quiñones, "Toward a Perspective on Chicano History," *Aztlan* 2 (Fall 1971): 1–51.

8. Manuel G. Gonzales and Cynthia M. Gonzales, eds., *En Aquel Entonces: Readings in Mexican-American History* (Bloomington: University of Indiana Press, 2000).

9. Rodolfo Alvarez, "The Psycho-Historical and Socioeconomic Development of the Chicano Community in the United States," *Social Science Quarterly* 53 (March 1973): 920, 926, 931.

10. Mario T. García, *Mexican Americans: Leadership, Ideology, and Identity, 1930–1960* (New Haven, CT: Yale University Press, 1989), 4.

11. David G. Gutiérrez, "Significant to Whom?: Mexican Americans and the History of the American West," *Western Historical Quarterly* 24 (November 1993): 519–39.

12. David Nasaw, "AHR Roundtable: Historians and Biography. Introduction," *American Historical Review* 114 (June 2009): 573.

13. Lois Banner, "AHR Roundtable: Biography as History," *American Historical Review* 114 (June 2009): 580.

14. Ibid., 584.

15. Americo Paredes, *With His Pistol in His Hand: A Border Ballad and Its Hero* (Austin: University of Texas Press, 1958).

16. Juan Gómez-Quiñones, *Sembradores: Ricardo Flores Magón y el Partido Liberal Mexicano: A Eulogy and Critique* (Los Angeles: Aztlán Publications, 1973).

17. This list of biographical works includes a number of works by Mario T. García, such as *Mexican Americans: Leadership, Ideology, and Identity, 1930–1960* (New Haven: Yale University Press, 1989); *Memories of Chicano History: The Life and Narrative of Bert Corona* (Berkeley: University of California Press, 1994); *Ruben Salazar, Border Correspondent: Selected Writings, 1955–1970* (Berkeley: University of California Press, 1995); *The Making of a Mexican American Mayor: Raymond L. Telles of El Paso* (El Paso: Texas Western Press, University of Texas at El Paso, 1998); *Luis Leal: An Auto/biography* (Austin: University of Texas Press, 2000); *A Dolores Huerta Reader* (Albuquerque: University of New Mexico Press, 2008); with Francis Esquibel Tywoniak, *Migrant Daughter: Coming of Age as a Mexican American Woman* (Berkeley: University of California Press, 2000); and with Sal Castro, *Blowout!: Sal Castro and the Chicano Struggle for Educational Justice* (Chapel Hill: University of North Carolina Press, 2011).

18. Richard Griswold del Castillo and Richard A. Garcia, *César Chávez: A Triumph of Spirit* (Norman: University of Oklahoma Press, 1995); Thomas H. Kreneck, *Mexican American Odyssey: Felix Tijerina, Entrepreneur and Civic Leader, 1905–1965* (College Station: Texas A&M University Press, 2001); Ignacio M. García, *Héctor P. García: In Relentless Pursuit of Justice* (Houston: Arte Publico, 2002); and Elliott Young, *Catarino Garza's Revolution on the Texas-Mexico Border* (Durham: Duke University Press, 2004).

19. Vicki L. Ruiz and Virginia Sánchez Korrol, eds., *Latina Legacies: Identity, Biography, and Community* (New York: Oxford University Press, 2005); Donald E. Chipman and Harriett Denise Joseph, *Notable Men and Women of Spanish Texas* (Austin: University of Texas Press, 1999); Jesús F. de la Teja, ed., *Tejano Leadership in Mexican and Revolutionary Texas* (College Station: Texas A&M University Press, 2010); and Teresa Palomo Acosta and Ruthe Winegarten, *Las Tejanas: 300 Years of History* (Austin: University of Texas Press, 2003).

INTELLECTUALS AND ETHNIC CONSCIOUSNESS

Figure 1.1. José de la Luz Sáenz in military uniform. José de la Luz Sáenz Papers, Benson Latin American Collection, General Libraries, University of Texas at Austin.

1

José de la Luz Sáenz

Experiences and Autobiographical Consciousness

Emilio Zamora

Portions of this essay appeared in my introduction to Sáenz's edited and translated diary, published by Texas A&M University Press in 2014 as *The World War I Diary of José de la Luz Sáenz*.

Introduction

José de la Luz Sáenz, according to Alonso Perales, was "one of our most distinguished and honest leaders in the United States of America."[1] Sáenz certainly stands out for his highly regarded civil rights work during the first half of the twentieth century as well as for his association with other equally remarkable leaders, some of whom also appear in this anthology. He is best known as a cofounder of the League of United Latin American Citizens (LULAC) and the author of a World War I diary, *Los méxico-americanos en La Gran Guerra y su contingente en pro de la democracia, la humanidad y la justicia*. Researchers have begun to acknowledge Sáenz's contributions to civil rights history as a member of an emerging group of largely upwardly mobile and US-born leaders

DOI: 10.5876/9781607323372.c001

from Texas. His political cohort, the so-called Mexican American generation, grew up at the turn of the century, set in motion a new form of ethnic politics in the 1920s, and sustained it at least until the early 1960s as a prominent cause for equal rights in the larger social movement.² Although Sáenz played a central role in the emergence of this group, researchers have not yet thoroughly examined his biography.³

This essay examines the life and work of Sáenz from experiential and autobiographical approaches. It recounts selected formative experiences to orient the reader on his trajectory from the poor rural experience of his youth to a teaching career and a life as a socially engaged adult. Recounting his experiences establishes a frame of reference to understand the sociohistorical context for his intellectual and political development, his place in the protest community, and his assessment of his life and political work. The judgments that Sáenz made over select experiences reflected his autobiographical consciousness, or self-awareness.⁴ His salient life experiences and configuration of self appear in three major autobiographical accounts: a World War I diary published in 1933 and two unpublished manuscripts, one authored in 1940 and another in 1944. The following sections that address his biography are based primarily on his 1944 manuscript, "Yo, Omnia Mea Mecum Porto," and his war diary. Subsequent segments address Sáenz's autobiographical consciousness, mostly in "Yo," the war diary, and his 1940 text *Realismo Misterioso: Estudio Psico-Teosófico.*⁵

Raised in Realitos

Sáenz was born May 17, 1888 in the South Texas town of Realitos, in present-day Duval County, and died at the Veterans Hospital in Corpus Christi, Texas, on April 12, 1953. He gave special importance to his formative experiences as a youngster in Realitos to explain his life as an adult. The principal autobiographical account that tells of these experiences is "Yo," the 120-page manuscript that he wrote for his son, Eduardo, who once asked him to talk of his years as a child. Sáenz penned "Yo" at fifty-six, when Eduardo was probably in his early teens. He took care to offer fatherly advice to his son, but he mostly spoke in a reflexive, didactic, and moralizing tone on issues like racial discrimination, inequality, identity, human behavior, and basic norms on human rights. His major purpose, in other words, was to recount his life experiences as a way to explain his ideas, values, and civil rights work.

Realitos had been a military outpost in the mid-1700s. It was located along one of the northeastern routes of the Camino Real, approximately fifty miles from the present-day Tamaulipas-Texas border at Mier and Camargo, colonial towns that appeared in the mid-1700s and extended their municipal reach into the area around Realitos and San Diego, the current seat of Duval County.[6] By the 1860s, Realitos had a small population of mostly Mexican families employed by nearby ranchers with familial ties to original Spanish and Mexican land grantees living along the border region. The population grew to 400 in the late 1880s primarily in response to the increased demand for workers to construct the Texas Mexican Railway, connecting Gulf of Mexico trade at Corpus Christi with Mexico-San Antonio commerce at Laredo.[7]

Sáenz's family arrived in the 1860s at a ranch close to San Diego. Marcelina, his widowed grandmother, had worked for a wealthy ranching family from Mier named Hinojosa, and she secured employment at another Hinojosa ranch in Texas. According to Sáenz, she feared that her sons would follow the political example of their grandfather Eugenio. The renowned Texas-born general Ignacio Zaragoza had recruited him on the border to fight in Mexico's momentous Battle of Puebla in 1862. He continued fighting alongside other Mexican patriots in the national cause to oust the French invaders and even participated in an early undetermined political cause against Porfirio Díaz, another hero from Puebla and would-be president of Mexico.[8]

Sáenz recalled that his father, Rosalío, was born on the Mexican border in 1864 and that he practically "became a man" working alongside his mother at the Hinojosa ranch in Duval County. The reference to becoming a man alongside his mother meant that Rosalío began working at a very young age, most probably in the ranch owner's home. Sáenz also stated that his father later worked "like a slave" as a ranch hand and "on halves" as a shepherd for local Mexican landowners, including Hinojosa. His point: that ranchers exploited Mexicans with hard work, long hours, and low pay. Life, however, was not always difficult and uncompromising.[9]

Rosalío, like other Mexicans from the area, built a meaningful life through his close personal relations. Sáenz's endearing story of how his father and mother met and fell in love bears out this other side of life. Cristina and her family were from San Antonio; they arrived by wagon at the Hinojosa ranch in 1880. The Hernández family had selected the ranch as a stopover to earn money for their trip to Mexico. Rosalío and Cristina, both young teenagers at the time, met while working at the ranch. They quickly developed a close relationship. The Hernández family left—never to be seen again—but not before they allowed their daughter to stay behind and marry Rosalío. The young couple moved to Realitos, and Rosalío became a laborer with a Texas Mexican Railway construction crew on the Texas-Mexican Railway. Although Rosalío supplemented his family's earnings by building adobe homes for other poor families in the area, they did not live any better than their neighbors.

The young Sáenz family lived a hardscrabble life that depended on Rosalío's meager earnings. His job took him away for two- to three-week periods, and strong willed and caring Cristina managed their home and raised their eight children with the chickens, pigs, goats, cow, and vegetable patch that she tended. Sáenz recalled that Rosalío had attended primary grades in Mier and taught Cristina to read and write. She used her newfound skills to correspond with Rosalío and school her children. Sáenz remained grateful to Cristina for being his first teacher and for insuring that the family survived recurring financial difficulties. He was especially moved by Cristina's difficulties in giving birth to a large number of children. She lost five of them over an approximately ten-year period. The image of a self-sacrificing mother became deeply etched in the family's memory when she succumbed while giving birth in 1896. Rosalío honored her by naming the child Cristín.[10]

Sáenz expressed equally profound respect for his older sister Marcelina, who inherited her mother's responsibilities after her death. She began caring for the children when she was eleven, mostly without adult supervision, because Rosalío's railroad work continued to take him away from home. Despite her young age, Sáenz's sister maintained Cristina's household routine and continued to care for the children long after their mother had passed. When not under the direct charge of his sister or father, Sáenz spent much of his preteen life with one of the local "gangs" of shoeless and rambunctious youngsters who were largely left on their own to lord over the area with rough play, exhilarating escapades, and tested relationships. Sáenz often had to depend on his wits to survive the frequent taunts from other boys and the dangers of the natural and "wild-like" surroundings that he frequented. He also remembered that some unfriendly and even cruel adults sometimes unwittingly taught him of life's adversities and the need to take care of himself and his loved ones. Family love and support, close reliable friends, and caring adults, on the other hand, provided Sáenz a happy and rewarding life in Realitos.

Rosalío married Petra Rámos in 1898, but not before the children, especially Marcelina, had grilled Rosalío on the conflict that could occur between her and his new wife. She had been like a mother to her siblings for six years and had become very protective of them. After some extended discussions, the children consented to the marriage. They demanded, however, that Marcelina continue her motherly duties and that Petra concern herself primarily with her own children and Rosalío. His children, especially Marcelina, had been raised to be willful and independent partly because of Rosalío's work-related absences. He also must have encouraged them to be self-sufficient because he allowed them to have a say about his second marriage and even agreed to their conditions. The arrangement apparently worked because the children and their new mother eventually made peace and, according to Sáenz, lived a happy life together.[11]

Sáenz's world began to change in another way soon after Petra joined the family. His father convinced a railroad supervisor to hire Sáenz to guard the storage depot with the workers' food and cooking utensils. The job required that he fend for himself against wild animals and the occasional malicious traveler who tried to take advantage of the eleven-year-old youngster. The experience reinforced his self-reliant and independent spirit, but the job ended quickly, possibly because the Texas Mexican Railway completed construction in 1899 or 1900. When Sáenz reached twelve, the age of early manhood in the working-class world of South Texas, he accompanied his father and older brother on the migratory trail that took them by horseback to "the outside world" of San Diego, Beeville, and González. Taming horses; clearing the land of brush and hardwood trees with a pick, ax, and shovel under an unrelenting sun; and picking tall cotton plants with sacks that grew heavier with every passing hour taught Sáenz the meaning of hard work. He also claimed to have learned that Anglo farmers continually exploited the large Mexican workforce and disregarded the difficulties that the long work hours and low pay visited on their lives.

Moving Up to Alice

Rosalío made a decision in 1900 that greatly influenced Sáenz's life. He moved the family to his new source of employment in Alice, a small town located approximately thirty miles northeast of Realitos. The local railroad station provided more than permanent employment and improved earnings for Rosalío. Alice also offered Sáenz better schooling opportunities.[12] Sáenz excelled at Alice High School, but he seemed more interested in telling stories about mean-spirited Anglos than about his accomplishments. A case in point involved an Anglo teacher who made an anti-Mexican remark to the students, which provided Sáenz the opportunity to demonstrate his sense of pride and strength of character. The teacher had complained that "if I had known that I was going to teach English to the Mexicans, I would not have come from so far away."[13] Sáenz responded by refusing to answer the teacher's questions to the class. According to Sáenz, everyone understood that his behavior was an outright affront because he was the highest achieving student at the time and was more than capable of engaging the teacher.

When a school inspector from a major unnamed university visited the school, Sáenz took the opportunity to further embarrass the teacher by volunteering to recite an oration by a famous person before the assembled teachers and students. He impressed everyone with his performance. The purportedly humbled teacher congratulated Sáenz, and even befriended him years later, suggesting that he had learned his lesson. Although Sáenz may have exaggerated the teacher's changed demeanor and his own defiance, he was clear about his early resolve to challenge persons "who in the grand scheme of things deny us our equal rights and the opportunities to life and progress accorded to all human beings." His point was that his youth was fraught with racism and that combating it prepared him for civil rights work as an adult.[14]

Sáenz's account of the racist teacher set the stage for one of his most far-reaching statements on race thinking and Mexican-Anglo relations:

> Some people do not know us as a race, do not care to understand us, and consequently will never be in a position to appreciate whatever value there may be in our potential ethnical qualities. Thus, mistakes have been made in rendering judgment as to our true worth. This is and has been the principal cause for the historical and racial prejudice that has existed in Texas and some other

States of our Union. Many of our fellow citizens yet through mere aberration of theirs deny the fact, but a finger will never cover the sun.[15]

High school teachers Nat and Alice Benton also left a deep impression on Sáenz—not for insulting and dismissive behavior, but for their acts of kindness and encouragement.[16] Even under such positive circumstances, however, race loomed large over Sáenz's relations with Anglos. Nat stood out in Sáenz's autobiography as a kind and caring school principal because he advised Sáenz and his Mexican classmates to be patient and restrained with racist Anglo teachers and students. Nat may have been more concerned with preventing racial tensions from escalating into embarrassing and disruptive conflict than helping Mexican youth, but Sáenz credited him for his understanding and goodwill. Alice, Nat's wife and a fellow teacher, took a bolder approach to the racial tensions that weighed heavily in Sáenz's life. She reportedly told Sáenz that he was more American than "the Anglo enemy of my people," meaning that he was a descendant of the original inhabitants of the American continent, and Europeans—including Spaniards but especially Anglos—disregarded his history and placed themselves above indigenous communities and their Mexican descendants.

Sáenz appeared taken aback by Alice's response, although he was also impressed that she described racial tension in broad terms. He had previously summoned the more moderate view of Nat to validate his reasoned approach to racial conflict; now he recalled the unvarnished opinion of Alice to proclaim his more defiant and broader understanding of race relations. Sáenz may have implied deep-seated racism by casting race relations in such broad terms, but he also wanted to appear measured in describing his formative years in Alice. Obviously concerned that he might leave the impression of unrelenting racism and overpowering feelings of racial resentment, Sáenz expressed gratitude to the community of Alice for supporting their "official" school and, with a touch of irony, thanked Alice High for preparing him for the profession that gave him "the pleasure of fighting for bettering the lot of my people."[17]

Mexican teachers also appeared in Sáenz's autobiographical account. He made special note of Pablo Pérez and Eulalio Velázquez. Pérez taught Mexican history, arithmetic, language arts, and literature in a private Mexican school, all in Spanish. Sáenz apparently studied with Pérez only briefly, but he held his teacher in high regard. On several occasions in his autobiography, as well as in other writings, Sáenz lamented that he had not received enough instruction in Spanish and that his command of the language could have been better; but he was grateful to have learned much from such an accomplished teacher as Pérez. Velázquez, a publisher, accountant, and teacher, may have played an even more important role in Sáenz's development.

Velázquez had built a reputation as a successful businessman, teacher, and journalist while in Laredo. He moved to Alice in 1903 and continued to publish his popular newspaper, *El Cosmopólita*, from the first floor of a building that he constructed soon after his arrival. The second floor housed his private coeducational elementary school, and he offered night classes for adults on agriculture and business. Sáenz did not attend the school, but he joined several of Velázquez's students who sought him out. Velázquez encouraged them to use his private library and guided them in their readings on Mexican history and historical figures like Benito Juárez, the famed Zapotec Indian who served as the lead justice and president of the Supreme Court, the president of Mexico, and the head of Mexico's nationalist cause against French intervention in the 1860s. Velázquez may have inspired Sáenz and his friends to organize a public celebration in honor of Juárez in 1906. Velázquez, no doubt impressed with the students' interest and abilities, assisted them in preparing the program with additional reading materials on oratory and patriotic celebrations. Sáenz's memory was especially clear when recounting the importance of the public program.

Sáenz had always claimed that he and his father descended from the Aztec civilization that had emerged in the ancient city of Tenochtitlán, in present-day Mexico City. He now took a special interest in honoring a fellow indigenous person who had attained high stature and contributed so much to the history of his country. Preparing and participating in the public program also gave Sáenz valuable experience in developing his oratorical skills in Spanish and in demonstrating his leadership abilities before the Mexican community. The program was a major success. The students rented a hall, decorated it with bunting and photos, and gave spirited talks on the historical significance of Juárez before a large Mexican audience. Sáenz indicated that the festivities had given him much satisfaction because he had honored Juárez and acknowledged his indigenous heritage before the people of Alice.

The Call to Teach

Some Mexican families from a nearby railroad workers' community—called El Palo del Oso by the Mexicans and Rogers by the Anglos—took special notice of Sáenz in a newspaper account of the Juárez festivities. When Sáenz accompanied his father to Oso, parents asked the eighteen-year-old to help them establish a private Mexican school to teach their children during the day and adults at night. The parents may have had a building at their disposal, but they were too poor to equip it. Sáenz turned to a Mexican businessman from Corpus Christi for assistance. The benefactor supplied the school with furniture and teaching materials. Sáenz had not yet graduated from high school and apparently devoted a limited amount of time to the school. His first teaching job at Oso, however, prepared him for a long career in the classroom.[18]

Sáenz graduated from high school in 1908 and immediately made plans to attend a business school in San Antonio, but he did not have the funds to pay the tuition. His family once again appeared prominently in his manuscript: his brothers and sisters decided to help him raise the money by picking cotton that summer. Unfortunately, some of them became ill, and they spent their hard-earned money on medical expenses. Marcelina again entered the picture. She sold the Realitos home that Rosalío had bequeathed her and gave Sáenz the full amount—$60—so that he could pursue his dream. Sáenz subsequently visited Velázquez, who was apparently associated with the San Antonio business school, paid him the required tuition, and headed for the city. He did not finish the story without writing to his son of the profound gratitude that he felt toward his sister. He built Marcelina a $500 home four years later.[19]

Sáenz completed his studies in bookkeeping and shorthand in six months and obtained a teaching certificate. Soon thereafter, he began teaching in the Central Texas area until he joined the military in 1917. He also attended what he called a "Teachers' Summer Normal" in San Antonio, most probably a teacher institute organized by John W. Knox, a popular teacher from the area who was to become his mentor during the 1910s. While in the military, Sáenz taught fellow Mexican soldiers to read and write in English. When he returned from the war, he resumed teaching and attended college for at least a year. During a teaching career that lasted thirty-four years, Sáenz taught all grades in thirty public schools and served as a principal in several elementary schools and high schools in La Joya, Benavides, and Oilton.

According to his grown children, Sáenz moved often because he riled influential persons when he protested the segregation and undereducation of Mexican children. His commitment to education extended beyond the classroom. He also believed in a more public form of education as a social cause for the Mexican community. With this in mind, he established the Academia Comercial Sáenz, a business school that offered basic office training "to carry out a job that can allow you to live comfortably and honestly."[20] This idea of public education was evident in many of his writings, including a concluding statement in his autobiography: "I see a greater need to strive to educate ourselves and raise our intellectual level but also to raise as many of our own as we can."[21]

Throughout his adult life, Sáenz penned articles in Spanish-language and English-language periodicals on school discrimination, the low enrollment of Mexican youth in public schools, and their inability to achieve parity with Anglo youngsters. His articles appeared in the *McAllen Evening Monitor*, *La Prensa*, *La Verdad*, *La Voz*, and the *Texas Outlook*. Some of his more moving remarks appeared in his diary. After completing basic training at San Antonio and while traveling by rail to France, he wrote about the schools in Comal County, where he taught, "I have struggled a great deal and I could not help but feel sympathy for those children who are unattended, unappreciated, ignored, and, worse, misunderstood." Other civil rights leaders addressed schooling issues with equal passion and sophistication, but Sáenz lent his voice to the cause for equal educational rights with the firsthand experience of a classroom teacher.

Soldiering Abroad and At Home

Sáenz's visibility and importance as a leader in the emerging Mexican civil rights movement grew when the United States entered World War I. He was working in a segregated Mexican school close to New Braunfels at the time that the government announced that able-bodied men were to register for military duty. Sáenz would not have been drafted; he was already married to María Petra Esparza and the father of three children when he volunteered for duty.[22] He was inducted at the Comal County Courthouse and reported for training at Fort Sam Houston on January 12, 1918. Soon after he completed his tour of duty on June 17, 1919, he began assembling the pages that he had been writing for eleven months—from the time of his induction until his release from military duty—and published his diary.[23] Sáenz never explained why he took fifteen years to publish the book. His family responsibilities and civil rights work no doubt contributed to the delay. The cost of publishing the manuscript may have also slowed his work. This may explain why he turned to friends for advanced book payments. At least 187 persons responded, and their names appeared in the published diary. Most of them were fellow veterans and civil rights activists from South Texas.[24]

The publication is the only known war diary published by a Mexican in the US military. Sáenz's chronicle is an extraordinary firsthand account of military service and speaks eloquently of the war as a crucible in the fight for equal rights for "humanity" as well as for Mexicans in the United States. The war, according to Sáenz, had given the United States the opportunity to join the global conflict on the side of democracy and justice and to affirm these principles among Americans on the home front. The war of principles, as Sáenz often described the fighting, also provided marginalized groups the opportunity to initiate a discourse on equal rights that focused on their battlefield contributions. Fellow civil rights leaders reiterated this argument beginning in the interwar period, suggesting that Sáenz had either refashioned a popular view or constructed an original line of reasoning. In either case, he articulated the earliest known formal statement on military service as a demonstration of loyalty that entitled Mexicans to social equality. Other members of LULAC and, later, the American GI Forum, agreed with this moral logic, especially when noting the ultimate sacrifice that many Mexicans paid on the battlefield. The contention that war contributions could be used to bargain for equality may have surfaced without Sáenz's encouragement. Sáenz, however, added singular elements to his arguments.[25]

Sáenz described military service and battlefield sacrifice as expressions of patriotic loyalty. This was no doubt meant to counter a popular view among Anglos that the large immigrant population in the Mexican community and the radical political activity that some Mexicans espoused gave them sufficient cause to question their loyalty. Sáenz, however, elevated the question of Mexican loyalty to a higher discursive level than the popular and limited patriotic allusions to flag and country. Mexicans, he insisted, served and fought for the democratic values and principles reflected in international norms and enshrined in the foundational documents of the United States. These values and principles, of course, had universal meaning and accommodated soldiers of all nationalities who defended them, including the Mexican nationals who served next to their US-born brethren. Sáenz added an important note to his sense of Mexican loyalty: they regularly faced racial affronts and indignities yet still accepted their duty to serve and fight.

Sáenz made yet another original contribution to the wartime language of justice and democracy. He analogized the cause for equal rights at home with the fighting in Europe and suggested that civil rights leaders represented the country's egalitarian heritage while segregationists undermined its promise of social equality. This inverted relationship theoretically allowed civil rights activists to present themselves as the authentic proponents of the United States' underlying wartime purpose: to insure justice and democracy for all people around the world, including Mexicans in the United States. Sáenz seemed to be saying that all Mexicans, regardless of whether or not they had served in the military, could now use a renewed moral authority to point out the contradiction between official pronouncements in favor of justice and democracy at the front lines and the reality of discrimination and inequality at home.

The language divide that separated Mexicans and Anglos meant that Sáenz was primarily speaking to Mexicans in his Spanish-language diary and in the articles that he wrote for Mexican newspapers during the interwar period and World War II. He also wrote in English-language periodicals, although with less regularity, and he tried without success to publish an English translation of his diary. Other leaders that made similar wartime arguments probably influenced the larger society to a greater extent than Sáenz ever could. We may never know if his chronicle of World War I experiences and his invigorating ideas might have appeared differently outside the largely insulated monolingual world that he inhabited. We do know that Sáenz thought it necessary that Mexicans know the significance of contributions by Mexican soldiers and that they should make them their own in calling for equality and the end to racial discrimination in Texas.

After World War I, and while he was preparing his diary for publication, Sáenz used the idea of battlefield contributions in a different way. He led a statewide campaign to establish a memorial in San Antonio for Mexican World War I veterans. Although he mostly feared that the public would forget that Mexicans had fought bravely in the war, he sought to construct a monument to formally recognize all the soldiers who had served in Europe.

Other pressing issues in the area of education, however, also drew his attention. He worked with organizations in the San Antonio area that lent assistance to the legal challenge against racial segregation at the Del Rio public schools in 1930. Sáenz's war memorial was never built, in part because he turned over the money that had been raised to the attorneys who handled the Del Rio case. While supporting this legal challenge, Sáenz also joined with other civil rights leaders who sought to build regional unity by consolidating the political work of different organizations throughout the state. LULAC emerged from these efforts.

The preparations for an organizational meeting began with a speaking tour in the Rio Grande Valley that included Sáenz, Alonso Perales, and José Antonio Canales.[26] They called the first meeting at Harlingen in 1927, but they were unable to overcome generational differences that plagued the organization for years to come. Sáenz, Perales, and Canales reportedly proposed that the organization emphasize US citizenship and Mexican contributions in US history as a way to call for an end to discrimination and to promote the incorporation of Mexicans into society on an equal basis. An untold number of delegates saw the proposed ethnic approach to civil rights as pandering to nativists. Apparently the division at the meeting was so significant that the mostly Mexican-born delegates representing mutual aid societies and other working-class organizations refused to continue working on the proposal. Undaunted by the letdown at Harlingen, Sáenz, Perales, Canales, and others called for a second meeting in 1929 at Corpus Christi. This time, the delegates established LULAC.[27] According to Rosaura Sánchez, the founding convention adopted the now famous preamble that embraced the dominant values and political perspective dictated by US society: "To develop within the members of our race the best, purest and most perfect type of true and loyal citizen of the United States of America."[28]

Sáenz's central role in the establishment of LULAC places him in the liberal pluralist tradition of the Mexican civil rights movement. His supposed authorship of the preamble represents a departure from the previously noted broad conceptualization of equal rights that he pronounced in his diary. The seemingly inconsistent views of a struggle for the principles of democracy and justice and a cause for Mexicans as a loyal ethnic group, however, appeared concurrently in his autobiographical essays, suggesting that political identities in the Mexican political struggle do not always fit into our neatly formulated categories of analysis. Sáenz's public identity as a Latin American, and his more private use of the word *indígena* suggest that he and others may have reconciled inconsistencies by using separate identities, depending on the different social and political settings that they inhabited. Sáenz's formulation of Mexicans as Americans—in the original or hemispheric sense of the word—during the Second World War represents yet another departure from the narrow ethnic identity that historians have attributed to LULAC.

World War II and the US Good Neighbor Policy in Latin America gave Sáenz another opportunity to apply his language of justice and democracy. This time he claimed that Mexicans were members of the larger Spanish-speaking population in the Americas and, as such, deserved to be included in the official wartime initiative for goodwill and improved understanding. Contemporaries like Perales also called on the United States to bring the benefits of the Good Neighbor Policy home. Consequently, it is difficult to determine if Sáenz achieved prominence in the discourse of good neighborliness at home and abroad with singular views on discrimination, inequality, and the role of the state in resolving these problems.

For Sáenz, Americanism, the expression of inter-American unity that reached wartime importance in the hemisphere, called on Mexicans to expand their sense of entitlement. The call for hemispheric unity also required that the United States demonstrate an improved regard for Latin Americans in the application of the Good Neighbor Policy. Sáenz, not unlike other Mexican civil rights leaders, also promoted the use of the self-referents "American" or "Latin American" to underscore hemispheric unity and to place Mexicans at the center of a continental form of patriotism. In some cases, members of LULAC and other community organizations may have used the term *Latin American* to avoid the negative connotations that segregationists associated with *Mexican* or *Mexicano*, but many others, including Sáenz, spoke more broadly and creatively.[29]

Although it is still too early to attribute a special Americanizing voice to Sáenz, he set himself apart from his fellow continental-minded activists in two ways: as the well-known diarist of the First World War and as a self-described "indigenista." When he spoke about the Good Neighbor Policy's promise of improved relations at home, he occasionally conjured the memory of the "sacrificing" Mexican soldiers during World War I and used his well-established authority as a Mexican veteran and diarist to strengthen his renewed call for an end to discrimination and inequality. He was less forth-coming with his indigenous identity and outlook, but he used it with some regularity. In a letter to newspaper editors, Sáenz underscored this view:

> We see no reason why we should keep on playing the fool calling them so [Indian] just because a Genoese Sailor might have had need to use it as a com-placent subterfuge. Why not call them the Genuine One Hundred Percent Americans?"
>
> Our ancestors (the Aztecs) fought the Spaniards, the French, and the Anglo Americans to uphold our racial decorum. We have fought America's wars against despots such as William II, Emperor of the Germans, Mussolini, Hitler, and Hiroshito, etc., because of their racism theories. Why should we not fight it here within the limits of our nation?[30]

Sáenz did not confine his work to overarching ideological constructs like the civil rights cause as an adjunct to worldwide or hemispheric causes for democracy and justice. He also endorsed candidates for political office, con-demned the segregation of Mexican youth in public schools, participated in campaigns for greater parental participation in the education of Mexican children, supported efforts to secure legislation for a civil rights law in Texas, critiqued the exploitation of Mexican workers, and embraced the allied cause during World War II. Moreover, he did not limit his membership to LULAC. During his more than forty years of activism and public service, he worked with organizations such as the American GI Forum, the Veterans of Foreign Wars, the American Legion, the American Council of Spanish Speaking People, La Sociedad Mutualista of Sacred Heart Church (McAllen), and the Texas Good Relations Association.[31]

The Good Relations Association deserves special attention because Sáenz, Perales, and Carlos Castañeda, the noted history professor from the University of Texas, founded the organization in the early 1950s in part to seek broad-based unity within the Mexican community as well as between Mexicans and other groups in the state. According to Perales, the association promoted "the progress and well-being of Texas residents of Mexican origin and Hispanics in general, and act to bring unity between our people and Texans of other racial stock."[32]

This purpose statement minimally suggests that the generational category of the so-called Mexican American generation must be used carefully, if at all, when examining the life and work of leaders like Sáenz, Castañeda, and Perales. They may have used their US citizenship and, in some cases, an official designation of Mexicans as "white" to leverage change, but this does not necessarily mean that they abandoned a cause of unity with Mexican nationals and African Americans. Sáenz and other members of LULAC may have leveled a critique of US immigration policy that came close to castigating the immigrants themselves, but they allowed Mexican nationals to join their organization and the Good Relations Association with the understanding that they would seek naturalized citizenship. This suggests that the Mexican civil rights leaders of mid-century were more complex than we have assumed and that it might be useful to begin asking who they said they were.[33]

I Am All That I Carry Within

The autobiographical narratives that Sáenz wrote are more than a recounting of personal experiences. He suggested self-awareness in the selection and telling of his experiences, as the previous sections have demonstrated, but his autobiographical accounts also offer explicit views of himself. This section revisits his 120-page manuscript that he titled "Yo," as well as selected letters, fragments of his World War I diary, and the manuscript titled *Realismo Misterioso: Estudio Psico-Teosófico*. The purpose is to offer a more direct examination of Sáenz's autobiographical consciousness.

Sáenz's deep-seated sense of parental responsibility is evident throughout the autobiography as he consistently offered moral and practical advice to his son and shared his memory of the love and kindness that his parents showed their children. Other records located elsewhere—in his archives at the University of Texas, for example—indicate that he consistently expressed this personal quality in both word and deed. This self-defining behavior was also evident in the caring and affectionate letters that he wrote in 1944 and 1945 to another son in the military. At a later point in his life, Sáenz also suggested that he had enrolled at Sul Ross State University to help and continue enjoying the company of another son who was studying in West Texas.

Sáenz made special note of the love and caring from his father, mother, and sister Marcelina and the consequent emotional stability that they nurtured in the family to explain the confidence and self-assuredness that characterized his public life as a civil rights leader. He also described his rough-and-tumble experiences with other youngsters in Realitos as a source of strength; he often attributed his independent and self-reliant spirit to these challenging yet fulfilling relationships. On the other hand, Sáenz suggested that the poverty in the community and the tensions that it created in families and among individuals, including youth, led him to appreciate the need for improving social conditions and promoting a deeper sense of moral responsibility around the educational needs of children and their parents. He believed that education provided the best means for individual improvement and collective advancement.

His devotion to a career in teaching explains his preoccupation with the under-education of Mexican youth, as well as his own story of schooling, as a way of escaping a world of poverty and even *"miseria,"* a word that he often used to underscore the general experience of hardship and destitution among Mexicans at the turn of the century. He acknowledged that life in the predominantly Mexican region of South Texas meant limited educational opportunities, and rural, isolated, and poverty-stricken places like Realitos often reproduced social relations in successive generations of Mexicans filling positions as low-wage ranch hands and migratory farm-workers. Sáenz also made it a point to remind his son that caring and helpful adults (including teachers) and his father's fortuitous decision to move to Alice explained his entry into the profession. He did not confine his lament to his youth; he also used his autobiography to critique the continuing problem of undereducation, racial discrimination in schools, and uncaring adults in the Mexican community and the larger society. This echoed his determined political work as a teacher activist who always insisted on incorporating the claim for educational equity and access into the nascent Mexican civil rights movement.

Sáenz also authored his narrative as a self-conscious Mexican intellectual with the capacity to draw knowledge and understanding from history, literature, and his own everyday experiences. Although he clearly sought to influence his son to be inquisitive and discerning, he used his narrative to construct an identity as an intelligent and learned person. His reference to historical figures, writers, and local organic intellectuals, however, did not necessarily mean that he simply sought to impress his son with his knowledge and analytical skills. Sáenz's overriding intent was to call on his autobiographical consciousness to affirm selected parts of his identity.[34]

Of Mexico's major historical figures, Juárez captured his attention the most. His autobiography recounted the public program about Juárez that he helped organize to underscore his abiding respect for the man, a concern for educating the public on Mexican history, and his unshakable indigenous identity. Sáenz also referred to authors, titles of works, and literary topics or concepts to illustrate important points. He noted characters in works by writers such as Hans Christian Andersen and Juan Antonio Mateos to describe striking behaviors or pronounced characteristics among persons from his childhood. A similar allusion to Bucephalus, Alexander the Great's famous horse, revealed Sáenz's view of the fine steed that his father had bought for him. While in Laredo, a family received him and his father as if they belonged to the royal line of the Chinese Celestial Empire, and their beautiful daughters guided Sáenz through town with such magical ease that they seemed to be saying "open sesame" and "close sesame" wherever they went. Alice, the city that exceeded Realitos in educational opportunities, also received accolades from his pen. The overwhelmed Sáenz considered it as he would the world-renowned Bagdad of the Orient. The howling coyotes at the railroad workers' supply station, on the other hand, seemed bigger than the big, bad wolf that ate Little Red Riding Hood's grandmother.

Sáenz's preoccupation with his ability to speak Spanish and to deploy a repertoire of information regarding Mexican history and its contemporary sociocultural setting was obviously important to a leader like him who needed to be linguistically and culturally proficient among the largely monolingual and socially marginalized Mexican population. Knowledge of the English language and a sound familiarity with the larger, mostly Anglo, population was also necessary if he was to successfully translate the needs and interests of his people and convince Anglo sources of power and influence to allow change in the racially unequal world of South Texas. Sáenz, of course, did not set out to become a biculturally adept person in order to overcome racial differences and divisions and ameliorate the distressful living and working conditions in the Mexican community. He preferred to think that he emerged "naturally," albeit impressively, from social surroundings that both nurtured his development and challenged his sense of what he believed was right and just.

Sáenz also used history and his community's place in it as a basis for making judgments about racialized social relations. He was especially concerned to demonstrate in his autobiography and diary that Mexicans constituted a charter community by virtue of their lineage from indigenous communities and early colonial settlements. He had obviously inherited the historical consciousness of border residents in communities like Mier that continue to attract much genealogical interest throughout South Texas. The popular history of the border region, as scholars like Jovita González and Américo Paredes have demonstrated, focused on the Spanish side of this border history—that is, it virtually excluded indigenous communities that predated colonization and coexisted and intermarried with the residents of the border community in the nineteenth and twentieth centuries. Castañeda may have echoed popular references to "el León Español" and "las Águilas del Anáhuac," but his focus on the Spanish side of colonial history reflected a biased interpretation of history.[35] Sáenz, on the other hand, was more even-handed. He emphasized their history as the original inhabitants of the Americas and as a colonized community. He interpreted this history as an indigenous person when telling an inherited family story that rings like a creation myth.

According to Sáenz, a group of indigenous survivors fled to the north soon after the Spanish military had conquered the Aztec defenders in what is now Mexico City, but they faced starvation in the unforgiving desert. Another group tried to escape by way of an early trade route to the Caribbean and the southeastern section of the present-day United States, but the presence of Spaniards at Vera Cruz persuaded them to follow the coast in a northern direction until they reached the mouth of the Pánuco River, on the boundary between the states of Veracruz and Tamaulipas. They found Spaniards there and faced the same problem further up the coast, in the town of Soto la Marina, Tamaulipas. Their only alternative was to reenter the mainland and traverse the Sierra Madre and its valleys. They finally reached a location six or ten miles south of Ciudad Victoria, where they established a town in remembrance of the ancient Toltec capital of Tollán (now called Tula, in the state of Hidalgo). When Spaniards arrived in 1617, they moved again into a canyon alongside an area where the mountains ended. Some of them eventually established settlements along the Río Bravo, probably during the late 1700s or early 1800s. "From here," Sáenz added, "it was very easy to cross and roam over the grassy prairie land of the Tejas [Indians]. This will explain well enough of how I came to be born in Realitos and being at the same time an Aztec."[36]

The pilgrimage story explains why he always claimed to be an indigenous person in his speeches and writings. Although usually reticent to express this identity, Sáenz made it especially evident in his diary, beginning with his photograph at the front of the book. His appearance—dark complexion, high cheekbones, and pronounced bridge on his nose—was unmistakably indigenous. He also spoke in endearing terms about fellow indigenous soldiers—"brothers in arms"—from Oklahoma who served with him in the Ninetieth Division. Moreover, he declared that the First World War represented a moment in history when Mexicans had helped form the first contingent of armed indigenous soldiers to bring justice and democracy to Europe. This kind of discerning and prescient view, informed as it was by a pan-tribal identity, no doubt contributed to the broad American identity that he promoted during World War II to legitimate the Mexican voice and reinforce the call for equality.

Sáenz also used history to explain the widespread poverty among Mexicans in South Texas. Anglo settlers arrived in the mid-1800s, entered into marriages and business ventures with landed Mexican families, and began securing vast amounts of land. Violence—meted out by the Texas Rangers and federal troops—against Mexico in 1846–1848 and against the resident Mexican population during the rest of the nineteenth century, made way for new waves of Anglo newcomers. The eventual Anglo takeover, according to Sáenz's autobiography, influenced all aspects of social relations. Even poor Anglos who had worked and lived among Mexicans came to believe "that their red sun-baked skin made them better than us with our skin the color of clay, and they forgot to be grateful and responsible." His personal experiences with discrimination consequently became part of a larger narrative that he described in the preface to his diary as a "conflict between two opposing races." Sáenz, however, did not make much note of the violent responses by the Mexican community to the socioeconomic transformations in South Texas and Mexico.

The 1892 revolt led by Catarino Garza against Mexican President Porfirio Díaz did not receive attention from Sáenz in his writings, although this may have been the uprising that his grandfather had joined. The armed action was primarily directed toward Mexico and was organized along the border and in the area surrounding San Diego. Garza received financial support from influential Mexican ranchers and merchants, and ranch hands from the area joined the insurgent army. Sáenz also overlooked the violent response by authorities, including the Texas Rangers that he openly despised. Sáenz failed to acknowledge yet another set of important political activities. This included labor organizing and strike activity, as well as exiled political activity in the area of Central Texas and San Antonio, where he lived in the 1910s. He does mention the San Diego revolt in his diary and even stated that he understood why some Mexicans were driven to take such drastic action, but he did this to critique armed action and to argue that US military service would gain greater support for the Mexican cause. It did not matter that the revolt was planned in a meeting at San Diego and that it attracted supporters from the area at the time when he was seventeen years old and working nearby. Sáenz's omissions and partial acknowledgments represent a self-defining measure of his moderate views regarding the Mexican condition and its social cause.

Although Sáenz did not write much about radical Mexican politics or the general reaction to discrimination and inequality in his diary, he did speak briefly of German saboteurs who influenced untold numbers of Mexicans to escape to Mexico as a way to avoid the draft and of seditious leaders who believed that armed action could bring to Mexico the territory it lost in the war with the United States. The exodus of agricultural workers and the armed revolt that exploded in 1915, according to Sáenz, contributed to the charges of disloyalty and damaged relations with Anglos in Texas. He added that differences within the Mexican community also led to serious divisions. His diary clearly stated where he stood: "We become divided when we should have built a united front like we are known to singularly do when faced with the understandable sense of responsibility to the nation."

Sáenz's righteous sense of the world obviously sprang from the parental guidance that he received as a young boy. Other sources of knowledge and inspiration also influenced his general outlook on proper social behavior that he used as a frame of reference in his political work. He made special note of the numerous "good deeds" that he observed as a young boy. He especially remembered a special act of kindness by a man named Rafael Arredondo that influenced him to work with children. It happened when a traveling show of clowns, singers, and acrobats arrived in Realitos, and Sáenz waited outside the site of the performance with other children who could not pay the entrance fee. Arredondo, his father's childhood friend, surprised Sáenz when he told him, "Go in, I paid for you." The unexpected and kindhearted act affected the boy so deeply that he resolved to help other poor children throughout his life as a way of returning the favor.

Sáenz, like many of his contemporaries, also used his Catholic beliefs and Christian faith to guide his work. His most telling statement of the divine as a source of inspiration and wisdom appeared in his 101-page manuscript, *Realismo Misterioso*, that narrated his thoughts during a near-death experience.[37] At the age of fifty-two, Sáenz suddenly fell into a coma that may have been triggered by exhaustion and over-prescribed medicine for fatigue. When he regained his faculties, he wrote of an altered state of consciousness during which he traveled back and forth between a purgatory-like spiritual world and his bedridden reality in his McAllen home. While his days seemed to pass like years—alternately slow then fast—he moved deeper into the world of spirits but retained the ability to see and understand his surroundings even as he was declared clinically dead, and his loved ones made preparations for his funeral. This extraordinary but "real" experience allowed him to speak of death as the spirit's "sweet" departure from the body and God's divine welcome into the eternal home of rest. Years later, he would continue to defy death with his faith: "Why fear death if it is the only thing between me and God?"[38]

Broadly speaking, *Realismo Misterioso* is evocative of the magical realism of more contemporary Latin American writers like Alejo Carpentier and Juan Rulfo, who blurred the line between the magical and the real and offered reasonable, familiar, and believable representations of a new synthetic "reality." A closer examination of the manuscript reveals an unsettled Sáenz slowly entering a comatose state while remaining fully conscious as the priest, his wife, and other relatives and close friends could only assume that he was dying. Sáenz could see and hear people witnessing his deteriorating condition while simultaneously engaging the good and bad spirits fighting over his body and soul. As his health worsened, he witnessed even more fantastic scenes, including the rapid passing of time, the accelerated aging of persons, and bolder bad spirits that appeared with the faces of friends and loved ones. Sáenz, however, survived by calling on God's love and mercy and on his own understanding of human behavior that he had learned in his public life.

Realismo Misterioso and other records in Sáenz's archival collection, demonstrates religion and faith to be an important part of his life. He and his contemporaries often pointed to God's love and mercy over his entire creation in support of moral arguments against discrimination and inequality. The trust and confidence that he obviously drew from his religion and faith to handle his profound coma-induced crisis points to a genuine devotion to the divine in his political work. Sáenz, however, also turned to his experience as a civil rights activist to make critical and lifesaving judgments about human behavior in the other world. He described the fight for equal rights as a replay of the spiritual battle and suggested that the responsibility of an effective leader was to watch participants in the social movement closely and patiently to determine their sincerity and honesty. Sáenz, in the end, lived the life that he imagined in his coma: a back-and-forth movement between unsettling experiences in life and the spiritual sources of meaning, inspiration, and purpose. He also fashioned a seamless sense of the world defined by his faith in divine justice and a belief in a purgatory-like form of accountability associated with the Catholic Church.

Although Sáenz often referred to divine inspiration to explain his righteous sense of purpose in the social setting that he inhabited, he also invoked the nonreligious spirit world to bring his imagination to life. On one occasion, for example, he narrated a dream in which a dove flew to him until "there was nothing else to do" but "to take her into my hands" and receive from her red feet two writing feathers, one white and one green. Although the colors already suggested an obvious nationalistic purpose, he underscored it when he added that the dove magically transformed itself into "the inseparable brother of our Aztec people—the mockingbird." Sáenz, in other words, used nationalist and indigenous symbols to transform his personal decision to write on behalf of Mexicans as a heroic duty and to display this self-validating act to his family and whoever else would read his accounts.[39]

Conclusion

Sáenz's autobiographical accounts are important because they tell us of the life experiences that led him to prominence as a teacher, writer, and civil rights leader. His ability to emerge with such success was all the more significant when seen against the general trends of poverty, discrimination, and inequality plaguing the Mexican community of the first half of the twentieth century. This is not to say that his personal qualities and abilities solely explain his educational, professional, and political achievements. Certainly, his confidence, determination, and studiousness inform much of his success. It would be a mistake, however, to divorce these qualities from his supportive family, his parents' fortuitous decisions, the mentoring and help from other influential adults, the meaningful relationships with fellow civil rights leaders, and the educational and professional opportunities that appeared along the way. He was equally challenged and motivated by widespread prejudice and discrimination, his lack of resources, political differences and divisions in the community, and resistance to change by persons in positions of political power and influence. The sociocultural world that Sáenz inhabited, in other words, explains the difficulties and encouragements that guided his life.

Sáenz's telling of his experiences also provides explanations for his ideas and life trajectory. However, he did not limit himself to the obvious formative experiences of challenges and opportunities in his life. He also expressed an autobiographical awareness of his position as an oppositional voice in the South Texas world of Mexican marginalization and Anglo dominance and as an architect of a new ethnic identity that sought to make use of political opportunities in Texas. This projection, from personal experiences and motivations to the larger social world of civil rights activism, involved inconsistent as well as earnest exercises in self-configuration and various explanations of the sociocultural world that he shared with other like-minded and non-concurring Mexican political leaders.

Sáenz's narratives—autobiographies, war diary, letters, speeches, and newspaper articles—reveal another key point of oppositional self-awareness. He sought to write himself and the Mexican community into a history that dismissed and disparaged them. This act of text writing involved more than retrieving a favored past to rejoin the dismembered parts. Sáenz also infused the recovery enterprise with the righteous sense of setting things right that drew added meaning from a personal quest for dignity and self-respect. Projecting a private, highly moralistic discourse on group identity and history—no doubt understood as such by Mexican audiences who were also apt to see social issues in personal terms—strengthened and popularized his reasoned observations and arguments regarding discrimination, inequality, an indigenous past, wartime contributions, democratic principles, unity, schooling, and a broadly defined American identity.

We can also see Sáenz as a self-defining political actor who joined other civil rights leaders in constructing a new ethnic or Mexican American identity that elbowed aside the Mexicanist political identity within their communities and countered the popular disparaging view of Mexicans as a largely foreign and disloyal population. His participation in this process reveals the give and take at the public square and in a Mexican civil rights community that was fragmented and even divided, not unified. Despite his own multidimensionality, Sáenz emerged as a fairly consistent proponent of a new language of democracy and justice for this emerging identity. He used creative moral arguments and discursive propositions that defined patriotism, civic culture, and American identity in broad and politically effective ways.

Faith and religion in particular provided Sáenz with a source of meaning and purpose in his personal and public life. Divine justice and the cultural discourse of community in the Catholic Church strengthened his resolve to work on behalf of Mexican rights, especially among children. His account of the afterlife was especially instructive in understanding the significant psychological pressures that leaders like himself encountered and tried to resolve with the use of faith and religion as well as with a related spiritual sense of identification with the Mexican community. Moving between the real and the imagined revealed profound complexities and uncertainties in José de la Luz Sáenz's life as well as in the community that he sought to reconstruct.

Notes

1. Alonso Perales, "Arquitectos de Nuestros Propios Destinos; Interesante Carta de un Gran Líder Mexicano," *La Verdad* (September 14, 1952): 1. Perales was himself one of the best-known Mexican civil rights leaders of the first half of the twentieth century and a reliable authority on leadership in the Mexican community. His fame owed much to his role as a cofounder of the League of United Latin American Citizens and the author of three tomes on civil rights issues: *En defensa de mi raza*, 2 vols. (San Antonio: Artes Gráficas, 1936–1937); and *Are We Good Neighbors?* (San Antonio: Artes Gráficas, 1948).

2. Mario T. García has proposed a generational framework for the study of Mexican American history in the twentieth century that focuses on the protest community and its succeeding political identities, with the "Mexican-American Generation" constituting the group that emerged in the 1920s and is mostly associated with LULAC and its brand of ethnic politics. *Mexican Americans: Leadership, Ideology, and Identity, 1930–1960* (New Haven: Yale University Press, 1989).

3. The following publications address various aspects of Sáenz's life and political work: Carole E. Christian, "Joining the American Mainstream, Texas Mexican Americans during World War I," *Southwestern Historical Quarterly* 92 (April 1989): 559–95; Emilio Zamora, "Fighting on Two Fronts: José de la Luz Sáenz and the Language of the Mexican-American Civil Rights Movement," in *Recovering the U.S. Hispanic Literary Heritage*, ed. José F. Aranda Jr. and Silvio Torres-Saillant (Houston: Arte Público, 2002), 4:214–39; Emilio Zamora, *Claiming Rights and Righting Wrongs in Texas: Mexican Workers and Job Politics during World War II* (College Station: Texas A&M University Press, 2009); José A. Ramírez, *To the Line of Fire! Mexican Texans and World War I* (College Station: Texas A&M University Press 2009); and Jesús Rosales, "José de la Luz Sáenz: Precursor de la literatura del Movimiento Chicano," *Camino Real* 1, no. 0 (2009): 153–73. Researchers may also wish to consult the José de la Luz Sáenz Papers, located at the Benson Latin American Collection, General Libraries, University of Texas at Austin (hereafter Sáenz Papers).

4. I borrow the concept of autobiographical consciousness from Linda Guardia Jackson, a recent PhD graduate from the School of Education at the University of Texas at Austin. Although Jackson was not the first to use autobiographical narratives to study self-awareness and identity, her dissertation may have initiated this analysis among Mexican American bilingual teachers in our public schools. "Becoming An Activist Chicana Teacher: A Story of Identity Making of a Mexican American Bilingual Educator" (PhD diss., University of Texas at Austin, 2009). For additional examinations of autobiographical narratives authored by Mexican-origin persons, see C. Alejandra Elenes, "Chicana Feminist Narratives and the Politics of the Self," *Frontiers: A Journal of Women Studies* 21, no. 3 (2000): 105–23; Genaro M. Padilla, "The Recovery of Chicano Nineteenth-Century Autobiography," *American Quarterly* 40 (September 1988): 286–306; Genaro M. Padilla, *My History, Not Yours: The Formation of Mexican American Autobiography* (Madison: University of Wisconsin Press, 1993); Shirley K. Rose, "Metaphors and Myths of Cross-Cultural Literacy: Autobiographical Narratives by Maxine Hong Kingston, Richard Rodriguez, and Malcolm X," *MELUS* 14 (Spring 1987): 3–15; and Ramón Saldívar, "Ideologies of the Self, Chicano Autobiographies," chap. 7 in *Chicano Narratives, The Dialectics of Difference* (Madison: University of Wisconsin Press, 1990), 154–70.

5. *Los méxico-americanos en la gran guerra y su contingente en pro de la democracia, la humanidad y la justicia* (San Antonio: Artes Gráficas, 1933); *Realismo Misterioso: Estudio Psico-Teosófico*, 1940, Sáenz Papers; and "Yo, Omnia Mea Mecum Porto," 1944, Sáenz Papers. The 298-page diary includes daily entries for most of an eleven-month period that began with Sáenz's induction into the US expeditionary force in 1917 and his release from military service in 1919. He wrote the first unpublished manuscript to describe his journey into the spiritual world during a

near-death experience. The last work spans a fourteen-year period between his birth in 1888 and his family's relocation in 1904 to Alice, Texas.

6. The Viceroy of New Spain commissioned José de Escandón to lead a settlement effort in the late 1740s. It succeeded in establishing settlements along the current Texas-Mexico border. Many Mexican families from Texas and northern Mexico, as genealogy researchers will attest, trace their ancestry to these colonial families in places like Reynosa Viejo, Mier, Camargo, Revilla, and Laredo.

7. Martin Donell Kohout, "Realitos, TX," *Handbook of Texas Online*, accessed May 25, 2009, http://www.tshaonline.org/handbook/online/articles/hlro5.

8. Sáenz's recollections of the family history and his experiences growing up in Realitos and Alice, unless otherwise noted, are based on his autobiography "Yo."

9. The reference to "on halves" indicated that Rosalío and the rancher had entered into a contractual understanding whereby the owner would make available his land, sheep, and possibly feed while the worker would supply his labor. Like in the case of land renters or sharecroppers, the owner and the worker would share the fruits of the labor—in this case, the newborn sheep—at the end of a period, usually a year. Sáenz included in his archives a formal contract between Rosalío and the rancher Hinojosa that detailed the contractual understandings.

10. Sáenz remembered that two persons, a man named Collins and a widow named Panchita Martínez, schooled his brothers. He did not indicate receiving any schooling in Realitos.

11. Petra and Rosalío had seven children. José de la Luz Sáenz, "Short Autobiographical Sketch from 'I', By Myself," 1947, Sáenz Papers.

12. After its establishment in 1988, the town of Alice prospered quickly as the principal junction between the Texas Mexican Railway and the San Antonio and Aransas Pass Railroad, a tributary of the Missouri Pacific. Aside from the increased trade through Alice, the different railroad gauges that met in town required a workforce to load and unload the railroad cars. Alicia Salinas, "Alice, TX," *Handbook of Texas Online*, accessed June 27, 2009, http://www.tshaonline.org/handbook/online/articles/heao1.

13. "Si hubiera sabido que mi trabajo iba a ser enseñar inglés a los mexicanos, no hubiera venido desde tan lejos."

14. "que nos niegan iguales derechos y oportunidades en el gran tiroteo de la vida, por la existencia y el progreso de todo ser humano."

15. Sáenz, "Short Autobiographical Sketch."

16. Nat Benton became a leader in the professionalization of the teaching profession in the area. He organized at least one regional teachers' meeting in Alice in 1905, and thereafter became the Nueces County superintendent of schools and helped establish the Gulf Coast Educational Association. Although Alice Benton

has not been given credit for contributing to this work, she was her husband's constant companion. Cecilia Aros Hunter and Leslie Gene Hunter, *Texas A&M University–Kingsville* (Chicago: Arcadia, 2000).

17. "El placer de luchar por el mejoramiento de mi raza," 117. Sáenz described relations between Mexican and Anglo students as distant and with few opportunities to socialize and build close relationships. He does not mention any such relationships with fellow Anglo students, including J. Frank Dobie, the famed folklorist from the University of Texas, who, despite this distance, went on to become an authority on Mexicans from South Texas and once referred to them as "my people." See the following for a critique of Dobie's failure to fully engage the reality of racial conflict and his role as an apologist "for the violent Anglo-American colonization of South Texas": José E. Limón, *Dancing with the Devil; Society and Cultural Poetics in Mexican-American South Texas* (Madison: University of Wisconsin Press, 1994), 46–59. Quotes on pages 51 and 53.

18. The school was named after the businessman from Corpus Christi who responded with "great enthusiasm and generosity. José de la Luz Sáenz, "La Escuela Laica 'Vicente Lozano,'" *La Verdad*, February 23, 1951.

19. Many would-be teachers like Sáenz attended business schools in preparation for classroom work since few university teacher-training programs existed at the time. Once they finished their business school instruction and secured a job with a school, they often attended teacher-training institutes organized by experienced teachers to insure that the novices learned the trade. Sáenz probably attended well-known institutes organized by the Bentons in Corpus Christi or another master teacher and close friend from San Antonio named James Knox.

20. José de la Luz Sáenz, "A Nuestra Juventud Estudiosa Latinnoamericana" 1938, Sáenz Papers.

21. According to one of his daughters, the young family lived in the following towns from the late 1910s to the 1950s: Moore, New Braunfels, Pleasanton, Poteet, Alice, Premont, Peñitas, La Joya, and McAllen. Eva Olivia (Sáenz) Alvarado, phone conversation with author, October 4, 2009. Fidencio M. Guerra, a judge from South Texas in the 1960s and 1970 who Sáenz had mentored as a young man, underscored Sáenz's commitment to education: "He was a loyal American, a civic leader, a war veteran, a public speaker and a writer. But I remember him best in the profession of an educator. And I believe this is the role he liked best." Fidencio M. Guerra to the principal of the J. Luz Sáenz School, November 20, 1966, Sáenz Papers.

22. Sáenz took special pride in his mother's family history. María Petra was born in Pleasanton on August 1898, the daughter of Gregorio Esparza, the granddaughter of Manuel Esparza, and the great granddaughter of José María (Gregorio) Esparza. José María fought and died in the 1836 Battle of the Alamo, and his wife,

Manuela (Leal) Esparza, and his sons, Enrique, María del Jesús, and Manuel, witnessed the battle. The Esparza family founded and settled San Augustine, a community near the town of Pleasanton, on the Enrique Esparza land grant. The settlement may have been named in the language of its first settler, San Agustín. Sáenz and María Petra raised nine children, four sons and five daughters: Adán, María de la Luz, Evangelina Lucía, Eduardo Francisco, Enrique León, Eva Olivia, Cristina Antonia, Beatriz, and José de la Luz. George Benavides, phone conversation with author, October 4, 2009; Reynaldo J. Esparza, "Esparza, José María," *Handbook of Texas Online*, accessed July 12, 2009, http://www.tshaonline.org/handbook/online/articles/fes02; Linda Peterson, "San Augustine, Texas (Atascosa County)," *Handbook of Texas Online*, accessed July 12, 2009, http://www.tshaonline.org/handbook/online/articles/hrscf; (Sáenz) Alvarado conversation; and Benavides conversation.

23. "Connecting the Centuries, 50 Years of Learning, 1947–1997, J. Luz Sáenz Elementary School, Alice, Texas," program of the anniversary celebration of the school, Sáenz Papers. Sáenz wrote daily notes on loose-leaf paper, in the margins of military manuals, and on postcards that he mailed home for safekeeping. He also included correspondence with Knox and his loved ones as well as articles that he wrote as a war correspondent for the San Antonio daily *La Prensa*.

24. Sáenz toured the state and gave presentations on his book to many friends and acquaintances who contributed to the publication. He printed one thousand copies with the advanced payments that he received. José de la Luz Sáenz, "American Soldiers of Mexican Extraction in World War No. One," 1938, Sáenz Papers.

25. Much of the discussion on the significance of the diary and Sáenz's writings in the interwar period also appears in my previously noted publications: "Fighting on Two Fronts: José de la Luz Sáenz and the Language of the Mexican-American Civil Rights Movement" and *Claiming Rights and Righting Wrongs in Texas: Mexican Workers and Job Politics during World War II*.

26. Evan Anders, "Canales, José Tomás," *Handbook of Texas Online*, accessed October 4, 2009, http://www.tshaonline.org/handbook/online/articles/fcaag; and Cynthia E. Orozco, "Perales, Alonso S.," accessed October 4, 2009, http://www.tshaonline.org/handbook/online/articles/fpe56.

27. For a review of the early history of LULAC as an ethnic organization that offered the upwardly mobile and US-born a new opportunity to challenge discrimination and negotiate improved social relations, see García, *Mexican Americans*, 25–38. Juan Gómez-Quiñones offers a critique of the liberal pluralist approach in the history of LULAC. Gómez-Quiñones, *Chicano Politics: Reality and Promise, 1940–1990* (Albuquerque: University of New Mexico Press, 1990), 21–25. See also Cynthia E. Orozco, "Harlingen Convention," *Handbook of Texas Online*, accessed May 25, 2009, http://www.tshaonline.org/handbook/online/articles/pqh01; Cynthia E. Orozco,

"League of United Latin American Citizens," *Handbook of Texas Online*, accessed May 25, 2009, http://www.tshaonline.org/handbook/online/articles/wel01; and Cynthia E. Orozco, "Ladies LULAC," *Handbook of Texas Online*, accessed May 25, 2009, http://www.tshaonline.org/handbook/online/articles/wel06.

28. Rosaura Sánchez, *Chicano Discourse: Socio-Historic Perspectives* (Houston: Arte Público, 1994), 22.

29. See the following for Sáenz's exhortations that described Americanism as "true Pan American understanding" and an American as someone who "lives and will die to defend the standard ideals": "I Am An American," May 1941, Sáenz Papers. On another occasion, he noted, "Americanism cannot be a single nation's patrimony, but that which is practicable and mutually beneficial to each and everyone of the nations in the Western hemisphere." "Deductive Americanism," April 1944, Sáenz Papers.

30. José de la Luz Sáenz to the editor of the *San Angelo Times*, July 23, 1948, scrapbook, Sáenz Papers.

31. Alonso Perales, "Arquitectos de nuestros propios destinos; Una nueva sociedad para el progreso y bienestar de nuestro pueblo en Texas," *La Prensa*, May 11, 1952.

32. Ibid.

33. Sáenz often noted that the failure to enforce immigration laws and pay just wages contributed to social inequality as well as the accompanying prejudice against all Mexicans. The following is an example of this view: "If the wetback problem would be stopped by our federal and state agencies and appropriate wages are paid to native laborers, the theory of natural low standard of living of the Mexican population would disappear. Who can live decently and raise their norm of living when nothing but miserable wages are paid them?" "Voice of the People; Says 'Wetback' Problem is Ignored," *Denton Record-Chronicle*, June 19, 1952.

34. Agnes G. Grimm, "Velázquez, Eulalio" *Handbook of Texas Online*, accessed July 15, 2009 http://www.tshaonline.org/handbook/online/articles/fve04.

35. Alonso Perales, "Quiénes son los mexicanos que residen en Texas?," *La Verdad*, March 1952. Perales quotes a speech that Castañeda presented on March 16, 1952, at a meeting in Mission, Texas. The assembly discussed the formation of a statewide organization—La Asociación de Buenas Relaciones de Texas—that was established in a subsequent meeting in Alice on May 4, 1952.

36. Sáenz, "Short Autobiographical Sketch." The "I" in the title suggests that this two-page narrative was extracted from the previously noted "Yo." The short narrative, however, does not appear in the longer manuscript. Also, the documents were written at different times. "Yo" was written in 1944 and "Short Autobiographical Sketch" carries the year 1947. Sáenz "confirms" the veracity of the pilgrimage story

in 1946, when he participated in a three-week symposium for thirty teachers from Texas. The meeting, sponsored by the Secretaría de Educación Pública and held at La Escuela Rural de Tamaulipas "Maestro Lauro Aguirre," included a lecture by a noted historian from Tamaulipas named Candelario Reyes. Reyes, according to Sáenz, retold the familiar family story. José de la Luz Sáenz, "Mi Linaje Azteca," three-page typescript, Sáenz Papers.

37. Sáenz, *Realismo Misterioso*.

38. José de la Luz Sáenz, "Arnoldo Díaz: ante sus restos que fueron traidos de Puerto Rico," 1948, Sáenz Papers. "¿Por qué temerle a la muerte, si es lo único que me impide ver a Dios?"

39. José de la Luz Sáenz, "Importante," September 14, 1945, Sáenz Papers.

Figure 2.1. Alice Dickerson Montemayor, first feminist in LULAC; national vice-president general; associate editor of the *LULAC News*; and director general of Junior LULAC. Benson Latin American Collection, University of Texas at Austin.

2

Alice Dickerson Montemayor

Feminism and Mexican American Politics in the 1930s

CYNTHIA E. OROZCO

The history of Mexican-origin women in voluntary organizations is a history largely untold.[1] Women's historians have studied women's organizations (where most women have historically organized) but have given little attention to organizations composed of both women and men and those composed of Mexican-origin women.[2] In her book *The Grounding of Modern Feminism*, historian Nancy F. Cott refers to those activities outside of electoral politics in which women participated as "voluntarist politics."[3] Cott's analysis has little relevance for Mexican-origin women who belonged to no national women's organizations until the early 1970s. In fact, the first national Chicana gathering occurred in 1971, although women had opportunities to congregate before then at national meetings and conventions of mutual aid, civil rights, and labor associations.[4]

Chicano studies scholars have rarely addressed women in organizations.[5] In particular, historians of Chicanos have yet to fully study women's participation in the League of United Latin American Citizens (LULAC). LULAC is the oldest Mexican American civil rights organization in the United

DOI: 10.5876/9781607323372.c002

States.[6] Founded in 1929 in Corpus Christi, Texas, by Mexican American men, LULAC quickly evolved into a statewide and then a national organization.[7] By 1940 it had reached into New Mexico, Colorado, California, Arizona, and Washington, DC.

LULAC can be compared with the National Association for the Advancement of Colored People (NAACP). It is a middle-class organization that has diligently protected the civil rights of Mexican-descent people in the United States. In the 1930s, LULAC men filed the first class-action lawsuit against segregated public schools. They were also responsible for changing the classification of La Raza from "Mexican" to "white" in the 1940 US census. LULAC also moved the Federal Employment Practices Commission (the first federal civil rights agency) to protect La Raza from employment discrimination. At the local level, LULAC desegregated schools, pools, theaters, housing, and real estate.[8]

In 1933 LULAC extended full membership privileges to women through gender-segregated chapters (or councils) called "Ladies LULAC," and women typically organized only with women until the 1960s.[9] Ladies LULAC became especially important in Texas and New Mexico. The first Ladies Council was formed in 1933 in Alice, Texas, and in 1934 LULAC created the office of ladies organizer general to organize women's chapters. By 1940 these chapters numbered twenty-six while men's totaled one hundred. In the 1990s, women constituted over 50 percent of LULAC's membership, and they helped elect the first female national president in 1994.

This essay analyzes gender politics in LULAC in the 1930s, assessing LULAC's ideology as it related to the family and addressing women's participation. It focuses on LULAC feminist Alice Dickerson Montemayor, a member of Laredo's Ladies LULAC. I will discuss her activities and analyze her essays, which challenged the entrenched patriarchal nature of LULAC and of Mexican American society in the 1930s. At the time of her activism her roles encompassed wife, mother, worker, businesswoman, and middle-class woman. As a free-thinking, assertive, independent feminist, she belonged to LULAC at a time of strong patriarchal ideology. It is important to note that her husband, Francisco Montemayor, Sr., was not a member of LULAC.[10]

Many view LULAC as a men's organization because its leadership has been overwhelming male.[11] Others think that all women in LULAC belonged to ladies auxiliaries.[12] In 1983 historian Marta Cotera argued that women took "a more subdued club woman reformist approach channeled through female auxiliary groups."[13] These auxiliaries were thought to be composed of wives. Some believe all women participated in a gender-segregated Ladies LULAC. Others contend that for women, LULAC was "a social gathering for women to go drink coffee and get together."[14]

In sum, historians have hardly addressed Ladies LULAC. For instance, Julia Kirk Blackwelder's study of the Depression in San Antonio, Texas, mentioned middle-class women's volunteerism but did not cite any Mexican-origin women's voluntary organizations other than Beneficencia Mexicana.[15] Ladies LULAC, perhaps the largest Mexican American women's organization in the city (outside of unions), went unmentioned.[16] Richard A. Garcia's *Rise of the Mexican American Middle Class: San Antonio, 1929–1941*, which addressed San Antonio and LULAC in the 1930s, overlooked the San Antonio Ladies LULAC, which had the largest membership in the state. He addressed LULAC as a male institution, discussing women only as wives and family members.[17] Arnoldo De León's brief treatment of Ladies LULAC in Houston in the 1950s should be praised.[18]

Mario T. García devoted a chapter to LULAC in *Mexican Americans: Leadership, Ideology, and Identity*, a book on Mexican American civil rights activism. He briefly addressed women as a group and identified several leaders. He emphasized the work of Ester Machuca, a ladies organizer general in the 1930s; he mistakenly believed she was the first such organizer. In actuality, Estéfana Valdez of Mission held that honor. García mentioned Montemayor, but he did not explain her significance.[19]

Benjamín Márquez's *LULAC: The Evolution of a Mexican American Political Organization*, the only book-length survey of LULAC, offers several paragraphs on women. Although Márquez noted that women constituted 50 percent of the membership, he did not analyze women's historical participation.[20] Yet among those who built LULAC were women from every locale where the League existed. These women constituted a diverse group. Not all had a familial or sexual tie to a man in LULAC. Many participated as single women, as married women whose husbands had no connection to LULAC, or as lesbians. Historically, the majority never participated in the ladies auxiliaries; rather, they belonged to Ladies LULAC and, after 1960, to councils composed of women and men.

Independent women—a few with feminist inclinations, like Montemayor—
could be found in the ranks of LULAC. Mexican American women had a
distinctive feminist heritage that countered a virulent patriarchal heritage. In
the 1930s, ideologies about the family were typically patriarchal in the United
States and Mexico and in Chicano society; LULAC reflected these three
influences. The organization first revealed its patriarchal tendency when it
excluded women in 1929, and it clearly conveyed its patriarchal ideology in
LULAC News. Member J. Reynolds Flores expressed the typical sentiment
about women's place in his 1932 essay, "How to Educate Our Girls," writing,
"The foundations of society rests on the homes. The success of our homes
rests on the wives. Therefore, first of all, teach our girls how to be successful
wives . . . Train them to do small things well and to delight in helping others,
and instill constantly into their minds the necessity for sacrifice for others'
pleasure as a means of soul development."[21]

Another LULAC publication, *Alma Latina*, a short-lived magazine for parents, included an essay titled "La Mujer." The author viewed women "como
madres, como esposas, como hijas o como hermanas" (as mothers, as wives,
as daughters, or as sisters), basing this description on Catholic doctrine,
especially on the story of Adam and Eve, where Adam represented *fuerza*
(strength) and Eve *amor* (love).[22]

LULAC men generally placed women on a pedestal. In 1938 Leo Durán of
the Corpus Christi men's council idealized "all mothers of Lulackers as the
ones responsible and ever watchful of all Lulackers and the teachers of future
generation that LULAC might start in all Latin homes."[23] A 1934 LULAC song,
"To Our Ladies Councils," noted, "Ladies councils are our inspiration head
and soul of our splendid LULAC."[24] But men made little effort to mobilize
women into chapters.

One LULAC member provided a progressive stance on men's familial
responsibility. An article entitled "Parents Are Fathers" in *Alma Latina* stated,
"Fathers often leave all of the raising of the small child to the mothers. This
isn't fair to any one concerned. It gives the mother too much to do, robs the
child of father's influence, and leaves the father, in a sense childless."[25] It is
unclear if the author was male or female. The article, however, was atypical
of LULAC members' ideology.

LULAC men's gender ideology reflected the thought of Mexico Texanos
and other Chicanos, a borderlands people whose thought reflected a blend

of US and Mexican thought. Women in the United States obtained the vote in 1920, and Mexico offered them the vote in 1958. Mexico Texanos, a product of two cultures and two nations, offered women full membership in LULAC (and thus the vote) in 1933. LULAC men were influenced by events in Mexico, as reported by the Mexican and Mexico Texano press. In 1929 *El Paladín*, another official LULAC organ, editorialized, "Es Justa la Aspiración de la Mujer de Nuestro País," favoring women's right to vote in Mexico and betraying the fact that the author still considered Mexico his country.[26] The essay suggests that women's suffrage in Mexico influenced LULAC men. But patriarchal ideology in Spanish- and English-language newspapers also influenced them. *La Prensa*, the only statewide Spanish-language newspaper, espoused this patriarchal ideology. Feminist writers were few.

In the 1930s, few LULAC women espoused feminism. Besides Montemayor, only one other woman penned a feminist essay in *LULAC News* in the 1930s. Adela Sloss of San Juan, Texas, a high school graduate in 1927, belonged to one of several ladies auxiliaries that existed only briefly before Ladies LULAC was formed. In 1934 she wrote an essay titled "Por que en muchos hogares Latinos no existe verdadera felicidad" (Why Most Homes Are Unhappy). For Sloss, la mujer was heterosexual and married to a member of La Raza. Sloss challenged sexism in the home and male privilege. She wrote, "A la mujer latina desde niña se le aprisiona" (Since childhood, Latinas are imprisoned) and "El hombre Latino tiene todos los privilegios y derechos" (Latino men have all the privileges and rights). She argued that happiness existed in European American homes because in the home "ella es la compañera del esposo y no la esclava" (she is the husband's companion and not his slave).[27] Too, through her life she championed civil rights as an orator, organizer, and newspaper essayist in the lower Rio Grande Valley in Texas. She continued to challenge patriarchal family ideology when she married. She raised children and reorganized traditional family life by using day care and involved her children in her political activities. Sloss was no prisoner of her home or marriage, though she found no support for her vision of family life in LULAC.[28]

Alice Dickerson Montemayor followed Sloss as a critic of LULAC's family ideology. A committed member, Montemayor was a woman of many "firsts." In 1937 she became the first woman elected to a national office not specifically designed for a woman—the position of second vice-president general—the third-highest post in the organization.[29] She was also the first woman to serve as an associate editor of *LULAC News* and the first person to write a charter to sponsor a Junior LULAC (youth) chapter. She was an ardent advocate for the inclusion of youth, including girls. Moreover, she was an avid supporter of more Ladies LULACs from 1936 to around 1940.

Born on August 6, 1902, in Laredo, Texas, Alice Dickerson (known as Alicia) was a woman of mixed heritage, the only child born to Manuela Barrera of Laredo and Irishman John Randolph Dickerson, a native of New Orleans. She was a descendant of one of the first twenty-eight families who settled Laredo in the 1750s; her grandmother was Juana Inez de la Cruz. Her father had moved from New Orleans to San Antonio, where he worked as an engineer for the International & Great Northern Railroad Company (now the Missouri Pacific). He helped build the railroad from Austin to San Antonio and brought the first passenger train from San Antonio to Laredo. Alicia's mother had worked as a seamstress out of her home before she married Dickerson.[30]

Because she was born and raised in Laredo on the Texas-Mexico border, Alicia grew up with a Mexico Texano identity. She also claimed her indigenous and Irish heritage. Due to her part-Irish heritage, La Raza sometimes called her "gringa," although her brown color made her look like a *mestiza* (of Spanish and Indian descent). Unlike most of La Raza in the early twentieth century, she grew up in a bilingual home. Her command of English gave her an advantage over other Mexico Texanos while her mixed heritage privileged her. Her middle-class status also distinguished her from most of La Raza in Laredo.[31]

What life experiences help explain Montemayor's feminism and her rise in LULAC? Her education and extracurricular activities prepared her for an active, meaningful adult life. She attended the private Catholic school Colegio de Guadalupe (Guadalupe College, later called the Ursuline Academy). As a girl she constantly got in trouble because of her admittedly clownish behavior. At Laredo High School (now Martin High School) she participated in the Glee Club, the Nike Literary Club, the Science Club, and the debating team. During her junior and senior years she wrote editorials for the *Laredo High School Journal*, contributed to the humor column, and reported on girls' athletic activities. She also served as editor and columnist for *The Live Wire*, the student newspaper.[32]

Besides her intellectual pursuits, Dickerson developed her physical abilities. She played on the girls' volleyball, tennis, and basketball teams, serving as captain of the basketball team her junior and senior years. For four years the school selected her as "best girl athlete." These physical activities convinced her of girls' and women's capabilities.[33]

Dickerson's education made her an exception in the Mexican-origin community in Texas, especially women. She graduated from high school in 1924 and attended night school at Laredo Business College for a year.[34] A high school education was rare for the working class and Mexican Americans in the 1920s. In the 1910s, compulsory education brought more children of Mexican descent into Texas schools, although often in separate schools. Those attending college were few; 250 persons of Mexican origin attended college in 1930, most of them men.[35]

Barriers created by race and gender limited Dickerson's schooling, despite her desire for higher education. Southwest Texas State Teachers College in San Marcos accepted her, but she was unable to leave home; Laredo had no college in the 1920s.[36] (Later, when Laredo Junior College opened its doors in 1947, she attended night school for two years.)[37] Few of her intellectual influences are known; she read George Eliot and William H. Allen, author of "Women's Part in Government." Her role models through life would include Marie Curie, Amelia Earhart, Carry Nation, Frances Perkins, Eleanor Roosevelt, Helen Hayes, and Irene Dunne. Her Mexicana role model was Sor Juana Inés de la Cruz, the feminist nun and intellectual.[38]

After graduation, Dickerson considered four careers: lawyer, actress, author, and artist.[39] She contemplated going to college and law school, but her father died two days before her high school graduation, and she was "forced to earn her livelihood in order to support herself and her mother."[40] She gave up thoughts of acting because, although she had belonged to the high school drama club, her mother believed that women onstage were not members of "decent society." She achieved her dreams of writing in the articles she produced for *LULAC News* in the 1930s—articles through which her legacy is known— but she published no books of poetry or prose during her lifetime. She realized her talent for art much later in life. In 1973, with an ill husband at home and at the urging of her son, she finally picked up a paintbrush. By 1980 she was an acclaimed folk artist in Texas known to her admirers as Admonty, and she became the subject of a chapter in *Folk Art in Texas*. Chicana and Chicano artists embraced her as their own.[41] Although she never worked for pay as an artist, lawyer, actress, or author, she nonetheless left an imprint on the local community of Laredo.[42] Moreover, because of her work in LULAC, she impacted Texas and beyond.

Dickerson had been born into the middle class, and her education provided employment in that sector. She worked at a local dry goods store while she attended Laredo Business College. Western Union employed her as desk clerk from 1924 to 1927, her first full-time job. After a short time at Western Union, she became the supervisor of the messenger boys. On the job she met Francisco Montemayor of Nuevo Laredo, a bookkeeper at Banco Longoria, and they married in 1927 when Dickerson was twenty-two. She quit her job and shortly thereafter, in 1927, bore her first son, Francisco, Jr. Around 1930 she returned briefly to Western Union before taking on a supervisory job at Kress Restaurant.[43] Her employment patterns typified those of the Mexican-origin female middle class, whose occupations included teachers and clerks.[44]

In 1933 she became a social worker, a position that broadened her horizons. Traveling beyond Laredo, she encountered race discrimination. After taking a merit exam in Austin, she qualified as a caseworker for the Department of Public Welfare. During the Depression, she worked in Laredo, in broader Webb County, and in Cotulla, in adjacent La Salle County. When she arrived in Cotulla, the European American county judge refused to give her a key to her county courthouse office, and she worked under a tree for two weeks until he finally conceded. Even her clients discriminated against her; poor whites refused to reveal their financial circumstances to a "Meskin," and a bodyguard protected her. Still, in Cotulla she placed an estimated 400 to 500 Mexican Americans on the welfare rolls.[45]

During her fifteen-month stay in Cotulla, Montemayor challenged white privilege. She helped desegregate the county courthouse, which prohibited Mexicans on the second floor, personally escorting the first group to her upstairs office. She also questioned the practice of segregated masses at the Catholic Church, which had a 7 a.m. mass for Mexicans and a 9 a.m. mass for whites.[46] Reminiscing in 1986, Montemayor expressed the greatest job satisfaction with her Cotulla job; there, she said, she had "had to fight."[47]

In 1936 she opened Monty's Fashion Shop in Laredo, a business that typified the kind that a Mexican-origin woman might own, a small business in the service sector with a female clientele who purchased goods for themselves, their family, or their household. But apparently the dress store failed, and by September 1936, she was heading the business office of Montgomery Ward's fashion department in Laredo.[48]

Several anecdotes about her personal life reveal a rebellious streak. Despite her active life as a student, her mother wielded control over her, treating her like a "little princess." Beyond that, Catholic doctrine and family ideology mandated the "protection" of females, and young women were not to work outside the home or travel unaccompanied by a man. Thus, she was prohibited from going out and visiting others; even during her courtship with Francisco, a female cousin chaperoned her on a regular basis.[49] Perhaps these social restrictions made her rebel.

In any event, she began to break from expectations. Although Francisco's mother had asked her to wear a traditional long white wedding gown, the practical and rebellious Alicia wore a suit appropriate for her California honeymoon. She also defied her mother-in-law's belief that a mixed marriage would not work. She challenged the idea that because she was part Irish, the marriage would end in divorce. Even so, the new bride told her mother-in-law, "I'm not guaranteeing I won't get a divorce if my husband doesn't treat me right."[50]

Montemayor joined civic life around 1937 when Francisco Jr. was in school. Her participation in public life paralleled the traditional life cycle of many heterosexual women, which revolved around patterns of childbearing and child rearing. In 1936 Ladies Organizer General Ester Machuca, a member of Ladies LULAC in El Paso, contacted Montemayor. Along with Minnie Zamora, Juanita Villarreal, Adelina Domínguez, Mrs. O. N. Lightner, and Mrs. A. R. Marulanda, Montemayor helped charter a council in Laredo. Husbands Arnulfo Zamora, J. G. Villarreal, and Fred O. Domínguez belonged to the local LULAC men's council, which had existed there since 1929.[51]

Membership was limited, fluctuating between seventeen and thirty-four, and excluded of working-class women. Members had to be recommended, and most had a high school education. Most were married homemakers while others worked as secretaries for the city and the county. Unmarried members included Lucinda Coronado, Emma Hernández, Elvira García, Esperanza E. Treviño, and Elena Leal—probably all recent high school graduates.[52]

In the 1930s, Laredo Ladies LULAC was one of the most active councils. *LULAC News* noted, "What council in the League has shown most activity since the beginning of the present fiscal year and has obtained results?

Without hesitation we answer the Laredo Ladies Council No. 15."[53] The chapter encouraged women to vote, held citizenship classes, and urged members "to have aspirations to work away from home." Members helped the women in Cotulla organize a chapter, no doubt through Montemayor's contacts there. The educational committee helped the mother of second-grader Roberto Moreno obtain justice for her son, whom teacher Joyce Williams had "severely whipped." The council also sponsored benefits for the Laredo orphanage, raised $250 for flood survivors, bought school supplies for poor Mexican-origin children, sponsored a column in Laredo's major newspaper, and published an edition of *LULAC News*. Delegates traveled to LULAC's annual national convention out of town and sponsored a Junior LULAC chapter. Class defined their activism; no direct assistance went to the working class during these depression years.[54]

LULAC News reports indicate that Ladies LULAC largely worked independently of the Laredo men's council. It was definitely not an auxiliary. In a 1984 interview, Montemayor said, "[M]en's LULAC had nothing to do with us."[55] On two occasions, when the two councils cosponsored events, the division of labor fell along gender lines. For instance, when the national president general visited from New Mexico in 1939, Montemayor chaired the banquet decoration committee, to which only women belonged. Men were in charge of arrangements and guests, many of whom were political officials. On another occasion, at a jointly sponsored ceremony in 1938, both councils "enjoyed refreshments served by the different committees of Ladies."[56]

The group also functioned as a social club. The chapter met on Friday nights (probably over dinner) and for a time met at a room in the Hamilton Hotel at 8 p.m. They held "just Lulac parties for good Lulac members," some of which were fund-raising benefits. In March 1937, members entertained their husbands with a dinner party, although not all were married and not all of the members' husbands were LULAC members.[57]

Montemayor was the first secretary of the Laredo council and its president from 1938 to 1939.[58] As secretary, she reported the chapter's activities to the *LULAC News* column "Around the Shield," which focused on local councils. She wrote, "We have always said and we still maintain that at the back of progress and success the ladies take a leading hand."[59] Because of her diligence about sending in news, *LULAC News* staff member J. C. Machuca (Ester's husband) took notice. Moreover, Fred O. Domínguez, who came from her hometown and could speak in her favor, served as a *LULAC News* associate editor. Consequently, in June 1937, *LULAC News* named Laredo Ladies LULAC as one of two outstanding LULAC chapters. This should be attributed to the council's activism, Montemayor's reports and probably due to the fact that the chapter sold ads for the magazine and increased its circulation.[60]

Montemayor soon garnered national attention. She was one of two Laredo Ladies council delegates to the national convention in 1937 (Houston) and 1938 (El Paso). In Houston she was the only woman on the five-member finance committee. In 1937 the nominating committee, which consisted of one delegate from each council and was overwhelmingly male, named her to a national post. Albert Redwine of the El Paso men's council nominated her. Montemayor was a member of the nominating committee but recalled being out of the room when the appointment by acclamation occurred; it took her by complete surprise. The news of her sudden rise in LULAC began to spread.[61]

Between 1937 and 1940, Montemayor held three national positions: second national vice-president general; associate editor of *LULAC News*, and director general of Junior LULAC.[62] The position of second national vice-president general was not gendered; indeed, the first person to fill the position was Fidencio Guerra of McAllen, Texas. But from the time of Montemayor's ascension to that office in 1937 until the abolishment of the office in 1970, women continued to hold this post. Apparently, the position became defined by gender only after a woman held it. There is no evidence that women defined this position as their own.

Montemayor used her three positions to advocate for women and youth. As second national vice-president general she promoted the establishment of more ladies councils in her columns, speeches, and letters.[63] As associate editor of *LULAC News*, she also advocated for women, penning a stinging unsigned editorial titled "Son Muy Hombres(?)."[64] Two sexist incidents moved her to do so. An unidentified male LULACer had written a national officer, "I hope that President Ramón Longoria will get well soon. There are those of us who hate to be under a woman," a clear expression of fear that Montemayor would became national president. The second incident also involved a national officer, presumably Longoria of Harlingen, who ignored three letters from El Paso's Ladies LULAC, eventually prompting the group to withdraw from the League "rather than create trouble and friction." (The chapter later reorganized.) According to Montemayor, the inaction of the national office could be attributed to men who "are cowardly and unfair, ignorant and narrow minded." In her written critique of the incident, she appealed to the LULAC and US constitutions. She concluded her essay by asking any member to step forward and write an article favoring the suppression of ladies councils and their denial of equal rights.[65]

In 1937 Mrs. Charles Ramírez of San Antonio's Ladies LULAC developed the idea for Junior LULACs and sponsored a resolution to create the youth chapters. Ramírez and Mrs. Santos Herrera organized the first Junior LULAC, but Montemayor was the primary force behind the youth chapters. In August 1938 Montemayor began writing a series of essays in *LULAC News* encouraging senior councils to organize youth. Besides serving as a local sponsor, she penned several essays to foster their organization after she was no longer an associate editor or an official youth organizer, and she wrote the first charter for a youth chapter.[66]

Around March 1937 Montemayor organized the second Junior LULAC council at her house, and it proved the most active chapter. Its first president was Ezequiel D. Salinas, whose father was a LULAC member. In March 1938, officers included Perfecto Solís, president; Delia Dávila, vice president; Fernando Salinas, secretary; Gloria E. Benavides, assistant secretary; and Montemayor's son, Francisco I. Montemayor, Jr., assistant treasurer. Most of the twenty-two members were children of LULAC members. Their ages ranged between nine and fifteen. These Junior LULACers wrote articles for *LULAC News* and worked on raising funds for a drum and bugle corps.[67]

Montemayor recruited both girls and boys for Junior LULAC. She believed this was necessary so "by the time they are ready to join the Senior Councils they will abandon the egotism and petty jealousies so common today among our ladies' and Men's councils." Her son Francisco echoed his mother's sentiments, writing for the *LULAC News*, "We have heard that there is a Junior council of 'just girls.' Heck, we don't like that. We [would] rather have a mixed group like we have in Laredo, because we feel like there is nothing like our SISTERS." He warned against a majority of girls and rallied the boys to prevent this.[68]

Montemayor believed that leadership training was necessary to the formation of good citizens and future LULAC senior members. From Junior LULAC would come "good Americans" who would be capable public servants, skillful debaters, knowledgeable citizens, and literate, independent thinkers. Montemayor taught Junior members to debate and trained them in acting skills every Sunday. She also accompanied five Junior officers to the El Paso national convention.[69]

Montemayor's feminism even influenced the youth group. In 1938 Laredo Junior LULAC member Leonor Montes rallied for a girl president. She wrote, "Now that the publicity chairman is of the 'nervier' sex but HOW ABOUT A GIRL PRESIDENT this coming term? We want a girl president! We want a girl president! RAH! RAH! RAH! BOOM!" Montemayor's son called Montes "the little Monty of the Juniors" for "she too is always wanting for the girls to outshine the boys." He warned her this could not be done "aunque somos pollos, pero nosotros mandamos" (although we are young, we are still in charge).[70]

The organization of youth also suggested women's primary responsibility. In 1943, when George Garza of Laredo reorganized the Juniors, he changed the focus from preteens to teenagers, thereby removing the "babysitting" aspect of the work. Nevertheless, most Junior LULAC sponsors continued to be ladies councils. Men's councils, on the other hand, typically sponsored Boy Scout troops, which coexisted with Junior councils.[71]

Besides challenging the patriarchal nature of LULAC's method of political mobilization by including women and children, Montemayor also challenged patriarchal ideology through her essays. She wrote more articles for *LULAC News* than any other woman in the history of the organization, typically signing her name Mrs. F. I. Montemayor. She also penned several essays without a signature.[72]

Among youth and adults, Montemayor stressed independent thinking. She wrote, "having the ability to think for oneself and forming an opinion of your own is a necessity in our organization." She asked LULAC to recall the 1938 national LULAC election and asked, "Did we not have a hard time to think for ourselves about the candidates? Did not some of us have the desire to influence our fellow members to vote our own way?"[73]

In her first essay, "We Need More Ladies Councils," she pointed to many inactive LULAC councils and asked women to come to the rescue. "Sister LULACS," she wrote, "our brothers need a good big dose of competition." She noted that of the seventy-one men's and fifteen women's chapters, only twenty-six and four, respectively, had been represented at the annual convention. Competition with men became a rallying point for Montemayor: "Now that our brothers have given the women a chance to show them what we can do, let all the Ladies Councils that are active now try and revive the Dormant Ladies Councils, and the Ladies Organizers and Governors try and get more Ladies Council [sic] to join our League so that we may prove to our brothers that we can accomplish more than they can."[74] She believed men endangered this competition because of their allegations that they were superior to women.

But Montemayor also believed in the fundamental superiority of women. In "A Message from Our Second Vice-President General," she asked women to join the LULAC family. Women, she believed, had intuition. "Women wish to mother men just because it is their natural instinct and because they see into the men's helplessness." Women's common sense made them "able to see at a glance and penetrate into in a second what most men would not see with a searchlight or telescope in an eternity." She added, "Women are the possessors of a super logic. They hang to the truth and work with more tenacity than our brothers." She concluded that LULAC would not flourish until the women became involved to help the men.[75]

Montemayor also penned "Women's Opportunity in LULAC," which proclaimed, "The idea that 'the women's place is in the home' passed out of the picture with hoop skirts and bustles, and now it is recognized that women hold as high a position in all walks of life as do the men." She noted that among Greeks and Romans "the girl was not trained for public life, as that was left for the boys and men. She occupied no place in the activities of her country." She added, "no thought was given to the girls in anything other than the keeping of the homes." Rejecting woman's place as "entirely in the home," she defined women's place to be "in that position where she can do the most for the furthering of her fellow women." She called on "women LULAC" to "realize that it is now time to get into our League, and stay in it."[76]

The editorial "Son Muy Hombres(?)" appeared in March 1938. Despite the question mark, Montemayor did not doubt that machismo was prevalent in LULAC, but she had faith in men's ability to change. She noted there "has been some talk about suppressing the Ladies Councils of our League or at least relegate them to the category of auxiliaries." She attributed this reaction to the "aggressive attitude which some of our women members have adopted." She noted that men "fear that our women will take a leading role in the evolution of our League; that our women might make a name for themselves in their activities; that our MUY HOMBRES (?) might be shouldered from their position as arbiters of our League."[77]

Montemayor also noticed that gender lines were drawn on these issues. She noted, "What surprises us mostly is the attitude assumed by some of our General Officers and members. While some of them may not be in complete accord with the move, at least they countenance it. Others are noncommittal and remain painfully silent."[78] Male bonding and collusion were in effect, and *LULAC News* includes no articles written in support of Montemayor.

"When . . . and Then Only," another of Montemayor's articles, emphasized the necessity of organizing women youth. She wrote, "God gave Eve to Adam, because Adam was lonesome and needed a mate." "Back of the success of any man, there is a woman," she said, and "women are God's MOST PRECIOUS GIFT TO MEN, therefore let's organize more Ladies Councils. Ladies, let's organize more Junior LULAC councils, let's train our children." For Montemayor, heterosexuality was commanded by God, women were to assist their mates and bear and raise children.[79]

Competition and conflict could sometimes characterize relations between men's and women's councils. The February 1937 *LULAC News* hinted at a conflict in Laredo when it mentioned that the chapter had "weathered a storm" of local character, but the article did not detail the nature of the storm "since such things happen in the best regulated families."[80] In a 1984 interview, Montemayor recalled that the Laredo LULAC men "had no use for us . . . they didn't want us." In fact, according to Montemayor, the men "just hated" her, especially Ezequiel Salinas of Laredo, the national president from 1939 to 1940; the men, she claimed, refused to vote for her at the national convention.[81]

Still, Montemayor believed that she had the respect of some men's councils.[82] Indeed, she must have had their support because in 1937 she participated in the Corpus Christi ceremony honoring LULAC's deceased first president, Ben Garza. And she optimistically believed she had the support of men throughout Texas. She could count among her male allies J. C. Machuca, San Antonio attorney Alonso S. Perales, Brownsville attorney J. T. Canales, and Austin educator Dr. Carlos Castañeda. She also corresponded with San Antonio attorney Gus García. All of these supporters, however, were atypical

LULAC members: college graduates and well traveled.[83] LULAC's dismal record of gender politics suggests that Laredo men's attitude was the typical male sentiment.

After April 1940, Montemayor's name is absent from *LULAC News*, perhaps because of the temporary decline of LULAC, perhaps because of repression from macho LULACers, or perhaps because of changes in her family life. The League witnessed growth and expansion in the 1930s, but World War II proved disruptive to organizing efforts. Like men's councils, Ladies LULAC declined. National LULAC reorganized in 1945; ten men's councils attended the annual convention that year, but only Albuquerque represented women.[84]

In 1943 the Montemayors adopted a son, Aurelio, adding new familial responsibilities. In the mid-forties, Francisco Montemayor, Jr., a student at Texas A&M University, died in an accident.[85] For the next forty years, Montemayor gave her energies to community activities in Laredo and died there in 1989.[86]

Without a doubt, Montemayor left her mark. As early as June 1937, *LULAC News* wrote, "no wonder she has been cussed and discussed, talked about, lied about, lied to, boycotted, and almost hung, but she claims she has stayed in there, first because she is a LULACer, and next because she wanted to see what the heck would happen next."[87] A junior LULACer noted that she seemed like a "hard-boiled supervisor" but was really "the swellest dame."[88]

LULAC's method of political mobilization, its theory of political empowerment, and its familial ideology were patriarchal. Montemayor's activism and ideology challenged male privilege. She argued that women and children be mobilized by LULAC to empower La Raza. She defined women's place as extending outside the home and helping other women.

Her radical voice, however, proved a lonely one, and her local chapter did not promote her vision as a collective body, refusing directly to challenge male privilege or battle gender segregation. Montemayor may have influenced women in Laredo and in the national organization, but there is no evidence she attempted to garner their support for a united front. According to Aurelio, she was highly individualistic. By her own report, she was "very independent. Nobody tells me what to do. [But] I can take always advice from people I think are intelligent."[89]

What were the limitations of Montemayor's vision? She attacked male privilege and power but did not question family, marriage, or religion as oppressive institutions. Nor did she question separate councils for men and women in LULAC, although she insisted on integrated youth councils. Segregated councils allowed her—and women—to thrive in a distinctive women's political culture where they learned to organize, dealt with issues they deemed important, and socialized with other women in a safe, nonsexist environment.

Montemayor did not challenge the division of labor within the home, viewing women largely as heterosexuals and mothers. According to one of her supporters, "Her hobby is housekeeping, making that 'tenable' husband of hers, as well as her sonnyboy as comfortable and happy as possible."[90] The rearing of children she saw as the responsibility of women, a view she extended to the public domain through Junior LULAC.

Montemayor believed women were superior to men and, as an optimist, believed men could change their errant ways. She thought women should not quit LULAC when sexism surfaced. She favored cooperation and flatly rejected notions of male superiority: "I think a woman can do a better job than a man [in] many instances, "she said.[91]

How did Montemayor view LULAC and her place in the organization? As a staunch advocate of the League, she argued that it could "educate our race and make better American citizens out of every Latin American." It was "as much a vital organ to the Latin American women, as it is to the Latin American men," she said. To the end, she considered LULAC the most important organization in which she had ever been involved.[92] About her role in LULAC, she reminisced, "I was a very controversial person. Many men didn't want any ladies involved in LULAC."[93] She said, "The men just hated me . . . I guess men don't think women can do anything."[94]

As seen through articles in *LULAC News*, Alice Dickerson Montemayor introduced progressive ideas to LULAC, decrying women's oppression decades before the Chicana feminist movement. She challenged the notion of women's place as the home and by example showed the diligent work women were capable of in public and in political life. She questioned the myth of male superiority and argued that women were as competent as, if not superior to, men. She identified machismo in action and fought to eradicate it through informed feminist reasoning. While she exhibited a feminist consciousness, she also embodied a female consciousness in her concern for children and families.

By example, Montemayor disproves assumptions about women in LULAC, about wives, and about members of Ladies LULAC councils. Nevertheless, she was an anomaly in the history of LULAC: an open feminist long before other Chicana feminists.

Notes

I would like to thank Norma Cantú, for conducting an interview for me, and Aurelio Montemayor, for clarifying several issues. The Rare Books and Manuscripts staff of the Benson Latin American Collection at the University of Texas at Austin should also be thanked. A version of this paper was presented at the Women and Texas History Conference sponsored by the Texas State Historical Association in Austin, Texas, on October 5, 1990.

1. Studies focusing on women include Christine Marín, "La Asociación Hispano-Americana de Madres y Esposas," Renato Rosaldo Lecture Series Monograph 7, 1989–1990 (Tucson: Mexican American Studies and Research Center, 1985), 5–18; Thomas E. Kreneck, "The Letter from Club Chapultepec," Houston Review 3 (Summer 1981): 268–71; Mary Pardo, "Mexican American Grassroots Community Activists, Mothers of East Los Angeles," in Writing the Range Race, Class, and Culture in the Women's West, ed. and with introductions by Elizabeth Jameson and Susan Armitage (Norman: University of Oklahoma Press, 1997); Emma M. Pérez, "'A La Mujer': A Critique of the Partido Liberal Mexicano's Gender Ideology," in Between Borders: Essays on Mexicana/Chicana History, ed. Adelaida R. del Castillo (Encino, CA: Floricanto, 1990), 459–82; María Linda Apodaca, "They Kept the Home Fires Burning: Mexican American Women and Social Change" (PhD diss., University of California, Irvine, 1994); and Margaret Rose, "Gender and Civic Activism in Mexican American Barrios in California: The Community Service Organization, 1947–1962," in Not June Cleaver: Women and Gender in Postwar America, 1945–1960, ed. Joanne Meyerowitz (Philadelphia: Temple University Press, 1994). See also Cynthia E. Orozco, "Beyond Machismo, La Familia, and Ladies Auxiliaries: A Historiography of Mexican-Origin Women's Participation in Voluntary Associations and Politics in the United States, 1870–1990," Renato Rosaldo Lecture Series Monograph 10, 1992–1993 (Tucson: Mexican American Studies and Research Center, 1995), 37–78.

2. Karen J. Blair failed to list Chicana organizations in her recent bibliography of women's organizations. The History of American Women's Voluntary Organizations, 1810–1960: A Guide to Sources (Boston: G. K. Hall, 1989).

3. Nancy F. Cott, The Grounding of Modern Feminism (New Haven: Yale University Press, 1989).

4. Marta P. Cotera, *Diosa y Hembra: The History and Heritage of Chicanas in the U.S.* (Austin: Information Systems Development, 1976).

5. Key studies, all of which are male-centered, include Kaye Lynn Briegel, "Alianza Hispano Americana, 1894–1965: A Mexican-American Fraternal Insurance Society" (PhD diss., University of Southern California, 1974); Juan Gómez-Quiñones, *Sembradores: Ricardo Flores Magón y El Partido Liberal Mexicano: A Eulogy and Critique* (Los Angeles: Aztlán Publications, 1973); José E. Limón, "El Primer Congreso Mexicanista de 1911: A Precursor to Contemporary Chicanismo," *Aztlán* 5, nos. 1–2 (1974): 85–118; José Amaro Hernández, *Mutual Aid for Survival: The Case of the Mexican American* (Malabar, FL: Robert E. Krieger, 1983); Julie Leininger Pycior, "La Raza Organizes: Mutual Aid Societies in San Antonio, 1915–1930" (PhD diss., University of Notre Dame, 1979); Richard A. Garcia, *Rise of the Mexican American Middle Class: San Antonio, 1929–1941* (College Station: Texas A&M University Press, 1991); Mario T. García, *Mexican Americans: Leadership, Ideology, and Identity* (New Haven: Yale University Press, 1989); Carl Allsup, *The American GI Forum, Origins and Evolution* (Austin: Center for Mexican American Studies, University of Texas at Austin, 1982); Liliana Urrutia, "An Offspring of Discontent: The Asociación Nacional México-Americana, 1949–1954," *Aztlán* 15 (Spring 1984): 177–84; Kaye Briegel, "Alianza Hispano Americano and Some Civil Rights Cases in the 1950s," in *An Awakened Minority: The Mexican-Americans*, ed. Manuel P. Servin (Beverly Hills, CA: Glencoe, 1970), 174–87; Ricardo Romo, "George I. Sánchez and the Civil Rights Movement: 1940–1960," *La Raza Law Journal* 1 (Fall 1986): 342–69; Guadalupe San Miguel, Jr., *"Let All of Them Take Heed": Mexican Americans and the Campaign for Educational Equality in Texas, 1910–1981* (Austin: University of Texas Press, 1987); Ignacio M. García, *United We Win: The Rise and Fall of La Raza Unida Party* (Tucson: Mexican American Studies and Research Center, University of Arizona, 1989); and Ricardo Romo, "Southern California and the Origins of Latino Civil Rights Activism," *Western Legal History* 3 (1990): 379–406.

6. On LULAC, see Oliver Douglas Weeks, "The League of United Latin American Citizens: A Texas-Mexican Civic Organization," *Southwestern Political and Social Science Quarterly* 10 (December 1929): 257–78; Edward D. Garza, "LULAC: League of United Latin American Citizens" (master's thesis, Southwest Texas State Teachers College, 1951); Moisés Sandoval, *Our Legacy: The First Fifty Years* (Washington, DC: LULAC, 1979); San Miguel, *"Let All of Them Take Heed"*; Arnoldo De León, *Ethnicity in the Sunbelt: A History of Mexican Americans in Houston* (Houston: Mexican American Studies Program, University of Houston, 1989); Mario T. García, *Mexican Americans*; R. A. Garcia, *Mexican American Middle Class*; Benjamín Márquez, *LULAC: The Evolution of a Mexican American Political Organization* (Austin: University of Texas Press, 1993).

7. LULAC was organized in 1929 with a national vision. When it expanded outside of Texas, members considered it a national association. The 1939 constitution referred to the organization as a national entity, and in the early 1940s, the US government recognized LULAC as a voice for the Mexican and Mexican American population in the United States. See "The Constitution of the League of United Latin American Citizens," *LULAC News*, July 1939, George I. Sánchez Papers, Benson Latin American Collection, General Libraries, University of Texas at Austin (hereafter BLAC). See also, "Showdown Expected This Week in Shell Walkout Threat," *Houston Press*, April 23, 1945, folder "Adequacy of Housing," box 454, Tension Files, Federal Employment Practices Commission, National Archives. Most of the *LULAC News* can be found in the LULAC Archives at BLAC.

8. Cynthia E. Orozco, "The Origins of the League of United Latin American Citizens (LULAC) and the Mexican American Civil Rights Movement in Texas with an Analysis of Women's Political Participation in a Gendered Context, 1910–1929" (PhD diss., University of California, Los Angeles, 1992). See also Mario T. García, "Mexican Americans and the Politics of Citizenship: The Case of El Paso, 1936," *New Mexico Historical Review* 59 (April 1984): 187–204; Emilio Zamora, "The Failed Promise of Wartime Opportunity for Mexicans in the Texas Oil Industry," *Southwestern Historical Quarterly* 95 (January 1992): 323–50; Márquez, *LULAC*, and San Miguel, *"Let All of Them Take Heed."*

9. According to Moisés Sandoval, "In the Beginning, LULAC was a man's organization. The persons who gathered to found the League were all men." *Our Legacy*, 70. But women and girls attended the constitutional convention (considered the first annual convention) on May 18–19, 1929. Their names are available in a translated typescript of "The Convention Held in This Port on the 18th and 19th of This Month Was Tremendous Success," *El Paladín*, May 24, 1929, Oliver Douglas Weeks Papers, 1928–1965, Benson Latin American Collection [BLAC], University of Texas at Austin).

10. LULAC recognized Montemayor twice in the late 1930s with a *LULAC News* cover page and articles about her. See Alice Dickerson Montemayor, "A Message from Our Second Vice-President General," *LULAC News*, September 1937; and the special women's issue in May 1939, especially the article by Esperanza E. Treviño, "Mrs. F. I. Montemayor." See also Cynthia E. Orozco, "Alice Dickerson Montemayor," in *New Handbook of Texas* (Austin: Texas State Historical Association, 1996). According to the Montemayors' son, Aurelio, his father was not politically disposed to join LULAC. Moreover, as a resident alien, Francisco Montemayor, Sr., was not officially qualified to join the organization even though some Mexican citizens did. Aurelio Montemayor, phone conversation with author, August 29, 1995.

11. Lillian Gutiérrez, "LULAC—A Vehicle for Meeting the Political Challenge," *Intercambios Femeniles* 2 (Autumn 1984): 9–10.

12. For instance, see María Berta Guerra, "The Study of LULAC" (undergraduate paper, 1979, Rio Grande Valley Collection, University of Texas–Pan American), in which she refers to the McAllen Ladies LULAC council as a women's council and an auxiliary. Ladies auxiliaries were only one form of women's historical participation in LULAC; the auxiliaries existed primarily from 1932 to 1933.

13. Marta Cotera, "Brief Analysis of the Political Role of Hispanas in the United States" (paper prepared for the Women of Color Institute, Washington, DC, November 1983, BLAC); and Marta Cotera, "Hispana Political Tradition," *Intercambios Femeniles* 2 (Autumn 1984): 9.

14. José A. Estrada, interview by Belén B. Robles, April 26–27, 1976, 9, transcript, Institute of Oral History, University of Texas at El Paso.

15. Julia Kirk Blackwelder, *Women of the Depression: Caste and Culture in San Antonio, 1929–1939* (College Station: Texas A&M University Press, 1984). Blackwelder made little use of *La Prensa*, the most important Spanish language newspaper in San Antonio and the state of Texas, or *LULAC News*.

16. Orozco, "League of United Latin American Citizens"; and Cynthia E. Orozco, "League of United Latin-American Citizens," in *Readers Companion to U.S. Women's History*, ed. Wilma Mankiller, Gwendolyn Mink, Marysa Navarro, Barbara Smith, and Gloria Steinem (Boston: Houghton Mifflin, 2000).

17. R. A. Garcia, *Mexican American Middle Class*, xvi. Unfortunately, Garcia did not integrate his research on women onto his book. See also Richard A. Garcia, "The Making of the Mexican American Mind, San Antonio, Texas, 1929–1941: A Social and Intellectual History of an Ethnic Community" (PhD diss., University of California, Irvine, 1980); Richard A. Garcia, "Class, Consciousness, and Ideology: The Mexican Community of San Antonio," *Aztlán* 9 (Fall 1978): 23–70; Richard A. Garcia, "The Mexican American Mind: The Product of the 1930s," in *History, Culture, and Society: Chicano Studies in the 1980s*, ed. Mario T. García and Bert N. Corona (Ypsilanti, MI: Bilingual Press, 1983), 67–94; Richard Garcia, "Mexican Women in San Antonio, Texas: A View of Three Worlds, 1929–1941" (paper presented at the Pacific Coast Branch of the American Historical Association, Los Angeles, CA, 1980); and "Around the LULAC Shield," *LULAC News*, March 1938.

18. Arnoldo De León, *Ethnicity in the Sunbelt*.

19. M. García, *Mexican Americans*. García emphasized the role of Machuca because LULAC itself has mistakenly recognized her as the first ladies organizer general and a more significant figure than Montemayor. Moreover, he conducted much of his research in El Paso, and both the subject and author are natives of that community. See "First Ladies Organizer General," *LULAC News*, March 1979.

This special issue on women, the second such issue in LULAC history, featured Machuca on the cover. See also Cynthia E. Orozco, "Ester Machuca," in *New Handbook of Texas*.

20. Márquez, *LULAC*, 93.

21. J. Reynolds Flores, "How to Educate Our Girls," *LULAC News*, December 1931.

22. "La Mujer," *Alma Latina* 1 (April 1932), Paul Schuster Taylor Papers, Bancroft Library, University of California, Berkeley (hereafter Taylor Papers).

23. "Around the LULAC Shield," *LULAC News*, February 1938.

24. "To Our Ladies Council," *LULAC News*, May 1938.

25. "Parents Are Fathers," *Alma Latina* 1 (April 1932), Taylor Papers. "N. Augilar and Son" of San Antonio served as editors and publishers of *Alma Latina*.

26. "Es Justa la Aspiración de la Mujer de Nuestro País," *El Paladín*, October 25, 1929, microfilm, UCLA Chicano Studies Research Center Library, Los Angeles.

27. Adela Sloss, "Por que en muchos hogares latinos no existe verdadera felicidad," *LULAC News*, March 1934, 31–32.

28. See also Adela Sloss Vento and Arnold C. Vento, *Alonso S. Perales: His Struggle for the Rights of Mexican-Americans* (San Antonio: Artes Gráficas, 1977); and Cynthia E. Orozco, "Adela Sloss Vento" (unpublished manuscript).

29. *LULAC News*, March 1937. Fidencio Guerra of McAllen held the position from 1936 to 1937. On the Guerra family, see Evan Anders, *Boss Rule in South Texas: The Progressive Era* (Austin: University of Texas Press, 1982).

30. Alice Dickerson Montemayor, videotaped interview by Norma Cantú, January 26, 1986; Montemayor, "A Message"; Alice Dickerson Montemayor, interview by Andre Guerrero, January 1983, Alice Dickerson Montemayor Papers, BLAC; and Alice Dickerson Montemayor, interview by Norma Cantú, with questions written by Cynthia E. Orozco, January 24, 1984. Manuela Barrera was the granddaughter of Don Desiderio de la Cruz and Doña Apolonia Reyes, who helped found Laredo. In "A Message," Montemayor referred to her mother as a "clothes designer."

31. "Alicia D. Montemayor: Young at 82," *Laredo Morning Times*, July 15, 1984; Aurelio Montemayor, phone conversation with author, June 15, 1989; and Montemayor interview, January 1983.

32. Montemayor, "A Message"; and Montemayor interviews, 1984 and 1983.

33. Montemayor, "A Message"; and Montemayor interview, 1984.

34. Montemayor interview, 1983.

35. See San Miguel, *"Let All of Them Take Heed"*; and Herschel Thurman Manuel, *The Education of Mexican and Spanish-Speaking Children in Texas* (Austin: Fund for Research in the Social Sciences, University of Texas, 1930), 106.

36. Montemayor interview, 1986.

37. Ibid.; and Kathy Ariana Vincent, "'Monty' Montemayor: Portrait of an Artist," *Arriba*, 1980. *Arriba* is a Chicago arts and business newspaper in Austin.

38. Mrs. F. I. Montemayor, "Women's Opportunity in LULAC," *LULAC News*, December 1937; Mrs. F. I. Montemayor, "Let's Organize Junior Councils," *LULAC News*, August 1938; and A. Montemayor conversation, August 29, 1995. In 1937 *LULAC News* reported that she read educational books in her spare time and directed "all her efforts towards giving her son the advantages of an education." Montemayor, "A Message."

39. Verónica Salazar, "Alicia D. Montemayor," *San Antonio Express News*, October 28, 1979.

40. Montemayor told Andre Guerrero that her mother prohibited her from leaving Laredo to go to college. Interview, 1983. Montemayor, "A Message"; Salazar, "Alicia D. Montemayor"; and Montemayor interview, 1986.

41. Salazar, "Alicia D. Montemayor"; "Alicia D. Montemayor: Young at 82"; Agueta Canales and Lauro Canales, "A Tribute to Admonty," ca. 1979; and Amy Dawes, "Vibrant Artist, Vibrant Works," *Laredo Morning Times*, ca. 1988. Aurelio gave her paint for Mother's Day in 1976. Vincent, "'Monty' Montemayor"; Sandra Jordan, "Alice Dickerson Montemayor," in *Folk Art in Texas*, ed. Francis Edward Abernethy (Dallas: Southern Methodist University Press, 1985), 184–87. Montemayor was considered a Chicana folk artist, and the inventory to her papers at the Benson Latin American Collection refers to her as "Chicana Folk Artist." She expressed discomfort with the term *Chicana* but looked favorably on the Chicano movement. "Materials Related to the Paintings and Art of Alice Dickerson Montemayor, Chicana Folk Artist of Laredo Texas," Montemayor Papers and Montemayor interview, 1983.

42. Montemayor's greatest imprint on Laredo was not her work in LULAC or in art but as a local community builder. She worked as the school registrar at Christian Junior High School for sixteen years, from 1956 to 1972. She was also active in her parish, Our Lady of Guadalupe, where she played the organ, organized the first choir, trained altar boys, taught catechism classes, and helped at church jamaicas (bazaars or fundraisers). Salazar, "Alicia D. Montemayor."

43. Montemayor, "A Message"; and Salazar, "Alicia D. Montemayor." This article reports her first (presumably full-time) job with Western Union.

44. Vicki L. Ruiz, "Working for Wages: Mexican Women in the Southwest, 1930–1980," Working Paper No. 19 (Tucson: Southwest Institute for Research on Women, 1984).

45. Montemayor interview, 1986; and Salazar, "Alicia D. Montemayor." Montemayor set up three apple crates under a tree to conduct her work. The San Antonio newspaper noted that two other Mexican Americans had been sent to Cotulla "but were not accepted because they were Mexican Americans."

46. Aurelio Montemayor conversation, 1989.

47. Montemayor interview, 1986.

48. "Around the LULAC Shield, Laredo Ladies Council No. 15," *LULAC News*, June 1937; "Around the LULAC Shield," *LULAC News*, December 1936; J. T. Canales Collection, John Conner Museum, Texas A&M University–Kingsville; "Around the LULAC Shield, Laredo Ladies Council No. 15," *LULAC News*, February 1937.

49. Montemayor, "A Message"; Montemayor interview, 1983; and Montemayor interview, 1986.

50. "Alicia D. Montemayor: Young at 82."

51. "Outstanding Councils of the League, Laredo Ladies Council No. 15," *LULAC News*, June 1937; "Around the LULAC Shield, Laredo Ladies Council No. 15," *LULAC News*, July 1937; and Montemayor, "A Message." The first names of some of these women were not readily available.

52. Montemayor interview, 1984; and "Around the LULAC Shield, Laredo Ladies Council No. 15," *LULAC News*, December 1936.

53. "Around the LULAC Shield, Laredo Ladies Council No. 15," December 1936.

54. Montemayor did not vote on a Democratic or Republican ticket; she was an independent. Montemayor interview, 1984; and "Outstanding Councils of the League, Laredo Ladies Council No. 15."

55. Montemayor interview, 1984.

56. "President General and the Three Laredo Councils," *LULAC News*, December 1938; "Around the LULAC Shield, Laredo Ladies Council No. 15," *LULAC News*, February 1937 and August 1938.

57. Montemayor interview, 1984; "Around the LULAC Shield," *LULAC News*, March 1937, December 1936, February 1937, and July 1937.

58. "Around the LULAC Shield, Laredo Ladies Council No. 15," *LULAC News*, February 1937. According to the July 1937 *LULAC News*, Elena Leal had replaced Montemayor as secretary for 1937–1938. See "Around the LULAC Shield, Laredo Ladies Council No. 15," *LULAC News*, July 1937 and August 1938.

59. "Around the LULAC Shield, Laredo Ladies Council No. 15," March 1937.

60. Ibid.; and "Outstanding Councils of the League, Laredo Ladies Council No. 15," *LULAC News*, June 1937.

61. "Outstanding Councils of the League, Laredo Ladies Council No. 15"; "Minutes of the Tenth Annual Convention of the League of Latin American Citizens"; "Our Second Vice-President General," *LULAC News*, July 1938; "Convention Proceedings: Minutes of the Ninth Annual General Convention of the LULAC held in Houston, Texas, June 5th & 6th 1937," *LULAC News*, July 1937; and Montemayor interview, 1986. A nominating committee, not a general election, selected officers. See "Convention Proceedings," *LULAC News*, July 1937; and Montemayor, "A Message."

62. List of officers, 1939–1940, *LULAC News*, July 1939.

63. "We Need More Ladies Councils," *LULAC News*, July 1937. The article is unsigned but written by Montemayor. See also Montemayor, "A Message"; and Mrs. F. I. K. Montemayor, "Echoes of the Installation of Officers of Council No. 1., Corpus Christi, Texas," *LULAC News*, December 1937.

64. Mrs. F. I. Montemayor, "Son Muy Hombres(?)" *LULAC News*, March 1938.

65. Ibid.

66. Garza, "LULAC," 24; "Special Convention Minutes, Minutes of the Special Convention Held in Laredo, Texas, February 20, 1938," *LULAC News*, December 1937; "Around the LULAC Shield, Laredo Junior Council No. 1," *LULAC News*, February 1938; and Francisco I. Montemayor, Jr., "The Laredo Junior Council," *LULAC News*, December 1938. Mrs. Charles Ramírez became the ladies organizer general for Junior LULAC from 1937 to 1938. Montemayor served from 1939 to 1940. M. C. Gonzales, a man, replaced her in 1940–1941. The first two official field organizers of youth councils were Sergio Gonzales, Jr., a lawyer from Del Rio, and Fidencio M. Guerra of McAllen, but the men did not offer assistance until December 1938, when a Junior LULACer noted that now the groups would not only have "mamas" but "papas" as well.

67. F. I. Montemayor, "Laredo Junior Council"; "Around the LULAC Shield, Laredo Ladies Council No. 15," *LULAC News*, October 1937; Treviño, "Mrs. F. I. Montemayor"; "Laredo Junior LULAC Council," *LULAC News*, March 1938; Montemayor interview, 1984; "Around the LULAC Shield, Laredo Junior Council No. 1," *LULAC News*, December 1937; Perfecto Solís, Jr., "Laredo Junior LULAC Council," *LULAC News*, August 1938; Leonor Montes, "Who Is Who in Laredo Junior Council," *LULAC News*, August 1938; and Fernando Salinas, "My Junior LULAC Activities," *LULAC News*, August 1938. Although Laredo Junior LULAC members ranged in age from nine to fifteen, the organization was open to young people between the ages of eight and eighteen.

68. Mrs. F. I. Montemayor, "Let's Organize Junior Councils"; and "Around the LULAC Shield, The Laredo Junior Council," *LULAC News*, December 1938.

69. Montemayor interviews, 1986 and 1984.

70. Montes, "Who Is Who"; and F. I. Montemayor, "Laredo Junior Council."

71. "The Junior LULAC Council, Laredo, Texas," *LULAC News*, July 1945. As early as 1934, the national LULAC recognized a "director of Boy Scout activities."

72. Montemayor, "A Message"; "Take Stock of Yourself," *LULAC News*, September 1937; Montemayor, "Son Muy Hombres(?)"; Mrs. F. I. Montemayor, "Echoes of the Installation of Officers of Council No. 1," *LULAC News*, February 1938; Montemayor, "Let's Organize Junior Councils"; Montemayor, "President General and the Three Laredo Councils"; Mrs. F. I. Montemayor, "When . . . and Then Only,"

LULAC News, March 1939; Mrs. F. I. Montemayor, "Our Ladies Organizer General," *LULAC News*, May 1939; and Mrs. F. I. Montemayor, "Why and How More Junior Councils," *LULAC News*, April 1940. See also Montemayor, "A Message."

73. Montemayor, "Let's Organize Junior Councils."

74. [Montemayor], "We Need More Ladies Councils."

75. Montemayor, "A Message."

76. Mrs. F. I. Montemayor, "Women's Opportunity is LULAC."

77. Montemayor, "Son Muy Hombres(?)."

78. Ibid.

79. Montemayor, "When . . . and Then Only" and Montemayor, "Let's Organize Junior Councils."

80. "Around the Shield, Laredo Ladies Council No. 15," *LULAC News*, February 1937.

81. Montemayor interviews, 1984 and 1986. Carmen Cortés of Houston Ladies LULAC No. 14, a member in the 1930s, also mentioned Laredo men's opposition to Montemayor in an interview. Carmen Cortés interview by author and Thomas Kreneck, December 16, 1983.

82. Montemayor interview, 1984.

83. Montemayor, "Echoes of the Installation of Officers," "Dedicatoria del Nuevo Parque Ben Garza," *El Paladín*, March 3, 1939; Montemayor interviews, 1986 (here Montemayor named a "Dr. Canales" among her supporters, but I assume she was referring to two different men, Dr. Carlos Castañeda and J. T. Canales); and 1984.

84. "Sixteenth Annual Assembly of the League of United Latin American Citizens Held on June 17th and 18th at Corpus Christi, Nueces County, Texas," *LULAC News*, July 1945. There were ten councils, including one women's council and the first mixed-gender council in the United States, which was in Winslow, Arizona. The article listed leaders of each council, and the Winslow council had both men and women leaders. The Laredo men's council existed in July 1945, but the Laredo women's council did not.

85. Aurelio Montemayor conversation, 1989; "Alicia D. Montemayor: Young at 82"; and Montemayor interview, 1983.

86. "Alice D. Montemayor," obituary, *Austin American-Statesman*, May 16, 1989.

87. "Outstanding Councils of the League."

88. Salinas, "My Junior LULAC Activities."

89. Aurelio Montemayor conversation, 1989; and Montemayor interview, 1983.

90. Montemayor told Andre Guerrero during their 1983 interview, "A girl's most beautiful day is graduation day. Then when she gets married. Then when she has a baby. Or have you a career."

91. Montemayor interview, 1986.

92. [Montemayor], "We Need More Ladies Councils"; and Montemayor, "Women's Opportunity in LULAC."

93. "Alicia D. Montemayor: Young at 82."

94. Montemayor interview, 1986.

Figure 3.1. This photo (ca. 1940) captures Alonzo S. Perales as a man of visible character, elegant in style, and with a quiet arrogance as a result of his success as a lawyer, diplomat, public speaker, public intellectual, and founder and leader of the League of United Latin American Citizens (LULAC). Perales is shown with his wife and lifetime companion, Marta, enjoying a loving stroll on Houston Street in downtown San Antonio, Texas. Marta was a LULAC member and community activist. Selections from the Alonso S. Perales Papers, Special Collections, University of Houston Libraries, accessed October 16, 2013, http://digital.lib.uh.edu/collection/perales/item/5.

3

Alonso S. Perales

The Voice and Visions of a Citizen Intellectual

Richard A. Garcia

"We hold these truths to be self-evident, that all men
are created equal, that they are endowed by their
Creator with certain inalienable Rights, that among
these are Life, Liberty and the pursuit of Happiness."
Declaration of Independence, 1776

"Man is his own star, and the soul that can
Render an honest and a perfect man."
John Fletcher, "Upon an Honest Man's Fortune"

"The next condition of success is the apparent existence, in
large numbers, of minds who unite healthy-mindedness
with readiness for regeneration by letting go."
William James, The Religion of Healthy-Mindedness

I. Introduction: Perales's Quest: A New Paradigm

Alonso S. Perales was the most famous American of Mexican descent from
the 1920s until his death in 1960. He was the leading contributor to the philosophy and social theory of the League of United Latin American Citizens
(LULAC) at its inception in its first constitutional convention in Corpus Christi,
Texas, in 1929. Under Perales's leadership at the Texas convention, the newly

DOI: 10.5876/9781607323372.c003

formed LULAC passed a declaration of freedoms, called the Code, and its constitutional principles. Perales, as the main author of these two documents, intended them to be the guiding hand for Mexican Americans in Texas and throughout the Southwest. Aimed at American citizens of Mexican descent, as Perales referred to them, these documents represented an approach to democracy framed by a new social theory, with new principles, values, and themes.[1]

The purpose of LULAC was to make Mexican Americans the best citizens they could be while retaining a consciousness of being both American and Mexican. Perales was the main architect of this new intellectual and cultural paradigm. In later decades an anomaly was emphasized (*Chicanismo* of the 1960s), but the paradigm of Mexican Americanism remained. Perales and other LULAC leaders emphasized Democratic reform, not any radical or revolutionary ideology. Before 1929 most Mexican American organizations were not political. It was not until after World War I, with the influx of Mexican American veterans into the American middle class, that these veterans formed organizations that brought the idea of citizenship and full rights to their communities in Texas. Mexican Americans had gone to Europe to fight World War I. As President Woodrow Wilson stated, they had gone "to make the world safe for democracy." Mexican American soldiers returned to Texas conscious of what they had fought for in Europe, and they realized that fighting for democracy was their cause in Texas and throughout the Southwest.

At the beginning of the twentieth century, political and economic pressures from the upper classes, especially the profiteering of the captains of industry (the robber barons) and pressures from below (the working class's strikes and physical clashes with police and soldiers) produced general anarchy. The middle class, as a result, became a political force in the United States. The central catalyst for the Anglo-American middle class seeking reform and order was the Progressive movement, which sought democracy, equality, and personal freedom in the new age of urbanization, industrialization, and modernization. At the same time, the black middle class called for reform in the areas of racial discrimination and prejudice. World War I was the catalyst for the Mexican American middle class seeking reform and civil rights. In general, the middle classes, as historian Robert Wiebe wrote, were searching for order, reform, and democratization and a return to constitutional principles.[2]

In San Antonio, returning veterans formed four organizations. But they had no coherent philosophy, and they based their leadership on the Mexican tradition of *personalismo*, leadership by personality rather than by ideas, principles, and a fundamental philosophy. Their goals encompassed the achievement of economic, social, and racial equality, equality of opportunity (specifically in education), and political power. World War I veterans felt they were Americans, but Anglo Texans simply called them by the pejorative "Meskins." Texas had joined the Confederacy during the Civil War (1861–1865) and was similar to the states in the Deep South. Its racial laws and discriminatory practices against blacks—the "colored folks"—were well known. Mexicans were also perceived as "colored" and received the same treatment. For blacks, racism was *de jure*, by law, and for Mexicans it was *de facto*, by custom. The principal effects of racial discrimination were that it crushed self-esteem and brought to the forefront Mexican Americans' consciousness of identity, which emanated from their views and behavior and from Texas's "cultural climate and intellectual temper" of racial discrimination against blacks and Mexicans.

The issues of racial prejudice and discrimination, although of great importance, were merely a veil over the deeper issues of humanism, political freedom, and opportunities of equality. Perales sought to affect and reconstruct the hidden issues of identity, citizenship rights, and civic virtues. These categories and values were, in fact, central to Perales's own life and successes. Another hidden issue that was becoming a central paradox in twentieth-century American society was that while the Midwest, Northeast, and West were becoming more prosperous, Texas and the southern states remained places of racism, prejudice, and discrimination. As a result, Perales forcefully wrote,

> We Latin-Americans must organize. We must get out of the rut and forge ahead. Let us catch up with and keep abreast of our hard driving fellow-citizens of Anglo-Saxon extraction. To accomplish this, no man should be allowed to stand in our way. No man is big enough to block our progress. A fraction is not larger than the whole. For the sake of posterity and the good name of our race, let us get together, my friends, and begin to solve our great problems. We can only do it thru a well disciplined, solid, powerful organization.[3]

In the early 1920s, returning soldiers and other middle-class citizens formed three organizations in San Antonio: the Order of the Sons of America, the Order of the Knights of America, and the League of Latin American Citizens. In 1929 Perales and other leaders met in Harlingen, Texas, to discuss unification, and a national meeting convened in Corpus Christi to complete the process. All of the members accepted the League of United Latin American Citizens as the new umbrella organization, and Perales was nominated to be the principal writer of LULAC's constitutional principles and declaration of freedoms. Following the convention, Perales published an article in the newspaper *El Paladin*, outlining the broad purposes of LULAC. He wrote that "the purpose of the unification was to have one strong organization to shape the intellectual themes and contours of Mexican American Citizens, specifically in the areas of citizenship responsibilities, economic functionalism, self-responsibility, the pursuit of justice, liberal education, and a redefinition of self and community within a cultural and intellectual redemption of Lo Mexicano." He emphasized, "That day that the Mexican-American betters his own conditions and finds himself in a position to make full use of his rights of citizenship, that day he will be able to aid the Mexican citizens in securing what is due him and to help him assure himself of his won welfare and happiness." Pointing out the major problem of racism, Perales wrote, "Undoubtedly the two greatest obstacles for the Americanization of the Mexican Texans are the racial prejudice which . . . [he harbors] against us and certain customs which are repugnant to ours." LULAC mirrored Perales's mind, and his mind mirrored LULAC. Perales drew from two main sources in his writing: his own personal and intellectual life journey and the US Declaration of Independence, the Bill of Rights, and the Constitution.[4]

In 1948 Perales wrote a book titled *Are We Good Neighbors?*, detailing all the incidents of racial discrimination in Texas in the decades after World War I. Documents in the book included testimonies by Mexican Americans and Mexican nationals; affidavits; letters of support from judges, lawyers, politicians, clergy, and World War II veterans; and transcripts from federal committee hearings. The testimonies uttered the pain and tragedies of personal humiliation of the Mexican Americans in Texas. Perales intended his text to be a "sword of words"—the voices of the people—which he used to alert the federal government that it had never responded to the needs of Americans of Mexican descent after World War I. The book announced Perales's and LULAC's new practice of political action in the 1940s: directly asking for the federal government to pass laws, to create local and state-wide national offices to monitor civil and racial discrimination, and to direct national efforts to end racial discrimination. Through LULAC, Perales spent the decades between World War I and World War II working politi-cally as a citizen and an intellectual; he wrote letters, essays, and editorials in Texas Spanish-language newspapers and gave lectures and speeches on these issues.

In 1921, after his service in the Army, Perales became one of the first Mexican Americans to testify before Congress on the topic of racial preju-dice in Texas. Mexican Americans and Mexican nationals had experienced racial discrimination, prejudice, and, at times, physical hostility throughout South Texas since before World War I. In 1944 little had changed. Racial dis-crimination was still a major problem for Mexican American citizens, immi-grants, and Mexican nationals as well as Mexican American soldiers return-ing from the war. Ironically, twenty-four years after his first Congressional testimony on racial problems in Texas, Perales was again asked to testify before the Senate Education and Labor Committee on the topic of S. 101 and S. 459, bills which would prohibit discrimination because of race, creed, color, national origin, or ancestry. In his statements he exhibited anger, res-ignation, and a forceful will to continue his struggle. Addressing the com-mittee he said, "We, American Citizens of Mexican extraction designated as Spanish-Americans, Latin-Americans, Mexican-Americans, some 3,000,00 in Texas and the Southwest find that our effort to eliminate discrimination by mutual cooperation and education have accomplished nothing. We are discriminated against more widely today than 25 years ago—socially, politi-cally, economically, and educationally." In his testimony, Perales also empha-sized that Mexican Americans in Texas are called by many derogatory names. On the surface alone, these derogatory names denied Mexican Americans their dignity, although the problem is also philosophically deeper. Mexican Americans' individuality was being denied. These linguistic attacks had a direct impact on Mexican Americans' sense of identify and self-esteem, and, above all, it signified that Texans perceived Mexican Americans as *nothingness*.

If a Mexican American in Texas were asked in the 1920s and 1930s if he was a Mexican or an American, he would have answered, with hesitation, "Mejicano" or "Tejano." Then, acknowledging the sentiment of racial preju-dice and discrimination, he would have followed his answer with an ambigu-ous statement, "What are we, Mexicans, Mejicanos, Tejanos, or Americans?" The problem is that he tried to answer the most important question of the post–World War I era—in truth, of all American history since America's independence in 1776—the question of the intersection of immigration, citizenship, and identity. This idea puzzled even Americans of Anglo descent. A long lineage of great Americans have pursued this question, the same question that J. Hector St. John de Crèvecoeur, in his text on America, *Letters From an American Farmer*, asked about Americans in the early nineteenth century: "Who is the American?" (as opposed to the Englishman). Historian and public intellectual Henry Adams asked himself the question in his text *The Education of Henry Adams*, written at the end of the nineteenth century. Perales pursued a similar question in the 1920s: Who is this (Mexican) American? In the 1970s, Ernesto Galarza pursued the question in his book *Barrio Boy*. In the 1980s, public intellectual Richard Rodriguez pursued the question in his book *Hunger of Memory: The Education of Richard Rodriguez* and added to it the question of homosexuality. America is a web of ethnicities, a "braided rope" of differences. This question of identity is the perennial American question, and from its trunk spring many other branches of questions of acculturation, assimilation, patriotism, and ethnic nationalism. All deal with individual choice and necessitate a reflective analysis of one's life. Perales realized that the question had no absolute answers; each person's perspective of himself determined his answer. Perales used his life as the blueprint for LULAC's principles and objectives, and in its constitution can be found his philosophy.[5]

This essay examines why and how Perales analyzed his own life and how his self-analysis provided him with the framework of his philosophy and social theory, which would help Americans of Mexican descent have a successful life. However, his philosophy needed to be applied to see if it worked. LULAC would be his empirical instrument.[6] In other words, this essay examines the central question: *What is the impact of identity, citizenship rights, and racial discrimination on Mexican Americans?* By analyzing the character, life, ideas, desires, and educational experiences of Perales, we can see how they affected LULAC's philosophy. Perales was a citizen intellectual. He laid out the basic ideas of individual freedom, communal responsibilities, and the instruments for change that Mexican American citizens should follow. In his contributions to LULAC and its founding documents, he played a role similar to that of Thomas Jefferson and his contribution to America. The LULAC Constitution and Code became the basis for the new paradigm for Americans of Mexican descent signified by Perales's language.

II. Perales's Vision: "Let's Catch Up"

By the time Perales entered World War I, he had already imagined his role in life and had almost accepted his developing philosophy of humanism and need to critically think about Americanism and *Mexicanidad*, but he also wanted to implement his ideas for helping Mexican Americans. This form of thinking—doing rather than just thinking for the sake of thinking—was concretized during his university education and law studies and by his diplomatic work through his constant attention to the issues and problems of Mexican Americans in San Antonio and the rest of South Texas. He had grown up in the area, and it was where he now made his home. This area had the most Mexicans in the Southwest, although Los Angeles would claim this accolade in the early 1930s. Many decades after Perales's death in 1960, his sister and son would remember him as being everywhere—*ubiquitous* is the word that could be applied to him. His critical reflection of his own life allowed him to focus on the psychology of his behavior and high energy level, his intellectuality in his political observations, and his perception in solving individual and communal problems; his unwavering commitment to the goal of his desire and need for a university education would provide a depth of economic and political knowledge; and his desire to attend law school would give him an understanding of the legal system and the ability to think through legal problems and provide solutions. Later in his life, he and Gus García would be the only Mexican American lawyers to try a case in the US Supreme Court.[7]

Perales was foremost an intellectual who worked to provide the vision of a new democracy for Mexican American citizens. Ensuring citizenship rights—social, civic, and political—was the core of his vision. Although the US Constitution guaranteed all rights to Mexican American citizens throughout Texas and the Southwest, rights were systematically denied to them through poll taxes; separate schools, restaurants, and public spaces; racial violence; and overall social and class prejudice. In a 1924 essay on "The Ideals of Mexican Americans," Perales wrote,

> We would like equality of opportunity in the various battlegrounds of life as well as before courts of justice. We would like for persons of Mexican descent in violation of the laws that govern the country to be tried before a competent Court of Justice and to not be lynched, as was the case of the unfortunate young man Elías Villarreal Zárate in Weslaco, Texas, on November 1921. We

would like to go to a theater, restaurant, dance hall, or any other establishment whose doors are wide open to the general public, whenever we feel like
it. We do not want to be ousted, as is frequently done, with the mere excuse
of our racial origin. In one word, we ask for justice and the opportunity to
prosper. There you have our goal. There you have our objective.

Perales believed that his ideas, through LULAC, would be the catalyst to
change the lives of Mexican American citizens.[8]

Consequently, he focused on and analyzed his personal evolution and progress, both as an individual in American society and as a Mexican American
who had many opportunities for equality and the freedoms emanating from
his citizenship. His life journey proceeded in a multiplicity of stages: from
orphan to impoverishment, to university student, to lawyer, to diplomat, and
then to an imaginative intellectual and a citizen of action. At every stage he
comprehended his different "realities" but he also saw his "rational" and imagined glimpse of his desire and need to achieve and progress toward becoming educated, understanding legality, and bettering his and others' lives. He
wrote the conclusions of his self-analysis and the steps to understanding
and gaining his goals into the LULAC Constitution and its code of conduct.
Benjamin Franklin had done something similar in his own autobiography, giving Americans guiding principles—steps for success—from the lessons of his
life. Perales wanted to provide Mexican Americans with guiding principals
from the lessons of *his* life. Due to the power of his vision, historian Carlos E.
Castañeda, Perales's intellectual and LULAC contemporary, referred to him as
a "prophet" for the Mexican American civil rights movement.[9]

When Perales returned from World War I he was certain that his life
experiences, analytically distilled, would provide the blueprint for Mexican
American citizens to achieve personal success, however they defined it. He
did not necessarily want individuals to follow blindly the patterns of his
life; they needed to attain a new consciousness of empowerment as citizens
and individuals by reimagining the American promise as being intended for
them. The philosopher Philip Wheelwright has written that everyone uses
the capacity of his or her *outer eye*—that is, the physical eye—to perceive
reality as it is. But Wheelwright also wrote of an *inner eye*—one's will and
imagination—with the capacity to see the ideal and believe that ideas and
promises can be real. To Perales's outer eye, he began life as a poor orphan.
What allowed him to move through the stages of his life to become a lawyer,

diplomat, and citizen intellectual was that his inner eye allowed him to consciously envision the goals, principles, and values that he used to change the reality that confronted him.[10]

Before a Congressional committee hearing in 1939, Perales presented himself as an example of the Americanized Mexican who had realized the promise of America, and he pointed to other LULAC leaders as further examples. Perales went on to testify emphatically to the fact that a basic tension existed between the reality, as perceived in Texas, and the ideal of the American promise of what Texas and America could be. As the Declaration of Independence states, "all men are created equal, that they are endowed by their Creator with certain unalienable rights." Expressly, the document further underscores that "whenever any Form of Government becomes destructive of these ends, it is the Right of the People to alter or to abolish it." This statement was the legal foundation for Perales's work through LULAC: to alter the government that "becomes destructive of these ends." Perales asked Mexican American citizens to acknowledge the discriminations and inequality that they perceived through their outer eye but to go beyond this by consciously using their rationality and imagination to see the promises of America and of LULAC, and most importantly, to work toward making the promise a new reality.[11]

In addition to serving Mexican American communities, Perales sought to make LULAC function as a state and federal lobbying group. He understood that in order to attain their needs, wants, desires, and beliefs, Mexican Americans could not rely on just personal action. Their energy also had to be channeled into organizational action. It can possibly be said that Perales learned the power of organizational theory by his experiences in the Army, in university history or economics classes, and at law school. He almost certainly read *The Federalist Papers*. For instance, in No. 10, James Madison described American politics as a process of "factions"—in other words, lobbying groups—seeking power democratically rather than through the class conflict or tyranny that characterized Europe. Using this organizational method, Perales inadvertently drew on Madison's theory of factional parties as well as the themes of the Pragmatist philosophers William James and Charles Peirce. LULAC, Perales believed, was the organization that would be effective in the struggle against inequality and discrimination.[12]

In the late 1920s and early 1930s, for example, Perales approached the problems facing Mexican Americans by writing newspaper columns and essays;

going on lecture tours; recruiting middle-class Mexican American citizens to become LULAC members; corresponding with political leaders in Washington, DC; and speaking in front of House Congressional hearings. Other LULAC leaders did the same. By these methods, Perales put forth his philosophy and presented solutions to the many problems facing Mexican Americans. In short, LULAC members were speaking on the issue of racial discrimination and citizenship rights as the means of having Americans of Mexican descent join their local LULAC chapters and implement solutions in their own communities. By the late 1930s, Perales understood that despite the potential of this approach, it did not fully work. He and LULAC could not be effective while following LULAC's own restriction against engaging in politics as an organization. Consequently, Perales approached the problem pragmatically and by 1944 had found a way around these limits. He created satellite organizations, such as the Committee of One Hundred, to act as LULAC's political arm. No sooner had Perales engaged in politics then he found another "truth": power.[13]

Perales further observed the major paradox that while America in theory provided equality of opportunity, individual liberty, and the possibility for individuals to define their own success and happiness, Mexican American communities lived in a different reality. And whatever reality a person perceives to exist around them is the reality that impacts them. Nevertheless, regardless of racism, civil, and social discrimination, Perales understood that the central principles, values, and ideas in America's foundational documents were historically embedded in the American psyche in memories and daily realities. This is the reality that would win out in people's minds. Americans believed the general consensus that the core freedoms stemming from the axiom of "Life, Liberty and the Pursuit of Happiness" were assured for all citizens. For Perales, the promise of America had not failed; he had experienced and lived that promise, going from poverty to diplomat, as had many other LULAC leaders, even while the promise of "Life, Liberty and the Pursuit of Happiness" was not easily evident in many Mexican Americans' daily lives. Reenergizing the hope, faith, and vision of this promise had always been the underlying purpose of his life. For Perales, citizenship lay at the core of the America promise and was the first step to becoming a success in America. He had used his life lessons to serve as the empirical evidence to prove this truth; his life was the proof of its success. In short, Perales had used his life propositions and successes to suggest a theory for "making it" in America.

Both Benjamin Franklin and Perales had proposed the great American paths to success. Perales's life almost seems to have paralleled Franklin's advice for success, and, in turn, Perales codified his life's principles in the documents of LULAC.[14] Due to his strong belief in the American principles, Perales deduced that racial discrimination and prejudice in law and habit were not deeply ingrained in the American fabric. They were not part of the general consensus regarding the central principals of America and, in fact, were un-American. He believed that discriminatory habits could be changed. Accepting citizenship, and struggling for its inherent rights, was the first step for Mexican Americans to become part of American society and to achieve the promise of America. Perales wrote, "Let us catch up with and keep abreast of our hard driving fellow-citizens of Anglo-Saxon extraction. To accomplish this, no man should be allowed to stand in our way. No man is big enough to block our progress. A fraction is not larger than the whole. For the sake of posterity and the good name of our race, let us get together, my friends, and begin to solve our great problems. We can only do it thru a well-disciplined, solid, powerful organization." LULAC was the first Mexican American organization to hold the idea that in order to succeed, Mexican Americans had to embrace the Declaration of Independence, the Constitution, and the Bill of Rights. Thus, LULAC became part of the intellectual and cultural history of the United States in order to succeed. Perales had communicated his life propositions and principles as the "steps to success" in the LULAC Code for individual members and in the constitutional principles of the organization's goals. They were ideas to follow but also goals to be achieved, or as pragmatist John Dewey wrote, "ideas are instruments for change." In a 1929 issue of *El Paladin*, Perales wrote, "Mexican American citizens had to be taught, by guidelines, examples, and civil actions that both physical and psychological behavior had to be based on personal needs, desires and clear understanding of what had to be done for himself and others."

III. Perales, Citizenship, and Ethnicity

Adela Sloss-Vento remarked in her biography of Perales that as a young man he had witnessed a disturbing act of racial violence by a white person against a Mexican American man that not only startled him but seared his consciousness throughout his life. Sloss-Vento believed this was a turning point in his consciousness and perspective on the problem of racism and discrimination. From that moment, Perales made these the central issues in his thinking. He believed racial discrimination to be the major deterrent to functioning successfully as a citizen. He emphasized the importance of being a responsible and loyal citizen, even to the point of giving your life for your country. He strongly believed that while ethnicity was a given, Americanization (acculturation) was both a right and a goal. He stressed that while being an American citizen was a political designation that carried rights and duties, ethnicity was a memory and a heritage and that neither one defined the whole person. In fact, Perales was the example of an acculturated, functioning American who also embraced his heritage of Mexicanidad.[15]

The concept of the "citizen" is central to American intellectual history. It is a title given to the common man of the United States. Its use as a title began during the French Revolution in order to differentiate the men of the new republic from the nobility of the preceding monarchy. Perales's process of acculturation took him from his youth in the 1900s as a poor, orphaned Spanish speaker in South Texas (with its very large Mexican American population) to the point in the 1920s and 1930s that he was comfortable living in Washington DC, testifying before Congress, and serving as a US diplomat in Latin America. Perales believed, as he had learned throughout his life, that in order to be successful citizens, Mexican Americans needed a strong will, well-defined goals, a belief in themselves, and a strong sense of communal responsibility. He saw that the importance of American citizenship was its guarantee to all Americans of the birthrights and the natural rights promised by the Constitution—freedom, equality of opportunity, and freedom to maintain one's own ethnicity. Yet wherever Perales went he relished his continued pride and unapologetic sensibility for his "Mexican dad."[16]

As early as 1921, before a Congressional hearing on immigration, Perales presented his viewpoints, which would later become the central pragmatic constitutional issues of LULAC in 1929. He first made the following acknowledgment, "Being a Mexican by blood and being just as proud of my racial extraction as I am of my American citizenship, I feel it my duty to deny most emphatically that the Mexican race is inferior to any other race, and I have quoted authorities here in support of my statement." Then he presented the major themes of LULAC: "loyalty to the United States as citizens"; "loyal to the ideas [and] principles" of citizenship; "acquire the English language, the official language of the United States which is necessary for the enjoyment of our rights and privileges. We pledge ourselves to learn, and speak and teach the same to our children"; and "oppose any radical and violent demonstration which may tend to create conflicts and disturb the peace and tranquility of our country." He concluded with the following statement: "attempts have been made to keep us down. Therefore, our effort to organize ourselves into this organization known as The League of United Latin American Citizens, to the end that we may become better citizens, seems to me to be all the more commendable."

Before Congress, Perales affirmed the central beliefs and principles of US citizenship for himself and on behalf of Mexican Americans. As an intellectual thinker, he was skeptical of whether the American government would be responsive to the issues, problems, and needs of Americans of Mexican descent. Regardless of government support, LULAC leaders and members continued to write newspaper articles and letters to the editor on the issue of racism and the federal government. They pointed out that since the United States was fighting the Nazis because of their racial persecutions, why did the United States continue to uphold racism and discrimination at home? Why were the racial persecutions of Mexican Americans in Texas and the Southwest allowed to stand? Perales further argued that underlying Mexican Americans' search for freedom, civil rights, and equality of opportunity were the same principles naturally rooted in the traditions of freedom, liberty, and the protection of civil rights under the Constitution. He pointed out that in American philosophy and intellectual history, racism of any kind was not acceptable to any American, whatever their race or ethnicity. Perales clearly understood the subversive nature of racism to democracy and citizens' civil rights as well as its negative psychological impact on all people, specifically Latinos.[17]

Perales understood that with citizenship came the responsibility of civic virtue and political commitment. In an essay in 1939 titled "Our Rights And Duties As Citizens," he wrote,

> Ours is a cosmopolitan country where more than one hundred and twenty million human beings reside who have united to struggle for a great IDEAL, namely, the IDEAL of Liberty, Progress and Justice. All the races of the world are represented among these inhabitants. Thus there are a great number of citizens of Mexican, Spanish, Anglo-Saxon, Irish, Scotch, Italian, German,

African and other extractions. Our forefathers came here to establish a common country under the guarantees offered by our democratic form of government. It is quite obvious that as citizens we have duties to perform and rights and privileges to enjoy. Now, then, we cannot claim our rights frankly and freely if we do not fulfill our duties as citizens. By the same token, we must not, under any circumstances, fail to claim our rights and privileges if we have performed our duties because it is just as grave an error to fail to perform our duties as it is to permit our rights and privileges to be violated. It was the intention of the founders of our Republic to establish a country where we all should have *equal duties and also equal rights and privileges.*[18]

Since the 1920s, Perales and LULAC had pledged to fight against any organizations or ideologies that sought the downfall of the United States. Perales pointed out very clearly in 1938, in a series of articles in Romulo Mungia's newspaper, *El Pueblo*, on the issue of the correct philosophy of Mexican American politics. There should be no support or voting for radical labor unions; pecan sellers' strikes; or Communist, Socialist, or Nazi leadership; and no membership in any organization with Communist affiliations, such as the Congress of Industrial Organizations and the Worker's Alliance of America (Emma Tenayuca was a member). Ironically, most Communist, Socialist, and Mexican radical labor groups ceased to be viable in America after World War II.[19]

In America, citizenship is public and ethnicity is always private, wrote Richard Rodriguez in his book *Hunger of Memory*. This conceptualization formed American reality. Charles Peirce wrote, "All realities influence our practice, and that influence is their meaning for us." In America, the "practice" is to hold citizenship and ethnicity separate and to value citizenship above ethnicity. However, Perales wanted a fusion of the two spheres. He wanted the American reality to be more than equality between conceptual words such as *Mexican* and *American*. He wanted the "pouring of ethnicity" to infuse the word *American*. Thus, the concept of ethnicity would be, for example, an American of Mexican ethnicity. Being a citizen, Perales understood, meant being American—not linked to ethnicity but infused with it. One could say that America was "pregnant" with ethnicities but not coexisting with them. Perales's argument pointed to an America rooted in a multiplicity of ethnicities. It did not mean ethnicity first and American second. Ironically, this position, of American first and ethnicity subsumed within it, was similar to that of M. C. Gonzales, who rivaled Perales in leadership ability and had personal differences with him. In *El Paladin*, Perales wrote an essay titled "Our Attitude toward History," calling for a redefinition of the American "self" and the need to have a relationship to Mexican traditions. He wrote, "we solemnly declare once and for all to maintain a sincere and respectful reverence for our social origin of which we are proud. This ought to be our proof that our efforts to be rightfully recognized as citizens do not imply that we wish to become scattered or much less abominate our Latin heritage." In the late 1930s, the US Office of Education sponsored a series of radio broadcasts titled "Americans All, Immigrants All," focusing on the contributions of ethnic minorities. The series focused on the collective America spirit embodied in each individual maintaining the consciousness of their ethnicity, their separate spheres of descent. Perales would have agreed.[20]

However, he also believed that Mexicans without naturalized papers would continue to be loyal to Mexico, segregate themselves, and not learn English or pursue citizenship rights. To Perales, the rising middle class of Americans of Mexican descent was the foundation for LULAC. When they became more successful in achieving the goals laid out in their constitution, then they could help Mexican nationals. Perales understood that a movement for citizenship rights had to focus on developing the middle class of lawyers, doctors, printers, journalists, merchants, and vast numbers of teachers throughout Texas and the Southwest and have them become politically involved as LULAC members in the struggle for citizenship rights and against racial discrimination.

Racism, discrimination, and color were central questions in Perales's philosophy and social theory. In his book *En defensa de mi raza*, Perales wrote that he "sought for Mexican Americans to be classified as Caucasians in the 1940 Census, instead of persons of color." Those who believed in the principals of LULAC found the label "persons of color" to be insulting and detrimental to their goal of acculturating into American society. For Perales, refusing to call himself a person of color was a pragmatic stance, not a denial of his ethnic roots. To be designated as "colored" would ingrain prejudice in law. This was the same problem that Perales and the other founders encountered when deciding on their name, the League of United *Latin* American Citizens. The word *Latin* was less caustic to the American ear than *Mexican*, which sounded too close to the Texan Meskin.[21]

Perales's book *Are We Good Neighbors?* presented essays regarding citizenship and the inhumanity of racism, such as one by Robert E. Lucey, the archbishop of San Antonio, who wrote,

> If the Mexican is sometimes illiterate, whose fault is it but the fault of those who denied him an education and drove him out to work in the days of his youth? If the Mexican is sometimes diseased and delinquent, whose fault is it but the fault of those who from his birth condemned him to the unwholesome atmosphere of poverty and squalor? If the Mexican is sometimes not a good American, what can you expect from a man who during all his life was socially ostracized, deprived of civil rights, politically debased and condemned to economic servitude? If some Mexicans seem to be inferior it is because we made them so. God gave them rights and gifts like all the rest of us but we have degraded them.[22]

In these comments, Lucey said what Perales would not say publically: that Mexican Americans were a social and political construction. This was what many black intellectuals were concluding about themselves in the decade of the 1920s in New York's Harlem Renaissance. While Lucey believed that all rights derived from God, Perales differed. He believed that the Declaration of Independence, the Constitution, and the Bill of Rights gave men and women citizens rights that might ultimately be rooted in nature.

The belief that rights were not given by God moved Perales away from traditional Catholic theological beliefs that man was subservient to God and existed by his will alone toward the secular beliefs of the Enlightenment of natural rights without God and where man acts through his own free will. The last two intellectual frameworks have as their central belief that man, theologically and philosophically, is his own ultimate authority and is responsible for his own actions. Above all, Perales sought to make Mexican Americans accept the idea that they determine their lives by their own free will and rationality, not God's will. They did not need to believe in a predetermined fate. By this shift of ideological and theological emphasis, Perales had accepted the basic premises of the American way.[23]

IV. Perales and Pragmatism

Pragmatism in twentieth-century American society gave birth to moral relativism and quickly ushered in the developing changes in manners, morals, and technology—the modernization process in the United States. Pragmatism was a philosophy that fit the United States history. This philosophy of *practicalism*, as some called, or *commonsense* as people in general referred to. Pragmatism became known as "the philosophy of no philosophy," or as James had suggested it was just a *method*. Peirce, James, and Dewey are considered the fathers of pragmatism. All three sought a philosophy that was not religious, socialist, or Marxist, one in accord with American thought and culture at a time when science, technology, and secularism were becoming prominent. Against the relativism of pragmatism, Perales argued for the need of a public "moral compass" based on religious values and civic virtues.[24]

Perales emphatically declared his philosophy of pragmatism and his social theory of humanism and freedom of the individual in certain of his writings. He wrote,

> We consider ourselves to be aware Mexican-Americans from any point of view, [and] as American as any other; and we challenge anyone to prove to the contrary. We do not intend to disown our race. To the contrary, we feel proud to carry our Mexican Blood in our veins. And it is not our purpose to ask, much less beg, Anglo-Saxons, to permit us to mix with them socially. What we desire is progress [as American citizens] and nothing should impede us from it. We want the rights and privileges. We believe in [being] respected. We desire equality of opportunity in the different areas in the struggle for life, and equality before the courts of Justice. In a word we ask for Justice and the opportunity for progress. There you have our objective. There you have our ideal![25]

Perales did not propose a radical or ideological approach to solving the problems of Mexican Americans. Instead, his philosophy pragmatically fused ethnicity and citizenship. Perales followed Peirce's argument that "our beliefs are really rules for action, said that, to develop a thought's meaning, we need only to determine what conduct it is fitted to produce: that conduct is for us its sole significance." In using the philosophy of pragmatism and his life journey of ideas and judgments, Perales established principles and ideas that would lead to action. Peirce and James's method of pragmatism was ingrained in American thought and culture by the beginning of the twentieth century.[26]

The other main philosopher of pragmatism, John Dewey, introduced the concept that ideas were "instruments" for change. He introduced this concept into American schools, from the lower grades to universities and law schools. As a result, Dewey became known as the Father of American Education, since the concept of using ideas as tools for change became central to education. To teach students to not just learn ideas in a vacuum fit the American intellectual and cultural experience. Consequently, Perales and his generation knowingly or not became pragmatists through their education and general osmosis: it was in the general discourse and behavior of American culture. Rodriguez's *Hunger of Memory*, Perales writings and lectures, and Galarza's *Barrio Boy* analyzed each author's identity and the American story of success. All guided generations to answer their own questions of identity as American citizens. Some ordinary citizens called this approach practical or common sense due to their limited perspective and understanding.[27]

Using this philosophy of pragmatism, Perales applied his ideas to reality, but instead of accepting the relativism inherent in pragmatism, he maintained his traditional core of religious values as a humanist to use as his moral compass. Perales could, therefore, focus on his civic-social work while still being religious and not becoming a pragmatic relativist.

Using this method of analytical self-reflection, Perales was inadvertently not only drawing on James but from Peirce, who proposed that man's perception allows him to understand himself in relationship to his impact and change on society and culture. Perales, like James, believed pragmatism to be a method for illuminating problems and focusing on solutions. Perales emphasized this American philosophical framework of pragmatism—James called it a method for "settling metaphysical [and social] disputes." The central issues that LULAC focused on, such as the rights of citizenship and racial discrimination, were guided by Perales's vision and belief that changes are initiated by man (through organizations), and the direction and definition of progress is based on one's perspective on the world, philosophy for change, a theology of a god that was not omnipotent, and for religious values and virtues that would provide a moral compass as the basis for change.[28]

Perales believed in the separation of church and state but still argued for individuals to maintain moral principles as they struggled in the civic arena. Given his bachelor's and law degrees, his diplomatic missions in Latin America, and his life experiences in Washington DC, he understood James's arguments in his 1907 essay on pragmatism. The key question in formulating a policy was *Does it work?* The consequence, not the approach, is the emphasis, with workability and usability the central aim. If it does not work, one returns to the "pool of ideas" and selects new ideas for a new approach. This kept with James's belief that "all realities influence our [life] practice[s] and that influence is their meaning for us." Perales had used this method to guide his life decisions, and he knew that "truth" led to success.[29]

These ideas were drawn from his American cultural and intellectual life and his university education and law school. They were, in fact, Peirce and James's method—the philosophy of pragmatism—that established principles and ideas would lead to action, especially against racial discrimination, which was, Perales clearly understood, dehumanizing. James preferred to call pragmatism a method rather than a philosophy because it addressed problems and approached them with a method to solve. For example, Perales applied his ideas to reality in a method that linked his beliefs and ideas to actions that focused on changing the secular problems of American society. Texas posed many problems for Mexican Americans, so Perales wanted to apply ideas to problems that were suggestive of a solution to such problems as racial discrimination. Perales wanted to find solutions and not ideological guidelines.

Perales also did not want to accept the relativism that was inherent in pragmatism. Thus, he emphasized that individuals adopt a moral compass as a litmus test to judge the possible solutions that would be used. This suggestion was the residue of his Catholicism and his ethnicity of Mexican traditionalism that focused on right and wrong: nothing was relative in Mexican intellectual thought; certainty was always sought. This was a problem.[30]

Perales, in addition to his position against relativism and his argument for American acculturation and functionalism, understood the need for the concept and use of the phrase "of Mexican descent" after the word *American*. This arrangement of language indicated adherence to the new country as well as to an immigrant's roots, their ethnicity. His use of the term was similar to what sociologist Werner Sollors has argued when he wrote, "ethnicity . . . emerges not as a thing itself, but as the result of interactions." Perales's central interpretation of these "interactions" was that Mexican American individuals and communities were in a constant *telos*—linear and always progressing toward their goals of American progress and acculturation while still being constantly linked to Mexican traditions, rituals, religion, and historical and personal memories. Underscoring this principle of individual and collective freedom, Perales wrote an editorial in *LULAC News* in the 1930s, stating, "We should endeavor to develop aggressiveness of the right sort and be able to pursue our own initiative, instead of waiting for someone else to do the things"[31]

In short, Perales, through LULAC, emphasized that each individual's personal life as a functional American should be existentially free. Sollors also makes this basic argument. He writes, "Ethnicity does not serve as a totalizing metaphor but simply as a perspective onto psychological, historical, social, and cultural forces." Perales further argued that in order to fully exercise personal and public freedoms of choice, individualism, and opportunities, Americans of Mexican descent had to first be accepted as equal citizens, with the full range of civil rights and responsibilities as granted in the Declaration of Independence, the Bill of Rights, and the Constitution. He imprinted all of these ideas and concepts in LULAC's guiding documents for the organization and for its members.[32]

V. Perales and Eclective Fusionism

Perales's approach to solving the problems of Mexican Americans was eclective. He shaped LULAC's founding documents by mixing the themes of American Enlightenment democracy—emphasizing rationality and free will to make choices—and the belief in a personal and collective memory of Mexican thought and culture. These themes were not simply abstract ideas written in LULAC's founding documents; they were codified and prescriptive principles for action. Since 1929 these themes had been the central paradigm for all Mexican American citizens. On one hand, Perales infused LULAC with a pragmatic approach to solving community problems. On the other, he wrote into the founding documents a social theory based on a philosophy that bordered on existentialism. He fused nineteenth-century classical liberalism, with its emphasis on the individual; twentieth-century liberalism, with its emphasis on the power of the federal government; and neo-liberalism, with its emphasis on ethnicity (traditional folkways, mythologies, and personal and collective memories). Perales bridged the theology of church and the secularity of states. He merged the perspectives of William James, Charles Peirce, and John Dewey in order to create a method of solutions where ideas were the instruments of change. These mergers were products of the experiences of his life[33]

Perales knew that San Antonio, and Texas in particular, needed an activist organization to promote the rights of Mexican Americans, even though some LULAC members felt that they would be called activists and organizers, which had overtones of communism or radicalism. Adela Sloss-Vento wrote about Perales, "He had a noble dream. The unity of Americans of Mexican descent was the dream of attorney Perales; [He was] A man of high morals, ethics and principles, who did not like to compromise his principles for material gain. Since [he was] young he had to struggle for the rights of his existence today." And in her eulogy, Perales's wife, Marta Pérez, stated, "Formar la liga fue su ideal disde su juventud" (Forming the League was his dream since his youth). His principals and political beliefs derived from a more coherent Enlightenment philosophy and were intertwined and tempered with his beliefs in virtues, religious values, community, self-understanding through self-introspection, and the acceptance of acculturation while retaining continuity with ethnic tradition.

In a letter to Sloss-Vento, Perales wrote, "My only purpose in forming the said organization [LULAC] . . . [was] to bring about the rapid intellectual, social and political evolution of Americans of Mexican descent, to promote the social welfare of all Latin people residing in Texas and to produce the highest type of American citizen." He understood that citizenship is part of a rarified constellation of concepts at the core of the American consciousness and that it is significant not for any spiritual meaning, nor for its "use-value"—for instance, in the economic realm—as Karl Marx states in *Das Kapital*. Instead, Perales believed that citizenship is significant for its relation to what Dewey, in "The Experience of Knowing," termed "experimental value"—the question *Does it work?* Peirce wrote, "our beliefs are really rules for action, said that, to develop a thought's meaning, we need only to determine what conduct it is fitted to produce: that conduct is for us its sole significance." For Perales, being a citizen signified the key to membership in a democratic society and access to all the political and civil rights as well as the ability to pursue life, liberty, and happiness. He and many of the LULAC leadership accepted the philosophy of pragmatism as a method but extended its focus to *For whom does it work and how?*[34]

Perales believed that Americans of Mexican descent could be American citizens and retain their ethnicity. He emphasized his acculturation, which had enabled him to function successfully in American society. For instance, his fluency in Spanish sustained the presence of an ethnic collectivity in his soul while his fluency in English served as a vehicle for the public expression of his worldviews. This is what Perales meant when he wrote that he wanted to make Americans of Mexican descent functional citizens in US society, with a personal and collective memory of their ethnicity—"the best that each could be." As a result of such acculturation, Perales could be American while still retaining his personal desires, his conceptualizations of future and past, and his goals. His successes and his personal and public experiences and decisions had became the cornerstones of his life, resulting in his tendency to act pragmatically, which was the basis of the LULAC philosophy. He articulated his sentiments in his 1939 testimony before the House Committee on Immigration: I have always been an "American citizen of Mexican descent and was proud of it."[35]

Perales's philosophy and central ideas of citizenship rights, cultural functionality in American society, love and respect for Mexican heritage, and embracement of American culture and thought, breathed life into the LULAC Code. LULAC, in turn, infused the community with similar hopes and dreams. As a result, Perales's philosophy and social theory for change became the philosophical bible for the emerging middle class of Americans of Mexican descent. LULAC not only provided the blueprint for a philosophy of freedom and equality but for the liberation of Mexican Americans and Mexican nationals from the "iron cage" of racism and discrimination. LULAC was the organization by which Mexican American citizens could walk a "shining path" to a new consciousness of hope and individual excellence, justice, and democracy. It was also the carrier of the word of the Enlightenment, the new human nature of rationality and individuality and adherence to the behavioral commandments of traditional Mexican values.[36]

Perales wrote into LULAC's constitution values to change the sociopolitical conditions of Mexican Americans to enable to flourish in them a new consciousness: one of hope and individual excellence, justice, and democracy. His speeches, newspaper articles, and books of the 1920s through the 1940s outlined his philosophical and political visions that became the intellectual and philosophical foundation of LULAC.

Perales formulated the major political, psychological, and philosophical tenets of the Mexican American mind. In 1931 he argued in *El México*

Americano y la política del sur de Texas that South Texas was a land forgotten in a state of poverty, discrimination, little education, and a politics of favoritism to Anglo-Americans, framed by a spirit of despair and without the freedom to vote. Elsewhere he wrote, "The consciousness of the younger generation of Americans [of Mexican descent], whatever their racial extraction might be, must be trained to be subservient to no one; to feel and act equal with all others; to grow into manhood upright, with no complexes of any kind, with loyalty to the [American] flag and respect to the constituted authorities, and an abundance of patriotism in their hearts; that is, if we are to have leaders among the Latin citizens of this country." In 1939 he wrote, "Unquestionably, I repeat, we Americans of Mexican descent must perform our duties as citizens, including that of giving our lives for our Country, whenever it may be necessary." He also wrote, "Yes, the Constitution [is] the charter of Freedom, the heart of our nation, the guarantee of our civil liberties, the fortress of our institutions, the bulwark of our security, and inspiration of our American way of life." These statements, together with the founding documents of LULAC and his ceaseless work in Mexican communities, show him to be what people said about him: a man of intellectual brilliance, integrity, and patriotism as well as industrious, imaginative, and respectful of his Mexican heritage.[37]

VI. Conclusion: "Americans All, Immigrants All"

In her biography of Perales, Adela Sloss-Vento captures a few of his notable qualities: "his intellectuality; his dedication to humanity, his devotion to all Americans of Mexican Descent and Mexican workers, and, in spite of all his responsibilities, his ability to be and live free," adding that Perales had all the "qualities of a patriot, a humanitarian, and one who loves justice and seeks to protect the rights of others." Sloss-Vento further states that Perales "within his soul bears the courage and the indomitable faith to conquer all obstacles for the good of the people, his country and humanity."[38]

In the early 1950s, Spain honored Perales in a special ceremony at San Antonio's Spanish consulate, awarding him the rank of Commander of the Spanish Order of Civil Merit. The Spanish consul stated that Perales was "a distinguished lawyer who had dedicated his life to the struggle for justice and the extermination of racial discrimination against the Spanish Speaking of this country [the United States]." Also at this ceremony, Archbishop Robert

E. Lucey took the opportunity to underscore Perales's love of humanity. Gus García, one of the new leaders of LULAC, acknowledged Perales's importance, stating that he was "a genuine leader because he constructed a better future for the new generation."[39]

Since the 1920s, Perales and LULAC had pledged to fight against any organizations or ideologies that sought the downfall of the United States. He focused on solving the problems of Mexican Americans and their communities through democratic means. Perales contended that LULAC was an American organization that emphasized that Mexican American citizens accept and learn the methods of democratic action, which prescribed pragmatic social change rather than ideology. As a result, he sought to bridge religion, citizenship, and civic or political action.[40]

By the end of World War II, Perales had turned LULAC from a force in communities, only—for membership drives, social activities, and a central organizer of social, educational, and other community needs—to the active voice for Mexican Americans in their local communities and in Washington DC. He also added the political arm Committee of One Hundred. Formerly, LULAC allowed its members to engage in political action, but not under its own banner. The Committee of One Hundred, with Perales as its founder and chair, entered the political arena as a sanctioned representative of LULAC.

Perales's university education, intellectual cosmopolitism, and American acculturation led him away from the traditional beliefs and theology of the Catholic Church. However, by analyzing and reflecting on his life journey from orphan to diplomat, he grew to embrace a *philosophical* theology that emphasized rationalism, free will, and freedom of the individual. Nevertheless, he still assumed he was a Catholic. He attended daily Mass and received Holy Communion, the Catholic Church's mystical sacrament for man's redemption. In effect, what Perales had done was fuse Catholic ritual with Protestant theology.

He still believed in a metaphysical god and he accepted the belief that Catholicism had instilled in him a spiritual core of sacredness that served him with a moral compass to use in his secular life. Yet he refused to accept that God had predetermined his life, his fate. Sloss-Vento writes that, for Perales, being Catholic and acknowledging God was like "the air we breathe." It was a necessity for living. Granted, Perales always believed that he remained religious, regardless of his secular beliefs in Enlightenment rationalism, free will, and secularism, his pragmatic philosophy that man used his ideas as instruments for change, and his acceptance of a moral compass to navigate in the secular world. To an extent, these changes were also occurring to many Mexicans and Mexican Americans throughout the Southwest. Since the 1910s, many Mexican immigrants changed to Protestant religions. In addition, the rising generation of Mexican Americans became more acculturated through their lives, jobs, schools, and the fact that many were born in the United States. Historian George J. Sánchez points out that in the early decades of the twentieth century

> Protestantism flourished among the displaced, and served as a stabilizing force in a world rapidly being transformed by technology and transportation. Catholicism appeared to be an ancient religion rooted in a disappearing village life. The new order encouraged the adoption of new values, such as punctuality and the prohibition of alcohol—values which Methodism and other Protestant churches emphasized." It seems that Mexican Americans and Mexicans were seeking the Promise of America and were open to acculturation in their new country.[41]

By reenvisioning Mexican Americans as Americans of Mexican descent, Perales hoped to change their consciousness and beliefs. He wanted an *intellectual redemption* for Mexican Americans, whose lives were immersed in the Mexican Catholic faith of mysticism, mythology, rituals, and the central power of a commanding God. Specifically, he wanted their faith, hope, and desire to become more secular and add to their character the core American values that emanated from citizenship: the belief in liberty, equality, and justice. These were, Perales believed, the "guaranteed heritage" of all American citizens and the same desires that inspired him to imagine his goals and work to accomplish his "guaranteed" right to successes. From his self-analysis, he also understood the need for a moral code to guide his and LULAC's actions in a secular society.

In analyzing his life, Perales was also aware that he was not to be defined by how people perceived him, as a dark-skinned Mexican immigrant, rather than what he was, a lawyer, diplomat, leader, and intellectual. He wore his ethnicity. His booming voice commanded attention and announced his presence. Because he had encountered the cruelty of racism firsthand, he never forgot the prevalence of racial prejudice and discrimination, especially since Texas was a southern state.[42]

Perales was an eclective fusionist. He fused philosophies out of a desire for pragmatic results. He did not seek closed ideologies or theologies. His life and the foundation documents of the United States had imbued him with the belief that ideas would help Mexican Americans, even if these fusions created a paradox. He also fused political philosophies; he was an eighteenth- and nineteenth-century liberal in the vein of Thomas Jefferson, who emphasized the power of the individual, and a twentieth-century liberal in the vein of Franklin Roosevelt, who emphasized the power of the federal government to help the "common folk." He fused theology with existentialism— religious mysticism with the mystics of liberal democracy. Moreover, he fused idealism with realism and rationality with traditionalism. His eclecticism was what critical theorist Jürgen Habermas has called "communication action"—that is, the use of different theories or philosophies that are applied to the practical. William James and John Dewey, the pragmatist philosophers, would call Perales's eclective fusionism pragmatic while sociologists Gabriel Almond and Sidney Verba would suggest that Perales's eclectivism was part of a developing civic culture where rationalism and traditionalism coexisted as a "version of political culture and a practice of accommodation and compromise." In short, Perales was attempting to establish a workable "civic culture" of American-ethnic diversity—political democracy and public morality—and the acceptance of ethnic diversity as part of the American character. Perales advocated a new social theory of *Americanism* with "Lo Americano fused by Lo Mexicano." Americans All, Immigrants All. This fusion of philosophies and social theories validated what Perales saw in his life and the lives of Americans of Mexican descent: pragmatism, not ideologies.

Perales's essay "Our Attitude toward History," called for a redefinition of *American* to include ethnicity. He argued, "we solemnly declare once and for all to maintain a sincere and respectful reverence for our social origin of which we are proud. This ought to be our proof that our efforts to be rightfully recognized as citizens do not imply that we wish to become scattered or much less abominate our Latin heritage"[43] Historian Cynthia E. Orozco has written of Perales, "He was [a] major political leader from the 1920s until his death [in 1960] and was one of the most influential Mexican Americans of his time. Perales saw himself as a defender of 'la Raza,' especially battling charges that Mexicans were an inferior people and a social problem."[44]

Historian Anthony Quiroz has identified the start of the Mexican American movement and political consciousness to "claim citizenship" as beginning in the 1920s, with the return of World War I veterans (who were seeking democracy in their communities) and the rise of the middle class (who urged Americanism). Quiroz calls this political consciousness a "quest for legitimation" and a struggle against any limitations put on their rights as citizens. In fact, Quiroz strongly argues—via Perales's 1929 LULAC Constitution and Dr. Héctor P. García's 1947 American GI Forum—that the acquisition of full citizenship is the fundamental pursuit of the Mexican American population. Quiroz also points out that regardless of the radical rhetoric and behavior of the Chicano movement of the 1960s, it was basically seeking full citizenship rights and a "quest for legitimation in American society.[45]

If Perales were asked the central question in American history—*Are you an American?*—he probably would have explained, as a pragmatist would, I am what I did. I was a citizen intellectual. I used my vision and my voice to help my fellow Mexican American citizens receive their constitutional and civil rights, and I helped them to be proud of who they are: American citizens of Mexican descent.

Notes

1. This essay has its thematic foundation in my text, *Rise of the Mexican American Middle Class, San Antonio, 1929–1941* (College Station: Texas A&M University Press, 1991), 282–89, which is the section on Perales but with an emphasis in analyzing his philosophy and social theory and incorporating it into the broader themes of American intellectual and political history. Perales's life narrative, experiences, historical context, and political and social evolution in the public sphere enabled me to analyze and interpret his ideas and thoughts as sources of his self-reflective themes and categories. See the introduction and essays in part 3 of Craig Calhoun, ed., *Habermas and the Public Sphere* (Cambridge, MA: MIT Press, 1992); and Jürgen Habermas, *Knowledge and Human Interests* (Boston: Beacon, 1968). See also Jürgen Habermas, *Theory and Practice* (Boston: Beacon, 1973); and the works of Charles S. Peirce, William James, and John Dewey.

Perales's three books were central to examining and interpreting the themes and nuances of his thoughts, reflections, and observations. Alonzo S. Perales, *El México Americano la política del sur de Texas* (San Antonio: n.p, 1931); Alonso S. Perales, *En defensa de mi raza*, 2 vols. (San Antonio: Artes Gráficas, 1936–1937); and

Alonso S. Perales, *Are We Good Neighbors?* (New York: Arno, 1974). See also Adela Sloss-Vento, *Alonso S. Perales: His Struggles for the Rights of Mexican Americans*, 2nd ed. (Austin, TX: Eagle Feather Research Institute, 2009).

This essay also draws on some of the arguments and themes in the following texts: Richard A. Buitron, *The Quest for Tejano Identity in San Antonio, Texas, 1913–2000* (New York: Routledge, 2004), 28; Craig A. Kaplowitz, *LULAC, Mexican Americans, and National Policy* (College Station: Texas A&M University Press, 2005); Anthony Quiroz, *Claiming Citizenship: Mexican Americans in Victoria, Texas* (College Station: Texas A&M University Press, 2005); Arnoldo De León, *Mexican Americans in Texas: A Brief History* (Arlington Heights, IL: Harlan Davidson, 1993), 88–94; Mario T. García, *Mexican Americans: Leadership, Ideology, and Identity, 1930–1960* (New Haven, CT: Yale University Press, 1989); Guadalupe San Miguel, Jr., *"Let All of Them Take Heed": Mexican Americans and the Campaign for Educational Equality in Texas, 1910–1981* (Austin: University of Texas Press, 1987); Ignacio M. García, *Héctor P. García: In Relentless Pursuit of Justice* (Houston: Arte Publico, 2002); Arnoldo De León, *Ethnicity in the Sunbelt: A History of Mexican Americans in Houston* (Houston: Mexican American Studies Program, University of Houston); Cynthia E. Orozco, *No Mexicans, Women, or Dogs Allowed: The Rise of the Mexican American Civil Rights Movement* (Austin: University of Texas Press, 2009); Cynthia Orozco, *The Handbook of Texas* online, Texas State Historical Association, http://tshaonline.org/handbook/online; and Henry A. J. Ramos, *The American GI Forum: In Pursuit of the Dream, 1948–1983* (Houston: Arte Publico, 1998).

2. R. A. Garcia, *Rise*, 204–7, 255–68, 281; Buitron, *Quest*, 19–25; De León, *Mexican Americans in Texas*, 86–94; F. Arturo Rosales, *Testimonio: A Documentary History of the Mexican American Struggle for Civil Rights* (Houston: Arte Publico, 2000), 157–71; William James, *Pragmatism and Other Writings* (New York: Penguin, 2000), 337–39; José de la Luz Sáenz, "Racial Discrimination: A Number One Problem of Texas Schools," *Texas Outlook* 30 (December 1946), reprinted in Perales, *Neighbors*, 29–36, 136, 121–23, 257, 276–77; Arnoldo De León, *They Called Them Greasers: Anglo Attitudes toward Mexicans in Texas, 1821–1900* (Austin: University of Texas Press, 1983); and Perales, *Neighbors*, 139–69.

3. Perales, *Neighbors*. In 1944 Perales testified before the Senate Education and Labor Committee. He addressed them under the new organization that was the political arm of LULAC, the Committee of One Hundred. Perales announced this "turn left," which meant that LULAC would not just recruit members who would be political but individuals, since the LULAC Constitution stipulated it was not to engage in direct politics. Perales was chairman of the new political arm, which allowed only 100 members to participate. The members were the elite leaders in Mexican American and Anglo communities. Anglo-Saxon members were allowed

only if they were political or leaders in their communities. But the organization never expanded; its membership remained at 100. In 1974 it "turned further left," meaning that LULAC (using its own name) could now pressure members of Congress—or lobby—directly. Perales sent letters directly to Franklin Roosevelt and the governor of Texas, which are printed in Rosales, *Testimonio*; and Perales, *Neighbors*.

On the subject of "turn left" see Perales, *Neighbors*, 114–20; Perales, "Senate Committee Hearings on S. 2048 and S. 459 August 30–September 6–8, 1944"; and Perales, *Neighbors*, 86–90, 92–98. Perales's testimony on the lack of attention to bills on racialism can be found in Perales, *Neighbors*, 114–17. Perales quoted in Lupe S. Salinas, "Legally White, Socially Brown: Alonso S. Perales and His Crusade for Justice for La Raza." This and other papers were presented at the dedication of the opening of the Alonso S. Perales Papers (hereafter Perales Papers) at the University of Houston Libraries on January 13, 2012, and are online at http://digital.lib.uh.edu /collection/perales.

4. Buitron, *Quest*, 20, 19–23; Orozco, *Handbook of Texas*; Perales, *En defensa de mi raza*, 1–3, 130–31; San Miguel, *"Let All of Them Take Heed"*, 68; J. Hector St. John de Crèvecoeur, *Letters From an American Farmer* (1904; repr., New York: Penguin, 1981), 9; Henry Adams, *The Education of Henry Adams* (1918; repr., New York: Time Inc., 1964); Ernesto Galarza, *Barrio Boy* (1971), 69–70; and Richard Rodriguez, *Hunger of Memory: The Education of Richard Rodriguez* (1982).

5. See Perales, *En defensa de mi raza*; and Perales, *Neighbors*, 44–45. For short biographies of Perales, see Perales, *Neighbors*, 5–9, 11–16, 17–20, 34–36, 53–57, 59–63, 114–17, 228–29; Perales, *El México Americano*; Sloss-Vento, *Perales*; Josh Gottheimer, ed., "Alonso S. Perales," in *Ripples of Hope: Great American Civil Rights Speeches* (New York: Basic Civitas, 2003), 156–58. Robert F. Sayre, *The Examined Self: Benjamin Franklin, Henry Adams, Henry James* (Madison: University of Wisconsin Press, 1988), ix–xxx; and Robert Denoon Cumming, ed., *The Philosophy of John-Paul Sartre* (New York: Vintage, 1965), 51–58.

6. Perales's sister, interview, Perales Papers; R. A. Garcia, *Rise*, chapter 1; and Perales's son, interview, Perales Papers.

7. Alonso S. Perales, "Our Rights and Duties as Citizens," in J. Montiel Olvera, *First Year Book of the Latin-American Population of Texas* (N.p., 1939), 21–22; "LULAC Constitution No. 10," in R. A. Garcia, *Rise*, 258–69; and Sloss-Vento, *Perales*, 1, 6, 9, 22, 29–30, 62, 66–67, 72, 78, 80.

8. Perales, *El México Americano*; De León, *Mexican Americans in Texas*, 91–94; and "LULAC Constitution and Code," in R. A. Garcia, *Rise*, 259, 268–69, 273, 282–85. Many Americans in Texas felt Perales was a "revolutionary," but LULAC leader José de la Luz Sáenz, in opposition to this sentiment, wrote, "We are not rabble rousers, impulsive, uncontrollable . . . We are and have [always] been genuine Americans."

Sáenz quoted in Sloss-Vento, *Perales*, 77. See also Perales, *Neighbors*, 5–8, 91–92 and Rosales, *Testimonio*, 167.

9. Philip Wheelwright, *Metaphor and Reality*; R. A. Garcia, *Rise*, 266–69, 273–75, 283–84; Sloss-Vento, *Perales*, 29–30, 67; Buitron, *Quest*, 31; Orozco, *Handbook of Texas*, entries on Perales and LULAC; Perales, "Our Rights and Duties as Citizens," in Olvera, *Year Book*, 19, 39, 21–22 (in Spanish on page 21); and M. C. Gonzales, "No Segregation," 17. The Spanish title is "Iguales, No Segregados" (iguales translates as "equals"), in Olvera, *Year Book*, 16–19.

10. Sloss-Vento, *Perales*, 30–31, 65–66. Sloss-Vento writes "that for him, God was like the air we breathe [part of daily life]." *Perales*, 66. Sloss-Vento writes that both Perales and Castañeda believed that God was part of everyday life and culture, 53–54. See also M. García, *Mexican Americans*, 35; Kaplowitz, *LULAC*, 22–23, 27; Habermas, *Knowledge*, chapter 3; David Carr, *Time, Narrative, and History* (Bloomington: Indiana University Press, 1986), introduction, chapters 1, 3; Werner Sollors, ed., *The Invention of Ethnicity* (New York: Oxford University Press, 1989), ix, xx; Jean Paul Sartre, *Essays In Existentialism* (New York: Citadel, 1993); and John E. Smith and William Kluback, eds., *Josiah Royce: Selected Writings* (New York: Paulist, 1998), 101–21.

11. Perales, "The Ideals of Mexican Americans"; and "The LULAC Constitution," in Rosales, *Testimonio*, 91,118–19, 165–67; Perales, "LULAC Constitution and LULAC Code: A Philosophy for Living," in R. A. Garcia, *Rise*, 268–69, 273; and Buitron, *Quest*, 31–32.

12. Ibid.; Philip P. Wiener, ed., *Charles S. Peirce: Selected Writings* (New York: Dover, 1966), 15–72, 180–202; Habermas, *Knowledge*, 15, 17, 43–44, 308–14; R. A. Garcia, *Rise*, chapter 9; Buitron, *Quest*, chapters 1–4; William James, *Pragmatism and the Meaning of Truth* (Cambridge: Harvard University Press, 1978), 95–113; William James, *Essays in Pragmatism* (New York: Hafner, 1968), 141–45, 146–58; John J. McDermott, ed., *The Philosophy of John Dewey* (Chicago: University of Chicago Press, 1981), chapters 3, 8; John Dewey, *Freedom and Culture* (New York: Paragon, 1979), chapters 1, 5, 7; and Patrick Kiaran Dooley, *Pragmatism as Humanism: The Philosophy of William James* (Totowa, NJ: Littlefield, Adams, 1975), chapters 4, 5.

13. Orozco, *Handbook of Texas*. For comparative views of immigrants, ethnicity, and the promise of America, see John Bodnar, *The Transplanted: A History of Immigrants in Urban America* (Bloomington: Indiana University Press, 1987), chapters 4–7; Benedict Anderson, *Imagined Communities: Reflections on the Origin and Spread of Nationalism* (London: Verso, 1983), introduction, chapters 5, 7; Arthur F. Corwin, ed., *Immigrants—and Immigrants: Perspectives on Mexican Labor Migration to the United States* (Westport, CT: Greenwood, 1979); and R. A. Garcia, *Rise*. For examples of class and status layering, see parts 2 and 3 of M. T. García, *Mexican Americans in Texas*, chapters 1, 2; Arnoldo De León, *The Tejano Community, 1836–1900*

(Albuquerque: University of New Mexico Press, 1982); and Quiroz, *Claiming Citizenship*, ix–xiii, xv–xxv, xii, 77.

14. R. A. Garcia, *Rise*, chapter 9; M. T. García, *Mexican Americans in Texas*, chapter 2; Buitron, *Quest*, chapter 2; and Kaplowitz, *LULAC*, chapter 1.

15. Orozco, *Handbook of Texas*; Matt S. Meier, *Mexican American Biographies: A Historical Dictionary, 1836–1987* (New York: Greenwood, 1988), 174–75; R. A. Garcia, *Rise*, 282–83; Sloss-Vento, *Perales*, 67–80; and Perales, *Neighbors*, 115–16.

16. Olvera, *Year Book*, 2–91.

17. Ibid.; Sloss-Vento, *Perales*, i–vii, 1–9; Kaplowitz, *LULAC*, 28–31; and R. A. Garcia, *Rise*, 259, 268–69, 273. While others, such as J. T. Canales and M. C. Gonzales, contributed to the LULAC documents, most of the themes were from Perales. Perales, *Neighbors*, 88–90; and Rosales, *Testimonio*, 91–92.

18. J. Montiel Olera, *Primer Anuario de los Habitantes Hispano-Americanos* (n.p.: 1939), author's emphasis.

19. R. A. Garcia, *Rise*, chapter 9; Olvera, *Year Book*, 22; M. T. García, *Mexican Americans in Texas*, chapter 2; Button, *Quest*, chapter 2; and Kaplowitz, *LULAC*, chapter 1.

20. Perales, "The Pioneer in Mexican Americanism," in Rosales, *Testimonio*, 168–69; Perales, *Neighbors*, 131; and Richard Rodriguez, *Lecture* (Santa Monica, CA: Santa Monica College, 1995). In his lecture, Rodrigues referred to acculturation "by osmosis" when one is living American life.

21. Buitron, *Quest*, 25, 28, 31, 35, 32; Peter L. Berger and Thomas Luckmann, *The Social Construction of Reality: A Treatise in the Sociology of Knowledge* (Garden City, NY: Anchor, 1966), 129–40, 173–78; James, *Writings*, 1–21; Carr, *Time*, 73–86; Habermas, *Knowledge*, chapter 3; and John J. McDermott, ed., *The Philosophy of John Dewey* (Chicago: University of Chicago Press, 1981), 160–239.

22. Rosales, *Testimonio*, 91–92, 164–70; Alexis de Tocqueville, *Democracy in America*, ed. J. P. Mayer (Garden City, NY: Anchor, 1969), 287; and Perales, *Neighbors*, 126–27, 131, 135–38.

23. Ibid.; Kaplowitz, *LULAC*, 27–28; R. A. Garcia, *Rise*, 260, 273, 284; and Buitron, *Quest*, 2.

24. Habermas, *Theory and Practice*, 1–39. Habermas argues for a critical approach that is "eclectic" by combining theories. Perales, in drawing from his self-reflection and self-analysis, as well as on his schooling and experiences, seems to have used an eclectic perspectivism. R. A. Garcia, *Rise*, 259–61; San Miguel, *"Let All of Them Take Heed,"* 71–72, 74; Kaplowitz, *LULAC*, 27–28; James, *Pragmatism*, 24–40, 41–57, 87, 124; Werner Sollors, ed., *Theories of Ethnicity: A Classical Reader* (New York: New York University Press, 1996), x–xliv, 156–67, 425–59; and Milton M. Gordon, *Assimilation in American Life: The Role of Race, Religion, and National Origins* (New York: Oxford University Press, 1964), xxi–xxii, xxvii–xxxiii, 60–83, 84–159.

25. Perales, "En defensa de mi raza" in Rosales, *Testimonio*, 167; see also Buitron, *Quest*, 91.

26. Perales, *Neighbors*, 86–91, 104–11, 114–33; and R. A. Garcia, *Rise*, 284–99.

27. Perales, *Neighbors*, 114–32; R. A. Garcia, *Rise*, 259–60; and San Miguel, "*Let All of Them Take Heed*," 71–74.

28. R. A. Garcia, *Rise*, 284, 281, 273, 289. Article 11 of the LULAC Constitution states that the organization and its members will oppose any radical action against America. See Buitron, *Quest*, 22–33 and Rosales, *Testimonio*, 91–92.

29. Perales, *Neighbors*, 63, 88–91. Perales and LULAC leaders had been very successful in organizing their chapters and working politically through the Committee of One Hundred, which listed hundreds of members and had political links to other California and Southwest Mexican American organizations, such as Eduardo Quevedo's Coordinating Council for Latin American Youth in Los Angeles. The Committee of One Hundred also accepted non-Hispanics to the organization. See Perales, *Neighbors*, 88–91. Perales and the rest of the LULAC elite were members and leaders of the Catholic political organization Council for the Spanish Speaking. Henry B. Gonzales was the president. Gonzalez became a US Congressman in the early 1950s until his death about forty years later. Perales, a practicing lawyer in San Antonio, was still the citizen intellectual for LULAC and other organizations. R. A. Garcia, *Rise*, 114, 127–32, 149–52.

30. Perales, "Letter to James E. Furgeson," in Rosales, *Testimonio*, 118–19; and Sloss-Vento, *Perales*, 25, 29–30, 58. Henry Steele Commager made this point in his American Intellectual History graduate seminar, which was filmed at Amherst College. I obtained this film from the Santa Monica film library where I was a faculty member in 1976.

31. See the texts cited in note 1. See also Manuel G. Gonzales, *Mexicanos: A History of Mexicans in the United States* (Bloomington: Indiana University Press, 2000); and Thomas Mernal, "The Chiasmus: Unamuno's Master Trope," *PMLA* 105 (March 1990), 251. There is an interesting theme that is linked to the conditions of Perales's theory of eclective fusionism. This was very close to what the Spanish philosopher Miguel Unamuno believed, as historian Thomas Mermail has written: Unamuno believed that "the fusion of interpenetration of contraries is actually dialectic without synthesis, since Unamuno is never prepared to relinquish his personal discrete identity, because fusion would be tantamount to spiritual death. Human life in all its forms only has meaning, Unamuno further believed, insofar as it struggles to affirm its individual unique qualities, and this struggle forces each polar identity into an unremitting tension with its own inherent and external opposites." Like Unamuno, Perales believed that the dialectic instead of leading to a Hegelian synthesis leads to an "interpretation of opposites—the individual and society. Therefore, according

to Unamuno, Mermail points out, this defines the self in relation to some form of otherness, releasing the potential identity and meaning of both with the ultimate dominance of neither." This is Perales's theory of eclective fusionism.

32. Rosales, *Testimonio*, 118–19; and R. A. Garcia, *Rise*, 284–89, 296, 297.

33. James, *Writings*, 2–8; Rosales, *Testimonio*, 167–68; Mario T. García, "Americans All: The Mexican American Generation and the Politics of Wartime Los Angeles, 1941–45," in Manuel G. Gonzales and Cynthia M. Gonzales, eds., *En Aquel Entonces: Readings in Mexican American History* (Bloomington: Indiana University Press, 2000), 192–99.

34. R. A. Garcia, *Rise*, 203–205, 287, 289.

35. Perales, *Neighbors*, 130–31; and Buitron, *Quest*, 31.

36. Olvera, *Year Book*, 21–22. The title page is also in Spanish as are a few of the articles. Being bilingual was still part of Mexican American communities in the 1930s, but this would change by the 1950s. The middle class would speak more English while the working people in the barrios would speak a combination of English and Spanish. Rosales, *Testimonio*, 91–92. For comparative points on B. T. Washington and W.E.B. Du Bois, see Henry Louis Gates, Jr., and Cornel West, *The Future of the Race* (New York: Vintage, 1996), vii–xvii, 133–77; and Gonzales and Gonzales, eds., *En Aquel Entonces*, 134–41.

37. Sloss-Vento, *Perales*, 71; R. A. Garcia, *Rise*, 283; Rosales, *Testimonio*, 118–19; and Henry Steele Commager, *The American Mind: An Interpretation of American Thought and Character Since the 1880's* (New Haven, CT: Yale University Press, 1974), 310–11, 414–16.

38. Rosales, *Testimonio*, 1–7; Carey McWilliams, *North From Mexico: The Spanish-Speaking People of the United States* (New York: Praeger, 1990), 91; and Richard Griswold del Castillo and Arnoldo De León, *North to Aztlán: A History of Mexican Americans in the United States* (New York: Twayne, 1997), 32.

39. Perales, *El México Americano*.

40. Rosales, *Testimonio*, 91–92.

41. James, *Pragmatism and Other Writings*, 74; George J. Sánchez, *Becoming Mexican American: Ethnicity, Culture, and Identity in Chicano Los Angeles, 1900–1945* (New York: Oxford University Press, 1993), 154–55.

42. Perales, *Neighbors*, 26; and Sloss-Vento, *Perales*, 79.

43. Olvera, *Year Book*, 22.

44. Ibid.; Orozco, *Handbook of Texas*; and Sloss-Vento, *Perales*.

45. Sloss-Vento, *Perales*, 68–69; Quiroz, *Claiming Citizenship*, xii–77. For a wider historical and intellectual view of pragmatism, see John Patrick Diggins, *The Promise of Pragmatism: Modernism and the Crisis of Knowledge and Authority* (Chicago: University of Chicago Press, 1994). I studied with Diggins.

Figure 4.1. Portrait of Jovita González, San Antonio, 1931. Courtesy of E. E. Mireles and Jovita González Mireles Papers, Special Collections and Archives, Bell Library, Texas A&M University–Corpus Christi.

4
Jovita González Mireles

Texas Folklorist, Historian, Educator

María Eugenia Cotera

In a thirteen-page memoir written near the end of her life, Jovita González recounts an incident that was to resonate throughout her career as a folklorist, historian, writer, and educator. In 1910, González's parents decided to relocate from her grandfather's ranch in the Lower Rio Grande Valley, to San Antonio in order to improve their children's educational prospects. Shortly before they made the move, González and her siblings traveled to Mier, a small town on the Mexican side of the Texas-Mexican border to pay a final visit to "Mamá Ramoncita," their great-grandmother and the family matriarch. "I have a clear picture of her lying in a four-poster bed," recounts González, "her clear-cut ivory features contrasting with her dark, sharp eyes." González recalls the meeting so vividly that she has recourse to cite her great-grandmother verbatim:

> "Come, get closer to me, children, so I can see you better," she said. "Your mother tells me you are moving to live in San Antonio. Did you know that land at one time belonged to us? But now the people living there don't like us.

They say we don't belong there and must move away. Perhaps they will tell you to go to Mexico where you belong. Don't listen to them.

Texas is ours. Texas is our home. Always remember these words: Texas is ours, Texas is our home." I have always remembered the words and I have always felt at home in Texas.[1]

Mamá Ramoncita was clearly attempting to inoculate her great-grandchildren against the distinctly anti-Mexican brand of "Americanism" that had come to dominate Mexican-Anglo relations in Texas during the early years of the twentieth century. And in the face of growing anti-Mexican racism in Texas, Jovita González, no doubt, had to remind herself continuously of the singular historical fact that in those last parting moments, Mamá Ramoncita had embedded in her great-grandchildren's consciousness. Indeed, she would encounter scores of individuals and institutions in the Southwest and beyond, who would have liked nothing better than to forget Mamá Ramoncita's claim to Texas. But González would not forget, nor would she allow her Anglo contemporaries to forget what, for her, was the *true* history of Texas.

González's long and varied career spanned perhaps the most politically complex years of Anglo-Mexican relations in Texas, and throughout, in her academic research and in her teaching, González remained committed to uncovering the vast historical legacy of *Mexicanos* in Texas. In so doing, she hoped to bring Anglos and Mexicans to greater consciousness of their shared history in North America, and to educate young Mexicanos themselves as to their rich linguistic and cultural heritage. But while González resisted Anglo-centered and anti-Mexican visions of Texas history and culture, like the other Mexican American intellectuals of her generation, she firmly believed that "better ethnic and race relations began with human understanding," and consequently stressed "what Anglos and Mexicans held in common rather than what divided them."[2] Though this pluralistic worldview would be constantly tested in the face of continued institutional racism against Mexicanos in Texas and the Southwest, González continued to insist, in both her writing and her pedagogical politics, that cross-cultural understanding was key to unraveling the knot of race relations in the U.S. Because of this perspective, the political contours of her rhetoric generally took the shape of a call to reform rather than revolution, and thus her writing has often been characterized as "assimilationist." But we should not let this label limit our understanding of González's importance to the legacy of Latina/o letters. In her

life and in her work, Jovita González challenged reductive readings of her
people and refused to accept the limitations placed upon her by individuals and institutions unwilling to imagine that a Mexican-American woman
could articulate a distinctive political voice.

Early Years

Jovita González was born near the Texas-Mexico border on January 18, 1904.[3]
González's father, a native of Mexico, came from a family of "educators and
artisans," but her mother's family had a much older provenance in Texas.
They had owned land on both sides of the border for over five generations,
and, according to González, her maternal grandparents were direct descen-
dants of the colonizers who had established the first settlements in "Nuevo
Santander" (the Rio Grande region of Texas) under the leadership of Don
José Escandón. Notwithstanding their instrumental role in the founding of
Texas, González's ancestors were forced to flee from Texas shortly after the
Treaty of Guadalupe Hidalgo was signed in 1848, ending the war between
Mexico and the United States. The family reestablished itself in Texas after
the Civil War, when González's grandfather—with financial support from his
widowed mother, Ramona Guerra Hinojosa (Mamá Ramoncita)—was able
to repurchase some of the land that was lost after 1848. On this land, located
in Starr County near Roma, Texas, he established "Las Víboras" (the snakes),
the ranch where González was born.

González's early life was filled with stories and legends from the people
that lived and worked in and around her grandfather's rancho. In her memoirs, González vividly recalls scenes and people from her childhood, many of
which reappear in her later writing.

> We went horseback riding to the pastures with my grandfather, took long
> walks with father, and visited the homes of the cowboys and the ranch hands.
> We enjoyed the last the most. There were Tío Patricio, the mystic; Chon, who
> was so ugly, poor fellow, he reminded us of a toad; Old Remigio who wielded
> the *metate* with the dexterity of peasant women and made wonderful *tortillas*.
> Tía Chita whose stories about ghosts and witches made our hair stand on end,
> Pedro, the hunter and traveler, who had been as far as Sugar Land and had
> seen black people with black wool for hair, one-eyed Manuelito, the ballad
> singer, Tío Camilo; all furnished ranch lore in our young lives.[4]

González remembers her Tía Lola with special fondness. Tía Lola was her mother's sister who came to live with them at Las Víboras as a young widow. It was the strong-willed Tía Lola who taught González and her siblings about their family's heritage in Texas, and, González implies, it was Tía Lola who ensured that their early education was rounded out with plenty of information about important women in history. As young girls, Jovita and her sister Tula memorized a poem in Spanish entitled "La Influencia de la Mujer" that charted a distinctly feminist historical heritage beginning with "Judith, the Old Testament heroine," and ending with "Doña Josefa Ortíz de Domínguez, the Mother of México's Independence." The girls also learned about Sor Juana Inés de la Cruz, and were familiar with her famous feminist poem "Hombres Necios" (Foolish Men).

Despite the nostalgic tone of her reminiscences, the years that González and her family spent at Las Víboras were not easy ones for Mexicans in south Texas. Indeed, the year of Jovita González's birth also marked a turning point in the economic and political destiny of the border communities. On July 4, 1904, the rail line from Corpus Christi to Brownsville was completed. Financed largely by Anglo ranchers and businessmen, the Saint Louis, Brownsville, and Mexico Railway finally connected Corpus Christi (and the Missouri-Pacific railroad system) to Brownsville, opening up the Valley to massive land speculation. The establishment of the railroad brought south Texas firmly into the fold of the market economy of the U.S., enabling wealthy Anglo ranchers to take part in the massive economic and social transformation that was taking place across the nation. As historian David Montejano notes, "with the railroad came farmers, and behind them came land developers, irrigation engineers, and northern produce brokers. By 1907, the three-year-old railway was hauling about five hundred carloads of farm products from the Valley."[5]

The railway was also hauling hundreds of Midwesterners into the region, latecomers to the promise of Westward expansion who were seeking to rebuild their lives in what was promoted as the "Magic Valley." These Anglo immigrants brought with them not only the hope for a new start in an unexploited territory, but also an understanding of race relations that was often at odds with the accommodative social relations that characterized the Anglo-Mexican ranching community of the late nineteenth century. Whereas the years immediately following the U.S.-Mexican War were marked by somewhat normalized relations between Anglos and Mexicans due to the relatively small Anglo population and the region's isolation from the world beyond the Nueces River, the new racial order that accompanied massive Anglo emigration into the area supplanted the accommodative race relations of the past with segregationist "Jim Crow" policies that regulated interracial contact, and created a caste-like system that separated Mexicans and Anglos in a variety of social spheres ranging from the educational system to public spaces like theaters and beaches.[6] While Anglo Mexican relations in south Texas had always been shot through with conflict regarding race and nationality, the type of "race thinking" that was at the root of the segregationist policies of the new social order represented a particularly pernicious amalgam of imported and indigenous racialist ideologies. The anti-Mexican sentiments generated by the bitter experiences of the Texas Battle for Independence in 1836 and the US-Mexico War in 1848 were now bolstered by popular eugenicist and Anglo-Saxonist theories of racial difference. Montejano notes that the distinct brand of "race thinking" that emerged in south Texas during the boom years was a pastiche of Western, southern, and Eastern racialist ideology: "Texan history and folklore, previous experience with other races, biological and medical theories, Anglo-Saxon nationalism—all furnished important themes for farm settlers in their dealings with Mexicans." Whether these racialist ideologies were "indigenous or imported in content," they contributed to a "culture of race thinking that made the segregated world a reasonable and natural order."[7]

After the entry of the railroad and the attendant agricultural "boom," it became clear to Texas Mexicans that social, political and economic relations in south Texas would never be the same. Indeed, the agrarian development of the Valley signaled the final blow to the remnants of Mexican hegemony in the region, and, according to Montejano, further "eroded the centuries-old class structure of the Mexican ranch settlements." Within fifteen years of the construction of the railway system the Texas Mexican people of the border region, with a few exceptions, were reduced to the "status of landless and dependent wage laborers."[8] In the end, the modernization process which brought south Texas into the national and international flow of goods and services led to the demise of the world that Jovita González knew, "the world of cattle hacendados and vaqueros," and eventually led to the rise of "a world of commercial farmers and migrant laborers." By the mid 1920s horses and carts had been replaced by automobiles and highways; and segregated public parks, movie houses, and drugstores took precedence over the plazas, churches, and haciendas as places to meet and exchange news.[9]

Early Education

In her memoirs, González recounts that her family moved away from the border region in 1910 so that she and her siblings might receive an "education in English," but there can be little doubt that the need for a more standardized education was precipitated by the dramatic economic and cultural changes taking place in the borderlands during this period. Despite the worsening conditions for Mexicanos in south Texas, things could not have been much better in San Antonio, where Anglos had come to dominate political and economic life some fifty years earlier. In the outline notes to her memoirs, González includes the phrase "some unpleasant incidents" in the section dealing with her early years in San Antonio. In the final draft of her memoirs no mention of these "unpleasant incidents" is made, but it is easy to imagine how difficult it must have been for a young Mexican girl from the borderlands to adjust to the new racial order of Anglo-dominated San Antonio. Nevertheless, González persevered in the face of culture shock and her lack of English proficiency. Thanks to the informal ranch-house schooling in English that she received at Las Víboras and her somewhat more thorough education in Spanish, González was able to advance to the fourth grade by the age of ten and, by attending school in the summer, finish her high school equivalency by the age of eighteen.

González's somewhat circuitous path through higher education in the early 1920s is testament to the financial and institutional barriers limiting the professional aspirations of Mexican-American women of her generation. Though the pursuit of a university education was never in question for González, she lacked financial resources of her own to support such an endeavor, and thus was under constant pressure to come up with money to finance her education. Her family's shaky financial situation only compounded these difficulties. González's educational career is pockmarked by interruptions caused either by her own lack of funds to continue her schooling, or the need to dedicate what little funds she did have to the support of her family. Upon graduation from high school, González decided that she would have to return to south Texas and work as a teacher in order to earn money for her college fund. She enrolled in a Summer Normal School, earning a teaching certificate two years later in 1920, and then took a teaching position in Rio Grande City where she lived with her aunt and uncle. This arrangement allowed her to save up enough money to enroll at the University of Texas in the fall of 1921.

After finishing her freshman year as a Spanish major, González was forced to return to her parent's home in San Antonio because of lack of funds. Again she turned to teaching to raise money, this time in Encinal, Texas, where she served as Head Teacher of a small two-teacher school. After two years of teaching, González decided to return to college, though not to the University of Texas. She enrolled in summer school at Our Lady of the Lake College in San Antonio in 1924, where she was offered a scholarship for the following year in exchange for her services as a Spanish teacher in their affiliated high school. The deal was too good to pass up: "For teaching two hours a day and a class of teachers on Saturday, I would get a private room, board, and tuition. My worries were over." Despite this ideal situation, González yearned to return to the University of Texas where she had begun studies in "advanced Spanish" under Lilia Casis a few years earlier, "once having her as a teacher I could not consider anyone else."[10] So González added yet another job to her already cramped schedule: she began tutoring fellow students at Our Lady of the Lake College in order to earn enough money to enroll for summer school at the University of Texas.

González's dedication eventually paid off. In the summer of 1925, her mentor, Lilia Casis introduced her to J. Frank Dobie, the man who had put Texas folklore studies on the map. This introduction was a turning point in Jovita González's life. "Heretofore," she writes, "the legends and stories of the border were interesting, so I thought, just to me. However, he made me see their importance and encouraged me to write them, which I did, publishing some in the *Folk-Lore Publications* and *Southwest Review*."[11] González is far too modest in this account. The story of her involvement with J. Frank Dobie and the Texas Folklore Society was certainly much more complex. Indeed, this fateful meeting had far-reaching implications for the ways in which the dialogue over Texas culture and history would be played out over the rest of the century.

Jovita González and the Texas Folklore Society

When Jovita González came to folklore studies in the late 1920s she found a congenial community of scholars who were consumed by the giddy possibilities that the modernist revolution in regionalist writing had created. These were "boom years" for Texas folklore studies; with public interest in regional traditions at an all time high, the Texas chapter of the American Folklore Society was leading the way in the movement to popularize the study of "the folk." J. Frank Dobie and his cohorts proposed the collection of the folklore of "the four peoples that have mingled their lore in the Southwest": the "Anglo-Saxon," the "Negro," the "Indian" and the "Spanish." Dobie hoped that by bringing the legends and lore of these rural folk communities to the public he might provide modern regional authors with the basis for the development of a reinvigorated and uniquely American literary form.[12]

Dobie's romantic investment in the "folk" of his region, and his antipathy to more scientific approaches to folklore studies not only reflected the general aesthetic values of his period, but also his personal background. A native son of the Anglo ranching community, Dobie was fascinated by what he figured was a "vanishing" way of life. As a young adult (Dobie was born in 1888) he witnessed the wave of agricultural development that had consumed the open ranges of his childhood and transformed formerly sleepy Texas towns into booming mercantile centers. Like González, Dobie recognized that the rugged ranch life that characterized his informal education was quickly disappearing. His experiences as a young man working on his uncle's ranch in south Texas also reinforced a deep and abiding respect for the largely dispossessed *vaqueros mexicanos* who worked the ranch. However, about Mexicans Dobie was ultimately ambivalent: on the one hand, because he had grown up on a ranch worked almost entirely by Mexicans, he idolized "vaqueros" for their "simplicity," their nearness to the land, and their unabashed masculinity; on the other hand, he was a son of the Anglo ranching elite, the very community that had (often violently) dispossessed the "freedom loving *vaquero*."[13]

Dobie's contradictory nostalgia structured the pursuit of knowledge about the Mexican folk in Texas for over thirty years. Under his direction, the Texas Folklore Society turned increasingly to the collection of the folklore of the dispossessed with special attention to the folk traditions of Mexicans in Texas. However, their renditions of folklore tended toward the ahistorical and apolitical—focusing, for example, on plant and animal lore, *curanderismo*, and legends of lost treasure—the forms of cultural poetics that, in Dobie's estimation, offered his general readership the true "flavor" of the folk. Thus, while Dobie's focus on Mexican folklore traditions during this period did promote general interest in Mexican culture, it rarely moved beyond the "appreciation" of Mexican arts, crafts, and narrative traditions. The "beauty" of Mexican culture was celebrated while the political and social valences at the heart of Mexican cultural poetics in Texas were left largely unexplored. As folklore historian James Charles McNutt observes, "beyond the purpose of collecting and presenting the materials for literary use, there was little conscious attention to the question of what folklore was supposed to mean for the people whose spirit it presumably expressed."[14]

In spite of the contradictions at the center of its formation—or perhaps because of them—the brand of romantic folklore studies that Dobie created at the University of Texas in the 1920s and 1930s did initiate "a liberating exploration of the boundaries which separated the various "folk" of the Southwest." And, even though the Texas Folklore Society generally "kept racial and ethnic conflict conveniently in the romantic past," the very process of exploring culture across ethnic and racial lines brought increasing interaction between these groups and a newfound respect for the cultural poetics of Mexican Americans in Texas. In fact, the methodological innovations that Dobie and his cohorts brought to the study of the folk in Texas and the Southwest permanently transformed the political and aesthetic landscape of regional folklore studies. More significantly, because Dobie and his liberal Anglo colleagues promoted "a limited but important encouragement of collection by non-Anglo folklorists," they ushered in a period of unprecedented dialogue between Anglo and "ethnic" public intellectuals.[15] For the first time in the tradition of knowledge production about culture and history in Texas, Mexicans were a part of the conversation, and a new generation of Mexican American scholars entered into this dialogue. People like Carlos E. Castañeda, Lilia Casis, and Jovita González played instrumental roles in the organizational structure of the Texas Folklore Society, and contributed significantly to the production of knowledge about their communities. Moreover, the flexibility that Dobie built into the research methodologies of the organization enabled a greater number of nonprofessional Mexican American folklorists (like Adina de Zavala) to collect material on the folk practices of the neighborhoods, towns, and ranches.

For Dobie, González embodied the virtues of the ideal collector of folk-lore: her fine literary abilities in combination with her "authentic" insider knowledge of the intimate customs of ranch life granted her a certain degree of ethnographic authority within the field of Texas folklore studies. On the occasion of her first contribution to the *Publications of the Texas Folklore Society* (*PTFS*), an article titled "Folklore of the Texas-Mexican Vaquero," Dobie played up González's personal history, noting somewhat hyperbolically, "Her great-grandfather was the richest land owner of the Texas border . . . Thus she has an unusual heritage of intimacy with her subject."[16] Dobie clearly believed that his readers would appreciate González's contributions more if they knew that she had actually lived among the rancheros and vaqueros of South Texas. Indeed, González's authenticity as a daughter of ranchero culture constituted the very foundation of her ethnographic authority, and she was not beyond capitalizing on this patina of authenticity to further her own position within the mostly white and largely male world of folklore studies at the University of Texas.

For Dobie, González might have represented a more "safe" and "sani-tized" version of his idealized vaquero. As an educated daughter of the ran-chero elite, she was removed from the more violent contradictions of Anglo Mexican ranching culture on at least two levels: her gender relegated her to the feminized internal world of the rancho, the world of plant-lore, legends and folk remedies; and her presumably "elite" status brought her in line with Dobie's ideological vision. But González refused to remain within the clois-tered walls of the hacienda. Her first contributions to the *PTFS* focused on the songs and legends of the masculine world of the vaqueros, and though, as José Limón has noted, she sometimes adopted the "superior, often conde-scending and stereotyping colonialist tone" of her mentor in these articles, "it is an idiom that at times appears to be repressing a certain sense of admira-tion for these classes and an acknowledgment of the state of war." Indeed, in his analysis of González's early folklore writing, José Limón uncovered "key instances of a counter-competing vision on questions of race, class, and gen-der domination."[17] But there are other indications that in spite of their friendly relationship, González did not always agree with Dobie's (and, by extension, the TFS's) version of Texas history. In a 1981 interview with James Charles McNutt, González revealed that she avoided Dobie's classes because the two shared such disparate views on Texas history: "You see, it was an agreement that we made, that I would not go into one of his classes because I would be mad at many things. He would take the Anglo-Saxon side naturally. I would take the Spanish and Mexican side." González acknowledged that many of her Mexican colleagues at the University of Texas were careful not to contest the "official history" promoted by Dobie and his cohort: "teachers couldn't afford to get involved in a controversy between Mexico and the University of Texas . . . but if the history of Texas were written the way it actually was . . . because things, some of those things that happened on both sides were very bitter. So we just didn't mention them. You just forget about it."[18]

Despite her protestations to the contrary, there was at least one instance during this period when Jovita González *did* insert her voice rather forcefully into this public dialogue. In 1929, just two years after completing her B.A. at Our Lady of the Lake, González, by now a full-time Spanish teacher at Our Lady of the Lake, was granted a Lapham Scholarship to take time off from teaching to conduct research along the border in order to pursue a Master's Degree at the University of Texas. González spent the summer of 1929 traveling through the remotest regions of Webb, Zapata, and Starr Counties and collecting notes for what would become perhaps her most vocal native-born critique of ethnographic, sociological and historical representations of Mexicans in south Texas, her master's thesis, "Social Life in Cameron, Starr and Zapata Counties" (1930).[19]

Although she is best known as an expert in Texas folklore, when Jovita González decided to pursue an advanced degree she did so in History under the begrudging guidance of Eugene C. Barker. Although we may never know the reason why she decided to pursue her master's degree in History as opposed to English (where she would have studied under her mentor, Dobie) or in Spanish (under Lilia Casis), we do know that Barker was singularly unenthusiastic about the thesis she submitted to him for approval. According to González, he was "somewhat hesitant at first to approve the thesis," but relented after the intervention of Dr. Carlos E. Castañeda, a family friend, who insisted that the thesis would be "used in years to come as source material." When he finally approved the thesis, Barker commented to González that it was "an interesting but somewhat odd piece of work."[20] Barker's reluctance to approve the thesis is not so unusual given the counter discursive tone of González's account of "social life" on the Texas Mexican border, an account that focuses on the lives of its Mexican inhabitants, resists Anglo ethnological assessments of Mexican people, and offers a highly polemical, counter hegemonic narrative of Texas history. In this respect, "Social Life in Cameron, Starr, and Zapata Counties" represents perhaps the earliest attempt (within the institutional discourse of Texas history) to intervene against colonialist representations of the Mexican community on the lower Rio Grande. Indeed, the narrative structure of González's thesis closely mirrors that of perhaps the earliest ethnohistorical representation of the Texas-Mexicans, "The American Congo" (1894), a xenophobic and terribly misinformed tract written by ethnologist John Gregory Bourke. "Social Life in Cameron, Starr, and Zapata, Counties" is quite literally dialogic, in that it addresses, point by point, John Gregory Bourke's representation of border culture, strategically rewriting his imperialist ruminations on the people and culture of the Texas Mexican border.[21]

After completing her M.A. in History, Jovita González dedicated herself to the business of promoting folklore studies in Texas, and it seems that at least in these early years of her involvement with Dobie and the Texas Folklore Society, González truly believed in the libratory possibilities presented by the new, more dialogic temper of folklore studies. Judging from her correspondence with J. Frank Dobie during these years, González and her mentor shared a great friendship and an intense professional camaraderie. From the moment that they met and for the next twenty years, Dobie "nurtured and mentored her, soliciting and editing her manuscripts, engaging her in sustained evening discussions of the subject [of Mexican folklore] in his home, underwriting bank loans for her field trips."[22] He also encouraged her increasing level of involvement in the Texas Folklore Society. With Dobie's support González assumed the vice-presidency of the group in 1928, and was elected president in 1930 and again in 1931, an astounding achievement given that at the time the Texas Folklore Society was dominated by white male Texans. She was also a regular contributor to the *Publications of the Texas Folklore Society* and offered lively presentations of her research at the annual meetings. She followed her first contribution to *Texas and Southwestern Lore PTFS VI* (1927) with "Tales and Songs of the Mexican Vaquero" in *Man, Bird and Beast, PTFS VIII* (1930) "Among my People" in *Tone the Bell Easy, PTFS X* (1932); and "The Bullet-Swallower" in *Puro Mexicano PTFS XII* (1935). By the late 1930s, under Dobie's mentorship, and through her own considerable determination, González was considered a national expert on the Mexican

Americans of the southwest, and was "one of the first native scholars of Mexican-American cultures and very probably the first woman."[23]

In 1934, with the help of letters of recommendation from Paul S. Taylor and Dobie, and her own growing national notoriety in the field of folklore studies, González was awarded a Rockefeller grant to complete a book-length manuscript on the folklore and culture of South Texas Mexicans at the turn of the century. The manuscript which she entitled *Dew on the Thorn* remained unpublished during González's lifetime, but has recently been recovered by José Limón, and is now in print.[24] *Dew on The Thorn* opens in 1904, the year of González's birth, and documents the changing lives of rancheros, vaqueros, and *peones* during a three-year period. That González chose to document the years between 1904 and 1907 in her folkloric treatment of Mexicano communities is significant for a number of reasons. First, the period correlates with her own childhood in south Texas, and thus offers an almost autobiographical narrative of a world she knew well. The primary figures of her childhood, the pastor Tío Patricio, the nursemaid Nana Chita, her father (as represented by the schoolmaster Don Alberto), and of course, Mamá Ramoncíta, the great-grandmother who cautioned her great-grandchildren to "never forget that Texas is our home," all appear as central figures in the text. The period is also significant in that it marks the beginning of the final decline of Mexicano political and economic dominance in south Texas. González documented this process in her master's thesis and locates its origins (as does David Montejano) in the completion of the Saint Louis, Brownsville, and Mexico Railway on July 4, 1904. Through accounts of folkloric stories and personal narratives, the protagonists of *Dew on the Thorn* chronicle the period in which Anglo Americans asserted economic and political authority over the region through the penetration of national markets and the settlement of Anglo citizens from the national core.

As José Limón has suggested, *Dew on the Thorn* should not simply be read as a literary rendition of the folkloric practices of the Mexican people on the border, but as an immanently *political* text, in which the primary objective is to use folklore and history as a tool to influence the discourse on race relations between Anglos and Mexicans. In her grant application to the Rockefeller foundation González indicated that she hoped her research would help Anglo-Mexican race relations by clarifying dominant misconceptions about "Latin-Americans" among the Anglo community. She also hoped that the manuscript would build pride within the Mexican-American community regarding its long history and important cultural heritage in Texas. Through the literary use of folklore, González hoped to appeal to two political constituencies at once, and thus to shape cultural politics both externally and internally. Moreover, insofar as it is deployed as a response to both the historical contradictions of the borderlands in general and the internal contradictions of patriarchal Mexicano culture in particular, the literary use of folklore in *Dew on the Thorn*, moves beyond its 'local color' manifestation in much of Texas folklore studies and becomes a critique of the expansion of American imperial power in the region as well as a device through which González explores the divisions of race, gender, and class within the border Mexican community itself.[25]

These early writings demonstrate that though the contours of her argument with the mostly Anglo, largely male voice of Texas folklore studies shifted along with the changes in the discipline and the strengthening of her consciousness as a gendered subject under colonialism, it remained, from the start, and to the end, an argument against those scientific and popular discourses which had sought to describe, contain, and dispossess her people. While "Social Life in Cameron, Starr, and Zapata Counties," offered a direct historiographical and sociological response to Victorian ethnological representations of the Mexican communities in the borderlands, *Dew on the Thorn*, offered a much more literary and impressionistic (one might even say pastoral) representation of the social life and people of the border. In both cases, González virtually rewrites the master narratives of the discipline, offering a native-born response to the changing colonialist imperatives of Texas folklore studies.

Back to the Borderlands

By the late 1930s Jovita González began to distance herself more and more from her friends at the Texas Folklore Society. Her correspondence with Dobie dropped off precipitously after 1938, and her presentations at Texas Folklore Society meetings and scholarly contributions to the *Publications of the Texas Folklore Society* all but ended by 1940. This may be due to the fact that in 1935, at the rather advanced age of 31 (for the standards of the time) Jovita González finally decided to marry. She met her husband, Edmundo

Mireles, when they were both students at the University of Texas, most likely through their mutual friend, Carlos E. Castañeda. Edmundo Mireles was a true citizen of the borderlands, his mother was a sister of the Mexican revolutionary leader, Venustiano Carranza, and while still an adolescent, Mireles had served with Carranza's revolutionary forces. Shortly before their marriage in 1935, Edmundo had been appointed as the principal of a high school in the newly established San Felipe Independent School District in Del Rio, Texas, and was spending his evenings training recently arrived Mexican immigrants in American citizenship and English at a night school he established on the border. Mireles's educational activism would unavoidably shape Jovita González's politics and her career choices after their marriage. Quite apart from Edmundo Mireles's influence though, it appears that González's sanguine view of the Texas Folklore Society and their "revolution" in folklore could not withstand the realities of Anglo-Mexican relations in Texas. By 1937, though her relations with Dobie and others were still cordial, González issued a very public critique of the Texas Folklore Society's cultural politics in "Latin Americans", her contribution to a collection entitled *Our Racial and Ethnic Minorities*. In this essay, González pointedly noted that while Anglos were willing to celebrate the cultural contributions of "Latin-Americans," they persisted in denying them equal rights:

> When one sees the great sums of money spent to reconstruct the Spanish missions and other building of the Latin-American occupation in our country, one cannot help but wonder at the inconsistency of things in general. *If Anglo-Americans accept their art and culture, why have they not also accepted the people?* Why have not the Latin Americans been given the same opportunities that have been given other racial entities in the United States?[26]

This transformation in González's feeling regarding the power of cultural appreciation to change racist sensibilities should be understood not simply as a result of her increasing involvement in the battle for educational equity for Mexicanos that her husband championed, but also her own maturing understanding of the limits and possibilities of folklore studies itself. While Texas folklore studies offered Anglos an opportunity to "appreciate" certain contributions that Mexicans had made to Texas history and culture, it did little to address the wretched circumstances in which many Mexicanos found themselves during the Depression. During this period, González struggled to find new ways of addressing the inequities of American culture through writing. She rightly sensed that the mere celebration of Mexicano folklore was a one-sided affair that ultimately relegated Mexicanos to a fixed, primitive, and highly romanticized past, and she searched for some other way in which writing could intervene in the system of racialized thinking that had come to dominate contemporary social realities in Texas.

An unpublished short story that González wrote in 1935 on the eve of her marriage to Edmundo Mireles offers us evidence of the tentative creative steps that her thinking began to take toward an ideology of pluralism that was not merely a celebration of multiculturalism or cultural "difference" but constituted a model for race relations based on mutual respect, reciprocity, and understanding. In "Shades of the Tenth Muse" González narrates the interchange between two ghostly women who have a dialogue in her study while she dozes. These women, two eminent poets and theologians of the Americas, Sor Juana Inés de la Cruz and Ann Bradstreet (both of whom came to be known as the "Tenth Muse of the Americas") disagree on many points, but in the end, they are able to bridge the cultural gap that divides them by sharing their experiences and, more importantly, their poetry. The aesthetic interchange outlined in "Shades of the Tenth Muse" seems to suggest a collaborative model of cultural pluralism based on mutual understanding and respect as opposed to one-sided "appreciation." This understanding of race relations came to dominate González's thinking in later years, structuring her approach to writing, educational activism, and her political outlook.

After her marriage, Jovita González moved to Del Rio, Texas where she headed the English Department at San Felipe High School and worked intermittently on various writing projects. She and husband had a tremendous impact on the small community of Del Rio where they "helped bring about a renaissance of language and culture and established a Latin Club which put on *zarzuelas*, or operettas, as a reinforcement of high culture as well as part of the formal education of young people."[27] During this period (1938–39) González explored the possibility of applying to Ph.D. programs at Stanford, California-Berkeley, or the University of New Mexico, and even solicited letters of recommendation from Dobie and Paul S. Taylor, "but following what were likely complicated marital negotiations," she eventually decided to move to Corpus Christi, Texas with her husband.[28] Though it is unfortunate that González did not pursue a Ph.D., these years were certainly not wasted, because sometime between 1936 and 1938 Jovita González embarked upon a project that would eventually lead to her most important work of fiction and her reemergence in the 1990s as an icon of Latina writing.

In 1936 González put together a special display of photographs, short biographical narratives, and material culture for the Texas Centennial celebration in Dallas. The historical display, entitled "Catholic Heroines of Texas" focused on the role of Mexicanas in the founding of Texas. It was perhaps her research on this subject, as well as the triumphalist mood of Anglos during the centennial year, that inspired González to begin working on *Caballero*, a historical novel that traced the lives of a group of ranchero families living on the border during the U.S.-Mexico War. González chose to write this novel in collaboration with a close friend of hers, Margaret Eimer. Not much is known about Eimer except that she was married to C. L. "Pop" Eimer, the owner of a Del Rio gun shop, and that she most likely met González through a group of Del Rio teachers that met for social occasions.[29] While many critics underplay Eimer's involvement in the drafting of *Caballero*, assigning her the role of editor rather than coauthor, her collaboration with González is actually instrumental to understanding both the aesthetics of the novel and its underlying politics. Indeed, *Caballero* is much more than a historical novel, it is a political project that embodies the very ideology it seeks to narrativize. Through both its form and content González and Eimer used *Caballero* to explore the politics of collaboration, to lift from it the stigma of betrayal, and to demonstrate how collaboration (or in contemporary feminist terms, coalition) might offer mortal combatants a way out of the resistance/assimilation binary. To this end, the novel traces a number of different kinds of collaborations: from the romantic love that binds its hero and heroine, Captain Warrener, the dashing southern gentleman who falls in love with a daughter of the rancho, Susanita; to the rather more pragmatic negotiations between Susanita's sister, Angela, who wants to do good works for her community and her Anglo suitor, "Red" McLane, who will provide her the money to do so in exchange for her agreement to marry him so that he can gain prestige among the conquered rancheros; to the artistic collaboration between the young ranchero Luis Gonzaga and an older army doctor, Captain Devlin, an artist himself, who recognizes Luis's talent and wishes to help him develop it. All of these peaceful collaborations, and the many others that populate the novel, are juxtaposed against the rigid ideologies of those Anglos and

Mexicans who refuse to see the world in any other way than black and white, and whose resistance to the politics of collaboration leads to death and bloodshed on both sides of the border.[30]

Scholars have noticed a proto-feminist critique in all of this, and this critique is given voice in two of the most vividly drawn characters in the novel, Don Santiago, the patriarch of the rancho and his widowed sister, Doña Dolores. These characters spend the better part of 350 pages sparring over both gender politics and territorial politics. In their extended debate we may witness not only a critique of the patriarchal standards that governed Mexican life in the nineteenth century, but also a critique of male-centered resistance strategies in general, a critique that applies to González's own period, and even to the nationalist movements that arose in the post–Civil Rights era. Because of the undeniable feminist undertones expressed in its powerful critique of the patriarchal social order, many feminist critics feel that *Caballero* represents an early example of what Chicana scholar Sonia Saldívar-Hull has termed "feminism on the border."[31]

González and Eimer worked on *Caballero* through the 1940s and 1950s writing, editing and re-writing, the manuscript, sharing it with enthusiastic friends, and submitting it to less-than enthusiastic publishers, to no avail. After the Mireles's move to Corpus Christi in 1939, and Eimer's move to Joplin, Missouri sometime in the early 1940s, the co-authors began to correspond with less frequency until finally, in the late 1960s their correspondence seems to have ended. Though *Caballero* remained unpublished during González's lifetime, it was uncovered by a recovery project in the early 1990s, and has significantly shifted our understanding of this foundational Mexican-American scholar.

In her memoirs Jovita González spends less than three paragraphs on her life after the move to Corpus Christi in 1939. Given this cursory treatment, one might get the impression that her life after Del Rio was somewhat uneventful, but nothing could be further from the truth. Though she published less frequently and made fewer public appearances, Jovita González and her husband Edmundo Mireles played an enormously important role in establishing Spanish education programs in Texas and the Southwest. And though they met with much resistance at first—as González notes "this was a period when the walls of racial prejudice still had to be torn down"—they ultimately succeeded in establishing one of the first elementary-level Spanish programs in the country.[32] In fact Edmundo Mireles is considered by many to be the father of bilingual education because of the role that he and Jovita played as advocates for Spanish education in the public school system of Corpus Christi. González and her husband also collaborated with educator Roy E. Fisher on a series of Spanish textbooks entitled *Mi Libro Español* (1941) and *El Español Elemental* (1949) designed for teaching Spanish at the grade school level.

González spent a total of twenty-one years as a Spanish teacher at W.B. Ray High School and Miller High in Corpus Christi, where her students remember her as a vibrant and compelling educator and role model. During this period González dedicated her summers to training teachers in the Mireles method for teaching Spanish and to traveling in Mexico with her husband. For González and Mireles, Spanish instruction meant something more than just developing language proficiency. Their unique instructional method combined González's encyclopedic knowledge of Mexican and Spanish culture, history, and folklore and Mireles's considerable linguistic skills in a potent mix that taught young children the fundamentals of communicating in Spanish as well as an understanding and appreciation of Mexicano culture. This pedagogical approach was mirrored in the social activity that took up the greater portion of their free time, the establishment and promotion of a quasi-political social club called the Pan American Council whose principal aims included the study of "Spanish, Latin America, its people, history, geography, population, customs, habits and way of life," the fostering of "good relations between Anglo Americans and Latin Americans" and the encouragement of Latin-American professionals to "contribute to the welfare of their community."[33] The Pan American Council also aimed to establish junior Pan American Clubs and Pan American Parent-Teacher organizations in area schools. During this time, González also dedicated herself to the promotion and continuation of Mexicano cultural traditions, directing *pastorelas*, pageants and Christmas *posadas* with Mexican children from the Corpus Christi community until she retired from teaching in 1967.

Jovita González spent the last years of her life trying unsuccessfully to write her autobiography. Plagued by diabetes and chronic depression, she was never able to finish the project, completing only a scant thirteen-page document before her death in 1983. What we can know about this early Latina intellectual must be gleaned from her published folklore studies and the pages of her recently uncovered manuscripts, *Caballero* and *Dew on the Thorn*. This body of work demonstrates that González was one of the first Mexican-American scholars to carefully think through the philosophical and political contours of Borderlands Studies. Moreover, like the generation of Latina scholars that emerged in the 1980s, Jovita González moved beyond the rigid binaries governing traditional thinking in this area to elaborate a concept of the borderlands as a transnational "contact zone" wherein different cultures, languages, histories, and genders collide and recombine into new forms of politics and poetics.

Notes

1. Jovita González, "Jovita González: Early Life and Education," *Dew on the Thorn*, ed. José Limón (Houston: Arte Público P, 1997), xi.

2. Mario T. García, *Mexican Americans: Leadership, Ideology, and Identity* (New Haven, CT: Yale University Press, 1989), 240–41.

3. Citing Texas Folklore Society records, Leticia Garza-Falcón lists González's birthdate as 1899. However, University of Texas student records list González's date of birth as 1904, indicating that González herself provided 1904 as her birthdate in her university application. Though certain chronological inconsistencies in González' memoirs (in which she rarely gives exact dates) support Garza-Falcón's assertion, others do not, so it is impossible to say with any degree of certainty whether 1904 or the 1899 is the correct birth date. Leticia M. Garza-Falcón, *Gente Decente, A Borderlands Response to the Rhetoric of Dominance* (Austin: University of Texas Press, 1998).

4. González, "Jovita González: Early Life and Education," x.

5. David Montejano, *Anglos and Mexicans in the Making of Texas, 1836–1986* (Austin: University of Texas Press, 1987), 107.

6. Jovita González, "Social Life, in Cameron, Starr and Zapata Counties" (MA thesis, University of Texas, 1930)," 108.

7. Montejano, *Anglos and Mexicans*, 161.

8. Ibid., 114.

9. Ibid., 161.

10. González, "Early Life and Education," xii.

11. Ibid.

12. Roger Abrahams and Richard Bauman, "Doing Folklore Texas Style," in *"And Other Neighborly Names:" Social Process and Cultural Image in Texas Folklore*, ed. Richard Bauman and Roger D. Abrahams (Austin: University of Texas Press, 1981), 4–5.

13. James Charles McNutt, "Beyond Regionalism: Texas Folklorists and the Emergence of a Post-Regional Consciousness" (PhD diss., University of Texas, 1982).

14. McNutt, "Beyond Regionalism," 235.

15. Ibid., 226.

16. *Texas and Southwestern Lore*, in Publications of the Texas Folklore Society VI, ed. J. Frank Dobie (Austin: Texas Folklore Society, 1927), 241.

17. José E. Limón, *Dancing with the Devil: Society and Cultural Poetics in Mexican-American South Texas* (Madison: University of Wisconsin Press, 1994), 62.

18. McNutt, "Beyond Regionalism," 350–51.

19. For a full analysis of Jovita González's Master's Thesis see: María Cotera, "A Woman of the Border," in Jovita González, *Life Along the Border, a Landmark Tejana Thesis*, ed. María Cotera (Corpus Christi: Texas A&M Press, 2006).

20. González, "Early Life and Education," xiii.

21. María Cotera, "Refiguring the 'American Congo': Jovita González, John Gregory Bourke and the Battle Over Ethnohistorical Representations of the Borderlands," *Recovering a Mexican-American West*, special issue of *Western American Literature* 35, no. 1 (Spring 2000): 75–94.

22. Limón, *Dancing With the Devil*, 61.

23. Ibid.

24. Jovita González, *Dew on the Thorn*, ed. José Limón (Houston: Arte Público Press).

25. José Limón, "Folklore, Literature and Politics," unpublished essay, 4.

26. Jovita González, "Latin American's," *Our Racial and Ethnic Minorities: Their History, Contributions, and Present Problems*, ed. Francis J. Brown and Joseph S. Roucek (New York: Prentice Hall, 1937), 509 (emphasis added).

27. Garza Falcón, *Gente Decente*, 78.

28. José Limón, "Introduction," *Dew on the Thorn*, xxiv.

29. In an earlier version of this essay, I speculated that "Pop" Eimer was Margaret's father. Since that time, new information has emerged about Margaret Eimer that clarifies her relationship to "Pop" Eimer, who was her husband.

30. I offer an extended analysis of the politics of collaboration in *"Caballero"* in my book, *Native Speakers*. See María Cotera, "Feminism on the Border: *Caballero* and the Politics and Poetics of Collaboration," in *Native Speakers: Ella Cara Deloria, Zora Neale Hurston, Jovita González and the Poetics of Culture* (Austin: University of Texas Press, 2008), 199–224.

31. Sonia Saldívar-Hull, *Feminism on the Border: Chicana Gender Politics and Literature* (Berkeley: University of California Press, 2000).

32. González, "Early Life and Education," xiii.

33. Garza Falcón, *Gente Decente*, 97–98.

Figure 5.1. CIO labor leader and civil right advocate Luisa Moreno as a young woman. Courtesy of Vicki L. Ruiz.

5

Of Poetics and Politics

The Border Journeys of Luisa Moreno

Vicki L. Ruiz

Over a quarter century ago, between my first and second year of graduate school, I spent part of the summer in Guadalajara, Mexico, interviewing Latina labor and political activist Luisa Moreno.[1] Early one morning, we boarded a bus that took us to a poor, fairly isolated *colonia* outside the city. After walking a few blocks, we entered a plaza of sorts. We had come on market day, and women, dressed in traditional indigenous garb, were busy selling their wares—richly colored chiles, mangoes, other fruits, vegetables, and live poultry. As I followed Luisa as she made her purchases, I became entranced with the idea that I had gone back in time decades, perhaps centuries, into the world of an Indian market. Of course, we had not made it halfway through the vendors when my ears picked up chords of a familiar melody. No, it was not a traditional folksong—it was not even Mexican pop. Fleetwood Mac's "Dreams" was blaring from a boom box a few yards away amidst the chiles and the mangoes. My illusion shattered, I then began to muse (actually, "pontificate" is a better word) about the tentacles of US consumer culture and its impact on the peoples of the Americas. Today I

DOI: 10.5876/9781607323372.c005

would have behaved differently. Instead of mouthing on and on about cultural hegemony, I would have approached the vendor with the boom box and attempted a conversation regarding what she liked about US popular music, where she had purchased stereo, and if she, or any relatives, had lived in the States (*al otro lado*). Certainly, I would exhibit a greater appreciation for the transhistoric, transnational marketplace I was privileged to encounter. Moreno teased me mercilessly on the way back to the city, laughing at my naïve polemics. What I have read of struggles for justice, she had lived. To her considerable credit and generosity, she continued to share her stories with me. Indeed, on the last day of my stay, I blurted out, "I know what I'm going to do for my dissertation. I'm going to write about you." She shook her head and said, "No, no. You are going to write your dissertation on the cannery workers in southern California. You find these women." I did and that's how my life work in history began.

Touching my scholarship at every turn, Luisa Moreno was an invaluable mentor for me, a woman of uncompromising principles, integrity, and honesty. Crafting her biography represents both a professional and personal challenge given the fragmentary nature of available archival evidence and my friendship with Moreno and later with her daughter. How does one narrate the life of another with any sort of speculative certainty? What degrees of revelation are necessary for the historical record? Where are the boundaries of discretion? I am reminded of the words of writer Tobias Wolff. "Memory is a storyteller and, like storytellers, it imposes form on the raw mass of experience. It creates shapes and meaning by emphasizing some things and leaving others out."[2] Mixing narrative and narrativity, I rely on the collective and individual memories of Moreno, her daughter, her close friends, and myself in chronicling and interpreting a life well-lived.

Luisa Moreno was one of the most prominent women labor leaders in the United States, comparable in stature to Mother Jones, Elizabeth Gurley Flynn, and more recently, Dolores Huerta. From the maw of the Great Depression to the chill of the cold war, Moreno journeyed across the United States mobilizing seamstresses in Spanish Harlem, cigar rollers in Florida, beet workers in Colorado, and cannery women in California. The first Latina to hold a national union office, she served as vice president of the United Cannery, Agricultural, Packing, and Allied Workers of America (UCAPAWA), in its heyday the seventh largest affiliate of the Congress of

Industrial Organizations (CIO). Moreno also served as the principal organizer of El Congreso de Pueblos de Habla Española (the Spanish-speaking
Peoples Congress), the first national US Latino civil rights conference, held
in Los Angeles in 1939. Her legacy, however, remains generally unknown
outside of Latino studies. And even within this interdisciplinary field, scholars (myself included) have tended to mention her only within her US trade
union and civil rights work, paying scant attention to her background and
activism outside the United States.[3] Relying extensively on oral interviews
and Moreno's own writings, this chapter moves beyond the iconography
of the labor heroine to interweave her poetry with her politics to render a
more complicated understanding of this remarkable transnational organizer
and intellectual, a courageous, totally human individual who made history.
Indeed, while exceptional in many ways, Luisa Moreno embodied a quintessential transnational subject, given her movement across discordant spaces,
physical and intellectual, where she invented and reinvented herself.

Born Blanca Rosa Rodríguez López on August 30, 1907, Luisa Moreno had
an improbable upbringing for a fiery labor leader. The daughter of Ernesto
Rodríguez Robles, a powerful coffee grower, and his socialite wife, Alicia
López Sarana, Rosa grew up in a sheltered world of wealth and privilege in
her native Guatemala. As an example of her family's opulent lifestyle, at the
wedding reception for one of her siblings, the large fountain on the estate
flowed with French champagne, Veuve Cliquot, to be exact. Rosa Rodríguez
received a boarding school education at the Convent of the Holy Names in
Oakland, California. Dashing her father's hopes that she would enter religious life, she returned home at the age of thirteen. Fluent in Spanish, English,
and French, Rosa attempted to pursue her studies beyond private tutors, but
soon discovered that the doors to a university education in Guatemala were
closed to women. Refusing to be dissuaded and taking matters into her own
hands, she organized other heeled, ambitious young women into Sociedad
Gabriela Mistral in order to push for women's rights, especially in the area
of education reform. These adolescents gathered signatures on petitions and
engaged in political lobbying, using their class status to affect concrete (and
radical) institutional change. Members of Sociedad Gabriela Mistral also
published a literary magazine and, as part of an evolving mission, they began
to include like-minded men into their ranks. One Guatemalan history book,
La Patria de Criollo, paid them tribute as "una generación que hizo historia"

(a generation that made history). During the early 1920s as US suffragists rejoiced in the passage of the Nineteenth Amendment that extended the franchise to women, Rosa Rodríguez and her compatriots celebrated their own feminist victory with Rodríguez herself admitted to the first entering class of university women. Yet, she never enrolled. Deciding to pursue her love of poetry and the arts in a more experiential fashion, she fled to Mexico City to join a burgeoning cultural renaissance taking place around the capital in the aftermath of the Mexican Revolution.[4]

Rejecting her family's wealth and no doubt the constrained gendered expectations it entailed, Rosa Rodríguez by the age of nineteen earned her livelihood as a newspaperwoman in Mexico City. She also belonged to the bohemian cultural avant-garde traveling in the same circles as Diego Rivera and Frida Kahlo. A Latina flapper, Rosa pursued her gifts as a poet and in 1927 published *El Vendedor de Cocuyos* (Vendor of the Fireflies). Barely twenty when her book appeared in print, Rosa Rodríguez conveyed in her poetry youthful abandon, passion, and desire without artifice or pretense. Her poems have an elemental quality with trees and flowers as recurring metaphors. Reflecting her youth, the verses were often introspective, expressing personal emotion and self-awareness. One Guatemalan admirer considered her a bright light in women's literature both in her home country and throughout Latin America, even comparing her favorably with the legendary Gabriela Mistral. Like most writers, Rosa treasured her good reviews; throughout her many travels, she kept a small bundle of news clippings and correspondence. On the occasion of her twenty-second birthday, one newspaper article made reference to her beauty, poetry, and vanguard feminism.[5]

One of her poems, "Literatura," provides a sense of her dedication to craft as it captures the struggle of every obsessed wordsmith staring at a blank page (or in our day a computer screen). An excerpt follows in English translation:

> Literature, literature . . .
> I have succumbed to your madness and at your altar
> I have sought the expression
> of a love,
> a dream
> and a religion . . .
>
> . . .

And still in my head
There is a hunger for madness
And all my road is
Shadowed by ghosts
Of not being able to say!
not being able to say!
Literature, literature . . .
Bitter and sweet,
Shadow and light . . .
O great flowering mystery!
In your madness
I have sought the expression
of a love,
a dream
and a religion.[6]

In November 1927, Rosa Rodríguez married Miguel Ángel de León, a Guatemalan artist sixteen years her senior. From a prominent family, de León, as a young man, had also escaped their effete social world, but instead of running away to Mexico, he had joined the French Foreign Legion. When he met the young poet, he was well ensconced in the arts scene of Mexico City. Theirs would be a tumultuous marriage, and if her poems provide an indication, their courtship was marked by passion and pain. In "El milagro" (The Miracle), Rosa wrote, "And I have lived, / I have dreamed / held in the fire of your arms."[7] However, in "Tu amor," she revealed:

I know
that you are a tear in my life
That your hands will strip off my petals
and break my stem . . .[8]

Soon after their marriage, the couple became expectant parents and suddenly and daringly decided to set sail, literally, on a new adventure far from their Mexican cultural refuge. They boarded the SS *Monterrey* and landed in New York harbor on August 28, 1928. In November, Rosa Rodríguez de León gave birth to her "Latin from Manhattan," a daughter, Mytyl Lorraine.[9]

Though fluent in three languages, including English, they found New York a difficult place to earn a living, especially with the onset of the Great

Depression. Within months of Mytyl's birth, Rosa would find herself bending over a sewing machine in the garment sweatshops of Spanish Harlem. It is within this context that her political awakening occurred. The tragic death of a friend's infant (a rat had gnawed on the baby's face) spurred her to action. She joined Centro Obrero de Habla Española, a leftist community group in Spanish Harlem, and in 1930 the Communist Party, USA.

She also organized her *companeras* into La Liga de Costureras, a small-scale garment workers' union. Reflecting on her days as a "junior organizer," she proudly related how at a time when only a few men's unions had "ladies auxiliaries," she had created a fraternal fund-raising group composed of male relatives and friends of Liga members. But making the union a family affair did not apply to her own. An absentee mother by circumstance and choice, Rosa Rodríguez de León also found in her radicalism and escape from a disintegrating marriage. In the midst of leftist political meetings, she struck up a friendship with Gray Bemis, a handsome young labor activist who had ventured far from his Nebraska farm boy roots. Drawn to him romantically, she refused to act on her emotions. "I liked him but he was married and I was married. Although I was in a miserable marriage, I did not fool around with married men."[10]

In late 1935 Rosa Rodríguez de León made a momentous decision, actually several—she left her husband, New York City, and the Communist Party. She accepted a job with the American Federation of Labor (AFL) to organize African American and Latino cigar workers in Florida. Arriving by bus with her daughter, Mytyl, she chose yet another transformation—she became "Luisa Moreno."

Deliberately distancing herself from her past, she chose the alias "Moreno" (Dark), a name diametrically opposite her given name, "Blanca Rosa" (White Rose). I contend that Luisa Moreno conjugated her identity. "Conjugating identity" refers to an invention or inflection of one's sense of self, taking into account such constructions as race, class, culture, language, and gender. It represents a self-reflective, purposeful fluidity of individual subjectivities for political action. Simply put, Moreno made strategic choices regarding her class and ethnic identification in order to facilitate her life's work as a labor and civil rights advocate. With her light skin, education, and unaccented English, she could have passed; instead, she chose to forego any potential privileges predicated on race, class, or color. Importantly, she made these changes in the Jim Crow South, where segregation and white domination was a way life. Moreover, the first name "Luisa" could be interpreted as a political statement, perhaps homage to Puerto Rican labor organizer and feminist writer Luisa Capetillo, who had preceded her in Florida twenty years earlier and whose legacy Moreno undoubtedly knew and built upon in organizing cigar workers.[11] Luisa Moreno was the professional persona. Her close friends called her Rosa, and as a graduate student conducting research, I quickly realized myself as a friend of Rosa's (not Luisa's) created an almost instant rapport with her compañeros in the labor movement. "Rosa" signified a level of intimacy and trust.

In Florida Moreno quickly grasped the challenges ahead. During her days as a labor organizer, Moreno penned two surviving poems in English.[12] With subtle tones, her poem "On the Road" revealed an awareness of African American life in the US South:

> Unpainted gray boards
> Formed the church
> By the poor Negro shacks.
> Voices sang in the evenings
> Hammock songs to the air.
> Hopeful words—hunger sounds:
> Sorrow, love, and despair.
> And near by bled the trees
> In the forest of pines.
> Negro peons raised their arms,
> Powerful arms to the skies,
> While the preacher's soft voice
> Told the tale of a white man
> Full of patience and love.
> And they dreamt of a new world
> In the turpentine country,
> As near by bled the trees
> In the forest of pines.[13]

With sympathy and irony, the images echo each other. African American turpentine workers bleed the trees while the white bosses bleed them.

On an immediate level, Moreno was cognizant of the role of the local Ku Klux Klan in suppressing labor militancy, including its involvement in the murder of Florida political activist and friend of labor Joseph Shoemaker in November 1935, just weeks before Moreno's arrival in early 1936. According to Moreno, her superiors believed that the Klan would think twice before harming a woman organizer. I would further note that fair complexion, as well as her gender, afforded her added protection. Slender and under five feet tall, Moreno possessed a delicate beauty, but her physical appearance belied her brilliance and steely determination.

Given her fears about the Klan as well as the challenges and erratic schedules inherent in trade union work, Moreno decided to board her daughter with a pro-labor Latino family. From age seven until almost thirteen, Mytyl would live apart from her mother as she was shuttled from one informal foster family to the next from Florida to Pennsylvania to Texas. In some households, she received kind treatment, maybe even love, but in others she was molested—in Florida by the head of her very first foster family and later in Texas by an elderly neighbor. Decades later, Mytyl related these incidents with a rawness that had not abated with time. Moreno visited infrequently and to my knowledge remained ignorant of the abuse her daughter suffered. Mytyl Moreno carried a sense of profound loneliness throughout her life, always seeking a deeper spiritual connection with others initially through religion and later through political activism. Contemplating a childhood where she lived apart from her mother and lost all contact with her father, Mytyl recalled "having the feeling of being alone."[14]

Although she lived in Florida for less than two years, this is where Luisa Moreno honed her skills as a labor leader. Organizing "all races, creeds, and colors," she negotiated a solid contract covering thirteen thousand cigar workers from Ybor City to Lakeland to Jacksonville in 1936. When AFL officials revised the agreement to be friendlier to management, an infuriated Moreno urged the workers to reject it. As punishment for her insubordination, the AFL transferred her to Pennsylvania. In 1937 she resigned from the AFL to join its newly established rival, the Congress of Industrial Organizations (CIO), and a year later she joined the United Cannery, Agricultural, Packing, and Allied Workers of America (UCAPAWA-CIO). The union's commitment to rank-and-file leadership and to inclusion, recruiting members across race, nationality, and gender, resonated with Moreno. Indeed, as part of the UCAPAWA pledge, members swore "never to discriminate against a fellow worker because of creed, color, nationality, religious or political belief."[15]

Moreno's first assignment as a UCAPAWA representative in 1938 was to take charge of the pecan shellers' strike in San Antonio, Texas. The shellers earned miserable wages—less than two dollars a week in 1934—and in 1938 they had reached their limit, for as many as ten thousand workers went on strike. Their union, El Nogal, was an UCAPAWA affiliate, and their leader was the fiery secretary of the Texas Communist Party, a young native of San Antonio by the name of Emma Tenayuca. UCAPAWA's national president, Donald Henderson, sent Moreno to help solidify the local, to move it from street demonstrations to a functioning trade union. As an outsider from the East Coast and a Latina (not a Tejana or Mexicana), Moreno at first had to gain the strikers' trust; but rather quickly she organized them into a united, disciplined force that employers could no longer ignore. Five weeks after the strike began, management agreed to arbitration with a settlement that included recognition of the UCAPAWA local and piece rate scales that conformed to the new federal minimum wage of twenty-five cents an hour. Tenayuca had stepped aside to give Moreno a wide berth, but she had done so very reluctantly and, as a result, the working relationship between these two legendary figures in Latino history was strained at best.[16]

After settlement, Moreno next traveled to the Rio Grande Valley of Texas. While organizing Mexicana migrants in dire straits, she too had few resources. She lived with farmworkers, slept under trees, and shared her groceries with those around her. Moreno encountered what she termed a "lynch spirit" among rural white residents. Lynching affected both African Americans and Mexicans in Texas. According to historians William Carrigan and Clive Webb, 597 Mexicans died at the hands of vigilante mobs from 1850 to 1930, almost half of these murders (297) occurred in Texas. While 597 represented a mere fraction of the 3,386 recorded lynchings of African Americans for the same time period, this specter of mob violence was embedded in the lexicon of Tejano collective memory. Perhaps drawing on border folklore, *corridos* (ballads), and stories told in the migrant camps and influenced by the haunting lyrics of Billie Holiday's "Strange Fruit," Moreno made a stark reference to lynching with the line "a brown and gruesome form" in her unpublished poem "1939."[17]

> His soul—a winter scene,
> Where thoughts
> Were leafless boughs reflecting on the stream
> A brown and gruesome form.

The earth was cold and quiet
The sky a plate of steel.
I waited for a word
A single word,
But nothing came
The fallen leaves went rolling by . . .
No more was there to say.
I gambled every claim
On a foolish dream.[18]

Composed during or immediately after her sojourn in South Texas, this poem raises several questions. Was this poem primarily about a deep disappointment or self-doubt? Was Moreno lamenting a lost romance, possibly with Gray Bemis? Or was the imagery of unrequited love simply a guarded metaphor for a feeling of abandonment by the national union or by the principles of the Communist Party?

When UCPAWA pulled her out of South Texas after only a few months in 1938, she took a leave of absence in order to organize a Latino civil rights conference. Traveling with Mytyl, she ended up in Los Angeles working with a small group of like-minded community and labor activists—Josefina Fierro, Eduardo Quevedo, and Bert Corona. These four would form the leadership for the national convention.

On April 28 through 30, 1939, the first national civil rights conference for US. Latinos was convened—El Congreso de Pueblos de Habla Española. Although the majority of the one thousand to fifteen hundred delegates hailed from California and the Southwest, women and men traveled from as far away as Montana, Illinois, New York, and Florida to attend the convention. Over three days, they drafted a comprehensive platform. Bridging differences in generational and ethnic backgrounds, they called for an end to segregation in public facilities, housing, education, and employment and endorsed the rights of immigrants to live and work in the United States without fear of deportation. While encouraging immigrants to become citizens, delegates did not advocate assimilation but rather emphasized the importance of preserving Latino cultures, calling upon universities to create departments in Latino studies. Despite the promise of the first convention, a national network of local affiliates never materialized. While Moreno had taken the lead in organizing the 1939 national meeting, Josefina Fierro was vital in buoying the day to day operations of the fragile southern California chapters. Fierro, a vibrant Los Angeles activist, descended from long line of rebellious women as her mother and grandmother were staunch supporters of Juan Flores Magón during the Mexican Revolution. Fierro was married at the time to Hollywood screenwriter John Bright (later a member of the blacklisted "Hollywood Ten"), and she used her celebrity contacts to raise funds for El Congreso and various barrio causes. Lifelong friends, Moreno and Fierro emphasized the dignity of the common person and the importance of grassroots networks, reciprocity, and self-help. As Fierro commented in an interview with historian Mario García, "Movie stars such as Anthony Quinn, Dolores Del Rio, and John Wayne contributed money, 'not because they were reds, . . . but because they were helping Mexicans help themselves.' "[19]

The stands taken by Moreno, Fierro, and El Congreso delegates must be placed in the milieu of the deportations or repatriations of the early 1930s. Between 1931 and 1934, an estimated one-third of the Mexican population in the United States (over five hundred thousand people) were either deported or repatriated to Mexico even though the majority (an estimated 60 percent) were native US citizens. Viewed as foreign usurpers of American jobs and as unworthy burdens on relief rolls, Mexicans were the only immigrants targeted for removal. From Los Angeles, California, to Gary, Indiana, Mexicans were either summarily deported by immigration agencies or persuaded to depart voluntarily by duplicitous social workers who greatly exaggerated the opportunities awaiting them south of the border.[20] Thus, advocating for the rights of immigrants was a courageous course given the recent history of intimidation and removal. In Washington, DC, Luisa Moreno spoke before the 1940 Conference of the American Committee for the Protection of the Foreign Born, a national left-of-center political group that grew out of the American Civil Liberties Union in 1933. Her only surviving speech, "Caravans of Sorrow," bears witness to her power as an orator. An excerpt follows:

> Long before the "grapes of wrath" had ripened in California's vineyards a people lived on highways, under trees or tents, in shacks or railroad sections, picking crops—cottons, fruits, vegetables—cultivating sugar beets, building railroad and dams, making a barren land fertile for new crops and greater riches . . .
>
> One can hardly imagine how many bales of cotton have passed through the nimble fingers of Mexican men, women, and children. And what conditions have they had to endure to pick that cotton? . . . Once a cotton picker

told me . . . [that] she remembered so many nights, under the trees in the rain, when she and her husband held gunny sacks over the shivering bodies of their sleeping children—young Americans.

These people are not aliens. They have contributed their endurance, sacrifices, youth, and labor to the Southwest. Indirectly, they have paid more taxes than all the stock holders of California's industrialized agriculture, the sugar beet companies and the large cotton interests that operate or have operated with the labor of Mexican workers.[21]

That same year (1940) Moreno accepted a desk job with UCAPAWA in Washington, DC, serving as the editor of its Spanish-language newspaper. I contend that she took this post in an attempt to establish a relationship with her daughter, now almost a teenager. Moreno and Mytyl celebrated their first Christmas together in years—an East Coast holiday that Mytyl always recalled with great fondness.[22] A year later the duo would live in Los Angeles, where Moreno, newly elected vice president of UCAPAWA, took charge of consolidating the cannery locals there. She threw herself into this task, earning the nickname "the California Whirlwind." Capitalizing on the gendered networks on the shop floor, Moreno would harvest unparalleled success, as food-processing operatives under the UCAPAWA banner significantly improved their working conditions, wages, and benefits.

The California canning labor force included young daughters, newlyweds, middle-aged wives, and widows; 75 percent of cannery workers were women, 25 percent were men. Occasionally, three generations—daughter, mother, and grandmother—worked together at a particular cannery. Entering the job market as members of a family wage economy, they pooled their resources to put food on the table. "My father was a busboy," Carmen Bernal Escobar recalled, "and to keep the family going . . . in order to bring in a little more money . . . my mother, my grandmother, my mother's brother, my sister, and I all worked together at Cal San." One of the largest canneries in Los Angeles, the California Sanitary Canning Company (Cal San), employed primarily Mexican and Russian Jewish women. Working side by side, they were clustered in specific departments—washing, grading, cutting, canning, and packing—and paid according to the production level. Standing in the same spots week after week, month after month, women workers often developed friendships crossing family and ethnic lines. Their day-to-day problems

(slippery floors, irritating peach fuzz, production speed-ups, arbitrary supervisors, and sexual harassment) cemented feelings of solidarity. Cannery
workers even employed a special jargon when conversing among themselves,
often referring to an event in terms of when specific fruits or vegetables
arrived for processing at the plant. For instance, the phrase "We met in spin-
ach, fell in love in peaches, and married in tomatoes" indicates that a couple
met in March, fell in love in August, and married in October.[23]

In 1939 Cal San employees staged a dramatic strike led by UCAPAWA organizer Dorothy Ray Healey. Wages and conditions improved at the plant as
workers nurtured their union local, and they jealously guarded their closed
shop contact. When Luisa Moreno arrived, she enlisted the aid of union members at Cal San in union drives at several Los Angeles-area food-processing
firms. Workers organized other workers across canneries, ethnicities, generations, and gender. The result would be Local 3, the second-largest UCAPAWA
affiliate in the nation. Moreno encouraged cross-plant alliances and women's
leadership. In 1943 the southern California cannery women held twelve of
the fifteen elected positions, with eight won by Mexican women. In addition
to higher wages and improved conditions, they negotiated innovative benefits such as a hospitalization plan, free legal advice, and, at one plant, man-
agement-financed day care. In 1944, UCAPAWA became the Food, Tobacco,
Agricultural, and Allied Workers of America (FTA). During an era when few
unions addressed the concerns of women, UCAPAWA / FTA blazed a new path.
By 1946, 66 percent of its contracts nationwide contained equal pay for equal
work clauses. A fierce loyalty to the union developed as the result of rank-and-
file participation and leadership. Four decades after the strike, Carmen Bernal
Escobar declared, "UCAPAWA was the greatest thing that ever happened to
the workers at Cal San. It changed everything and everybody." As an example
of women's leadership, Moreno herself rose in the ranks of the California
CIO, becoming the first Latina to serve on a state CIO council.[24]

Moreno's home life did not match her professional success. In 1941 she wed
a local Los Angeles dry cleaner, but the marriage lasted only a few months.
Mytyl was in no mood for a stepfather, and the friction within the household became intolerable. "I wanted my mother all to myself," her daughter
explained; "She was nobody else's. She was mine." Mytyl grew into a rebellious teenager, ditching classes and cajoling sailors into buying her booze.
Moreno worked behind the scenes raising money for the legal defense of

the young Mexican American men unjustly convicted in the Sleepy Lagoon murder case, men the press had characterized as dangerous, zoot suit-wearing *pachucos*. However, she would not tolerate her own daughter dressing in pachuca-style clothing, personally taking a pair of scissors to one outfit. In 1945, Mytyl, just shy of her seventeenth birthday, eloped with returning veteran Edward Glomboske, the older brother of a girlfriend. During one of our interviews, Moreno remarked "I had a choice. I could organize cannery workers or I could control my teenage daughter. I chose to organize cannery workers and my daughter never forgave me."[25]

The year 1945 would also mark Moreno's greatest professional challenge. She would organize cannery workers in northern California in a head-to-head battle with the International Brotherhood of Teamsters. In May 1945 the AFL national president turned over its northern California cannery unions to the Teamsters; as a result, disgruntled local leaders approached FTA. Directing an ambitious drive that extended from San Jose to Sacramento to Modesto, Moreno handpicked her organizing team, and within three months the team had collected fourteen thousand union pledge cards and helped to establish twenty-five functioning locals. Under Moreno's leadership, FTA decisively won the National Labor Relations Board (NLRB) election that covered seventy-two plants. In February 1946 the NLRB, under intense political pressure, rescinded the results of the 1945 election and called for a second tabulation. The Teamsters began a campaign of sweetheart contracts, red baiting, and physical assaults. Amazingly, Moreno and the FTA narrowly lost the second election. This Teamster victory marked the beginning of the end for FTA. In 1950, the union, battered by red baiting, was expelled from the CIO for alleged Communist domination.[26]

Luisa Moreno retired from public life in 1947 and married Gray Bemis. A naval officer recently divorced, Bemis rekindled his relationship with Moreno at a CIO dance held in San Francisco. Their devotion to one another was apparent to all who knew the couple. As her attorney and friend Robert Kenny wrote in a letter to Luisa after Gray's death in 1960, "Certainly the story of your marriage and devotion is a love story that most novelists would want to claim as their own creation."[27]

Their happiness in the United States would be short-lived. In 1948 she faced deportation proceedings. According to Moreno, she was offered citizenship in exchange for testifying against legendary Longshoremen union leader Harry

Bridges, but she refused to become a "free woman with a mortgaged soul." Although high-profile journalists Carey McWilliams and Ignacio López chaired her defense committee and put forth a valiant effort, the result was almost a foregone conclusion. With Gray Bemis at her side, she left the United States in 1950, under terms listed as "voluntary departure under warrant of deportation, "on the grounds that she had once belonged to the Communist Party.

In preparing for the Immigration and Naturalization Service hearings, Luisa Moreno clearly articulated her own legacy. "They can talk about deporting me . . . but they can never deport the people that I've worked with and with whom things were accomplished for the benefit of hundreds of thousands of workers—things that can never be destroyed." As retired California labor activist Doris Walker related in a memorial message in 1992, "Luisa Moreno has been an example for me ever since 1946, when she was a leader and I was a young green organizer . . . her indomitable courage and perseverance will continue in all of us who had the privilege of knowing and working with her."[28]

Luisa Moreno "died" when she crossed El Paso's Stanton Street Bridge into Ciudad Juárez on November 30, 1950. Rosa Rodríguez de Bemis would live on, participating in many activities associated with the progressive government of Guatemalan president Jacobo Arbenz. In particular, she organized a literacy campaign in the hinterlands, teaching basic reading, writing, and math skills to Indigenous women. During the CIA-sponsored coup that the toppled the Arbenz government, Rosa Rodríguez de Bemis went into hiding; and although her brother had secured asylum for her in El Salvador, she and her husband fled to Mexico in their Studebaker. As a forty-seven-year-old woman in 1954, Rosa Rodríguez de Bemis would shift her identity once more as she began another round of travel and migration. From 1954 to 1960 she and Gray Bemis raised chickens in a radical American expatriate community near Mexico City. With Gray's death in 1960, she moved to Cuba, where she translated economic materials from English into Spanish. She missed her daughter and grandchildren and so returned to Mexico in 1963. The Immigration and Naturalization Service issued a "Look Out Notice for Luisa Moreno," stating, "since deportation, she has continued her communist activity in Latin America including service in Cuba as one of Castro's bodyguards." When I shared this document with her in 1984, she burst into laughter: "Imagine me, a big, bad bodyguard."[29]

In the mid 1960s she managed an art gallery in Tijuana. Dolores Huerta and Cesar Chávez visited her on occasion as they sought her advice during their early days of organizing farmworkers. Later on she settled in Guadalajara. In failing health and failing finances, she was denied entrance to the United States for medical treatment in 1984. Refusing to cross the border under any subterfuge, she had no choice but to move in with her brother and his family in Guatemala. Perceived as the prodigal sister, the woman with a radical past, she did not physically live with the family, but resided instead in the children's playhouse on the grounds of the estate.[30]

My last contact with Rosa revolved around her poetry. Through her close friend Elizabeth Eudey, I had received from her a gift—her sole copy of *El Vendedor de Cocuyos*. A few months later Eudey forwarded to me a copy of the poems in English, translated by Abbott Small, a Spanish teacher and published poet who had spent his boyhood in Mexico as a part of the American expatriate community. His parents, Berthe and Charles Small, had known Rosa Rodríguez since her organizing days in Florida. María Lucía Gómez, a poet from Columbia, also took a turn at translating the verses. In 1991 Mytyl Glomboske carried both sets of translations along with a copy of the original poems to her mother in Guatemala. Although debilitated by a stroke, she asked her daughter to read each version aloud; and then after examining each text, she wrote simply "Rose" by the translation she preferred.[31]

In retrospect, she had chosen politics over poetry, considering the latter a luxury she could no longer afford as a labor leader. Yet, it is precisely through her poetry that one can catch a glimpse of her passion, intellect, and spirit, hints of the woman (or women) she would become. Her gift of *El Vendedor de Cocuyos* signified not only a special trust between us but also a readiness to share Rosa Rodríguez, the poet and intellectual, alongside the very public Luisa Moreno. According to her daughter, she was thoroughly engaged in selecting the translations, though it required a great deal of stamina from an eighty-four-year-old woman in failing health. Possibly, she felt a sense of closure, of her life coming full circle. This dance of remembrance was captured by the poet herself in "La ausencia" (The Absence), written during her days as a feminist flapper:

> When we are far apart
> And I think of you,
> The light of the memory of you

Will open out in the night of absence,
Like a fan of sunlight . . .
Distance,
Watching over you in its black cape,
Will not have the power
To separate us . . .
And like the stars
Spilling out on the dark thread of my life,
Luminous waterfalls,
Your eyes,
Your mouth,
Your whole body!
Will open the dawn of enchantment
Along all of my road . . .
When we are far apart,
And from invisible censers there left
The golden spirals
Of memory . . .[32]

Rosa Rodríguez de Bemis died on November 4, 1992. Several weeks later, I received a phone call from Mytyl Glomboske. She had in her possession a package from Guatemala. We talked as she unwrapped it contents. It was a blue suitcase, containing the remaining effects of her mother's life. She asked me to open the case with her the next morning and I readily agreed. We stared at the old suitcase for a moment before Mytyl pressed the metal latches. Inside there was an array of neatly packed items—two photo albums, assorted sheets of unpublished poetry and drafts of poems, correspondence and news clippings related to her poetry. Gray Bemis's death certificate and assorted business papers, and a hand-crocheted blue *rebozo* (shawl). The most surprising of all was a bundle of note cards. She had saved every letter and greeting card I had ever mailed to her (no matter how silly or inconsequential). And there at the bottom of the suitcase lay my dissertation. As an oral historian who tends to fret over issues of reciprocity, I to this day remain moved beyond words. Not only had Rosa Rodríguez (aka. Luisa Moreno) profoundly influenced my own life professionally and personally, but I had also mattered to her.

Notes

I would like to express my deep appreciation to my sister scholars of the Meaning and Representation of Women and Work in the Lives of Women of Color Research Group, especially Nancy Hewitt and Lynn Bolles. I also thank Virginia Sanchez Korrol and Sharon Block for their careful comments. Most importantly, Valerie Matsumoto, my dear friend and critic, pushed and prodded, encouraging me to think about the poems in ways I had not imagined. I look forward to working with Albert Camarillo on our joint venture in crafting a full-fledged biography on Moreno. And thanks to my biggest fan, Victor Becerra, who never tires of my "Rosa" stories.

1. I use the term *"Latina/Latino"* as a US-specific umbrella term, as a descriptor for all people of Latin American birth or heritage in the United States.

2. *New York Times*, April 28, 2001. My approach to biography has been profoundly influenced by the works of Mary Felstiner and Greg Sarris. See Mary Lowenthal Felstiner, *To Paint Her Life: Charlotte Salomon in the Nazi Era* (New York: Harper Collins, 1994); and Greg Sarris, *Mabel Mackay: Weaving the Dream* (Berkeley: University of California Press, 1994).

3. As an example, see Vicki L. Ruiz, *From Out of the Shadows: Mexican Women in Twentieth-Century America* (New York: Oxford University Press, 1998).

4. "Data on Luisa Moreno Bemis," file 53 (Robert W. Kenny Collection, Southern California Library for Social Studies Research, Los Angeles [hereafter referred to as the Kenny Collection]); interviews with Luisa Moreno, August 4, 1984, and July 27, 1978, conducted by the author; "Handwritten Notes by Robert Kenny," file 53 (Kenny Collection). Interview with Berthe Small, Alba Zatz, and Asa Zatz, September 28, 1996, conducted by the author; e-mail correspondence from Patricia Harms to the author, April 5, 2004. After the first references (which include the interviewer's name), all interviews will be cited by the last name of the interviewee and the year. Note: In a move that no doubt further disconcerted their elders, Sociedad members began to advocate for the rights of indigenous people. According to Latin American women's historian Patricia Harms, several Sociedad members would continue their feminist activities in Guatemala well into the 1940s.

5. Moreno interview, 1984; Rosa Rodríguez López, *El Vendedor de Cocuyos* (México: Imprenta Mundial, 1927); letter from Guatemalan admirer (signature illegible) to Rosa Rodríguez, October 23, 1927; Marco Augusto Recinos, "El Vendedor de Cocuyos," *ALMAMÉRICA*, n.d.; "Cumpleaños," unidentified news clippings, ca. August 30, 1929. All referenced materials are in author's possession.

6. "Literatura," in Rodríguez López, *El Vendedor de Cocuyos*, 71–72. The original is as follows: "Literatura, literature . . . / Yo he succumblo a tu locura / y en tu altar / he buscado la expression / de un amor, / un sueño / y una religión.

"Y todavía en mi cabeza / hay hambre de locura / y en todo mi comino / sombrean los fantasmas / íde no poder decir!

"Literatura, literature . . . / Amarga y dulce. / Sombra y luz . . . / ¡Óh gran misterio en flor! / En tu locura / he buscado la expresión / de un amor, / un sueño / y una religión . . ."

All English translations courtesy of Abbott Small, poet and friend of Rosa Rodríguez.

7. Moreno interview, 1984; *Jacksonville Journal*, September 23, 1943; *French Foreign Legion Handbook of Miguel Ángel de León* (in author's possession); interview with Luisa Moreno. August 5, 1976, conducted by Albert Camarillo; "Data on Luisa Moreno Bemis"; "El milagro," in Rodríguez López, *El Vendedor de Cocuyos*, 25. The original verse follows: "Y he vivido, / he soñado / en el fuego de tus brazos."

8. "Tu amor," in Rodríguez López, *El Vendedor de Cocuyos*, 33. The original verse follows: "Yo sé / que eres lágrima en mi vida. / Que tus manos / deshojarán mis pétalos / y romperán mi tallo . . ."

9. "Data on Luisa Moreno Bemis"; interview with Luisa Moreno, August 12–13, 1977, conducted by Albert Camarillo; Moreno interview, 1976.

10. Moreno interview, 1976, 1977, and 1984.

11. Ibid. This concept of conjugating identities derives from interviews with Luisa Moreno and her daughter, Mytyl Glomboske, as well as my reading of the scholarship of Rebecca Lester, Michael Kearney, Chela Sandoval, Stuart Hall, Paula Moya, and Ramón Gutiérrez. I also owe an enormous intellectual debt to all of my compañeros in the University of California Humanities Research Institute "Reshaping the Americas" Residency Group (Spring 2002). Moreover, I thank Nancy Hewitt for bringing to my attention the importance of Luisa Capetillo's organizing in Florida to Moreno's efforts twenty years earlier. Note: I surmise that she left the Communist Party out of expediency, given her new position with the American Federation of Labor. Her commitment to Marxism never wavered.

12. If Moreno composed verses in Spanish as a labor leader, they did not weather her many travels, as all but one of the Spanish-language poems she saved during her lifetime appear to date from her youth in Mexico. Moreover, among her effects at her death were fragments of two scrawled poems she composed as an elderly woman.

13. Luisa Moreno, "On the Road" (unpublished poem, 1935, in author's possession).

14. Interview with Mytyl Glomboske, August 27, 2001, conducted by the author; "Handwritten Notes"; Small, Zatz, and Zatz interview, 1996; Moreno interviews 1977, 1978. For more information on the radicalism of the Tampa workers, see Nancy A. Hewitt, *Southern Discomfort: Women's Activism in Tampa, Florida, 1880s–1920s* (Urbana:

University of Illinois Press, 2001); and for more information on the role of the Ku
Klux Klan, see Robert Ingalls, *Urban Vigilantes in the New South: 1882–1936* (Knoxville:
University of Tennessee Press, 1988).

15. Moreno interviews, 1977, and 1978; Vicki L. Ruiz, *Cannery Women, Cannery
Lives: Mexican Women, Unionization, and the California Food Processing Industry,
1930–1950* (Albuquerque: University of New Mexico, 1987), 44.

16. Moreno interviews, 1976, 1977, 1978. For more information on the pecan
shellers' strike, see Zaragosa Vargas, "Tejana Radical: Emma Tenayuca and the San
Antonio Labor Movement during the Great Depression," *Pacific Historical Review* 66
(1997): 553–80; and Ruiz, *From out of the Shadows*, 79–80.

17. William D. Carrigan, and Clive Webb, "Muerto por Unos Desconocidos
(Killed by Persons Unknown): Mob Violence against African Americans and Mex-
ican Americans," in *Beyond Black and White: Race, Ethnicity, and Gender in the US
South and Southwest*, ed. Stephanie M. Cole, and Allison M. Parker (College Station:
Texas A&M Press, 2003), 65–66. For information on lynching in Tejano collective
memory, see Américo Paredes, *With Pistol in His Hand: A Border Ballad and Its Hero*
(Austin: University of Texas Press, 1958); Julian Samora et al., *Gunpowder Justice*
(Notre Dame: University of Notre Dame Press, 1979); María Eva Flores CDP, "The
Good Life, the Hard Way: The Mexican American Community of Fort Stockton,
Texas" (PhD diss., Arizona State University, 2000). On the resonance and meanings
of the song "Strange Fruit," in American memory and popular culture, see Angela
Y. Davis, *Blues Legacies and Black Feminism: Gertrude "Ma" Rainey, Bessie Smith, and
Billie Holiday* (New York: Pantheon, 1998).

18. Moreno interviews, 1977, 1978; Luisa Moreno, "1939" (unpublished poem in
author's possession).

19. Moreno interviews, 1977, 1978; interview with Josefina Fierro de Bright,
August 7, 1977, conducted by Albert Camarillo; Carlos C. Larralde, and Richard
Griswold del Castillo, "Luisa Moreno: A Hispanic Civil Rights Leader in San Diego,"
Journal of San Diego 14 (1995): 284–310. For more information on El Congreso, see
David G. Gutiérrez, *Walls and Mirrors: Mexican American, Mexican Immigrants, and
the Politics of Ethnicity in the Southwest, 1910–1986* (Berkeley: University of California
Press, 1995); George J. Sánchez, *Becoming Mexican American: Ethnicity, Culture, and
Identity in Los Angeles, 1900–1945* (New York: Oxford University Press, 1993); Albert
Camarillo, *Chicanos in California* (San Francisco: Boyd & Fraser, 1984); Mario García,
Mexican Americans; Leadership, Ideology, and Identity, 1930–1960 (New Haven: Yale
University Press, 1981). Quote from García, *Mexican Americans*, 158.

20. Camarillo, *Chicanos in California*, 48–49; Abraham Hoffman, *Unwanted Mexican
Americans in the Great Depression* (Tucson: University of Arizona Press, 1974), 43–46;
Francisco Balderrama, *In Defense of La Raza: The Los Angeles Mexican Consulate and the*

Mexican Community, 1929–1936 (Tucson: University of Arizona Press, 1982), 16–20. The most comprehensive survey of the Mexican deportations and repatriations during this period is Francisco Balderrama, and Raymond Rodríguez, *Decade of Betrayal: Mexican Repatriation in the 1930s* (Albuquerque: University of New Mexico Press, 1995).

21. Luisa Moreno, "Caravans of Sorrow: Noncitizen Americans of the Southwest," in *Between Two Worlds: Mexican Immigration in the United States*, ed. David Gutiérrez (Wilmington, DE: Scholarly Resources, 1996), 120, 122.

22. Moreno interview, 1976, 1977, 1979; Glomboske interview, 2001.

23. See Ruiz, *Cannery Women*, 21–39

24. This discussion is taken from Ruiz, *From out of the Shadows*, 80–82; and Ruiz, *Cannery Women*, 69–85.

25. Carey McWilliams, "Luisa Moreno Bemis" (August 1949), file 53, Kenny Collection; "Data on Luisa Moreno Bemis"; "Handwritten Notes"; Glomboske interview, 2001; Moreno interview, 1984.

26. Ruiz, *Cannery Women*, 103–107.

27. Moreno interview, 1984; Small, Zatz, and Zatz interview, 1996: Glomboske interview, 2001; Robert W. Kenny to Luisa Bemis, February 11, 1950, file 56, Kenny Collection.

28. Ruiz, *Cannery Women*, 113–118; "The Case of Luisa Moreno Bemis," *Labor Committee for Luisa Moreno Bemis* pamphlet (in author's possession); US Department of Justice, immigration and Naturalization Service, "Closing INS Report (Los Angeles District) on Luisa Moreno," December 6, 1950; Steve Murdoch, *Our Times*, September 9, 1949, file 53, Kenny Papers; letter from Doris Walker to Luisa Moreno Memorial Committee, November 29, 1992.

29. Moreno interviews, 1976, 1977, 1979, 1984; Small, Zatz, and Zatz interview, 1996; US Department of Justice, Immigration and Naturalization Service, "Look Out Notice for Luisa Moreno," July 15, 1965 (cancellation date August 1977).

30. Moreno interview, 1984; Glomboske interview, 2001.

31. Unfortunately, this bilingual volume remains unpublished.

32. "La ausencia" in Rodríguez López, *El Vendedor de Cocuyos*, 51–52. The original is as follows:

> "Cuando estemos lejos / y piense en ti, / se abrirá en la noche de la ausencia, / como abanico de sol, / la luz de tu recuerdo . . .
>
> 'La distancia, / velándote en su capa negra / no tendrá la fuerza / de apartarnos . . .
>
> "Yo como estrellas, / vertiendo en el hilo oscuro de mi vida, / cascadas luminosas, / tus ojos, / tus manos / y tu boca, / ¡tu cuerpo enterol! / abrirá la aurora del ensueño / en todo mi comino . . .
>
> "Cuando estemos lejos, / y se alcen de invisibles pebeteros / los dorados espirales / del recuerdo . . ."

Figure 6.1. Private Félix Longoria's graduation picture after basic training, spring 1945. Courtesy of the Jeff and Mary Bell Library's Special Collections at Texas A&M–Corpus Christi.

6

Separate Tejano/Texan Worlds

*The Félix Longoria Controversy, Racism, and Patriotism
in Post–World War II South Texas[1]*

Patrick J. Carroll

Private Félix Longoria died from a sniper's bullet on the island of Luzon in the summer of 1945. Four years later, the War Department shipped the body back to his hometown of Three Rivers, Texas, for reburial. Three Rivers had but one funeral home. Because of some friction between his widow, Beatrice Moreno de Longoria, and her in-laws, she decided to wake Félix in the funeral parlor's chapel instead of in his parents' house. Tom Kennedy, the director then the owner of the funeral home, refused to honor her request because "the whites would not like it." This denial sparked a furor that involved Anglos and Mexican Americans in South Texas, statewide Anglo political factions, the US State Department, and the Mexican government. It caught the attention of the national press and radio. Accounts of the unfolding conflict appeared in print throughout the Americas. It threatened the successful extension of the US-Mexico Bracero Program.[2] It thrust Dr. Héctor Pérez García and his newly formed American GI Forum into the forefront of the Mexican American civil rights movement. It forged consensus and focus within the Mexican American community. It first threatened and

DOI: 10.5876/9781607323372.c006

then advanced the political career of the new US senator from Texas, Lyndon Baines Johnson.

But what made this "affair of honor" so much more public and influential than numerous other cases of discrimination against Tejanos in this setting? To answer this question, we must consider a number of things, not the least of which is the very nature of the Longoria incident itself.

The Mexican Consul in Corpus Christi characterized the Longoria affair as a case of "social" discrimination. To him, that made it less onerous than physical and legal discrimination.[3] No physical abuse occurred. No one's legal rights had been denied. And no prejudicial laws had been passed to institutionalize racism. An Anglo funeral director had merely refused a Tejana widow's request to use his chapel to wake her dead Mexican American husband. Such actions were not against the law in 1949.[4] Yet this socially discriminatory act elicited louder and more widespread protest than acts of physical, economic, and political persecution, suggesting that in and of itself, the incident does not explain the strong public reaction to it. Indeed, it was but a small part of a larger historical whole that shaped traditions of Anglo / Mexican American and Texan/Tejano interaction in South Texas.

Three Rivers fell within the northern boundary of the "Valley," as Texans call it, a zone "bordered on the north by a line stretching from Del Rio to San Antonio to Corpus Christi and on the south by the Rio Grande."[5] Prior to about the turn of the twentieth century, the Valley was still a lightly populated subsistence farming and commercial ranching area. During the latter part of the nineteenth century, however, it began to undergo an economic transformation. New Midwest US migrants moved into the area in search of cheap land. They brought with them a commitment to commercial agriculture—something that, beyond raising livestock, had never been successfully practiced in the region. Oil production and refining soon spread into the Valley. These changes expanded and diversified the production sector of the economy, increasing the demand for workers. From south of the border came waves of Mexican nationals fleeing the death and destruction of a revolution that raged off and on between 1910 and 1929 and seeking new employment opportunities in the Valley.[6] The consequences of these altered production conditions and the heightened Mexican immigration drastically affected the lives of Mexican American citizens within the region.

García's family was among those who fled the destruction and carnage in Mexico. In 1917 his parents packed up their transportable belongings and, with young Héctor and nine other siblings in tow, made their way north from Llera, Tamaulipas, across the border to Mercedes, Texas, the home of Héctor's uncle.[7] Like so many other Mexican refugees, the Garcías sought a more secure life in the Valley. The number of Mexican-born individuals within the state rose from just over 70,000 in 1900 to an estimated 125,000 in 1910. During each of the next two decades, the number of Mexican national residents more than doubled, reaching 688,681 by 1930, and the Valley held the heaviest concentration of them.[8] They provided the region with a comparative economic advantage—cheap and malleable workers, Anglo employers' labor of choice. As one South Texas commercial farmer explained, Mexican refugee workers "don't live on anything . . . they ask for less . . . and they work cheaper."[9] Along with the growth and diversification of the production side of the local economy, these newly arriving Mexican nationals greatly contributed to the economic expansion of the region.

David Montejano provides perhaps the best explanation of how these demographic and production changes altered relationships between Anglos and Hispanics in South Texas during the first half of the twentieth century. Montejano contends that a new commercial and impersonal economic order replaced an older and more benign patron-peon labor system.[10] This newer and harsher labor relations environment did provide the region with a comparative advantage that allowed it to compete successfully with other regional economies in the Southwest and the rest of the nation but at great cost. Hispanic laborers lost their dependent status and became mere wage laborers, often-transient workers. No more could they count on the support of their *patrón*. This depersonalization of the workplace had a disastrous effect on Mexican Americans in the region. It dehumanized and converted them into mere production units in the eyes of their new Anglo farmer and oil company employers. The result everywhere was the same: where commercial agriculture and petroleum production grew, Anglos' treatment of Mexican Americans worsened. Mexicans Americans now found themselves treated as an inferior race, segregated into their own town quarters and refused admittance to restaurants, movie theaters, barbershops, swimming pools, and so on.[11]

The 1930s and 1940s witnessed the emergence of what Mario T. García calls the "Mexican-American Generation." These rising leaders launched "the first significant civil rights movement by Mexican Americans in the United States."[12] According to García, a small number of US-born Mexican Americans obtained middle-class status by the 1930s, either through university educations and/or business acumen.[13] He and other Chicano scholars reason that World War II had a dramatic impact on the thinking and activism of this group.[14] García maintains that its members "identified with the World War II slogan: 'Americans All'" and redoubled their efforts to achieve equality for Mexican Americans within mainstream US society.[15] They tried to accomplish this through Anglos' and Tejanos' recognition of Mexican Americans' whiteness. They saw this as a necessary prerequisite to following the path that white ethnics had traditionally taken to integration and equality within the broader US society. Prominent Mexican American leaders like Alonso S. Perales of San Antonio advised disassociation from causes of nonwhite and foreign groups—black Americans and Mexican nationals.[16] As Benjamin Márquez put it, "In a society that judged individuals on the basis of skin color (Hispanics) sought to avoid the stigma of minority status."[17] If Mexican Americans got too close to issues affecting nonwhite and non-US groups, white Americans might begin to define Mexican Americans as nonwhite and un-American, and that would make Tejanos' goals of integration and equality tough to accomplish.

Three Rivers, Texas, and the rest of Live Oak County experienced these demographic and socioeconomic shifts. There, as in the rest of South Texas, Mexican American labor did not have the opportunity to effectively resist these changes until World War II and the labor shortages it created. Incidents like the Longoria controversy mobilized Tejanos/as in the region and provided them with political and social leverage to fight the erosion of their socioeconomic standing and reclaim their citizenship.[18]

By the outbreak of the war, South Texas had cleaved into two markedly separate communities. One was white and spoke English first; one was brown and spoke Spanish first. Just as important to understanding evolving relations between the two populations, as Eric Wolf has pointed out, is the realization that group identity, as well as individual identity, was the product of ongoing negotiation between intergroup and interpersonal identification.[19] In whites' eyes, it no longer mattered which side of the border Hispanics came from, all were "Mexican."[20] Carlos E. Castañeda, a history professor and librarian at the University of Texas commented on this identity transformation in 1948, just months before the outbreak of the controversy over Longoria's wake:

Under the term "Mexican" are included those who have recently come from Mexico and those who have lived in Texas and the Southwest for generations, those who are American citizens . . . and those who are citizens of Mexico; those who speak English without an accent and those who speak nothing but Spanish. In the mind of the average (Anglo) citizen the Mexican is a "Mexican."[21]

Such thinking clearly advantaged Anglos. It paid them what David R. Roediger, in another context, called a "wage" for their racism. By cleaving the overall population along racial lines and then discriminating in favor of the white half, Anglos earned all the advantages and privileges and Tejanos paid all the "wages" derived from such a prejudicial power dynamic.[22] This racist social climate explains Kennedy's perception that "whites would not like" his waking Longoria's body in his funeral chapel.

Fortunately for Mexican Americans, a set of political conditions had developed by 1949 that enhanced Hispanics' political influence. A split had appeared within the Texas Democratic Party. Texas "Regulars" stood for states' rights and white supremacy. "National" Democrats favored Franklin Delano Roosevelt's New Deal and the federal government's authority over state governments. In 1946 Regulars supported the state's native son, Vice President John Nance Garner, in his split with President Roosevelt and the Nationals. Garner quit the Democratic ticket in disgust when Roosevelt decided to run for a third term as president, thereby dashing any hopes of the vice president succeeding him.[23] As a result, Texas Democrats divided along Regular/National Democratic Party lines. García used this split to negotiate Anglo political support for the Mexican American civil rights movement. The Longoria incident provided García the opening to do this.

The day after becoming involved in the Longoria dispute, García fired off seventeen telegrams to state and national officials as well as a number of media celebrities. One of those messages went to the newly elected democratic senator from Texas, Lyndon Baines Johnson. Johnson had emerged as a prominent member of Texas's Democratic faction. Months earlier he had defeated former Governor Coke Stevenson, a Texas Regular, for his Senate seat, in one of the most contested elections in the state's history. The new junior senator was one of the logical people for García to contact. Besides being a National, he sat on the Senate Armed Services Committee and enjoyed a good reputation among the Valley's Mexican American community.[24] Johnson had taught at a Tejano school in Cotulla, just south of Three Rivers, and he had successfully courted the Mexican American vote during his 1948 senatorial race.[25] The senator had also served in World War II.

In his note to the senator, García first explained the circumstances surrounding the Longoria incident, then requested an "immediate investigation and correction of the un-American action of the Manor-Rice Funeral Home" for "denying the use of its facilities for the re-interment of Félix Longoria."[26] García assured Johnson that if another funeral home had existed, the Longorias would have gone there, and the matter would have never come before the public eye. The doctor charged that the incident revealed "discriminatory practices which occur intermittently in this state."[27] He reminded Johnson that he had seen such prejudice firsthand while teaching at Cotulla.[28]

In an intra-office memo, John Connally, chief of staff of Johnson's Senate office, wrote that on January 11, the day after receiving García's telegram, Johnson telephoned Robert Jackson, publisher of the *Corpus Christi Caller-Times*.[29] The senator read the doctor's wire to the newspaperman. Johnson then asked whether Jackson knew anything about the incident. The publisher replied that he did. Jackson said that his newspaper "already had a story about it." Johnson asked if García's account rang true. Jackson said it did and summoned Bob McCracken, the managing editor, and George Groh, the reporter covering the story. Johnson individually read each of them the telegram and asked them the same question. They too corroborated García's story. Satisfied, Johnson composed his reply to the doctor. "This injustice and prejudice is deplorable," Johnson wrote. He expressed his sympathy and deep "regret to learn that the prejudice of some individuals extends even beyond this life." He further stated that although he had "no authority over civilian funeral homes nor does the federal government," he had made arrangements to rebury Longoria at either Fort Sam Houston National Cemetery or Arlington National Cemetery. If Longoria's widow wanted him reburied at either site, Johnson advised that she send him a collect telegram before the body's scheduled arrival in San Francisco on January 13.[30]

Johnson was the only one of the seventeen recipients of García's telegrams to become directly involved in the incident. The others simply sent polite notes of regret with no offers to help in any way. This decision to intervene placed Johnson in a precarious political position, one many of his Texas Anglo constituents, especially Texas Regulars, would not appreciate. Regulars were committed to states' rights. They were especially sensitive to National Democrats and the White House meddling in Texas's social environment.[31]

When the outcry emerged over the Longoria incident, Johnson had to exhibit either uncommon courage or imprudence to stick out his neck so soon after his close election in November. Anglo constructions of this incident broke down along the same lines Anglo politics did. One faction from outside South Texas, National Democrats in the main, saw what happened as discrimination against a World War II soldier and his family. Texas Regulars from South Texas and other parts of the state interpreted the incident as a misunderstanding perpetuated by unreasonable Latinos, ambitious National Democrats, and ignorant outsiders who were unfamiliar with the logically and naturally developed apartheid order that existed within the region. When Johnson offered his sympathies to the Longoria family and encouraged the collective reaction of South Texas's Mexican American community, his behavior appeared reckless, even traitorous, to Texas Regulars. From the perspective of the Texas establishment, Johnson's liberal good intentions had gone too far.[32] This not only explains the political undertones that became attached to the incident, it also implies another factor that added to its significance. Inherent in this set of political conditions was the fact that different groups interpreted the controversy within a context that seemed appropriate to them.

Texas Regular Democrats and others who shared their views saw little to criticize in the funeral director's actions. They recognized two worlds in the Valley—one Anglo and the other Mexican. Both communities might peacefully coexist, but neither wanted to mingle with the other. Anglos who saw the incident in this light interpreted it as either a misunderstanding resulting from an ignorance of South Texas ways or a trumped-up charge instigated by liberal rabble-rousers. Travis Bryan represented a good example of this type of thinking. He wrote Johnson that Mexicans, like Sicilians and Negroes, loved to "funeralize." He "never became entangled in any of their family brawls [an apparent reference to the purported estrangement between Beatrice Longoria and her in-laws], misunderstandings or disagreements which is usually the case even when they go to lay away a dear one."[33] The funeral director had acted sensibly and reasonably. Mexicans were different from white folks. Mixing the two, whether through use of a common funeral chapel or anything else, made little sense.

William Chesnutt of Kennedy voiced similar views. He cautioned Johnson that most Anglos in his town interpreted the incident far differently than the senator did. Chesnutt, however, put a slightly different speculative twist on the Anglo segregationists' justification. He shared a rumor circulating among Kennedy Anglos that the funeral director had not really denied use of his chapel; he had merely suggested that the Longoria family wake Félix in the local Catholic Church for two reasons. First, that was what Mexicans normally did, and second, the funeral chapel was too small to accommodate a large "Mexican" wake. Chesnutt concluded that the whole controversy represented nothing more than a misunderstanding that troublemakers had blown out of proportion.[34] W. G. Luce of Tilden agreed. Johnson had erred in his stand on the matter. This was just another instance of "hot headed Latins yelling prejudice, over everything." In America, a businessman like Tom Kennedy had the right to deny service to whomever he liked. Luce volunteered that Johnson's involvement in the protest would cost him Anglo support across the state. He ended with a friendly warning: "for Pete's sake, quit sticking your neck out in situations where you do not first inquire *carefully* into all angles and get all the information possible from *both* sides (Luce's underlining)."[35]

Many Anglos, those living in Three Rivers and others in the Valley and beyond, went further in their criticism of García and Johnson. They saw a conspiracy in the incident. The two had deliberately tried to embarrass the town, the region, and the state in the eyes of the nation. To these people, Johnson had shamefully distorted the truth. They complained that as a result "hate mail poured into Three Rivers."[36] To these Anglos, segregating the funeral parlor did not represent prejudice; it merely reflected the voluntary separation that existed between Texans and Tejanos in all facets of life in Three Rivers and South Texas.[37] Anglos lived on one side of the railroad tracks running through town; Mexicans lived on the other side. Anglos got haircuts at one barbershop; Mexicans got haircuts at another. Anglos went to one grammar school; Mexicans went to another. Anglo dead lay on one side of the fence running through the middle of the cemetery; Mexicans lay on the other side of the fence. Much of this negative publicity about these "facts of life" might have stemmed from statewide and national ignorance of the "way things were" in South Texas. Johnson and García were agents of the National Democrats, who were bent on slandering Texas in order to strip it of its state sovereignty.

Texas Regulars decided to fight back.[38] J. F. Grey, Texas House Representative from Live Oak County, led them to battle. In collusion with Texas Regular Governor Beauford Jester, Grey moved the legislature to appoint an investigative committee to look into the matter. Its real task, however, was threefold. It aimed to exonerate Kennedy and Three Rivers of the charge of racism. It sought to prove García's and Johnson's complicity in fabricating the Longoria controversy. And in accomplishing the first two tasks, it hoped to publically embarrass the newly elected liberal National Democrat, Senator Johnson. In order to facilitate these three ends, Grey and Jester stacked the investigative committee's membership with four Regular Democrats and only one Johnson supporter. The governor then allotted the committee a meager $1,000 budget and requested an investigation and written report within three weeks.[39]

The investigative committee's outcome was predictable. Only the four Texas Regular members of the committee signed its final report. As planned, it cleared Kennedy from any wrongdoing, finding no racism in his or the town's actions toward the Longoria family. Frank Oltorf, the lone National Democrat on the body, authored and presented his own minority report. This surprised the Regulars. Worse, Oltorf's report proved so convincing in its alternate conclusion that Kennedy had acted in a racist manner that one of the four Regulars, Rep. Byron Tinsley of Greenville, was so embarrassed that he asked the committee chair, Cecil Storey, to remove his signature from the majority report.[40] Anglos' counterattack had ended in failure and humiliation for Texas Regulars rather than National Democrats.

All Anglo-Texans and citizens across the nation did not construct the incident in racist terms. In the shadow of the country's World War II experience they saw Kennedy's refusal as unpatriotic. He had denied use of his funeral chapel to wake a decorated US soldier. Their letters of support arrived at the senator's office in far greater numbers than those offering criticism. They also swamped the correspondence coming into the offices of the Three Rivers funeral director and the town's elected officials. Robert Pampa of West Orange, New Jersey, quipped in his letter to Johnson, "any man good enough to die fighting on foreign soil is good enough to be buried anywhere in this country." Members of the American Legion James A. Edmond Post No. 21 in Waco sent Johnson a resolution stating, "Whereas, we hang our heads in shame for the un-American treatment of Three Rivers Funeral Parlor in refusing to accept and do honor to the soldier's remains who has given his life so that we may now live." The cover letter mentioned that a copy of the resolution had been sent to the state legislature and governor. Claude Bryant of Stephenville praised the senator for his intervention on behalf of the Longoria family and added, "I am a lot stronger Johnson man now." Charles Mumm of Laredo wrote, "The Three Rivers Funeral Director insulted her [Beatrice Longoria], her son [husband] and every dead G.I. by refusing the use of his chapel." George Long, a philosophy professor at the University of Alabama, mentioned that he used the public protest over the incident in a lecture as a positive example of patriotism and democracy in action.[41]

State, national, and international newspapers added their voices to the public outcry. The *Dallas Morning News* observed, "The story (of the incident) exploded over America and Mexico."[42] The Fort Worth *Star-Telegram*, the *San Antonio Express*, the *Corpus Christi Caller-Times*, the *Austin American-Statesmen*, the *Valley Morning Star* (Harlingen, TX), the San Angelo (TX) *Standard*, *The New York Times*, the *Detroit Free Press*, the *Chicago Tribune*, the *Santa Fe New Mexican*, the *Washington (DC) Times-Herald*, and *The Philadelphia Inquirer*, to mention but a few, carried multiple articles on the controversy. Virtually every one of their bylines stressed the same theme that pervaded the Anglo protests at whatever level. Kennedy was wrong because he had discriminated against an American soldier who had fought and died for his country in World War II.[43] The Longoria incident, coming as it did on the heels of the US-led victory, connected with the still-fervent US patriotism across the nation.

Latin American presses, unlike most of those in the United States, shared the Mexican American perspective on the incident. Mexican newspapers such as *Excélsior*, *Novedades*, and *El Mundo* all carried articles on the controversy as it unfolded. *The Havana Post*, *El Mundo* (Puerto Rico) devoted coverage to the incident. *La Estrella de Panamá*, the *Correo da Manhã* (Rio de Janeiro), and *La Nación* (Buenos Aires) also ran articles on it. In each case, the thrust of Latin American news coverage was the same. Although it decried the unpatriotic nature of events in Three Rivers, the Latin American press even more strongly condemned the pervading racial discrimination inherent in these events.[44] Through the war, Mexican Americans had become Americans in everybody's eyes but those of Anglos in the Southwest. Hispanics from South Texas to southern Patagonia linked the Longoria controversy to racism first and to lack of patriotism second.

Latin American reaction to an incident such as the Longoria affair would normally have attracted little attention in the Valley, perhaps only a sidebar to a story in local newspapers. That general pattern did not hold in this case. Mexico, the neighboring Latin American country that devoted the most attention to the incident, was in the midst of delicate negotiations with the United States over extension of the Bracero Program. In 1942, in order to aid the allied war effort, Mexico signed a pact with its northern neighbor to allow Mexican nationals to cross the border and fill labor gaps created by the departure of millions of US workers for the military to fight on foreign shores.

In hindsight it is hard for us to imagine Mexico's agreement to this program as a sacrifice, but it was in the 1940s. During this period, Mexico perceived itself as an underpopulated country. Sixteenth-century conquest and the introduction of Old World diseases had decimated the population so much that Mexico did not reach the number of inhabitants it had in 1519 until 1946![45] This created a centuries-old perception of labor shortages, especially in areas with low population density like northeastern Mexico, an area that shared a common border with Texas. This same region was in the midst of industrial and commercial agricultural expansion by 1942. In Mexicans' minds during the 1940s, the Bracero Program required them to surrender workers needed for the development of the southwestern US economy at the expense of the development of Mexico's northern economy. During the war, that sacrifice seemed justified. Afterward, it did not. Thus, when the US government pressed its Mexican counterpart for extension of the Bracero Program after World War II's end, Mexican negotiators used every means at their disposal to delay, avoid, or restrict this commitment. The Longoria incident offered Mexicans such an opportunity to stall the renewal negotiations in 1949.[46] Widely circulated Mexican newspapers such as *El Nacional*, *El Universal*, *El Popular*, *La Prensa*, *Novedades*, *La Prensa Gráfica*, *Excélsior*, and even the English-language newspaper Mexico *Herald* demanded that the Mexican government either withdraw from the negotiations or, minimally, continue to blacklist Texas from participation in the program.[47] That meant the loss of valuable labor for the US Southwest and for Texas, in particular.

In response, the US State Department placed pressure on two offices connected to the State of Texas in order to arrive at a quick resolution to the controversy. The State Department needed a solution that would dispel the popular Mexican perception that the Longoria incident reflected rampant and deep-seated racist discrimination against Mexicans and persons of Mexican descent (Mexican Americans) in Texas. One of those offices was that of Senator Lyndon Baines Johnson. The other was that of the Good Neighbor Commission, a very public but politically powerless state agency set up to strengthen the state's ties with Mexico and improve Anglo-Mexican American relations. Paul Reveley, the State Department's chief of the Division of Mexican Affairs, maintained ongoing communications with Johnson throughout the incident, making suggestions and requesting updates on the situation. Reveley even went so far as to bring Tom Sutherland, the executive secretary of the Good Neighbor Commission, to Washington and provide him with a State Department office, in order to better coordinate the two agencies' efforts in dealing with the Longoria controversy. This undoubtedly strengthened Johnson's commitment in the affair.[48] It does not, however, explain his initial decision to enter the controversy. The State Department's pressure on Johnson did not come until well after he had publicly committed to the Mexican American side of the dispute.

Johnson's motives aside, these national and international economic and political conditions provide another piece of the overall explanation for the unusually widespread and strong reaction to the Longoria incident. As long as the controversy raged, Mexico refused to negotiate the renewal of the Bracero Program, and the program's continuance was important to the economic well-being of Texas and the rest of the Southwest.

Valley Tejanos' reaction to the Longoria affair represented another major contribution to the impact of this incident. Like Anglos across the nation, Hispanics in the Valley were deeply insulted by the fact that Tom Kennedy had denied a US soldier use of Three Rivers' only funeral chapel. Yet they saw something more in the controversy than just an affront to patriotism; they saw racism too. This made the funeral director's actions doubly offensive. Tejanos believed that Longoria, a Mexican American, had bought racial equality with his life. Now "whites would not like it" if his body rested in their funeral home? The very people he had died for were denying him the rights his sacrifice had earned him. Kennedy's actions insulted Mexican Americans, and they offended the country's patriotism. This construction of the incident, and the widespread notoriety surrounding it, provided a much-needed post–World War II rallying point over a specific well-defined issue to unite and spur

Tejanos to action against Anglo discrimination. For as Benjamin Márquez points out, the Mexican American civil rights movement had fallen into a degree of disarray during the years leading up to World War II. The leadership's preoccupation with the fight for whiteness within US society and the consequent hands-off policies on the issues of white racism toward black Americans and the mistreatment of Mexican nationals had somewhat disaffected those in the vanguard of the movement from the Mexican American community at large.[49] The Longoria incident helped to bind these divisions.

Rank-and-file Tejanos saw in the Longoria controversy a reflection of their own lives and difficulties in the Valley—discriminatory attitudes and practices embedded in the regional Anglo culture that needed addressing. In their minds, racism was a tradition in South Texas, and so was Hispanics' struggle with it. The Longoria incident helped to reattach the area's long tradition of Mexican Americans' struggle for equality in the Valley that had somehow been sidetracked by seemingly esoteric issues, like whether the US Census Bureau and other government agencies were going to classify Mexican Americans as white or colored. The Longoria incident put the movement back on track. The story of the rise of Mexican American leadership in the 1920s and their partial disconnect from their constituents over these issues requires further explanation. This story illustrates the reciprocal roles played by the Mexican American community in raising the significance level of the Longoria incident and in uniting and enhancing the Mexican American community's effectiveness in its fight for Hispanic civil rights.

The war also had something to do with Mexican American leadership's ability to mobilize Tejanos more fully than in past incidents of discrimination. Mexican American soldiers integrated into existing combat units. They were not segregated like black soldiers.[50] These Tejano GIs, sailors, and airmen had experienced a measure of social equality in the military. This made them unwilling to suffer racial prejudice upon their return home, as they had before they left.

The text of García's initial January 10, 1949, telegram to Johnson soliciting support in the protest captures the impact of the war on Tejanos' thinking about the Longoria matter. Speaking for the American GI Forum (AGIF) membership as a whole, García stated that the funeral director's actions were "in direct contradiction of the principals for which this American soldier made the supreme sacrifice." He identified those principles as equality and individual liberty. He charged that the Longoria incident represented "a typical example of discriminatory practices which occur intermittently in this state."[51]

García's telegram successfully married the post–World War II patriotism of the nation to the revived Mexican American civil rights movement in South Texas and the rest of the Southwest. Messages from other persons of Mexican descent independently struck the same chord, suggesting that this common Hispanic interpretation of the affair was a natural outgrowth of wartime and post-wartime sentiments within the Mexican American community. Santos Delgado's letter to Johnson offers insights into these renewed feelings of opposition to racism within the collective Tejano psyche. A resident of Port Arthur, Texas, he started out by condemning discrimination against a dead American soldier. Delgado then solicited the senator's support for ending all discrimination against Mexican Americans:

> All of my life I have experienced this same discrimination and was wondering if you could do anything in Washington to stop such things that happen here (Texas) in a free country. I was borned [sic] in the United States of Mexican parentage and am a high school graduate and feel that I am as good as any other man and no better.[52]

García organized a public protest on the evening of January 11, at the Lamar Elementary School cafeteria in Corpus Christi. He admonished "all veterans, their families, and the general public to come, NO EXCUSES."[53] Local Spanish-speaking radio stations began reporting developments in the protest movement. Beatrice and Félix's daughter, Adela, came to the meeting along with the rest of the Morenos. The Longorias attended as well, as did hundreds of both families' neighbors and friends. García offered everyone three choices: wake Longoria at the funeral chapel (Kennedy had since relented and offered its use), and then bury him in his hometown's racially divided cemetery; conduct the burial at one of the national cemeteries within the state; or lay Longoria to rest in Arlington National Cemetery, with national and international dignitaries in attendance.

With Beatrice's permission, they put it to a vote. The choice was near unanimous. Denial of the funeral chapel had affronted the honor of Longoria, his family, and the Tejano community as a whole. Such an offense could only be forgiven by an act or acts honoring those injured. And the most honorific of the three choices was Arlington National Cemetery, the resting place of national heroes.

Soon the entire Mexican American community, from Corpus Christi to Three Rivers and southward to the border, got caught up in the impending burial arrangements. Once the Longoria family decided to lay Félix in the nation's most hallowed ground, García and the AGIF began soliciting contributions to send Beatrice, Adela, and other members of the Longoria family to this grand ceremony. The response overwhelmed AGIF officials. García had to refuse donations after a few days because too much money poured into his office. Virtually all of the contributions came in small amounts, with short notes written in Spanish attached to them. My translations do them injustice; much of the enthusiasm and poignancy is lost. Here are just a few examples of these letters. "I heard about the discrimination case and the Longoria family's needs on radio K.W.B.U. I am sending fifty cents for everyone in our family" (signed Juan Moya and his wife, $6.50 total.)[54] "I gladly contribute to Mrs. Félix Longoria to cover the costs of attending her son's funeral" (signed G. C. Flores of Brady, Texas.)[55] Roy Navarro and his family sent five dollars. By way of explanation he penciled in, "I was very sorry to hear about this boy funeral's not being admitted at this funeral home, I cried and kept looking at my brother's picture who died for the sake of this country to [sic]."[56] Some merely signed their names *"un amigo"* (a friend) and said they contributed to right a wrong.[57] Church groups held cakewalks and raffles. The League of United Latin American Citizens (LULAC) councils staged money-raising events. Principals of Mexican Ward schools took up collections, as did Mexican American businesses all over the region. Radio stations broadcast information and provided a forum for public comment on the controversy.[58]

Later, in describing what the incident had meant to him, García's response probably approximated the thoughts of the rest of the area's Tejano community: "We, as Veterans, did not fight a system like the Nazi Socialist system . . . in order to come back to our own state and live and tolerate such humiliation."[59] Second, he personalized the Longoria incident. He said he knew about general problems facing his people, such as high infant mortality rates, high unemployment rates, and low educational levels. But these statistics represented cold facts. They did not have voices and faces. They did not inspire emotional commitment. Félix Longoria was a person, a fellow soldier.

García knew members of his widow's family even before the incident. They were his patients. Beatrice's sister, Sara, belonged to a young women's club sponsored by the AGIF. García had intervened a year earlier when a skating rink denied her and her friends access because "Mexicans were not allowed." "This injustice [the Longoria incident] happened on my front door." To García, this was almost a "family matter."[60]

On February 16, 1949, just thirty-seven days after García fired off his telegrams that converted this private dispute over the use of a small-town funeral chapel into a national and international controversy over anti-patriotism and racial or ethnic discrimination, Longoria was buried in pomp and circumstance at Arlington National Cemetery. Johnson's office orchestrated the event; Johnson charged one of his staffers, Horace "Posh" Busby, with making the arrangements.[61] The members of Longoria's family represented a minority of those that came. High-ranking representatives of both the US and Mexican governments attended along with a large press corps from both nations. A lot was at stake: Texas state and US national images, the Bracero negotiations, and the private grieving of the Longoria family. Mexico sent its ambassador to the United States, the renowned historian Dr. Justo Sierra, and a Mexican military honor guard. Major General Harry Vaughan, President Harry Truman's personal military advisor, and Paul Reveley, the chief of the State Department's Division of Mexican Affairs and overseer of the US Bracero negotiations, represented the US government.[62] They led a US military honor guard who, along with their Mexican military counterparts, performed during the ceremony. Texas National Democrats, Johnson and his wife, Lady Bird, and US Representative John Lyle of Corpus Christi came too. Texas Regulars boycotted the burial. They clung to their perception that the incident was a trumped-up controversy to embarrass them and the state.

A light rain fell and a cool breeze blew during the entire ceremony. Both chilled the crowd. Busby had an awning and a small number of chairs set up to shield the Longoria family from the elements and to provide them comfort. Beatrice reserved two seats next to her for Johnson and his wife. Truman's office also requested seating in the front row for its two representatives and the Mexican ambassador. Busby faced a real dilemma. His president, the leader of the National Democratic Party, wanted prominent and public space for his representatives. The dead soldier's wife wanted Johnson and his wife seated at her side. Busby's boss rejected both requests and ordered him to reserve the tent for the Longoria family alone. Everyone else would stand in the rain. Johnson told Busby that he was not going to turn this moment of family grieving into a photo op for the president, for the National Democrats, for the State Department, for his own political gain and public image, or for US and Latin American presses. Busby and John Connally tried to reason with Johnson, but he was adamant on this point. They had no choice but to follow his orders. In the end, and to Busby's and Connally's chagrin, everybody but the Longoria family did stand in the rain throughout the burial. Johnson and his wife had positioned themselves next to a tree in a spot, according to Busby, that could not provide a photo angle that would capture them and any of the rest of the burial party.

With Longoria's burial at Arlington, the controversy faded from national consciousness. Ironically, the event that spawned it, a dispute over a dead soldier's family's right to wake him in a small-town funeral chapel, never took place. In the end, there was no wake. Denial of this private family ceremony resulted in a far more public event that redeemed wounded family and Mexican American public honor and post–World War II US patriotism.

Conclusions

The national US press had rallied behind this local Hispanic protest movement thanks to the efforts of Héctor P. García and the junior US senator from Texas. The efforts of García effectively connected a local event to the statewide Mexican American civil rights movement. García already knew, and in some cases had closely worked with, middle-class World War I– and World War II–bred activists such as J. T. Canales of Brownsville; Gus García, Alonso Perales, and Manuel González, San Antonio lawyers; Drs. Carlos Castañeda and George P. Sánchez, university professors in Austin; and John Herrera, a Houston businessman. The Longoria incident gave García the cause and his connections and experience gave him the means to reenergize the Mexican American civil rights movement in South Texas and beyond. He and other Mexican American middle-class professionals and businessmen had little trouble accomplishing this task because of the nature of the Longoria affront. Social discrimination was something Tejanos of whatever means had all experienced. Every Tejano could relate to this type of discrimination. As a result, the Hispanic community protested with levels of intensity and unity rare for the region. The Longoria affair focused Mexican Americans' varied and pent-up frustrations on a single incident, an affair of community honor.

But what made this "affair of honor" so much more public and influential than numerous other cases of discrimination against Tejanos in South Texas? What about the Longoria incident reversed a century-old tradition of relatively unchecked Anglo discrimination in South Texas? A number of factors did. Timing certainly played an important role in magnifying the impact of the Longoria incident on the Mexican American experience at local, state, national, and international levels. The controversy came during a fissure in Texas's political culture between Texas Regulars and Texas National Democrats. This opening provided an opportunity for subaltern or disempowered Hispanics to negotiate more privilege within the broader regional community by aligning themselves with one of these two competing Anglo political factions.

Ongoing Bracero Program negotiations also added to the importance of the incident. The controversy threatened to forestall this labor agreement that was so favorable to Texas and broader southwestern US economic interests. Mexican braceros contributed heavily to the Southwest's participation in the rise of the Sunbelt economy during the post–World War II period, stretching from about 1946 to 1964.

Leadership played a critical role in magnifying the importance of the dispute. The controversy broke during the emergence of two gifted leaders within the state. From the Texas Anglo community came Johnson, who a few months earlier had won a hotly contested US Senate race against former Governor Coke Stevenson, one of the most powerful figures in the Texas Regular camp. The fact that Anglos represented the bulk of the electorate, the controversy surrounding his election, and the timing of the Longoria dispute—just six days after Johnson was sworn in—made him an unlikely collaborator with García in this dispute. Johnson had too much to risk. Connally told him as much. Connally later remembered an argument they had during an elevator ride to Johnson's office over the senator's taking sides in the Longoria case. The two refused to speak to each other for two weeks afterward. Connally saw Johnson's participation in the dispute as a potentially mortal blow to his boss's rising political career; the senator saw it as the right thing to do. In Connally's mind, Johnson acted foolishly; he was politically vulnerable, a brand-new senator entering Washington politics under a cloud of dispute over his contested election victory.[63] This controversy could ruin his political career. Julie Pycior, a leading authority on Johnson's relations with Mexican Americans, argues that the senator's long association with the South Texas Hispanic community prior to January 1949 predisposed him to respond the way he did to García's telegram.[64] Johnson's own World War II naval experience likely played a role as well. Whatever his motives, Johnson contributed mightily to mobilizing national public support for Tejanos in the dispute.

The Longoria controversy provides us with important insights into the character and personality of Johnson, one of the most enigmatic figures in recent US political history. This 1949 controversy demonstrated that he was a far more complex man than many portray him. Some, like Robert Caro, paint him as an overly ambitious workaholic driven by a quest for power.[65] The Longoria incident reveals a very human side of the man, a side that sometimes could—and in this case, apparently did—override his personal ambitions. From the outset, Johnson went out of his way to risk his young and tenuous political career through his very public participation in the Longoria controversy. Then, at the end of the ordeal, he passed up the opportunity to reap merited public acclaim for his actions through his high-profile presence at Longoria's burial. Perhaps the complex personality revealed in this brief affair provides valuable insights into how this sometimes ruthless southern politician could later compile the record he did as president in successfully promoting the most ambitious civil rights agenda of the twentieth century. The extraordinary leadership of this young Anglo politician contributed to the surprising impact of the Longoria dispute.

A leader of equally remarkable courage and talent emerged from the Hispanic community at the same time Johnson rose from the ranks of the Anglo population. His name was Héctor Pérez García. An active member of the first chapter of LULAC, and founder of the American G.I. Forum just months before the onset of the Longoria affair, this young doctor and veteran was equally suited to lead and shape the Mexican American and national reaction to the controversy. García constructed the incident in such a way that it successfully married Mexican Americans' struggle for civil rights to post–World War II national patriotism. In so doing, he also helped to redefine Mexican American identity in the national consciousness. By exposing the racist and unpatriotic nature of the funeral director's actions, García redrew Americans' image of Mexican Americans from aliens to patriots. This transformation of Mexican American identity within the national consciousness became one of the cornerstones of the Mexican American civil rights movement, from 1949 to the present.

Two additional interrelated conditions made this case of "social" discrimination, as opposed to more disturbing physical or legal discrimination, so significant in the eyes of observers, like the Mexican Consul in Corpus Christi. First, the incident had drama, a story that captured and held the attention of an audience stretching from Argentina to Michigan. The dramatic nature of the controversy, with its well-defined heroes and villains, its international implications, its bigger than life actors—García, Johnson, Connally, Beatrice Longoria, Tom Kennedy, Representative Jeff Grey, and Governor Beauford Jester, several of whom went on to become major figures in the United States—all helped to capture the attention and imagination of nearly all the Americas.[66]

Second, by tying wounded Mexican American honor to wounded World War II US patriotism, this incident not only attracted public attention, it generated public emotion. This emotion, perhaps as much as any other factor, contributed to the unlikely importance of this otherwise mundane example of the social discrimination that South Texas Mexican Americans endured on a daily basis. Hardly a US family existed that had not suffered a wounded or dead loved one during World War II. This emotional connection with the affront visited on the family of Private Félix Longoria, a fallen hero, resonated throughout the nation. From California to New York, from Minnesota to Louisiana, people connected with this insult to a dead US soldier and his family as well as to South Texas Mexican Americans. And that connection brought with it personal pain that elicited a strong emotional outcry.[67] This widespread emotional response across the United States represented one of the most important explanations to the unlikely significance of the Longoria incident in Mexican American civil rights history. For a brief period, the Longoria controversy focused everyone's attention on what most considered a regional problem: Anglo discrimination against Mexican Americans.

Finally, the Longoria dispute confirmed in the minds of Mexican American activists the benefits of outside support in their struggle for citizenship and social equality. National and international backing enormously empowered

Tejanos in the Longoria dispute. In this sense, one implication latent in the incident went far beyond the controversy itself. This affair of honor helped to direct the thrust and tone of political activism within the Mexican American community after the 1940s toward a national audience. At the same time the incident helped to forge new political connections and strengthen old political alliances between emerging Mexican American activist leaders like García and rising Anglo politicians like Johnson. Forty years later, these were the significances García saw in the controversy. In his opinion, such developments accelerated the Mexican American civil rights movement and more closely linked South Texas to the national political environment. Lessons learned from the Longoria incident contributed to later developments like the rise of the Viva Kennedy and Viva Johnson movements as well as to heightened Mexican American participation in state and national politics.[68]

Notes

1. This essay is based on my previously published monograph, *Félix Longoria's Wake: Bereavement, Racism, and the Rise of Mexican American Activism* (Austin: University of Texas Press, 2003).

2. See box 2, folder Longoria, Félix, Paul J. Reveley to Johnson, March 8, 1949, Pre-Presidential Confidential File (hereafter PPCF), Lyndon Baines Johnson Presidential Library, Austin (LBJ Library).

3. See "Blacklisted Counties" (by the Mexican government), box 1989/19, file 9, City Discrimination Files, Good Neighbor Commission, Texas State Archives, Austin (hereafter TSA).

4. Beatrice Longoria, Adela Longoria de Cera, and Héctor P. García, interview by author, May 5, 1990, and Beatrice Longoria and Adela Longoria de Cera, interview by author, June 1, 1990, both in Dr. Héctor P. García Papers, Special Collections and Archives, Texas A&M University–Corpus Christi (hereafter García Papers); "Minority Report on the Longoria Investigation," April 7, 1949, 51st Legislature, *Texas House Journal*, 1424, TSA.

5. I borrowed my spatial delineation of the Valley from José Limón, one of the leading scholars of Mexican American culture and a native son of this region. See his introduction to Jovita González's *Dew on the Thorn* (Houston: Arte Público, 1984), xvi.

6. Michael C. Meyer and William L. Sherman, *The Course of Mexican History*, 5th ed. (New York: Oxford University Press, 1995), 552–53; Raymond Vernon, "Mexico's

Economic Development, 1910–1940," in *Revolution in Mexico: Years of Upheaval, 1910–1940*, ed. James W. Wilkie and Albert L. Michaels (New York: Knopf, 1969), 24–26; Roger D. Hansen, *The Politics of Mexican Development* (Baltimore: Johns Hopkins University Press, 1971), 29–30; and Alan Knight, *The Mexican Revolution*, 2nd ed. (Lincoln: University of Nebraska Press, 1990), 2: 406–7, 414–15.

7. Héctor P. García, interview by author, March 15, 1995 and Amador García, interview by author, March 26, 1995, both in García Papers.

8. Manuel Servín, *The Mexican-Americans: An Awakening Minority* (Beverly Hills: Glencoe, 1970), 32.

9. Paul S. Taylor, *An American-Mexican Frontier: Nueces County, Texas* (Chapel Hill: University of North Carolina Press, 1934), 128–29.

10. David Montejano, *Anglos and Mexicans in the Making of Texas, 1836-1986* (Austin: University of Texas Press, 1987), 110–13.

11. Ibid., 113–17.

12. Mario T. García, *Mexican Americans: Leadership, Ideology, and Identity, 1930–1960* (New Haven: Yale University Press, 1989), 1.

13. Herein I use the term *middle class* in a relative socioeconomic context. I say relative because the income and social status of these individuals did not necessarily equate with Anglo middle-class individuals of the time. Neither did they enjoy comparable social status to Anglos with similar training and occupations. Many of these individuals earned much less than their professional or occupational counterparts in the Anglo population. Within the Mexican American community, however, these new leaders did enjoy at least middle-level wealth and social rank. See García, *Mexican Americans*, 2–3, 16, 19, 21, and especially 227–231.

14. Ibid., 36–38. David Montejano, *Anglos and Mexicans in the Making of Texas, 1836–1986* (Austin: University of Texas Press, 1987), 260, 270–71.

15. García, *Mexican Americans*, 36–37.

16. Benjamin Márquez, *LULAC: The Evolution of a Mexican American Political Organization* (Austin: University of Texas Press, 1993), 28, 30–33, 40.

17. Ibid., 54.

18. Anthony Quiroz ably treats the theme of Tejanos' struggles for citizenship in *Claiming Citizenship: Mexican Americans in Victoria, Texas* (College Station: Texas A&M University Press, 2005).

19. Wolf cited in David J. Weber, *The Spanish Frontier in North America* (New Haven: Yale University Press, 1992), 13.

20. Social scientists and historians describe the growing sense of "otherness" resulting from ethnic discrimination by nativists in response to wide-scale immigration into an area. The immigrant and ethnically defined community concentrates itself in a defensive posture in response to nativist pressures. See Alejandro Portes

and Robert L. Bach, *Latin Journey: Cuban and Mexican Immigrants in the United States* (Berkeley: University of California Press, 1985), 33–34.

21. Carlos E. Castañeda, "The Second Rate Citizen and Democracy," in *Are We Good Neighbors?*, Alonso S. Perales (San Antonio: Artes Gráficas, 1948), 19.

22. David R. Roediger, *The Wages of Whiteness: Race and the Making of the American Working Class* (New York: Verso, 1991), 12–13.

23. George Norris Green, *The Establishment in Texas Politics: The Primitive Years, 1938–1957* (Norman: University of Oklahoma Press, 1979), 30; Julie Leininger Pycior, *LBJ and Mexican Americans: The Paradox of Power* (Austin: University of Texas Press, 1997), 43–44; and Rupert N. Richardson et al., *Texas: The Lone Star State*, 5th ed. (Englewood Cliffs, NJ: Prentice Hall, 1988), 387.

24. Héctor P. García, oral history interview transcript, April 5, 1974, LBJ Library and Pycior, *LBJ and Mexican Americans*, 48–49.

25. Stanford Dyer and Merrel Knighten, "Discrimination after Death: Lyndon Johnson and Félix Longoria," *Southern Studies* 17 (Winter 1978): 417–18.

26. Héctor P. García to Lyndon B. Johnson, January 10, 1949, PPCF.

27. Ibid.

28. D. B. Hardeman quoted in Merle Miller, *Lyndon: An Oral Biography* (New York: Putnam, 1980), 144–45.

29. John B. Connally, "Memo for the Files, Re: Félix Longoria, January 11, 1949, box 2, folder Longoria, Félix 2, PPCF.

30. Johnson to García, January 11, 1949, García Papers.

31. Green, *Establishment in Texas Politics*, 45–46. Actually, Green devotes an entire chapter to a detailed account and assessment of both Democratic and Republican opposition to Roosevelt's policies within Texas. See chapter 4, "Rebellion Against the New Deal, 1944."

32. Much of the description of Texas politics during the 1930s and 1940s herein is based on conversations with the late Texas historian Joe B. Frantz. Frantz, a senior at the University of Texas in 1937, was shocked when one of his instructors, Ray E. Lee, resigned his $1,800/year position to campaign for Johnson during his first Congressional campaign. In his undergraduate wisdom, Frantz exhibited shock at Lee's gamble. Later he watched Lee with envy as he represented US agencies in the Middle East and Jamaica. Lee eventually became postmaster of Austin before making a sizable living in the insurance industry. Frantz also became an intense Johnson watcher for the next thirty-six years. For more conventional documentation of this point, see Green, *Establishment in Texas Politics*; John B. Connally and Joe B. Frantz, interviews by author, April 1, 1991, García Papers; Allan Shivers and Joe B. Frantz, interview, May 29, 1970; Hobart Taylor and Frantz, interview, January 29, 1972; Coke Stevenson and Frantz, interview, date unknown; Jim Wright and Frantz, interview,

June 30, 1969; J. J. Pickle and Frantz, interview, May 31, 1970 (no. 1) and August
25, 1971 (no. 4); and Gerald Mann and Frantz, interview, October 12, 1968, all LBJ
Library; Homer P. Rainey, *The Tower and the Dome: A Free University Versus Political
Control* (Boulder: Pruett 1971); Evan Anders, *Boss Rule in South Texas: The Progressive
Era* (Austin: University of Texas Press, 1982); and Montejano, *Anglos and Mexicans.*

33. Travis Bryan to Johnson, March 21, 1949, box 3, file Longoria, Félix folder 2,
PPCF.

34. Ibid., box 2, file Longoria, Félix, folder 1, PPCF.

35. W. G. Luce to Johnson, February 3, 1949, box 3, file Longoria, Félix, folder 2,
PPCF.

36. Wick Fowler, "The Félix Longoria Incident," *Dallas Morning News*, January 31,
1949, in box 3, folder Longoria, Félix, PPCF.

37. *Herald* (Live Oak County), January 20, 1949, in García Papers.

38. Box 3, folder Longoria, Félix, PPCF.

39. Gus García to Johnson, April 16, 1949, box 3, folder Longoria, Félix, PPCF,
LBJ Library; *Dallas Morning News*, May 12, 1949, editorial page in the "Félix Longoria Burial Scrapbook," unnumbered pages, Texas Attorney General's Office, files
stored in the TSA; 51st Legislature's *House Journal*, April 7, 1949, 331, 334, 1420; Pycior,
LBJ and Mexican Americans, 71–72.

40. Frank "Posh" Oltorf, interview, August 3, 1971, 18, LBJ Library.

41. Box 2, file Longoria, Félix, folder 1, PPCF.

42. Fowler, "Félix Longoria Incident."

43. Box 3, file Longoria, Félix, folders 1–2, PPCF.

44. Loose bundles of newspapers covering the period January 11–March 31, 1949,
Collections Deposit Library, University of Texas Libraries, University of Texas at
Austin (hereafter Deposit Library).

45. Patrick J. Carroll, *Blacks in Colonial Veracruz: Race, Ethnicity, and Regional
Development* (Austin: University of Texas Press, 1991), table 6, 95; and Nicolás
Sánchez-Albornoz, *The Population of Latin America: A History*, trans. W. A. R.
Richardson (Berkeley: University of California Press, 1974), table 6.1, 184.

46. John B. Connally, "Summary of Conversations with Mr. Paul J. Reveley of the
State Department," February 25, 1949, box 2, file Longoria, Félix, PPCF.

47. *El Universal*, February 17, 1949, 6–7; Ibid., January 13, 1949, 5–6; Ibid., January
20, 1949, 7, 24; *El Popular*, February 17, 1949, 2–3, 5, 7; *La Prensa*, January 15, 1949, 1–2;
Ibid., February 20, 1949, 1–5; *El Excelsior*, January 13, 1949, 2; *La Prensa Gráfica*, January 14, 1949, 4–6; *Novedades*, January 14, 1949, 1–2; *Mexico City Herald*, January 15, 1949,
1–2, all in the Newspaper Collections Deposit Library, University of Texas at Austin.
Clippings of many of the articles listed can also be found in the previously cited
Longoria Burial Scrapbook.

48. Connally, "Summary of Conversations with Mr. Paul J. Reveley"; and Paul J. Reveley to Johnson, March 8, 1949, box 2, folder Longoria, Félix, both in PPCF, and John B. Connally, interview by Joe B. Frantz and author, April 4, 1991, García Papers.

49. Márquez, *LULAC*, 1, 15, 17 and R. Anthony Quiroz, "Claiming Citizenship: Class and Consensus in a Twentieth Century Mexican American Community" (PhD diss., University of Iowa, 1999), 138–39, 450.

50. Raul Morín, *Among the Valiant: Mexican Americans in WWII and Korea* (Alhambra, CA: Borden, 1963), 84.

51. Box 2, folder Longoria, Félix, PPCF.

52. Ibid., box 3, folder Longoria, Félix, file 2, PPCF.

53. Ibid.

54. Juan Moya to García, January 15, 1949, García Papers.

55. G. C. Flores and Pablo Estrada to García, January 13, 1949, García Papers.

56. Mr. and Mrs. Roy Navarro to Dear Sir, January 14, 1949, García Papers.

57. These letters can be found in the uncataloged sections of the García Papers.

58. Ibid.

59. Quoted in Guadalupe San Miguel, Jr., *"Let All of Them Take Heed": Mexican Americans and the Campaign for Educational Equality in Texas, 1910–1981* (Austin: University of Texas Press, 1987), 116.

60. Héctor P. García, interview by Robert Miranda, March 23, 1989, García Papers.

61. This account of Longoria's burial ceremony comes from six sources. Horace Busby and Michael Gillette, interview, August 16, 1988, Oral History Collection, LBJ Library; Longoria interview, May 5, 1990; Héctor P. García and Joe B. Frantz, interview, August 21, 1985, García Papers; Connally interview, April 4, 1991; "Burial at Arlington," *New York Times*, February 17, 1949, box 3, file Longoria, Félix, folder 2, PPCF; and Connally, "Summary of Conversations."

62. Pycior, *LBJ and Mexican Americans*, 71.

63. Connally interview, April 4, 1991, García Papers.

64. Pycior, *LBJ and Mexican Americans*, 68–73.

65. Robert A. Caro, *The Path to Power: The Years of Lyndon Johnson* (New York: Knopf, 1982), 170.

66. For more on the significance of drama in explaining strong public feeling and extraordinary action, see Victor Turner, *Dramas, Fields, and Metaphors: Symbolic Action in Human Society* (Ithaca: Cornell University Press, 1974), 2, 17, 19.

67. For more on the importance of emotion in explaining unusually strong collective responses to human events, see Renato Rosaldo, *Culture and Truth: The Remaking of Social Analysis* (Boston: Beacon Press, 1993), 14–15, 37.

68. García interviews, March 23, 1989 and March 15, 1995, García Papers.

LEGAL, POLITICAL, AND LABOR ACTIVISTS

Figure 7.1. Dr. Héctor Pérez García, founder of the American GI Forum. Dr. Héctor P. García Papers, Special Collections and Archives, Mary and Jeff Bell Library, Texas A&M University–Corpus Christi.

7

Dr. Héctor Pérez García

Giant of the Twentieth Century

Carl Allsup

Héctor Pérez García is the central figure of the Mexican American generation. Yet he remains unknown to most non-Latino Americans and inadequately recognized or understood by most Latino Americans themselves. This essay will highlight Dr. García's life and accomplishments in order to address this issue.

Héctor García was born in 1914 in Mexico. His father and mother, both teachers, were of the lower middle class. In 1912 the family was a part of the great Mexican migration of refugees from the chaos and violence of the Mexican Revolution of 1910–1920. Settling in Mercedes, Texas, by way of the nearby town of Thayer with his younger brother, Héctor's father shared work in the family *mercado* (department store) and eventually owned a clothing store.

Héctor and his siblings lived a lower middle-class life by *Mexicano*-Tejano standards; economic stability provided some consistency of life changes but still compelled work in the cotton fields. His parents mandated education above all. He came to understand that opportunity was influenced by

DOI: 10.5876/9781607323372.c007

environment and never accepted any Anglo notion of white supremacy or Mexican inferiority. As his siblings absorbed the same teachings, family life was organized around intellectual development and pursuit of opportunity. Because of his superior intellect, García was one of the handfuls of Mexican Americans to matriculate from the University of Texas at Austin during this time. He became a physician in 1942. His constant encounters with Anglo racism were always understood as just that: Anglo-American racism. One of the best examples of such oppression was the tri-level school system in Texas, which separated Anglos and African Americans by legal segregation and Mexican American students for presumed language deficiency despite minimal effort by Anglo administrators to evaluate any level of English or Spanish proficiency. As García traversed through this miasma and observed the economic oppression imposed by the agribusiness oligarchs and their political allies, he made careful note to prepare for what he understood would be his life mission: the betterment of his people. The precise vehicle emerged with the creation of the American GI Forum (AGIF) in 1948.[1]

From 1942 to 1945, García served in five combat zones in Europe during World War II. While stationed in Italy, he married Wenela (Wanda) Fusillo. After the war, he returned to Corpus Christi, Texas, as a young doctor and opened a medical practice that lasted for almost fifty years. He immediately engaged in community activities as a member of the League of United Latin American Citizens (LULAC), as a health practitioner and an advocate for Mexican American participation in Corpus Christi and South Texas society. A seminal moment occurred in 1947, when he experienced a serious medical condition that plagued him the rest of his life. While recovering he listened to an insulting and very critical radio program by South Texas Anglo school superintendents on the inferiority of Mexican American schoolchildren; García pledged to himself that through his faith he would devote his life to his people.[2]

The 1945 G.I. Bill of Rights was one of the most comprehensive social programs of the twentieth century. It provided benefits and opportunities for approximately 11 million US veterans. It significantly altered the economic and educational landscape for the US working class; it also incorporated all the nuance and less subtle characteristics of the ideology and material structures of the overwhelming Anglo belief in racial superiority. The massive bureaucracy and its administrators mostly ignored its failure to deliver the same level of services to veterans of color as it did to whites. The experience caused the coalescence of hundreds of Mexicano veterans in South Texas and, more specifically, Corpus Christi. Because of the G.I. Bill's need for local physicians, it allowed García to treat Mexican American veterans in Corpus Christi. Due to his interaction with these veterans, and because of his experience hearing public school administrators comment publicly on the radio waves about Mexican American inferiority, he led a push for the creation of a new organization in March 1948, when the AGIF organized in Corpus Christi.[3]

The immediate effects of the AGIF targeted a restoration of veterans' benefits and then proceeded, by the momentum of success, to seek redress through a broader push for civil rights. So why does, as Ignacio M. García so aptly states, the later scholarship largely dismiss this fundamental evolution of the Mexican American community?[4] From the inception of the AGIF its ethos is clear as is that of García and his fellow members. Prejudice, discrimination, oppression, and Anglo ideology based on a belief in racial superiority are understood. However, unlike the analysis of the subsequent Chicano movement, those realities are not considered fundamental or core characteristics of the American dream. Rather, as Martin Luther King, Jr., would present in his "I Have a Dream" oration of 1963, their elimination is not only possible but mandated by the founding principals of the Declaration of Independence and the Constitution of 1789. García had no doubt that reform, not reconstruction, was necessary and achievable. And as did King, he underestimated the narrow "promise" of these documents that had defended Anglo privileges for the past 200 years. At the same time, the climate of the postwar anti-communist hysteria that defined the Cold War gave mainstream society the language and ideology to resist changes as un-American. As a patriotic veteran, however, García and the founding Forumeers consciously chose the name American GI Forum to demonstrate a pragmatic response to the race-baiting anti-communist rhetoric of both political parties. It also incorporated a sincere belief in the fundamental principles of a society formed to represent and advance democracy, liberty, and individual opportunity (i.e., the American mythology). García never altered his commitment to including Mexican Americans in that society.[5]

In the next thirty years, this core belief would guide and center García's efforts on many issues as Mexican Americans confronted Anglo oppression.

García and the AGIF emphasized their patriotism and participation in World War II as the ultimate evidence of the right to full equality and participation in American society as fully qualified American citizens. In the violent context of anti-communist volatility, one is perplexed as to what other rational options existed. The embrace of Cold War liberalism fit the deep confidence that García held in the promise of what I earlier called "the American mythology." This worldview allowed for the first major triumph of García and the AGIF against the Texas Anglo oppressors in the Félix Longoria affair.[6]

Patrick J. Carroll's *Felix Longoria's Wake: Bereavement, Racism, and the Rise of Mexican American Activism*, is a master narrative and an analysis of this moment. As Carroll emphatically describes, it is the first moment in the postwar United States where the fact of the Mexican American struggle acquired national attention. In 1948 the refusal of the funeral home in Three Rivers, Texas, to allow the Longoria family to hold a wake for the veteran because of Anglo racism escalated to a national issue. The widow of Private Longoria sought advice from Longoria's sister, who knew of the initial efforts of García and the AGIF, and both women sought his help. García contacted the funeral home director, listened to his racialist rationalizations, and began a process that in many ways became a template for future activity. Immediate communication ensued with the forum membership, all state officials, Texas congressional representatives, and national leaders. Incorporating the themes of patriotism and sacrifice (the service and death of Longoria in the Philippines on a volunteer mission), the mythology of the American creed, Cold War tension, and the Mexican American right to claim citizenship, García and the AGIF established, for the first time in the twentieth century, a national context for Mexican American civil rights, as compared to the more Texas-oriented vision of LULAC. He also began a twenty-year relationship and quasi-partnership with Senator Lyndon Baines Johnson, who, with some risk, took up Longoria's cause and offered to bury Longoria in Arlington National Cemetery, an offer the family accepted.[7]

In phase two of this event, García encountered the common response of Anglo distortion and misrepresentation, overlaid with the clichéd charge against him and the AGIF as "outside agitators" disturbing the local racial harmony. It was particularly the courage of the Longoria family, most especially Longoria's father and widow, who stood against and denounced the all-too-frequent Anglo tactics of intimidation and fully acknowledged García as the inspiration for their response. After Longoria's burial, the Texas legislature conducted an "investigation" and promulgated a whitewashed report. They ultimately lost this confrontation when a member of the investigative committee (Frank Oltorf) refused to sign the report. Another investigator later recanted and wrote a critical "minority" report. The entire affair galvanized the Tejano community and Southwest Mexican Americans, catapulted the AGIF into a national organization within ten years, and identified García as a major Mexican American advocate.[8]

A further comment is merited. This moment is analogous to Rosa Parks's refusal to give up her seat on a bus in Montgomery, Alabama. That incident was crucial to the post–World War II African American civil rights movement. After Parks's arrest, the community of color erupted against the egregious acts of white racism in a manner similar to the reaction of Mexican Americans in 1949. But an important distinction separates this action from the Longoria affair. Martin Luther King, Jr., emerged from the Montgomery bus boycott as almost an accidental national leader (he had no role in the organized resistance of Parks). By contrast, García fully envisioned, organized, and implemented public reaction. Of course, the determination of the Longoria family is the primary reason for their success, but without the relentless commitment and García's calculated, skillful manipulation of national symbols and values, the Longoria affair could not have become the Rosa Parks analogy for the Mexican American community. And yet, the history is almost absurdly underplayed if even acknowledged in Chicano/Mexican historical studies. That gap represents a general failure to include Mexican Americans in a comprehensive narrative.[9]

As stated, the Longoria affair intensified the AGIF's organizational effort, and García was tireless as the central organizer. He attracted young men and women of the lower middle class and working class to create their own local AGIF chapters and sustain their growth. As witnessed by many of those people, García would speak to five Mexican American veterans or one hundred (there were no other membership restrictions except being a veteran). His presentations involved several thousand miles of travel in his automobile. The Cadillac he drove aroused criticisms of his middle-class values, but as he explained once, it was the biggest car to accommodate the most assistants and materials. He challenged local and regional Anglo power and mandated Mexican American advocacy. He received and ignored several death threats through the years. His message was consistent: one had to be a patriotic and lawful citizen, but Mexicanos had already achieved that status and should advocate that reality and resist with nonviolent, legal methods, but with emphatic clarity in the *equality* of Mexican *Americans* to any Anglo-American. García made considerable use of cultural values such as family, integrity, community history, collective identity, and religious faith (with frequent appropriate notice to reluctant or cautious Catholic clergy that anti-discrimination was an appropriate cause to pursue). Dues for membership were 25 cents per year. By 1958 the AGIF, with García as national chair, was in twenty states and a political force.[10]

The specific issues of oppression and exclusion confronted by García and the AGIF sometimes reflected regional circumstances, but the primary programs generated more often from the Texas experience. Thus, LULAC and the AGIF often combined forces to combat discrimination in several areas, including educational segregation. Texas school officials created and enforced a separate school structure within the legal white/black segregated system. It was based on "pedagogical deficiency" (i.e., the inability of the Mexican American children to speak English). Student evaluations supposedly occurred on a regular basis, and it was a "coincidence" that virtually all Mexican American students took four grades to acquire English language proficiency. Instruction could be in separate classrooms or buildings, but with the legal segregation of African American children, Texas employed a triple school system.[11]

In the issue of equal, quality education, opportunity is central to all movements of people of color in the United States, and it was central to García's goals and objectives. The glaring bigotry of the Anglo educational leadership resisted with the assuredness of their self-cherished entitlement and by their believed racial and class superiority. Hence, García joined with LULAC to demolish the separation of Mexican American students. The two groups provided a team of AGIF lawyers, who proved again and again the fraudulent core of the Anglo-devised process. One of the many horrific results of segregation was the placement of ten-year-old Mexican American students in the same classes with six-year-old Anglo students. Ten years of incremental success culminated in the *Driscoll* decision of 1957, where James DeAnda, the lead AGIF attorney in this struggle, proved that Linda Pérez did *not* speak Spanish when she was placed in the four-year English delinquent process.

The federal judge was particularly strident and harsh in his denunciation of Texas Anglo educational leaders.[12]

Guadalupe San Miguel depicts with great clarity the efforts of LULAC and the AGIF but seems to emphasize the work of LULAC as the sustaining force, when it was the energy and relentless activity of García, DeAnda, and other AGIF members in the surveillance and reporting of the constant attempts of Anglo school officials to circumvent the victories in state and federal courts to dismantle the triple school system. San Miguel rightly points out that the elimination of this fraudulent and bigoted structure did not bring about equality of education due to political impotence. But this is a startling and also obvious conclusion. García never proclaimed that the AGIF program was a complete success, but certainly the elimination of the triple school system was a major blow against the Anglo educational structure based on the ideology of white supremacy.[13] For example, no historian would conclude that equality of educational opportunity has been achieved by the African American community. And none would evaluate the *Brown v. Board of Education of Topeka* decision of 1954 as a failure. Certainly there is debate on all the effects of a history of oppression and the most difficult (at times, seemingly insurmountable) task of confronting those outcomes . . . but failure? García and the AGIF fixed the objective beyond LULAC English learning to equal participation as Mexican Americans. The point to be made here is the failure of most scholars (until recently) to address the enormity of the success of the *Driscoll* decision and the influence of the elimination of the triple school system legal structure in the continuing efforts of *all* Mexican American groups (the Mexican American generation, the Chicano movement, the Hispanic/Latino generation) to achieve the ultimate goal of complete inclusion.

Another significant accomplishment in confronting the US Anglo legal, racialized structure was the *Hernández v. Texas* case decided by the US Supreme Court in 1954. For the first time in American criminal jurisprudence, Mexicans were found to be treated with bias apart from the due process offered white America. Once again, LULAC and the AGIF joined forces to supply a team of attorneys to argue for Pete Hernández before the Supreme Court. At issue was the fact that he had been found guilty of murdering a man in Jackson County, Texas. During his trial, only Anglos were considered for the jury. Upon appeal to the highest court in the land, the county was found guilty of discrimination and Hernández was awarded a new trial. It is also not coincidental or happenstance that two weeks after the *Hernández* case, the Warren Court found 9–0 for *Brown* and rendered unconstitutional the "separate but equal" finding of *Plessy v. Ferguson* in 1896. Again, legal analysts and other American historians have overlooked the obvious; and, as has been commonplace, the leadership of García and the AGIF are virtually unacknowledged. One more vital step toward that goal was coerced by García and the AGIF by Mexican Americans from Anglo society.[14]

Perhaps the most dramatic (and still generally acknowledged in the metanarrative) impact is the leadership and participation of García in state and national political events. As the AGIF was established, and with the success of the Longoria affair, García was viewed by the state and national Democratic Party as a new player. Julie Leininger Pycior, in *LBJ and Mexican Americans: The Paradox of Power* demonstrates that as Johnson's political star rose, ending with his presidency, García fostered an ongoing relationship with him.[15] Even though the AGIF was nonpartisan and explained the political actions of its members as separate from the organization, obviously the members pursued goals and actions parallel to the organization. García was tireless in communicating with Texas and US political figures, and it is no accident that these persons showed up at state and national AGIF meetings and conferences, which is the beginning of a substantive (albeit still minimal) Mexican American presence in the Democratic Party. In 1960, after the defeat of Johnson by John F. Kennedy in the Democratic primary, García led the charge to create Viva Kennedy clubs around the nation.[16]

After the creation of the Viva Kennedy clubs, García and other Tejano political leaders conducted the first national voter registration campaign in the Mexican American community. With the simultaneous efforts in the African American community, stimulated by Kennedy's declared support of Martin Luther King, Jr., in their famous telephone call, the nation's two largest minority groups (African Americans and Mexican Americans) actively participated in the national Democratic Party. As is well known, the African American vote for Kennedy was fundamental to his narrow victory. Yet Anglo historians ignore the equal contribution to that victory by Mexican Americans. Despite the contributions of the Viva Kennedy clubs to his victory, Kennedy's administration failed to fulfill its promise to "reward" the Mexican American community with more appointments to the Democratic

Party and national institutions. This, in turn, caused a conflict and an enduring disagreement between García, the AGIF, and many of its allies, which found continued cooperation with the Democratic Party problematic.

Although stated several times by Johnson, and demonstrated by his clearly popular collaboration with García, there is minimal understanding of how the famous 1964 and 1965 Civil Rights Acts were shaped by García as well as the obvious and well-known influence of King and the African American civil rights movement. Further, Johnson felt limited by his own fight for African American civil rights and the fact that few at the time had any knowledge of, let alone interest in, Mexican American issues. Nevertheless, Johnson appointed Mexican Americans to governmental positions, and for the first time in American history, national civil rights legislation and activities included the Mexican American community. García was at the center of this inclusion, and he often colluded with Johnson's paternalistic personality. García did not ruefully or in any other way accept what he correctly perceived as Johnson's failure to adequately respond to Mexican American needs.[17]

In the well-chronicled, tumultuous period from 1966 to 1972, Johnson's Great Society programs faced challenges on many fronts. First, the programs collided with the chaotic tempest of the Vietnam War. The budget process, the emerging feminist movement, and the eventual countercultural divide in Anglo society severely impacted the already controversial projects. Exacerbating such pressures was the birth of a farmworker movement in California led by César Chávez. Chávez and his supporters resisted agribusiness' political resistance to the demands of Chávez and the United Farm Workers of America. The anger and organized response by Chicano movement supporters dramatically underlined the new, clear Mexican American / Chicano generation divide. Johnson typically dismissed that issue, as he also failed to appoint Mexican Americans at policy-making levels. García presented a strong statement from most major Mexican American leaders demanding a presidential assistant for Mexican American issues. California AGIF chapters picketed the Equal Employment Opportunity Commission (EEOC) to protest Johnson's refusal to appoint enough Mexican Americans to decision-making appointments. Johnson further ignored such specific criticism when he created a White House Conference on Civil Rights, "To Fulfill These Rights," without any reference to Mexican Americans. Finally, in March 1966, the AGIF and other organizations led by García walked out of a regional EEOC meeting. García, fully and with strong critique, condemned Johnson's indifference and failure of commitment. The president produced a 1967 conference on the Mexican American issue in El Paso in October 1967. And though the Chicano element boycotted the hearings, García did not. I have previously stated that both "sides" were right, and both stridently refused to recognize their similar distrust for the Johnson administration and the Democratic Party. But García appeared to be a sellout and a middle-class assimilationist to his Chicano critics (César Chávez excluded). García considered the Chicano movement's organizations naive and counterproductive because they failed to create a national base and emphasized militant rhetoric.[18]

Tensions between García and Chicano activists culminated with disagreements over the Vietnam War. García, like most combat veterans of World War II, Mexican American or otherwise, could not understand those who criticized or refused (draft resistance) to support the United States in war. Those of the Chicano movement were astonished that any group—racial, ethnic, or other—would accept a mandate to prove patriotism. Such requirements were particularly galling to a group that stood in defense of anticolonial movements. Still, García expressed ambivalence about the unfair nature of conscription with exemptions available to mostly middle-class college attendees or those "favored" (overwhelmingly Anglo) by draft boards. The California AGIF broke with the national organization and condemned the United States' use of people of color to fight a nation of color. García did not criticize the California AGIF position but did continually emphasize his support as a patriotic American.[19]

The final issue to be presented in this brief biography of García's participation in the Mexican American social justice movement is the most problematic, controversial, and volatile of his life: immigrant labor (documented and undocumented) and its effect on the Mexican American community. García's most emotional introduction to the terrible plight of migrant workers was when he treated a dying tubercular Mexican mother, laying with her children covered in her blood, in a horrific immigrant camp in 1947. This haunted García the rest of his life; he was quite aware of the exploitation by agribusiness of contract Mexican laborers, undocumented workers, and migrant Mexican American workers. He was also clear of its impact in South Texas. In the post–World War II United States, the presence of contract labor and undocumented workers lowered the prevailing wage for migrant workers. Only gaining an education would pull workers out of the fields and move them into other occupations.[20]

Mexican American workers were trapped by the exploitive power of the Anglo corporate structure. García's solution was to eliminate the "unfair" competition to Mexican Americans of the Mexican worker, contract or undocumented. García certainly understood the role of agribusiness in corporate exploitation but determined that the first solution was to end Bracero program "treaties" and stop the influx of Mexican workers before confronting the growers as oppressors of American workers. Consequently, the AGIF cooperated in projects designed to monitor working conditions, but at the same time demanded an end to the hiring of non-contracted Mexican workers. Chicano movement advocates were blistering in their critique and condemnation.[21]

The most troubling (then and now) moment in these efforts was García's support of, and AGIF participation in, Operation Wetback in 1954. Using basically all Anglo law agencies and agents and the Armed Services, a massive roundup of suspected illegal Mexican workers was conducted. According to official estimates, approximately one million suspects were detained and released to Mexico. These numbers are largely exaggerated, but the event is clear and too reminiscent of the repatriation boxcar roundups of the 1930s. García worked diligently to assure that Mexican American citizens were not arrested.[22]

Mexican workers were set out as threats to opportunity and the American way. García and the AGIF often described the Mexican worker as an unwanted presence who could bring promiscuity, a disease-ridden populace, and criminal activity. One may see this as implication of historic white nativism by a group seeking inclusion and a tactical response to Anglo racism against the Mexican American. Nonetheless, there is a tragic aura of Mexican American people of color playing a dangerous game and walking in the minefield of appeal to racism to confront racism. This contradicting strategy is best found in the AGIF propaganda written and distributed against undocumented workers.[23]

Ed Idar, author of the AGIF pamphlet "What Price Wetbacks," constructed an informational justification for the anti-Bracero program campaign that was rooted in strident race and class antagonisms. Idar clearly invokes Anglo race-based stereotypes of white superiority against the undocumented and their presence in the United States. While much more circumspect, García also used symbols of Anglo-American racial privilege and power.[24] A most incisive critique of the AGIF position regarding the color line of the United States is Michelle Hall Kells's *Héctor P. García: Everyday Rhetoric and Mexican American Civil Rights.* García's embrace of the 1954 anti-undocumented project and the accompanying anti-Mexican propaganda was a blatant contradiction of the human rights concern that he also enunciated. Kells suggests that a "pragmatic" approach led to the strategic "whiteness" that is unpersuasive and conflictive, as most Anglos viewed Mexican-origin people as a "racial" group. Also, it is seemingly contrasted with García's relentless attack on Anglo racism toward those of Mexican origin and this tireless determination to call Anglos to accountability and redress.[25]

Indeed, the whiteness conception to innate physical features (light skin, more European than indigenous, etc.) is nonsensical, as most members of the AGIF were indeed of "non-European" appearance. Yet, as Kells points out, García could advocate "racial solidarity as la raza and (in the same letter to a confidant), disassociate from Mexico" as being primarily American, and American citizens, not Mexican citizens.[26] Unfortunately, earlier analysts of this ambivalence underplay the reality of the socioeconomic plight of the majority of Mexican Americans. Historians Kells and Carlos Kevin Blanton point out the severe constriction that McCarthyism and the Cold War agenda, combined with the power of Anglo dominance, caused the evolving social analysis and rhetoric of García. Blanton, I. M. García, and I have emphasized that the working-class membership of the AGIF does not focus on their whiteness. By the latter 1970s, Héctor García was clear in his denunciation of white racism and the rejection of its use. The *mestizaje* was always a core theme of early AGIF organizational efforts; as some of its members advocated more middle-class aspirations, it was not anti-Mexican. García evolved as an un-conflicted advocate of universal human rights. His dynamic denunciation of Texas leaders and their failure to meet their responsibilities to Tejano Vietnam veterans is without ambivalence, ambiguity, or any social coding. His support of Chávez and the farmworkers, starting in the late 1960s, was as strong and unwavering as, ironically, the failure of his (and the AGIF's) attempt to lessen Anglo dependence on undocumented workers.[27]

García was, in the 1960s, the most powerful national Mexican American in terms of access and influence on national politics and politicians. None since have approached that position. His influence largely diminishes as the Vietnam era dissipates into the Great Society. The Nixon era and the fractioned chaos of the Chicano movement further removed Anglo attention from the Mexican American community. García certainly continued to pursue justice for Mexican Americans, but he became more vested in local and state issues, as the AGIF retrenched to a narrower base of Mexican American veterans. Ironically, and perhaps with some tragic connotations, García was awarded the Presidential Medal of Freedom in 1984 by Ronald Reagan, the antithesis of García's hope for democratic, liberal national leadership. In 1996, after another decade of seeking justice for his people, García died.[28]

In 2009 much has improved for Mexican Americans. However, the basic issues of social justice that García engaged remain the same. Economic opportunity, educational attainment, political representation (especially on a national level), equal jurisprudence in the criminal justice system, anti-Mexican/Latino attitudes, and Anglo antipathy are still crucial, embedded obstacles. The immigration—or more concisely, the anti-immigration—concerns of Anglos is as paramount as any movement in the last sixty-plus years. Unfortunately, there is no comparable Mexican American figure with the same vision, energy, and power that García brought to his community. No Mexican American organization today initiates, advances, or has comparable access to even regional, much less national, influence. The Chicano movement and its political extension, La Raza Unida, never developed these assets. Their focus on Mexican cultural identity stood against Anglo demands for conformity. Even though Chicano analysis was incisive and necessary, it did not segue into the structural development of material tools such as political power and economic influence. Clearly, to designate the activities of the Mexican American generation as failures because they did not achieve their goals is fatuous. By that standard, Martin Luther King, Jr., was a dismal failure.

García and the AGIF believed in the fundamental mythology of the promise of America. García embraced an ideal of equality and the possibility offered by the rhetoric of the Declaration of Independence and the Constitution of 1789. Essentialism seemed true and welcoming for Mexican *Americans*. However, this ideology (and it is such) of democratic liberalism did not prevent a fierce, and even ruthless, determination to confront obstacles of Anglo racism and class antagonisms. García could seem naive to later Chicano activists, for his anti-communist advocacy and policies in the AGIF, but 1948 or 1957 are *not* 1967, and the choices and actions possible are not those of 1967. Neglecting that difference can obscure and criticize the totality of García's vision and activities. While properly analyzed as at sometimes xenophobic and, sometimes, racialist, the crux of the anti-Bracero campaign was intended to address the plight of Mexican Americans, as was the successful effort to remove public school segregation in Texas. When one observes the still-existing problems in public education, despite at least minimal attention by the federal government, it is staggering to consider the frustration in confronting not only Anglo indifference but the strength of the historical embrace of the ideology of white supremacy. García and the AGIF established that battleground for mostly young Chicano activists to join.

In the national political ecology of the so-called turbulent 1960s, and the preceding 1950s, García, at a critical moment, was the most influential Mexican American in the United States. He provided the major impetus for the dramatic expansion and outreach of the American GI Forum. He was at the center of the most significant and volatile issues of social justice for the Mexican American community. His leadership and relationship with Lyndon Johnson was most significant for the inroads made in national Anglo legislative and judicial movement toward inclusion and opportunity for Mexican Americans. As access to national input lessened, García returned to his original focus on issues of equal access to quality education, ending public discrimination, and improving health care and equal treatment for all Mexican Americans, especially migrant and undocumented workers.[29]

Epilogue

Most poignantly, García led the charge for economic security, educational attainment, full justice under American law, and full citizenship. In so doing, he configured Mexican American understandings of progress.[30] The Hispanic generation, which has yet to produce such leadership, could begin by rejecting the ridiculous label "Hispanic." We should not be named by those of the historic and contemporary ideology of white supremacy and self-entitled claim to order and control. The Mexican American, as well as the Latino, population is not "of things Spanish." García (and the AGIF) offered their best, and it was more than adequate. He and they continued the activity of a pre–World War II LULAC and added their own dynamic and much-required energy and resolve to more directly confront the fundamental corruption of comprehensive racism and economic extortion and exploitation. The Public Broadcasting Service's News Hour in 2009 called upon a "national" Latino organization spokesperson to address the "Hispanic" problem and presented a six-minute debate with some virulent, anti-Mexican, right wing advocate; the timid nature of the Hispanic advocate mandates that we finally recognize Héctor Pérez García for who and what he was: "A Giant of the Twentieth Century."[31]

Notes

1. Carl Allsup, *The American GI Forum: Origins and Evolution* (Austin: Center for Mexican American Studies, University of Texas at Austin, 1982), 30–32; and Ignacio M. García, *Héctor P. García: In Relentless Pursuit of Justice* (Houston: Arte Público, 2002), 1–48.

2. Allsup, *American GI Forum*, 31.

3. Ibid., 34.

4. I. M. García, *Héctor P. García*, xii–xiv.

5. Allsup, *American GI Forum*, 29–38.

6. Ibid., 39–49.

7. Patrick Carroll, *Felix Longoria's Wake: Bereavement, Racism, and the Rise of Mexican American Activism* (College Station: Texas A&M University Press, 2002); and Allsup, *American GI Forum*, 39–49.

8. Carroll, *Felix Longoria's Wake* and Allsup, *American GI Forum*, 49.

9. The two exceptions are Allsup, *American GI Forum* and the exceptional *Felix Longoria's Wake* by Patrick Carroll.

10. Allsup, *American GI Forum*, 50–62.

11. Ibid.; and Guadalupe San Miguel, *"Let Them All Take Heed": Mexican Americans and the Campaign for Educational Equality in Texas, 1910–1981* (Austin: University of Texas Press, 1987). This is the second major scholarly work to utilize the archives of Héctor P. García and is dedicated to him. The first major work was Allsup, *American GI Forum*. See also Carlos Kevin Blanton, *The Strange Career of Bilingual Education in Texas, 1836–1981* (College Station: Texas A&M University Press, 2004.) Blanton's excellent analysis is representative of the most recent Chicano scholarship that is inclusive and insightful of the metanarrative of Mexican American / Chicano historical studies.

12. Allsup, *American GI Forum*, 95.

13. San Miguel, *"Let Them All Take Heed,"* 216–18.

14. Allsup, *American GI Forum,* 72–78.

15. Julie Leininger Pycior, *LBJ and Mexican Americans: The Paradox of Power* (Austin: University of Texas, 1997). This is perhaps the best example of the new comprehensive Chicano / Mexican American scholarship. It is the seminal work on Johnson as the best president in American history on civil rights, as it demonstrates the narrow, black/white axis of Anglo and African American scholarship. It also is the response to Robert A. Caro's abysmal minimalization of Mexican Americans.

16. Allsup, *American GI Forum,* 33–59, 130–31.

17. Ibid., 133–34; I. M. García, *Héctor P. García,* 244–48; and Ignacio M. García, *Chicanismo: The Forging of a Militant Ethos among Mexican Americans* (Tucson: University of Arizona Press, 1997), 102–6.

18. Pycior, *LBJ and Mexican Americans*; and Allsup, *American GI Forum,* 135–41.

19. Allsup, *American GI Forum.*

20. Ibid., 152–53.

21. Ibid., 124.

22. I. M. García, *Héctor P. García,* 253–87; and Ibid., 160–63.

23. Neil Foley, *The White Scourge: Mexicans, Blacks, and Poor Whites in Texas Cotton Culture* (Berkeley: University of California Press, 1997). Foley insists that "whiteness" is a central goal of Mexican Americans, when archival evidence of workers attitudes/ideas on whiteness is not sufficient to prove this. Clearly, García and the AGIF are ambivalent and, at moments, contradictory on the rhetoric of whiteness. David Roediger's *Working Toward Whiteness: How America's Immigrants Became White* (New York: Basic Books, 2005) demonstrates the comprehensive ideology of white (and embedded) supremacy that does not admit non-European people for membership.

24. Allsup, *American GI Forum*; Franciso E. Balderrama and Raymond Rodríguez, *Decade of Betrayal: Mexican Repatriation in the 1930s* (Albuquerque: University of New Mexico Press, 1995); and Juan García, *Operation Wetback: The Mass Deportation of Mexican Undocumented Workers in 1954* (Westport, CT: Greenwood, 1980). This work is lacking research and analysis on García and the AGIF, but it still provides an otherwise significant account of this post–World War II action against Mexican workers in the United States.

25. Michelle Hall Kells, *Héctor P. García: Everyday Rhetoric and Mexican American Civil Rights* (Carbondale: Southern Illinois University Press, 2006).

26. Ibid.

27. Jeff Felts, "Justice for My People: The Héctor P. García Story," Latino Public Broadcasting, 2007.

28. Ibid.

29. Ibid.

30. Anthony Quiroz, *Claiming Citizenship: Mexican Americans in Victoria, Texas* (College Station: Texas A&M University Press, 2005). This is an excellent example of the recent scholarship on Mexican American, working-class worldviews, showing commonalities across time and supposed class distinctions.

31. Pycior quoted in Felts, "Justice for My People."

Figure 8.1. Mexican American civil rights attorney Gus García. Dr. Héctor P. García Papers, Special Collections and Archives, Mary and Jeff Bell Library, Texas A&M University–Corpus Christi.

8

"I Can See No Alternative Except to Battle It Out in Court"

Gus García and the Spirit of the Mexican American Generation[1]

ANTHONY QUIROZ

The 1950s was a crucial decade for Mexican American identity formation. Led and supported by a growing middle class of professionals such as attorneys, businessmen, and working-class and middle-class organizations and a small handful of politicians (Anglo and Mexican American), the Mexican American community throughout the American Southwest asserted publicly its self-definition as first-class citizens. Filing lawsuits, organizing workers, becoming professionals (attorneys, physicians, professors, and the like), Mexican Americans fought openly for their rights to equal education and equal justice before the law. This struggle produced a conundrum in that many Anglo-Americans resisted Mexican American civil rights struggles in the name of preserving Americanism. Yet Mexican American activists argued that their intent was to force the nation to live up to a different brand of Americanism—one that extended its promise to all citizens, even the poor and dispossessed.[2] This work highlights one of the most charismatic and enigmatic among such actors, an attorney from San Antonio, Texas, named Gustavo "Gus" C. García.

DOI: 10.5876/9781607323372.c008

Gus García is a well-known figure among Mexican American historians, who have heard about his brilliant eloquence, legal insights, and profound courtroom arguments. Yet no one has set their scholarly sights solely on his career and his life. This likely stems from the fact that while he appears in bits and pieces of the historical record, García himself left behind little for us to study in terms of documentation. One relies on a hodgepodge of interviews, newspaper clippings, and other similarly discrete records. Save for a handful of folders at the Benson Latin American Collection at the University of Texas at Austin, no large-scale Gus García collection exists in any archive. This work pieces together these discrete documents from a range of primary and secondary sources in order to recreate and interpret the significance of García's life, beginning with the year of his birth.[3]

In January 1915, local authorities in San Diego, Texas (a small town that lies about halfway between Corpus Christi and Laredo), arrested a Mexican immigrant named Basilio Ramos. On his person, authorities found a document titled *el plan de San Diego*. This scheme called for an armed uprising of Mexican Americans, blacks, and Native Americans. The goal was to wrest from the United States all the land lost in the 1848 Treaty of Guadalupe Hidalgo. The newly freed territory would remain independent from both the United States and Mexico. The plan resulted in several attacks on Anglo farmers and ranchers. Ultimately, the plan failed miserably once the Texas Rangers swept in and murdered numerous Mexicans and Mexican Americans in the name of law and order. (Estimates range from 300 to over 3,000, but 1,000 seems to be the most likely number.) Gus García was born into this social tumult in Laredo on July 27, 1915. Just as turbulent as the social events of 1915, García's life proved similarly chaotic in its own way.

As with many Mexican Americans of his era, García was born into an immigrant family. Gus's grandfather, Alfredo García, Sr., had immigrated to Texas from Guerrero, Mexico and settled in the Laredo area. The Garcías had two sons, one of whom was Alfredo Jr., Gus's father. Alfredo Jr. married Maria Teresa Arguindegui, and together they had three children: Alfredo, María Teresa, and Gus. Life in the García household was rocky. Gus's father apparently suffered from alcoholism and kept irregular hours at home. Wishing to provide a more stable home life and better educational opportunities for her children, Maria Teresa moved the children to San Antonio in 1924, when Gus was just nine years of age.[4]

García proved his intellectual mettle early. In San Antonio, he attended St. Cecilia Catholic School for a year. He later attended St. Henry's Academy, moving to Hawthorne Junior High School in 1929. After completing middle school, García attended Main Avenue High School (the present-day Fox Technical High School). But in spring 1932, he transferred to the newly erected Thomas Jefferson High School, where in one short year he became a champion debater and graduated as the school's first valedictorian. He then received a scholarship to attend the University of Texas at Austin (UT). At UT he continued to pursue his love of debate. He became the captain of the university debate team that, under his leadership, went undefeated.

In addition to his bookish nature and intellectual prowess, he was also tall, thin, and good looking. Maury Maverick recalled, "He was a handsome man and the girls were forever 'escorting' him." García completed his undergraduate degree in 1936 at the age of twenty. He then attended the University of Texas School of Law, taking his LL.B in 1938. During his time in law school, García met and became friends with such future luminaries as John Connally and Alan Shivers, both of whom later became governors of Texas. In later years García enjoyed telling the story of how he helped Connally elope "by driving the get-a-way car." His wit and intelligence helped him make friends with a range of people, from a variety of backgrounds, wherever he went.[5]

The next several years were disruptive for García. Upon completion of law school, he passed the state bar exam and took a job in San Antonio as assistant city attorney under City Attorney Victor Keller. García later served as assistant district attorney for Bexar County.[6] But as was typical of men his age, a World War II draft notice drew him into military service. In the military he became a commissioned officer and spent the war stationed in Japan assigned to the US Army's Judge Advocate General's Corps in Yokohama. There he met and worked with another future friend, Ralph Yarborough. With a lively mind, good looks, engaging personality, and eloquence, García added continually to a growing list of important friends.[7]

After the war, García demonstrated that he also had a heart of gold. He took on a range of cases, defending the wealthy and privileged as well as the poorest of the poor. According to his best friend and fellow attorney, John J. Herrera of Houston, García believed that he could make enough money from his wealthy clients to help pay for his poorer ones.[8] Driven by his Catholic background, his sympathy for the oppressed, and his many talents, he quickly became a plaintiff's attorney, often working closely with the League of United Latin American Citizens (LULAC) and the American GI Forum (AGIF).

In 1947 the local School Improvement League of San Antonio helped elect García to the San Antonio Independent School District (SAISD) Board. Although he only served one term, he had a dynamic impact, helping to pass a school improvement bond issue and closing down dangerous buildings.[9] In this new phase of his career, one of his first targets was segregated schooling. To García and other attorneys, one key to defeating such entrenched bigotry involved filing court cases in order to force various school districts to stop segregating on the basis of language. In this way, they could force the courts to make legally binding statements prohibiting segregation as unconstitutional. García's first attempt at integrationist litigation occurred in 1947 while he was serving on the San Antonio School Board. In this instance, García filed in Cuero, Texas, a small town about 90 miles southeast of San Antonio. Through court action, he pushed the state attorney general to agree that segregation in Cuero was illegal.[10] This important decision brought about change in the Cuero school system, but other areas remained intransigent. That same year, another case was tried in a California federal court, *Mendez v. Westminster*, which established the precedent of disallowing segregation solely on the basis of national origin. The following year, Texas asked Attorney General Price Daniel to issue a pronouncement on the practice of segregation by ethnicity. Daniel issued a statement indicating that such practices were contrary to law. But the practice of segregation continued unabated in Texas nevertheless.

In 1948 García and others got a big break when Minerva Delgado sought assistance in filing an anti-discrimination suit in Bastrop, Texas. Although we know the case by the name *Minerva Delgado, et al. v. Bastrop Independent School District of Bastrop County, et al.*, official court documents listed numerous defendants, including the Elgin Independent School District (ISD), the Martindale ISD, the Travis County Board of School Trustees as well as the state superintendent of schools, L. A. Woods. Attorney General Daniel served as counsel for Woods and the State Board of Education. Delgado sued because the Bastrop ISD segregated Mexican children as a matter of course. District officials argued in court that they did so only in cases involving language deficiencies, but García produced Delgado herself, who spoke clear, perfect English. Based largely on her testimony, federal Judge Ben Rice found for the plaintiffs and ruled that the type of segregation that occurred in Bastrop and the other locales stood in violation of the Fourteenth Amendment and was therefore unconstitutional. Rice ordered the schools to cease and desist such practices. The judge allowed for segregation of native Spanish-speaking children, but only after they received individualized scientific testing and then only through the first grade. Further, the "Instructions and Regulations" section of the ruling stated, "The only requirements or authority for segregation of students in the public schools of the State of Texas on account of race or descent is based upon Section 7, Article VII, of the Constitution of Texas, and applies only to persons of Negro ancestry." Therefore, the document went on to argue, it was illegal to separate Mexican children on the basis of race.[11]

Since the 1930s, Mexican Americans had argued for inclusion as full citizens in part due to their official status as white, not black. In 1942 the United States suffered a severe labor shortage, particularly in the agricultural Southwest. That same year, Mexico and the United States developed the Bracero agreement, which allowed for documented Mexican workers to enter the United States as guest workers. Mexico originally refused to send workers to Texas, however, because of the state's history of discrimination. In response, the Texas Legislature passed the 1943 Caucasian Race Resolution, which identified Mexicans as Caucasians and forbade discrimination on ethnic grounds. But it took the *Delgado* case to embed the concept of Mexicans as Caucasians onto the state and national landscape. García and others would come back to this idea and build upon it later.[12]

Bastrop was a smashing victory for García and the other attorneys on the case. Now segregation solely on the basis of race and the presumptions that went along with that practice were declared illegal. Dr. Héctor P. García, founder of the AGIF, called it "one of the foremost decisions in this state." It affected the area around Austin but extended south to the districts around Corpus Christi as well.[13] This did not mean, however, that the educational struggle was over. Segregationist tendencies died hard in mid-twentieth-century Texas, and the forces of apartheid remained vigilant.

By May 1949, García's reputation had grown such that Herrera, his best friend, invited him to speak at a LULAC convention in Kingsville, Texas. Herrera argued that García's reputation, combined with his stature on the

SAISD Board, would make him a big draw.[14] Indeed, by this point, García had been involved in numerous public school lawsuits and was developing a reputation as a bit of a community hero.

At the same time, the virulent racism that justified segregation in the first place ran deeply in the veins of local school officials as well as the heads of the state educational machinery. In 1949 the Gilmer-Aikin Law replaced the elected office of superintendent of public instruction with a new appointive position, the state commissioner of education. The new commissioner, J. W. Edgar, immediately began a process of modern-day "redemption" by recovering the old order of Mexican American segregation. Previous Superintendent L. A. Woods had, for instance, investigated discriminatory conditions in the Del Rio Independent School District ultimately rescinding its accreditation. One of Commissioner Edgar's first acts in office was to reverse this decision and reinstate the district's accredited status. On May 8, 1950, the Texas Educational Agency (TEA) issued a formal "Statement of Policy Pertaining to Segregation of Latin-American Children," declaring that "the segregation of children of Latin-American descent from Anglo-American children in the public school program is contrary to law." Yet in that same issuance, the TEA also proffered that any charges of segregation had to go through the local school boards first. The TEA would only get involved after that point if the plaintiffs appealed. But this approach was viewed by Mexican American activists as a "dodge" of the issue by Edgar, who, it appeared, hoped that most or all complaints would die in a sea of localized red tape.[15]

The next year, the *Wharton Spectator* published a demeaning editorial that criticized Mexican labor while arguing that farm owners had the right to contract individually with workers rather than suffer government interference, as was the case with the Bracero program. García wrote to the publisher of the paper, Frank A. Shannon, laying out the basic principles that underlay his worldview and that of his generation. And in true García style, he opened by writing that if the publisher truly believed in freedom of opinion, he would publish his response. He then went on to demonstrate that the problems identified in the editorial were not the result of Mexican indolence but American social inequity. García laid out the notions of equality of opportunity in education, politics, and society. He embraced concepts of freedom of association and turned the editorial's theme on its head by noting how even those of a higher "class" were less worthy of emulation if they were morally bankrupt.[16] The *Spectator* editorial that prompted García's response closed with the remark, "I still reserve the right to choose my own social companions. And Mexican peon labor is not my type." García concluded his response, "Since we feel confident that you believe in the development of our American way of life we are enclosing an application blank for membership in LULAC and trust that, after you become familiar with our aims and purposes, you will see fit to file a formal application for membership in our organization." This episode offers evidence of how García's worldview represented that of his generation. These individuals were driven by desires for equal access and equal treatment. Unfortunately, educational segregation and the public attitudes that drove such practices were all part of a piece that included legal discrimination as well.

Education was not the only area in which Mexican Americans in Texas faced discrimination. Dating back to the nineteenth century, Mexican Americans often found themselves at odds with law enforcement. Police brutality ran rampant in many communities. As if police officers were not problematic enough, the court system, too, maintained a strong bias against Mexican Americans. One important example of such treatment occurred in Jackson County, a small rural community about ninety miles south of Houston. Jackson County had a 14 percent Mexican American population. Yet prior to 1951, not once in the county's entire history had a non-Anglo been allowed to sit on a jury. Civil and criminal defendants stood before all-Anglo juries, court officials, law enforcement officers, detention officers, and judges. To combat this state of affairs, García and attorneys such as Herrera and Carlos Cadena had been seeking a test case that would allow them to challenge the exclusion of Hispanics from juries. Such a victory would be a vital first step toward the integration of law enforcement and the court system.

But the attorneys faced a problem. Clients often refused offers of appeal because even if these attorneys won the case by arguing that the exclusion of Hispanics from jury pools had resulted in an unfair trial, the individual still had to stand trial again. This second time around, there were no guarantees that the jury or judge might not hand down a harsher punishment. Understandably, no one wanted to risk that outcome.[17] But in 1951, such a golden opportunity presented itself.

On August 7, 1951, Pete Hernández shot Joe Espinoza inside Chico Sánchez's Tavern in Edna, a small town about ninety miles southwest of Houston. It is not clear how Hernández secured the aid of García and Herrera. According to historian Ignacio M. García (no relation), Gus recalled the Hernández family coming to him and pleading for justice for Hernández. In any event, Hernández went to trial on October 11, 1951, with Herrera, García, and James DeAnda by his side.

In preparation for the trial, García and Herrera traveled to the Jackson County Courthouse to look for evidence that Mexican Americans had been excluded from jury pools. While investigating the facts of the case, García and DeAnda realized that the local sheriff was going to various businesses and telling them to take down any "No Mexicans" signs. But racism was so ingrained in Edna (the Jackson County seat) that it was impossible to completely eradicate. While conducting their investigation, García and DeAnda asked a groundskeeper where the men's bathroom was located, and he directed them downstairs. Much to their delight, there in the basement was a sign on the bathroom door reading "colored men and hombres aquí." What a gift! In the belly of the halls of Jackson County justice hung a sign for all to see that clearly indicated discrimination against Mexican Americans. The plaintiff's team also noticed a restaurant across the street from the courthouse bearing a sign denying service to Mexicans.[18] Meanwhile, the local district attorney, Wayne Hartman, refused to admit to the practice of excluding Mexican Americans from juries until Herrera and García began entering the various jury pool books they had found in the basement into the official record. At that point, the district attorney conceded that he would state in court "that never in the history of Jackson County has there been a Mexican-American-petit jury, Grand Jury, or Grand Jury Commission." García pressed him and made him accede to the fact that out of 50,000 calls for jury service, not a single Mexican American had ever been chosen.[19] In the end, Hernández was nevertheless found guilty by an all-Anglo jury and sentenced to life in prison.

The attorneys immediately filed an appeal. As they strategized their way to get past the Court of Criminal Appeals, they realized that they could not use the "black versus white" argument because in Texas, Mexican Americans were considered white by law. Building upon the *Delgado* decision of 1948 and the Caucasian Race Resolution of 1943, Cadena hit upon the argument of identifying Mexican Americans as a "class apart."[20] Cadena asserted that the attorneys should argue that yes, Mexican Americans were considered Caucasian but their continual exclusion from the jury pool in Jackson County proved that they were treated as a separate class within the white race. The precedent had already been set in California, when an aircraft mechanic named Carl Chessman was charged with rape, which was a capital offense in the state at that time. But Chessman's attorney proved that local officials had agreed to not choose aircraft workers to serve on jury pools because they missed too much work already due to surfing or otherwise seeking to leave work early. Hence, whenever it was learned that a local aircraft mechanic's name was eligible for the jury pool, it would be withdrawn. Cadena jumped on this issue and applied it to Hernández's case. In Texas, the exclusion of Mexican Americans as jurors stood not due to absenteeism but simply because officials believed that Mexican Americans would not make good jurors.[21]

After filing ineffective appeals in the Texas courts, the attorneys were finally granted a writ of certiorari to appear before the US Supreme Court in Washington, DC, in January 1954. The county argued that the absence of Mexican Americans from juries was merely happenstance, an argument that the court never found persuasive. García then brought into evidence the sign in the courthouse restroom and the "No Mexicans" sign in the window of the restaurant across the street from the courthouse. In this way he demonstrated that Mexican Americans were indeed identified as different from whites and that their status in society was subsequently determined by that identification.

In a Supreme Court hearing, the justices can disturb your concentration (made worse by nervousness brought on by arguing before such an august body) by stopping you at any moment and asking questions about how this issue relates to other cases and why yours is somehow different. This disconcerting possibility makes it easy to lose your train of thought. But when the justices asked how the *Hernández* case differed from *Alabama v. White* (a case in which Tony Pace, a black man, argued that an Alabama statute against cohabitation was unconstitutional because it applied different penalties for interracial couples as opposed to single-race couples), García noted that the *White* case involved discrimination based on race, whereas in this case, Mexican Americans argued that they were being mistreated as a separate class within the white race.[22] After expounding upon that line of argument, García then went back to his original train of thought without missing a step.

When arguing before the Supreme Court, each attorney receives a half hour to make his case. There are two lights at the lectern. One is green and another is red. The green light starts flashing once the attorney has five minutes left to speak. As García was trying to wrap up, he said, "After all, Justices of the Court, when after 50,000 calls for jurors, petit, Grand Jurors, and Commissioners, since memory of man runneth not to the contrary, and not a single Hispanic name being allowed to serve on such judicial bodies, I say to you there's a white man in the woodpile somewhere." Everyone in the room then burst out laughing and the red light flashed, indicating that his time had ended. Chief Justice Earl Warren, in a surprising move, said, "Mr. García, what you say is very interesting. Will you please proceed?" In this way, García became the first attorney in Supreme Court history to receive extra time at the lectern from the Chief Justice.[23]

Through the course of the hearing, García and the other attorneys proved that despite comprising 14 percent of the county's population, Mexican Americans had never served on a Jackson County jury of any sort. The Court ruled that due to Hernández's presence as part of a social class that was excluded from jury service, he had certainly been denied a fair trial by his peers, in violation of his Fourteenth Amendment rights, which guaranteed him equal protection under the law. And while the victory won a temporary reprieve for Hernández, he was eventually retried, convicted, and sentenced again to life in prison.[24]

Unfortunately, the world will never hear García's historic argument. There were no court reporters at the time because there was no appealing beyond the US Supreme Court. Beginning in January 1955, according to Herrera, the Court began to tape and sell copies of the proceedings. But this practice did not begin until a year after the historic *Hernández* case.[25]

The Supreme Court decision was significant on many fronts. Traditionally, Texas courts had identified two classes of citizens: black and white. Now it admitted for the first time that there were more than two classes. Mexican Americans comprised a class apart but within the white race. Second, it allowed Mexican Americans to begin accepting the rights and responsibilities of citizenship by serving on juries. Third, Gus García became the first Mexican American to argue a case before the US Supreme Court, a fact that made the victory all the sweeter.

García tried numerous cases in his career, but Pete Hernández seemed to haunt him. Evidence does not support that García kept in touch with any client the way he did with Hernández. As noted by historian I. M. García,

Gus wrote numerous letters to Hernández while he was in prison. Offering advice on how to maintain a clean record and work for early release, we see a compassionate side of the man that stands in contrast to his driven personality.[26] In a February 1960 letter to the Honorable Jack Ross, of the Board of Pardons and Paroles, García asked why Hernández had not been paroled. By this time Hernández had been imprisoned since 1951 and was given sixty-two months time off in 1955 for good behavior. García noted that Hernández had served ample time, especially in light of his willingness to "risk a possible death sentence upon the second trial of his case in order to help us establish a very important principle of law and civil rights for Latin Americans everywhere."[27] Five days later, García wrote to Herrera that he had spoken with Ross about Hernández, but it is "a long and complicated story." García was going to pursue the matter and send out mimeographed copies of a memorandum "for the benefit of all interested parties (assuming anybody other than you and I is interested in helping out this poor guy)."[28] After pressure from García, the state Board of Pardons and Paroles granted Hernández parole on June 8, 1960.[29]

The year after trying the *Hernández* case, García and his family moved to Kingsville, where he maintained a focus on educational equality. He had been working on some matters with friend and attorney Homer López, who had a law practice in the small South Texas town, located about forty miles southwest of Corpus Christi. As a result of his move, García's next case was against the Kingsville ISD for gerrymandering school zones to ensure future segregation. But the case was dismissed before it reached a conclusion.

After this, García's next big case came in 1957 and involved the Driscoll ISD. García convinced a federal court that segregationist practices in the school district were targeted at Mexican American children as a class and were therefore unconstitutional. After this, however, the AGIF and LULAC refused to fund any more educational lawsuits; the state's insistence on protecting local control ensured an almost endless potential for variations of subterfuge of the original *Delgado* ruling so that such efforts were deemed useless.[30] The long struggle for educational equality, fought so bravely and intelligently throughout the postwar years had finally come to an end. And with that end, García's career too began to wind down.[31]

The early 1960s appear to mark the beginning of the end for García. His behavior moved from erratic to outright strange. He had long since understood the need to make money and be responsible with it. He just couldn't do it. García's conscience caused him to decline a job offer from San Antonio District Attorney Charles J. Lieck, Jr., in February 1960. Grateful for having been offered the job, García nevertheless declined the offer on moral and economic grounds. He posited that he would feel guilty prosecuting the poor since he believed that juries often made decisions based on the lawyers rather than their arguments. García further noted that he needed more money than an assistant district attorney could make.[32] Then in 1961 he was disbarred for passing bad checks.

In early 1963, Herrera had lent García $5 that he said came in handy for a haircut and to pay his poll tax. In his thank you letter, García seemed despondent and desperate. García informed his friend, "This is the final turning point in my life, and whether I choose the right road or end up in the gutter or a suicide depends largely on the few friends I have left (which means the only true friends I ever had) such as you, Henry Castillo and Pat Henley." He proceeded, "Keep dropping me a line even a few words at a time. Everything helps, because I have so little to sustain me."[33]

In summer of that same year, Herrera tried to help his friend by writing to his ex-wife, Eleanor García, imploring her to allow García's two daughters to write to him. Herrera noted that García was in dire straits, "but a letter now and then would be of the greatest aid now that he needs it most . . . I am sure if the girls write to him it will away [sic] the scales in Gus' favor and he will feel that he has now more than ever a greater reason to fight for a full recovery."[34] Finally, in November, Eleanor wrote back to Herrera, criticizing her ex-husband for never having been a father to the girls but now wanting their affection: "If he wants to send them money (this may help ease his conscience), that is his business, but that doesn't mean we have to put up with him." She went on to argue, "If he ever comes around here I wouldn't hesitate to call the police."[35] And who could blame her? His pendulum-like mood swings drove a wedge between him and his family. She rightfully felt in danger for her children and herself.

The assassination of John F. Kennedy in November 1963 further drove García's downward spiral. García, LULAC, the AGIF, and other Mexican Americans had worked very hard to secure the presidency for Kennedy, a fellow Catholic who was viewed as a champion of civil rights. It is not exactly clear, but it appears as though the assassination was the final straw that sent

García's life into a tailspin. According to Herrera, García never got over Kennedy's death. From November 1963 until his death the following June, he stayed in a constant state of drunkenness. Indeed, Herrera regrets throwing him out of his house for showing up drunk one night with a complete stranger and asking if the two could spend the night. Herrera was infuriated with this request and stunned at his gumption for asking to allow another unidentified male companion to stay as well. Herrera ordered García, his lifelong friend, out of his home. The guilt stayed with Herrera until his dying day.[36] Drinking and the resultant malnourishment amounted to a death sentence for García.

For all his brilliance and eloquence, García struggled with alcoholism all his adult life. And as often happens with alcoholics, he rationalized his behavior by noting that he was a brilliant attorney who had a gift for public speaking and argument. Thus, according to Herrera, García also felt that others had no right to interfere with his business. Herrera speculates that García drank to cope with the pressures of having come from a broken home. His mother took the children to San Antonio when he was a boy because his father drank heavily. But Herrera notes that García also drank while he was a law student at UT. In that situation, García felt all the pressures of being the only Mexican American student, who had to fit in with the right crowd and prove himself to his peers. These areas were as important to him as learning the law and practicing his debate skills. After law school he entered the military, where drinking is often a fact of life for many of the men. Drinking became García's downfall.

García always understood that he had a problem. He entered rehabilitation numerous times in at least two different veterans' hospitals. Treatment never took despite the fact that a part of him honestly wanted to stay sober. Friends commented to each other about his struggles to remain on the wagon. It seems that among his friends and enemies, he was as well known for his drinking as for his judicial eloquence. Thus, it is no surprise that accounts of his passing focus so heavily on this unpleasant aspect of his complex life.

García's drinking became storied and professionally detrimental. He sometimes disappeared for days, weeks, and even longer toward the end of his life. He angered those around him because of his drunken remarks. Friends wanted him to stop because they could see that it was literally killing him. This sad fact was obvious to everyone, including García himself.

And to hear Herrera tell it, it was also a time when he and others felt so guilty about telling him to stop drinking that they blamed themselves for his personal misfortunes.

As his life wound down, García felt that he only had a handful of friends: Herrera, Castillo, and Henley.[37] Yet he must have had more. In his final months of life, he frequented the Casablanca Café, across the street from the Municipal Market in San Antonio. The café's owner, one Mr. Nuñez, had orders from García's friends (unnamed) that anytime he walked in he was to be served, and they would pay the bill. But this became a problem for Nuñez, as few, if any, of his customers at the time recognized "this unkempt man, unshaven, skinny, scrawny, trembling," who kept running back and forth to the bathroom because by that time he was so ill that he could not keep any food down. At this point Nuñez said to García, "'Por que no paras de tomar, Gus? Mira como te ves. No tienes miedo que algún día te hallen muerto en un callejón como un wino?'" (Why don't you quit drinking Gus? Look at yourself. Aren't you afraid that one day someone will find you dead in the alley like a wino?) And Gus stood up straight and looked Nuñez in the eye, saying, "'Qué chingados le importa a Ud.? Así mueren los hombres.'" (What the hell do you care? That's how men die.) And then Gus left the café.[38]

In the middle of the city of San Antonio is an area called Plaza de Zacate. It is called this because local farmers would come into town with their families and sell their wares, including rolled up grass, or *zacate*. The plaza was overseen by a "market master" who allotted space to the various vendors from an air-conditioned office. Since García was a very well-known political activist in town, whenever he had supported the current mayor, that mayor would tell the market master to tend to García's needs. Thus, it was at 5:00 a.m. on the morning of June 3, 1964, that García asked permission to sleep in the office of the market master to escape the summer heat. At around 10:30 or so, the market master went in to check on García and found him having a violent seizure. He immediately called for an ambulance, but it was too late. García had passed away. Local shoeshine boys, newspaper boys, and workers from the restaurant across the street where García frequently ate came rushing over to see what had happened. Amid the buzz of it all, some were asking what all the commotion was about. Who was this dead wino who enthralled everyone? The answer, of course, was that he was Gus García, a man who had shaped the course of Mexican American history. Here was a giant of a man who was the first Mexican American to successfully argue before the US Supreme Court and win. García fought school segregation, fought for those with no voice and no resources as well as for the high and mighty.[39] And few who witnessed his passing appreciated who he was or what he had accomplished.

Herrera was asked to handle the funeral arrangements and select the pallbearers. After careful consideration, Herrera realized that his friend had touched so many lives in so many ways that he should get representatives from each of the major groups with which García had been involved. So he chose John Solís of LULAC; Héctor García of the AGIF; Carlos Cadena, who had tried the *Hernández* case with Gus; Benito Juárez, nephew of the deceased; Mickey Herrera, Herrera's son; and Justice of the Peace Gutiérrez. All the lawyers who knew García wanted to speak at the funeral, but Herrera limited speakers to just three: Héctor García, Solís, and Cadena, each representing the AGIF, LULAC, and the bar, respectively.[40] García was buried with full military honors on June 8, 1964, at Fort Sam Houston National Cemetery.

García's early death robbed his people and the nation of the opportunity to have had a first-class Hispanic serve on the US Supreme Court. AGIF leader Vicente Ximenes once commented that, when asked by Lyndon Johnson to find people to suggest for federal positions, he immediately thought of García. "He would have been exactly what we were looking for because he did have that legal mind. Gus García was a genius," noted Ximenes in reference to García's handling of the *Hernández* case of 1954.[41] Beyond his intellect, he was well known for his uncompromising manner. He was a staunchly principled man who had no fear of retaliation. He wrote his own speeches and always spoke his mind. According to Ximenes, many Anglos "hated him for breaking with tradition—that is selling out for retainer fees and country club memberships." And while people were upset with him, there appear to have been no threats of violence or personal attacks against him. This was particularly surprising given his sometimes openly combative nature. In 1946 he invited Ralph Yarborough to attend an AGIF state convention in Austin. When Yarborough commented on the lack of dignitaries, such as the governor and the attorney general, García responded by saying, "Ralph, if they aren't for us, we don't invite them." Yarborough later recalled that García did not play the game of deference and hierarchy: "It was typical of Gus García's straightforward dynamic hard hitting positions, with no servility, no groveling, no pawing to kiss the foot of a Governor or sell a cause for tea in the Mansion, such as is so common among politicians in Texas."[42]

Yet to keep García in a proper historical light, one must also consider the broader social context in which he operated. Standing up, often alone, in hostile environments to argue for the underdog, García made many enemies. As if this weren't bad enough, many of his own people failed to give him the widespread recognition he so richly deserved. We, as historians, are aware of his struggles and those of the AGIF, LULAC, and others. It is easy, therefore, to get a sense of a groundswell movement, a brown wave of activism, so to speak. But the truth is that while we celebrate individuals such as Gus García, the majority of folks alive at the time were not nearly as interested. When an incident like the Félix Longoria affair in Three Rivers occurred, there was an obvious outpouring of sympathy and anger. The refusal of burial for Longoria, who died defending American freedoms and ideals in the Philippines during World War II, was an obvious affront to all Americans, Mexican and Anglo alike. The less flashy, but more legally significant, cases in which García took part went by largely unnoticed except by the handful of people who were involved directly. Julie Leininger Pycior notes how after the landmark Supreme Court decision in the *Hernández* case, García "return[ed] home unheralded." Eight years after his death, however, San Antonio memorialized him forever.[43]

One of the most important tributes involved the naming of a middle school in San Antonio in his honor in 1972. Even this wonderful homage was not without controversy. The school was to be built with money from the Department of Housing and Urban Development's (HUD) Model Cities Program, but when the original allotted funds fell far short of the necessary expenses in 1970, the school's future appeared to be in real danger. Then, in February of 1971, HUD released an additional $2.15 million, allowing for the school's completion. When the two-story school with thirty-eight classrooms, 700-seat auditorium, library, cafeteria, and gymnasium was dedicated on Sunday, October 8, 1972, it drew dignitaries from around the state. Héctor García, founder of the AGIF, gave an emotional talk in which he recited a litany of Gus's achievements and joined other key figures in remembering Gus fondly.[44]

This, then, was an overview of the life and times of Gus García. He was a man of depth, intelligence, and weakness. He made significant contributions to subsequent generations through his legal work. Too many of today's Mexican American students do not understand the depths of the racism experienced by their parents and grandparents. And while that is good for them—Gus would have wanted it that way—it is too bad that these folks are susceptible to claims that such behavior either never existed or was overexaggerated. It is for the sake of scholarship, but mostly for the sake of future generations, that we must preserve—nay, enshrine—the memory of Gus García and his accomplishments and the threatening environment in which he lived.

Notes

1. Gus García to George I. Sánchez, September 1, 1955, copied to Héctor P. García, Ed Idar, and Richard Casillas, box 19, folder 36, Dr. Héctor P. García Papers, Special Collections and Archives, Texas A&M University–Corpus Christi (hereafter García Papers).

2. García pointed out to an audience in Laredo, Texas, on January 15, 1959, that while Mexican Americans sought equality, ironically, their opponents embraced un-American beliefs and tactics. These ideas were expanded in a letter to Frank A. Shannon, publisher of the *Wharton Spectator*, November 4, 1949. Both the speech and the letter are in box 2, folder 22, John J. Herrera Papers, Houston Metropolitan Research Center, Houston Public Library (hereafter Herrera Papers). Also see Ignacio M. García, *White But Not Equal: Mexican Americans, Jury Discrimination, and the Supreme Court* (Tucson: University of Arizona Press, 2009), 10–12.

3. For more information on Héctor P. García, see Henry A. J. Ramos, *The American GI Forum: In Pursuit of the Dream, 1948–1983* (Houston: Arte Público, 1998); Ignacio M. García, *Héctor P. García: In Relentless Pursuit of Justice* (Houston: Arte Público, 2002); Craig A. Kaplowitz, *LULAC: Mexican Americans and National Policy* (College Station: Texas A&M University Press, 2005); and Michelle Hall Kells, *Héctor P. García: Everyday Rhetoric and Mexican American Civil Rights* (Carbondale: Southern Illinois University Press, 2006).

4. Abel A. Reyna, cultural advocate, Experimental Schools Project, Englewood Independent School District, "Short Biography of Gus C. García," n.d.; Abel A. Reyna, "Gus García Jr. High Dedicated," *City of San Antonio Model Cities News* 2, December 1972, box 107, folder 39, García Papers

5. Sam Kindrick, "Offbeat: Story of Gus García Deserves Retelling," *San Antonio Express*, June 10, 1970 and Gus García obituary, *San Antonio Light*, June 4, 1964, both in box 107, folder 33, García Papers; Héctor P. García, notes for a speech given

at the dedication ceremony for Gus García Junior High School in December, 1972, box 107, folder 14, García Papers; and "Gus García Junior High Dedicated."

6. Kindrick, "Offbeat: Story of Gus García"; and Reyna, "Gus García Junior High Dedicated."

7. Ralph Yarborough to Héctor P. García, July 16, 1974, box 107, folder 24, García Papers.

8. John J. Herrera, interview by Tom Kreneck, May 22, 1981.

9. Richard A. Buitron, *The Quest for Tejano Identity in San Antonio, Texas, 1913–2000* (New York: Routledge, 2004), 43.

10. Héctor P. García, speech given at dedication of Gus García Junior High School, December 1972, box 14, folder 117, García Papers.

11. For a detailed account of the case see Guadalupe San Miguel, Jr., *"Let All of Them Take Heed": Mexican Americans and the Campaign for Educational Equality in Texas, 1910–1981* (Austin: University of Texas Press, 1987).

12. Judge Ben H. Rice, Jr., "Final Judgment," *Minerva Delgado, et al. v. Bastrop Independent School District of Bastrop County, et al.*, filed June 15, 1948, box 107, folder 5, García Papers.

13. I. M. García, *Héctor P. García*.

14. John J. Herrera to Gus García, May 18, 1949, box 2, folder 20, Herrera Papers.

15. San Miguel, *"Let All of Them Take Heed,"* 129; and "Texas Education Agency Statement of Policy Pertaining to Segregation of Mexican-American Children," May 8, 1950, box 126, folder 67, García Papers.

16. García to Frank A. Shannon, November 4, 1949, box 2, folder 20, Herrera Papers.

17. Herrera interview.

18. James DeAnda, "Transcript of Judge DeAnda Remarks" lecture, *Hernández v. Texas* at Fifty Conference, Houston, TX, November 19, 2004, accessed September 28, 2006, http://www.law.uh.edu/hernandez50/Deanda.pdf.

19. Herrera interview.

20. We must keep in mind that this law passed in light of the fact that Mexico had blacklisted the state of Texas from the Bracero agreement, a contract that allowed for Mexican citizens to come to the United States as guest workers. But since Texas had the worst record of mistreating Mexican citizens, Mexico refused to allow her citizens to enter the state. In an attempt to alleviate such tensions, the legislature passed this law, which designated them as white and declared that it was illegal to discriminate against any white person. In reality, this was just a Band-Aid on a gaping wound. Discrimination continued unabated well into the future.

21. Herrera interview.

22. Ibid.

23. Ibid.

24. DeAnda, "Transcript of Judge DeAnda Remarks."

25. Herrera interview.

26. I. M. García, *White But Not Equal*, 193–94.

27. García to Jack Ross, February 12, 1960, box 20, folder 2, Herrera Papers.

28. García to Herrera, February 17, 1960, box 2, folder 20, Herrera Papers.

29. García to Pete Hernández, n.d. and G. García to H. P. García, George I. Sánchez, Herrera, Frank Jasso, James DeAnda, Judge Manuel V. López, and Anthony García, memo, June 8, 1960, box 2, folder 20, folder 20 (JJH HMRC).

30. San Miguel, *"Let All of Them Take Heed,"* 134, 217.

31. Ibid., 134.

32. García to Lieck, February 17, 1960, box 2, folder 20, Herrera Papers.

33. García to Herrera, January 28, 1963, box 2, folder 20, Herrera Papers.

34. Herrera to Eleanor García, June 1963, box 2, folder 20, Herrera Papers.

35. E. García to Herrera, November 13, 1963, and E. G. McCusker to Herrera, box 2, folder 20, Herrera Papers.

36. Herrera interview.

37. García to Herrera, January 28, 1963, box 2, folder 20, Herrera Papers.

38. Herrera interview.

39. Ibid.

40. Ibid.

41. Julie Leininger Pycior, *LBJ and Mexican Americans: The Paradox of Power* (Austin: University of Texas Press, 2002).

42. Vicente Ximenes, letter to the editor, *San Antonio Express*, December 25, 1970, box 107, folder 11, and Yarborough to H. P. García, July 16, 1974, box 107, folder 24, both García Papers.

43. Pycior, *LBJ and Mexican Americans*, 202.

44. "Gus García Junior High Okay," *San Antonio Express*, February 26, 1971, box 107, folder 47, and "Dedication Program for the Gus García Junior High School, Edgewood ISD, San Antonio, Texas," October 8, 1972, box 107, folder 9, both García Papers.

Figure 9.1. John J. Herrera, ca. 1950s, John J. Herrera Papers, Houston Metropolitan Research Center, Houston Public Library, MSS 160-138.

9

Mr. LULAC

The Fabulous Life of John J. Herrera

Thomas H. Kreneck

John J. Herrera (1910–1986) ranks among the extraordinary individuals in twentieth-century Texas Mexican history though by no means is he well enough celebrated. A Houston attorney and civic activist, he could lay claim as few could to being called "Mr. LULAC," a description earned from his involvement in and passion for the League of United Latin American Citizens, which he served faithfully from 1940 until his death. His heyday came during the 1940s through the mid-1960s, at a time when the Mexican American World War II generation made the Hispanic presence felt as never before. As part of that cohort, Herrera numbered among such Tejanos as Gustavo "Gus" García of San Antonio, Félix Tijerina of Houston, Dr. Héctor P. García of Corpus Christi, George J. Garza of Laredo, and the diverse legion of people who led the movement for Mexican American equality in other states across the nation. John J. (as he was popularly known) participated in significant events as an advocate, leader, and sometimes larger-than-life figure.

Herrera also lived a fabulous existence, much in the spirit of Betram D. Wolfe's depiction of Diego Rivera in his 1963 classic, *The Fabulous Life of Diego*

DOI: 10.5876/9781607323372.c009

Rivera. Wolfe captured the essence of that greatest of all Mexican artists by using the word *fabulous.* Wolfe noted, "His life was fabulous, his accounts of his life more fabulous still . . . His talk, theories, anecdotes, adventures, and his successive retellings of them" entered the realm of fable, sometimes to people's chagrin, but on the whole, beguiling and adding much to the richness of "his world, his time, his country, its past, present, and future." Rivera's life, as much as his painting, was art.[1]

While Herrera did not achieve the stature of Rivera (few do), so might such a description be made of John J. Much as Rivera felt passionate about his life and art, so did Herrera display exuberance about life and being in LULAC. He stands out as the most devoted advocate of LULAC that I, as an archivist historian, have ever met in over thirty years of documenting that organization and its adherents. Like Rivera, Herrera was eminently memorable. Tall, handsome, and flamboyant, his presence in the room, or his contributions to Chicano history, could not be ignored. In his own circles, he equaled Rivera in controversy. While Herrera inspired many Mexican Americans by his words and actions, likewise he had critics, just as Rivera both motivated and aggravated. But Herrera always lived grandly. A raconteur, he could tell a story in a manner mesmerizing to listeners.

Also like Rivera, Herrera often spoke in fable-like terms. He made fables of that which inspired him, the things he learned, and the events great and small that he experienced. His fables adhered to the definition of the word that says "A story about legendary persons or exploits." Through his stories, he did as much as any other participant to ingrain into the lexicon of Mexican American history at least two incidents: the seminal civil rights case *Hernández v. Texas* and President John F. Kennedy's visit with a LULAC audience at Houston's Rice Hotel on the evening before his assassination. He also, probably more than anyone else, celebrated the life of his friend and fellow attorney Gus García, elevating García into almost legendary status.

The reader by now has noted that I deviate from the standard academic practice of writing in the third person. As Wolfe knew Rivera, I had the good fortune of being friends with Herrera. While an archivist historian for the Houston Metropolitan Research Center during the 1980s, I acquired his papers for that institution and simultaneously conducted a series of formal interviews with him; in these recordings, he revealed his experiences, worldview, and zest for life. We had many casual conversations as well.

Equally important, I held Herrera in great respect. Befitting his station, he was always "Mr. Herrera" to me. He ranks among the most remarkable subjects that I ever met professionally. It is almost impossible for me to write about him in the third person because I sense his presence whenever I say or think his name. I learned much Mexican American history from him. So, like Wolfe in his treatment of Rivera, I am extremely invested in John J. Herrera as a topic. I am in his debt and feel obliged to let others know about him.[2]

Herrera's pedigree was the envy of any Texas genealogist and does much to explain him as a man. He proudly traced his ancestry to the Ruiz and Herrera families, who helped to establish San Antonio during the eighteenth century. The Ruiz clan claimed ties to the San Antonio area dating back to the 1730s. One ancestor, Francisco Ruiz, became San Antonio's mayor and a signer of the Texas Declaration of Independence in 1836. A forebear named Pedro Herrera fought in Juan Seguín's company with Sam Houston at the Battle of San Jacinto that same year. Undoubtedly a grand storyteller in his own right, Herrera's father, Juan José Herrera, regaled his son about the glory of old San Antonio and the Herrera-Ruiz family, whose members were buried in the ancestral cemetery near Garza's Crossing, some sixteen miles from San Fernando Cathedral.[3]

Although people recognized Herrera as a quintessential Houstonian (a designation connoting optimism and urban sophistication beyond other Texas citizens), he came to the city via a fabulously circuitous route that symbolized the migrations of many Mexican American people as well as other Houstonians of his time. His father, Juan José, was a San Antonio native and his mother, Antonia Jiménez, hailed from Eagle Pass. Juan José worked at times for both the San Antonio police force and its fire department.[4] Around 1908 he took his growing family to Cravens, Louisiana (Vernon Parish), where he served as the bilingual city marshal to protect and run a boardinghouse for the Mexican workers who cleared the swamps for the development of that region. In Cravens, John James Herrera was born on April 12, 1910.[5]

After approximately four years in Louisiana, the Herrera family returned to San Antonio. John always considered himself a seventh-generation native Texan who, as the saying goes, just happened to be born away from home. John's mother died in the influenza epidemic of 1918. This loss in conjunction with economic hard times caused John's father to take his family to Galveston in 1920, where he worked as a foreman during construction of the causeway linking that island city to the mainland. John attended school there for several years. The family went to Michigan in the spring of 1924 to labor in the beet fields. In December, fleeing the cold climate, the Herreras moved back to Texas and settled in Houston, where John would continue to attend school and spend the rest of his life.[6]

Many years later, John recalled that he had never really known discrimination until he came to Houston. The San Antonio he remembered seemed more hospitable to Mexican Americans, with its deeply rooted Hispanic traditions and large number of residents with Spanish surnames. John felt that the Houston of the 1920s, with its active Ku Klux Klan klavern, exhibited a hard edge of prejudice, much like the small towns in the surrounding region.[7]

The Herreras lived near downtown in a small neighborhood just south of Washington Avenue, which, to some extent, shielded him from prejudice. It contained an increasing number of Mexican Americans but also many other nationalities such as Greeks, Lebanese, and Italians; Houston, a port city, attracted various groups. John's neighborhood provided a buffer for the Mexican arrivals because, as he cleverly put it, "the Battle of San Jacinto didn't mean a damn thing" to its residents.[8]

John's father opened a small string of boardinghouses across town and a couple of barbershops to accommodate the many single Mexican workers immigrating to the Bayou City. The urbanization of the twentieth-century Mexican American population continued apace, and the Herreras took part in this demographic shift.[9]

Within a few years, as the Chicano community expanded westward, the family moved to the 1400 block of Washington Avenue. Young John found employment at the nearby Weingarten's grocery store. Working numerous jobs to help his family, he also shined shoes near downtown's Rice Hotel and hired out as a Western Union messenger at the Houston Coliseum during the 1928 Democratic National Convention.[10]

By 1928 John entered Sam Houston High School, one of its few students of Mexican descent. He took public speaking and civics from future President Lyndon B. Johnson, during his own brief tenure at the school. John's recollections of Johnson were the stuff of fable: "What we loved about Mr. Johnson was when we'd have our annual blood-letting football game with Heights [High School], [h]e would get up on [the] balcony . . . overlooking the play ground . . . and he'd . . . give us a pep talk. [H]e was dynamic." Johnson "would just infuse you with everything. And he was always in a hurry." John wanted to be on Johnson's debate team but was too busy with after-school jobs to participate in extracurricular activities.[11]

John's greatest early influence was Juan José. He would credit all his later work with civil rights advocacy and LULAC to his father because, as he put it, "my dad taught me to be fair. I always thought to be fair." Although he felt no direct personal discrimination while growing up, he saw the signs in certain sections of town where industries stated "No Mexicans Hired Here." More importantly, he accompanied Juan José when he approached then-Mayor Oscar Holcombe about putting him on the police department, as he had been in San Antonio. John recalled that Holcombe "laughed at him. Then, I began to see what discrimination meant."[12]

As the 1930s progressed, the Mexican American community in Houston, and the Herrera family in particular, experienced great economic difficulties. John left high school to work full time. His father's businesses began to fail, and Juan José moved back to San Antonio; but John remained in Houston and permanently linked his destiny to the Bayou City.[13]

At a young age, John knew he wanted to be an attorney. Like most grand individuals, everything of meaning had a story behind it. He recollected that as a child his mother read in Spanish the Bible passage regarding Joseph of Arimathea, *el consejero* (a counselor), who retrieved the body of Christ for proper burial. When young John asked his mother what the word meant, she answered, "that's a man that . . . settles disputes. He's a lawyer. He knows the law." This explanation made a lasting impression on John. He carried this remembrance with him throughout his life, as great storytellers often do.[14]

John heard more lighthearted accounts of lawyers from his father—like the one about "Leal of San Antonio." As John humorously recounted the tale, Leal would vow to stick by his clients all the way—even up the thirteen gallows steps in front of the old Bexar County Courthouse. At the twelfth step, however, John would note with a flourish, Leal pronounced, "Brother, this is as far as I can go." His dad told him another story about a blind man at San Antonio's Plaza de Zacate, the legendary square that flourished in the early days of the twentieth century for Mexican American music, food, culture, and social interaction. An attorney encountered this blind man and gave him a nickel, to which the recipient said, *"Gracias, licenciado"* (Thank you, lawyer). After circling the plaza, handing the man another nickel, and hearing these same words of appreciation, the attorney asked him, "How do you know I'm a lawyer?" The blind man responded that "everybody's a lawyer here. Even the dogs are lawyers." So from the sacred to the amusing, John's parents had instructed him on the presence and importance of attorneys in society.[15]

As a lad during the 1920s, John sold newspapers near Houston's Civil Courts Building to prominent attorneys and judges. These distinguished men impressed him greatly. In the 1930s, he and his father had even helped a young Percy Foreman in his unsuccessful election bid for district attorney. Foreman later became one of the most celebrated criminal defense lawyers in the United States.[16]

Unfortunately, Herrera's limited education held him back. When, in the early 1930s, he applied for admission to the South Texas College of Law, the institution rejected him because he did not have a high school diploma. Officials also told him that beginning in 1935 he would have to have a year of college, which would have been simply out of the question for Herrera. Thus, in 1934 Herrera made three big moves. At twenty-three years of age he went back to high school for the spring semester. After graduating, he married his fiancée, Olivia Cisneros, in July, sent her to live with her parents in Galveston, and went to work in the rice and cotton fields near Houston for the summer, where he earned enough money so that he and Olivia could set up housekeeping in Houston. On September 1, 1934, he entered the South Texas School of Law, a private institution founded in 1923 as a night program, catering mainly to young men working and raising families.[17]

Herrera recalled fondly his law school experiences. He appreciated the utilitarian nature of the law classes and that sitting judges and practicing attorneys served as the professors. At the time, the downtown YMCA building housed the institution. Herrera lived like most students on meager resources. He studied, drank coffee for a nickel a cup, and ate hot dogs for 5 cents each and chili for a dime a bowl at James Coney Island, a Houston culinary landmark, across the street from the school.[18]

In law school, a course Herrera took on legal ethics inspired him to have a loftier view of the world. He always saw himself as someone who aspired to be high-minded and not mired in petty prejudices or perceived insults. For example, when a professor could not master his Hispanic surname and called him "O'Hara," John responded good-naturedly by always wearing a shamrock in his lapel on St. Patrick's Day.

Herrera admittedly struggled in law school. Although his was a four-year program, he took six years to finish by attending classes three nights a week. A self-acknowledged C student because he had to work, he at times held down three jobs. Perhaps his most important place of employment was at the city water department as a ditch digger in maintenance for six years, 1934–1939, always part time.[19]

During that stint as a laborer, Herrera became involved in civic action through membership in a group called the Latin American Club of Harris County (LAC). Although LULAC Council No. 60 had been formed in 1934 in Houston, Herrera was still young, and he felt that the more established men of the council saw him and some of the other fellows as too inexperienced and meddlesome. He attended several of the broader LULAC functions held in Houston in the mid-1930s and was impressed with its founders, like M. C. Gonzales of San Antonio, who came for these events. But among Houston LULACers, as Herrera put it, "I was a young, upstart kid, so they wouldn't have anything to do with me."[20]

Moribund for several reasons by 1935, the decline of Houston LULAC Council No. 60 created a vacuum into which stepped some of the more strident young men around town, including Herrera. Together these gentlemen organized the LAC, which struck a more militant posture. LAC reflected Herrera's assertive nature. In 1937 the organization monitored the trial of two Houston police officers who allegedly beat to death Elpidio Cortez, a local resident and Mexican immigrant. Herrera attended the trial and gained infinite respect for all the attorneys involved in the proceedings. This experience helped to hone his love of the legal profession.[21]

In 1938 LAC protested the statement of city councilman S. A. Starskey, who in open session opined that he could not understand why the Mexican crew in the water department should be paid for the San Jacinto holiday, a day in which Mexicans faced defeat. Herrera told me years later that the official had actually made the comment directly to him when Herrera had protested the pay policy at a council meeting. On May 10, 1938, the *Houston Press* printed a letter to "The Mail Bag" by Herrera in which he deplored Starskey's "prejudicial statement" in the strongest of terms. Herrera's letter borrowed from his own heritage; he informed Starskey that people in the water department crew—"that gang of 37 men" of which he was one—could trace their ancestry "10 generations back on Texas soil, and one whose direct forefather signed the Texas Declaration of Independence." Herrera was no recent Mexican immigrant who felt pressure to be reticent. His letter took an extremely courageous, perhaps unprecedented, stand by a Mexican American in Houston, especially one only twenty-six years old. LAC's protest brought Starskey to apologize for his off-the-cuff remark.[22]

Herrera routinely called into question the differential wages and temporary status of the Mexican crew, and by his own account, his vocal nature resulted in his termination from this employment in 1939. But he stood tall in these public actions, and his fellow maintenance men good-naturedly dubbed him *abogado garras* (lawyer rags) because he was a law student / advocate who wore patched clothes to work.[23]

Herrera especially liked being in LAC because, as he said, "It was the first [Hispanic] club [in town] to ever have . . . guts enough to endorse candidates." Political aspirants came to speak at its meetings, sharpening Herrera's interest in the electoral process. He would always say, however, that LAC was "just a veritable voice in the wilderness" for voting rights, equal hiring practices, and advocating full citizenship under the law.[24]

After leaving the water department in 1939, Herrera took up taxi driving to support his family, and his cab served as a vehicle for other ventures into community action. First, he became involved in the taxicab drivers' union. At the behest of local liberal Democrats, he also helped to organize other unions in the refineries and ship channel industries, where substantial numbers of Mexican Americans worked. Despite his efforts, Herrera felt that the liberal Democrats (of which he always considered himself to be a part) never gave him his just desserts, a sentiment toward the Democratic Party common among Mexican Americans in Texas during those years. His opinion of the unions did not fare better; he felt that he had been "used" by them as well. He recalled that they only volunteered to buy him one "bowl of chili" in return for his efforts.[25]

Herrera's militancy took on a tempered edge in 1940 with the death of his father. When John returned to the Alamo City for the funeral, he experienced an epiphany. The burial took place, as his father had always wanted, in the family cemetery at Garza's Crossing, amid Herrera and Ruiz clan graves dating from 1800. John recalled that he then fully realized what Juan José had meant about "the glory that was early Texas" and how his illustrious ancestors had worked to build the state's foundations in cooperation with men like William B. Travis and Sam Houston. In short, after fifteen minutes at his father's grave, Herrera realized "what my heritage was, and that I was [now] sitting on a powder keg of injustice and prejudice."[26]

Herrera finally graduated in 1940 with his LL.B. He recalled that he was one of six Mexican Americans in his beginning classes, but only two of them finished. Yet he felt no discrimination and emerged with fond memories of camaraderie with many attorneys who would make their own mark on Houston. Herrera harbored no blanket animosities toward Anglos. He appreciated the complexities and subtle nature of interpersonal and interethnic relations.[27]

Between working and community action, Herrera found little time to study for the bar examination. As a result, he failed the test three times—in 1940, 1941, and 1942. School officials finally warned him in 1943 that if he failed it once more he would have to return to law school for another year. In response to this admonition, he moved his family to San Antonio and located himself in Austin to study. In 1943 he passed the bar on his fourth attempt, and the state licensed him to practice law at thirty-three years of age.[28]

As an attorney during World War II, Herrera's community activities increased. In the early 1940s he helped to rebuild the Houston LULAC Council that had been in hiatus. The "flying squadron" of San Antonio LULAC Council No. 2 had convinced the young men of LAC in 1939 to come back into the LULAC fold. Men such as Mauro M. Machado, Alonso Perales, Teodoro Góngora, and M. C. Gonzales told the young turks of LAC that they would have more clout within a larger organization; these LULAC leaders would forever hold a special place with Herrera. He threw himself into the organization and began to rise in its official ranks.[29]

Herrera soon also cemented his association with historian Dr. Carlos E. Castañeda, who had taken a position in 1943 with the Fair Employment Practices Committee (FEPC). Castañeda received a leave of absence from his position at the University of Texas to help rectify discriminatory labor situations within defense-related industries in Texas during World War II. Herrera had first seen Castañeda at various LULAC functions and had received encouragement from him while he studied for the bar in Austin.[30]

As an FEPC examiner, Castañeda contacted Herrera about possible instances of defense industry workplace discrimination. Herrera pointed to cases of flagrant abuse at the Humble Oil and Refining Company in Baytown.

He recounted that Castañeda had these conditions "stopped . . . right away." He also complained to Castañeda that the shipbuilding industries hesitated to hire Chicanos, which Castañeda likewise addressed. Herrera always maintained, with much validity, that these jobs added millions of dollars to the Mexican American economy.[31]

Herrera's bond with Castañeda strengthened the longer the two men associated. He recalled Castañeda as "the most learned man I ever met." One of the high points of Herrera's life came when he introduced Castañeda at a LULAC banquet during the war by noting that his work on behalf of home front workers made him "a man that's doing the work of at least two divisions." It was a turn of phrase that he would use again and again in honor of and deference to the great Castañeda. He even credited Castañeda with bringing him back to the church through Castañeda's example as a devout Catholic.[32]

When Herrera received his law license in 1943, he reportedly became the third Mexican American to practice law in Houston. He recalled having difficulty as an attorney at first because he did not know the ways of the courthouse or courtroom, especially as a Latin American defending Latino clients. He noted that he had to fall back on his intuition through understanding the traits of Mexican Americans and divining how they would have acted in given situations. While he dealt with prejudice and discrimination, key members of the Anglo legal establishment assisted him in numerous ways.[33]

As a young attorney and activist, Herrera had his critics. Some Mexican Houstonians thought him a publicity seeker. But Herrera saw things otherwise. He was no immigrant from a small town or Mexico with a retiring personality. Rather, he was a thorough Texan, conscious of his deeply rooted Tejano / San Antonio ancestry. He stood out in the crowd with his vibrant presence and confident urbane mannerisms.[34]

During the war, Council No. 60 kept LULAC alive in the Bayou City with Herrera as a principal figure in its activities. He rose steadily through the organization's ranks. Before he reached the ultimate office in the early 1950s, he would later note that he had held every position that LULAC offered. By 1942 he had become president of Council No. 60 and would hold that office at other times during the decade. For the next ten years, he was a self-described "work horse" for the organization. Already in the 1940s, Herrera and other members of the Houston council would go "LULACing" on the weekends—that is, they would travel to outlying towns along the Gulf Coast in Fort Bend, Brazoria, Galveston, Wharton, Victoria, and Jefferson Counties to organize. As he recalled vividly, "the further out we went . . . around Houston, the tougher the situation was."[35]

In 1943–1944 Herrera threw himself into the school desegregation of Pearland, a small community to the south of Houston. He led a Council No. 60 delegation that negotiated the eventual abolition of Pearland's substandard "Mexican School," one that had serviced the Hispanic children in the lower grades. For Herrera such a duty was "a labor of love." He reflected, "We didn't have money in those days. We dug out of our own pockets—left our own jobs" to participate.[36]

Herrera's actions with LULAC merged with his patriotic enthusiasm when the United States entered World War II. Although he was deferred from military service by 1943 as the father of three children, he named his second son Douglas MacArthur Herrera when the child's birth occurred on the day the media announced that General MacArthur had eluded the Japanese and reached Australia. He also began in 1942 to lead a LULAC delegation in laying a wreath at the San Jacinto Monument during the annual celebration of the 1836 battle. LULAC's participation commemorated the company of Tejanos who contributed to Sam Houston's defeat of General Antonio López de Santa Anna. In 1943 Herrera and Council No. 60 convinced the US Maritime Commission to name Liberty ships after Latin American and Mexican heroes. As a result, a Houston shipyard launched vessels named for Benito Juárez and José Antonio Navarro. By virtue of such leadership, by 1944 Herrera was LULAC district governor of his region.[37]

In the postwar years, Mexican Americans coming back from the service wanted to be full participants in society, and they accomplished this goal through organizational efforts. In Houston, LULAC Council No. 60 acted as the leading venue for such endeavors, and Herrera accelerated his advocacy. In this period, he truly earned the right to be called "Mr. LULAC." He embraced the organization like no one else in town. He had memorized its history and lore; he could and did readily recite the LULAC Code by heart.[38]

Houston LULAC, with Herrera in the fore, remained assertive during the immediate postwar period. He assumed the chairmanship of the local arrangements committee for the 1946 national LULAC convention in Houston hosted by Council No. 60. That same year, he led the pro bono defense team for Macario García, the highly acclaimed World War II Medal of Honor winner and Houston resident. García had been indicted for assault when he took umbrage at being refused service in a cafe in Richmond, Texas. In 1948 Herrera won election as the Texas LULAC regional governor. He headed the Houston delegation at the 1948 LULAC national convention in Austin, offering a resolution that called for reversing LULAC's constitutional restriction on political activity. Its proposal sought "to change our constitution so that all LULAC Councils have the right to openly engage in politics and to endorse . . . any candidate . . . of mutual good to our people." The resolution failed, but their statement was in keeping with that of LAC during the 1930s.[39]

During the late 1940s, Herrera also wrote businesspeople around Houston asking them to hire Mexican Americans in the many stores sprouting up as a result of postwar prosperity. For instance, he sent a letter to Glen McCarthy after the famous oilfield wildcatter opened the Shamrock Hotel on South Main in 1949. He politely requested McCarthy to add Spanish-speaking staff to make the new hotel more attractive to international guests. In response, Herrera proudly stated years later that McCarthy called him and said, "John, you just send them over here. I'll put 'em all to work."[40]

Herrera always criticized the racist policies the Houston police force practiced, including its refusal to hire Hispanic officers. In 1950 he played a crucial role in recruiting the first Mexican American, Raúl C. Martínez, for admission to the Houston Police Academy. Martínez became a uniformed police officer.[41]

These immediate postwar years also initiated Herrera's association and friendship with Gustavo "Gus" C. García of San Antonio. He had heard much about García—the San Antonian's years as an academic prodigy at the University of Texas, his gifts as an orator, his youthful graduation from law school and skills as an attorney, his association with LULAC, his experiences in the military during the war, his charisma, and his status as the fair-haired young up-and-comer. As Herrera put it, "Everybody knew that Gus was the man to watch."[42]

Herrera so readily identified with García that when they met in 1945, they embraced one another (*un abrazo*) as if they had known each other for years. Their San Antonio roots bonded them further. Even more flamboyant than Herrera, García made an immediate impression on everyone. As Herrera told me many times, "No one equaled Gus, and I've met 'em all. Gus could talk his way through a brick wall."[43]

From the start, Herrera learned from García. He credited García with helping him refine his oratorical delivery and achieve the sort of polish he wanted as an attorney. In turn, Herrera gave García succor during some of his most troubled times. They were kindred spirits and similar in many ways. They would be LULAC brothers and legal comrades-in-arms for the next two decades. Herrera and García were likewise political soul mates—that is to say, they were self-professed "yellow dog Democrats." Herrera remained one for his entire life. Both men campaigned for Democratic Party candidates from Allan Shivers to Adlai Stevenson.[44]

With García, Herrera became involved as one of the initial attorneys in the 1948 *Minerva Delgado, et al. v. Bastrop Independent School District of Bastrop County, et al.* lawsuit initiated by LULAC under the national presidency of Raoul Cortez, a San Antonio businessman. This case ruled school segregation of Mexican American children unconstitutional, and for activists in the 1940s, it represented a landmark decision. For Herrera, these years comprised a time of great enthusiasm for civil rights endeavors in the courts, even though the LULAC litigants routinely experienced setbacks.[45]

By the beginning of the 1950s, fellow LULACers knew Herrera as a diligent, committed stalwart and one who wanted to be national president. Never a person to be stopped by defeat, he ran unsuccessfully twice. He finally won on his third attempt, elected at the 1952 national convention in Corpus Christi with the support of delegates from the many councils he had organized.[46]

His presidency (1952–1953) was as productive as it could be given the limited resources that plagued LULAC. Herrera reflected many years later that often LULAC's "enthusiasm would go according to our pocketbooks." His tenure in office expanded the organization in Texas and New Mexico; he helped form or reorganize a total of thirty-one councils. During his presidency, LULAC began to lay the groundwork for fighting segregation of Mexican Americans in the schools of Pecos, Texas. Such discrimination in education still existed, regardless of the *Delgado* decision. Perhaps his most far-reaching move, however, involved helping to orchestrate joint policymaking between the national LULAC office and the American GI Forum. Herrera knew and respected Héctor P. García, the World War II veteran who had played the guiding role in the formation of the latter group in 1948.[47]

Despite Herrera's high level of enthusiasm, the perils of the national presidency took their toll. As he said later, "I had foolishly promised during my campaign speeches that I would go to every organization and visit at least once. So out of my own pocket, I had to go through Arizona, New Mexico, and Colorado, and by the time I got home, my practice was shot." He traveled by bus and by automobile, using any type of transportation he could acquire to reach his destination, taking in so many LULAC banquets (where he ate the obligatory chicken supper) that when he returned home, he asked Olivia not to serve him chicken. He went on the radio whenever he could to talk about LULAC, and he made legions of speeches at community meetings.[48]

At the end of his first term, he sought reelection vigorously at the national convention held in Santa Fe, but Alberto Armendariz of El Paso, who electioneered near his home turf, defeated him. Although disappointed, Herrera showed resilience. He soon concluded that another year in office would have left his personal finances in shambles. When Frank Pinedo, an Austin-based attorney, assumed the presidency in 1954, he appointed Herrera to the position of LULAC national organizer. Herrera simultaneously made three unsuccessful bids for the Texas State Legislature during the 1950s.[49]

In 1954, however, Herrera—as LULACer, attorney, and civil rights advocate—took part in a landmark event that would imprint itself upon his very being. This milestone, carried out with Gus García and others, was the decision handed down by the US Supreme Court in *Hernández v. Texas* (1954) that barred the exclusion of Mexican Americans from petit and grand juries.

While it is not within the scope of this essay to recite the particulars of this case (which has become the subject of articles, books, and documentary films), Herrera played a crucial role in its successful conclusion. Of the three attorneys who went before the Supreme Court, García and Carlos Cadena of San Antonio have received the most fanfare, for they made the verbal arguments to the justices. As the third attorney at the table, however, Herrera provided critical assistance.[50]

Herrera had served at the initial 1951 trial of Hernández with García in Edna, Texas. He also acted as a witness at that first trial regarding the segregation he found in the public restrooms at the Jackson County Courthouse. García had agreed to defend Hernández for the murder of a popular Edna Mexican American. Finding no support at the trial from Anglos or Latinos in the area, García later wrote, "I decided to contact the only man I knew who could possibly help me, namely, John J. Herrera of Houston, who, at the time was the first National Vice-President of the LULACs. I explained the situation to him. I told him that I was jittery and that I was in desperate need of help." Herrera never hesitated. García further explained that he "didn't even ask if there was money for expenses." Herrera thus accompanied García from almost the inception of the case. When the case reached the Supreme Court in 1954, he served as statistician (handing Cadena and García the notes they needed as they addressed the justices) and, perhaps more important, as a legal, steadfast, and moral force in the proceedings from Jackson County to Washington, DC.[51]

Equally significant, Herrera began to tell the story (and importance) of the decision almost from the moment the court rendered it, and he spoke about it for the rest of his life. While García had great oratorical skills and Cadena possessed a keen legal mind, they made few comments on the case after it transpired. García penned a concise factual account of it in the mid-1950s, but he would die in the mid-1960s, having had little time to philosophize about the case's impact. Cadena remained relatively quiet about the matter. Herrera, however, understood the significance of *Hernández v. Texas* just as well as the other two lawyers, and he played the major role in placing it into the narrative of Chicano history and lore. He presented it as the stuff of fable; he told about it in *fabulous* terms as a first-person participant.[52]

Herrera's statements about the *Hernández* case began in the June 1954 issue of *LULAC News*, when he wrote a letter to the "In Our Mailbox" section in which he reported on the decision as "cerró con broche de oro" (closing with a golden brooch) twenty-five years of LULAC's "fighting existence." He concisely related its history from the initial phase; the roles that García, James DeAnda, Cadena, and he played; and the actual arguments Cadena and García presented to the Supreme Court on that fateful day of January 11, 1954. He also had the entire decision printed in that issue for posterity.[53]

Herrera understood the primary role of Mexican American attorneys in community advocacy. He knew that lawyers could be more strident than Mexican American businessmen, the latter having to be careful for fear they would lose income. He would even foster the careers of civic-conscious young lawyers such as DeAnda, who would become a distinguished member of the bar and bench. Herrera hired DeAnda when the latter came fresh from law school at the University of Texas. Herrera had DeAnda assist in the Hernández case and later introduced him to Héctor P. García, who enticed DeAnda to Corpus Christi to begin a successful practice. DeAnda later became a federal judge for the Southern District of Texas.[54]

At the same time, Herrera realized that many Mexican American graduates from major law schools looked askance at individuals (like himself) who had attended lesser institutions. He held no grudge against them for their understated disdain. As a courageous advocate, he stayed active on many fronts and had no need to defer to anyone, even though he and other lawyers who "served in the trenches" did not always receive the respect they deserved from the Hispanic alumni of more prestigious schools. Herrera for the most part dismissed this condescension and did not allow it to interfere with his admiration for fellow LULAC attorneys.[55]

Herrera soon took on another adversary, this one within LULAC. In 1954 Félix Tijerina, Houston millionaire restaurateur, began the first of two terms as regional LULAC governor. From 1956 to 1960, Tijerina served four terms as LULAC national president. These two good men had known one another for many years, but they diametrically opposed one another's approach and had a mutual antipathy for the other. Their clash seemed natural, almost inevitable: Herrera, the outspoken advocate, and Tijerina, the more conservative entrepreneur, focusing on Mexican American preschool English language training. Tijerina's concern with education resulted in the creation of his famous Little School of the 400, an effort to teach Spanish-dominant children to master 400 basic English words required for academic success.[56]

Herrera initially supported Tijerina for LULAC national president, but the two soon sparred over a range of issues. After 1954 LULAC Council No. 60 members sided almost solidly with Tijerina. Even some of Herrera's protégés took sides against him and viewed him as an irritant. Herrera joined the opposition to Tijerina that sprang up among LULAC members from other geographic areas.[57]

After Tijerina left the national presidency in 1960, Herrera returned to the top echelons of LULAC as legal advisor to Alfred J. Hernández, the third national president of LULAC from Council No. 60 between 1952 and the 1960s. Hernández had been a loyal Tijerina supporter and tried to bridge the gap between the two men.[58] In the history of the Bayou City, especially during the late 1940s–1960s, Herrera stood as one of three giants in that organization, the other two being Tijerina and Hernández. At the risk of stretching an artistic analogy, scholars appropriately mention Herrera, Tijerina, and Hernández in the same paragraph when discussing the history of Houston and LULAC, much as writers list Diego Rivera, José Clemente Orozco, and David Alfaro Siqueiros together in Mexican history and revolutionary painting.

As for Herrera's association with Gus García, the two men stayed close. García would come from San Antonio to practice with Herrera and other Houston attorneys on numerous occasions between the time of the Hernández case and García's death in 1964. Relations between the two friends sometimes became rocky because of García's drinking problems, a condition which troubled Herrera.[59]

In 1960 the candidacy of John F. Kennedy captivated Herrera as much as it did Mexican Americans of his generation across the Southwest. The youthful, charismatic Roman Catholic struck a chord with him. Gus García had made Herrera aware of Kennedy in 1956 and had told him that this man would someday be president. During the 1960 election, Herrera toured with Gus, Héctor P. García, New Mexico Senator Dennis Chávez, and others to help Kennedy win.[60]

The high point of Herrera's association with the Kennedy presidency occurred on November 21, 1963, the night before the assassination, and it became an occasion that Herrera helped to sear into Mexican American history. In early October 1963, Herrera, veteran Houston LULACer David Adame, and John's son, Mike Herrera, came up with the idea of inviting the president and his wife, Jackie, and Vice President Lyndon Johnson and his wife, Lady Bird, to attend an evening function for LULAC state director Joe Garza on November 21 at the Rice Hotel. About that time, the presidential party was scheduled to be at a testimonial dinner in Houston in honor of longtime Congressman Albert Thomas. The Houston LULACers mentioned in their letters of invitation to the administration that many of the folks who would attend their event had been in the 1960 Viva Kennedy-Johnson clubs. Almost miraculously, the president and his party accepted, and they spent twenty-two historic minutes at the LULAC reception. Herrera served as emcee and became filled with emotion as he conversed with and then introduced the president and his wife to the audience. The following day, the president was murdered. That Kennedy had spent part of his last evening with

Mexican Americans—and with LULACers in particular—made the memory of the fallen president even more precious to Herrera. When he heard that Kennedy had been killed, Herrera went home and cried out in anguish to his family, "Han matado a mi presidente!" (They have killed my president!), a sentiment that could only be released by using what he called "the Spanish language of my fathers." He would recount these events in writing and conversation for posterity. The photos of that event, including ones of Herrera with Kennedy, are iconic.[61]

Herrera also witnessed the demise of his good friend Gus García. García had been in and out of Houston over the years and stayed frequently in hospitals to combat alcohol addiction; Herrera had helped in any way he could. When García died in early June 1964, his family called Herrera to San Antonio for the funeral. Believing that Herrera had been García's closest friend, they turned to him to coordinate aspects of the burial. Herrera chose the pallbearers as well as the people to speak at the graveside. This act of loyalty was not the last service he performed for his friend. As much, perhaps more, than anyone else, he helped to keep the memory of Gus García alive, and Gus now has become the stuff of conventional history.[62]

Herrera stayed civically active for the rest of his life in ways too numerous to list here. As Alfred Hernández once told me, "John was the type of man who accomplished more . . . by accident than most people did by trying." When I made acquaintance with Herrera in the 1980s, I gained glimpses into his world. I visited him in his downtown Houston office, where I overheard political hopefuls asking for his endorsement. He often gave legal advice over the telephone and spoke straight from the shoulder. Inscribed photos and campaign posters of Hispanic officeholders that acknowledged his pioneering role adorned the walls of his suite.

He and his wife had five children together but divorced later in life. He subsequently married Carmen García, with whom he had a son. Herrera reveled in his family, which included his three sons, three daughters, and grandchildren.[63]

Herrera never gave up on LULAC. He received an appointment as LULAC national legal advisor during the mid-1960s and again in the 1970s. He took sides in LULAC issues during the 1980s, even when his stances meant incurring the wrath of some of the membership. He took great exception with anyone who mistakenly portrayed the LULAC of old as a "country club organization."[64]

Herrera died on October 12, 1986, from the results of a stroke. Poetically, he passed from this earth on Columbus Day, which is also known as Día de la Raza, a traditional day of celebration of Hispanic heritage.[65]

I hold many fond memories of Herrera. The most lasting ones came from the LULAC history conference that the Houston Metropolitan Research Center and LULAC Council No. 60 held jointly in 1984, on the occasion of the fiftieth anniversary of LULAC's presence in Houston. As the elder past national president from the Bayou City, he served as the keynote speaker and also addressed the gala that evening. As he had done during his entire adult life, John J. Herrera, the lion-hearted, did not fail to impress. He was "Mr. LULAC," and his fabulous life will be remembered.

Notes

I wish to thank Arnoldo De León for his invaluable editorial assistance. I also wish to express my gratitude to Don E. Carleton, Kemo Curry, Joel Draut, Ignacio M. García, Joyce Herrera Harper, Douglas M. Herrera, John Michael Herrera, Louis J. Marchiafava, Chrystel Pit, Anthony Quiroz, Elizabeth Sargent, and Mikaela Selley.

1. Betram D. Wolfe, *The Fabulous Life of Diego Rivera* (New York: Stein and Day, 1963), 6.

2. I conducted four formal recorded oral history interviews with Herrera, including ones on May 22, 1981, October 29, 1981, November 5, 1983, and February 29, 1984. All four are in the Oral History Collection at the Houston Metropolitan Research Center. My many unrecorded conversations with Herrera took place at his office, by telephone, and at LULAC events.

3. Herrera interview, May 22, 1981; biographical article on John J. Herrera, *Pan American* (San Antonio), ca. 1940s, box 1, folder 2, John J. Herrera Papers, Houston Metropolitan Research Center, Houston Public Library (HMRC) (hereafter Herrera Papers); and "John J. Herrera Announces for Legislature Position No. 8," ca. 1952, box 10, folder 13 Herrera Papers.

4. Herrera interview, May 22, 1981, and John J. Herrera, resume, box 1, folder 3, Herrera Papers.

5. Herrera interview, May 22, 1981.

6. Ibid.

7. Ibid.

8. Thomas H. Kreneck, *Mexican American Odyssey: Félix Tijerina, Entrepreneur and Civic Leader, 1905–1965* (College Station: Texas A&M University Press, 2001), 38–39; and Herrera interview, May 22, 1981.

9. Herrera interview, May 22, 1981.

10. Ibid.

11. Ibid.

12. Ibid.

13. Ibid.

14. Ibid.

15. Ibid.

16. Herrera interview, November 5, 1983.

17. Herrera interviews, May 22, 1981, October 29, 1981, and November 5, 1983; and Herrera resume.

18. Herrera interview, May 22, 1981.

19. Ibid.; and Herrera interview, November 5, 1983.

20. Herrera interviews October 29, 1981, November 5, 1983.

21. Herrera interview, November 5, 1983; and F. Arturo Rosales, "Mexicans in Houston: The Struggle to Survive," *Houston Review* 3 (Summer 1981): 241–42.

22. Rosales, "Mexicans in Houston," 242; Herrera interview, May 22, 1981; and *Houston Press*, May 10, 1938, clippings scrapbook, Juvencio Rodríguez Collection, HMRC.

23. Herrera interviews, May 22, 1981, and November 5, 1983.

24. Herrera interview, November 5, 1983.

25. Herrera interview, October 29, 1981.

26. Herrera interview, November 5, 1983.

27. Herrera interview, May 22, 1981.

28. Herrera interview, November 5, 1983.

29. Ibid.; Herrera interview, February 29, 1984; and "LULAC Past National Presidents and Their Administrations," box 7, folder 9, Herrera Papers. The flying squadron was a group of San Antonio LULACers who organized councils in various parts of Texas during the 1930s.

30. Félix D. Almaraz, Jr., *Knight Without Armor: Carlos Eduardo Castañeda, 1896–1958* (College Station: Texas A&M University Press, 1999), 216–61; and Herrera interview, October 29, 1981.

31. Herrera interviews, October 29, 1981, and November 5, 1983.

32. Herrera interview, October 29, 1981.

33. Herrera interview, November 5, 1983.

34. Ibid.

35. Kreneck, *Mexican American Odyssey*, 103; LULAC banquet program, box 5, folder 1, Herrera Papers; and Herrera interviews, October 29, 1981, and November. 5, 1983.

36. Herrera interviews, November 5, 1983, and October 29, 1981.

37. Arnoldo De León, *Ethnicity in the Sunbelt: Mexican Americans in Houston* (Houston: Mexican American Studies Program, University of Houston, 1989), 92–93; Kreneck, *Mexican American Odyssey*, 102–3; John J. Herrera to Romeo Vera, Sr., September 28, 1967, Herrera resume, and clipping regarding Liberty ships, April 1943, all in box 1, folder 3, Herrera Papers; and Benjamín Márquez, *LULAC: The Evolution of a Mexican American Political Organization* (Austin: University of Texas Press, 1993), 53.

38. Kreneck, *Mexican American Odyssey*, 99–100, 102–3; De León, *Ethnicity in the Sunbelt*, 130–31; and Herrera interviews, October 29, 1981, and November 5, 1983.

39. Kreneck, *Mexican American Odyssey*, 93, 103–5; and Herrera to Arnulfo Zamora, n.d., box 5, folder 20, Herrera Papers.

40. Herrera interview, October 29, 1981.

41. Kreneck, *Mexican American Odyssey*, 132–34; Herrera to M. E. Walter, March 11, 1950, box 1, folder 8, Herrera Papers; and Herrera interview, May 22, 1981.

42. Herrera interview, February 29, 1984.

43. Ibid.

44. Ibid.; and Herrera interview, November 5, 1983.

45. Herrera interview, October 29, 1981; Herrera resume; John J. Herrera employment record, box 1, folder 3, Herrera Papers; and "John J. Herrera Remembers When," *Houston Post*, August 22, 1976, box 1, folder 4; and "For LULAC National President," n.d., box 5, folder 22, both in Herrera Papers.

46. Herrera interview, October 29, 1981; and "LULACs Name Houston Attorney," *Houston Chronicle*, ca. 1952, box 10, folder 15, Herrera Papers.

47. Herrera interview, October 29, 1981; *LULAC: Fifty Years of Serving Hispanics, Golden Anniversary* (n.p., n.d.); John J. Herrera, *Twenty First National President of LULAC, Houston, Texas*, 1952–1953; Ed Idar to Héctor P. García, November 18, 1952, folder 215.2, and Herrera to all LULAC officers and members, mimeographed circular, ca. 1952–1953, folder 216.1, both in Dr. Héctor P. García Papers, Special Collections and Archives, Texas A&M University–Corpus Christi (hereafter García Papers); *LULAC News*, August–September 1952, box 1, folder 3, Herrera Papers; and "A Message From Your National President," *LULAC News*, January 1953, *LULAC News* Collection, HMRC.

48. Herrera interview, October 29, 1981.

49. Ibid.; Mathew H. Kelly to Herrera, June 19, 1953, and Herrera to Neville G. Penrose, July 23, 1953, both in box 5, folder 20; "Continue LULAC's Progress," June 12–14, 1953, box 5, folder 22; clippings, box 10, folders 13 and 15; and "Resume of John J. Herrera, Political Activities," box 1, folder 3, all in Herrera Papers; and Carole E. Christian, "Herrera, John J.," *The New Handbook of Texas*, vol. 3 (Austin: Texas State Historical Association, 1996), 575.

50. Major examinations of *Hernández v. Texas* that have appeared coinciding with its fiftieth anniversary include Michael A. Olivas, ed., *"Colored Men" and "Hombres Aquí"*: Hernández v. Texas *and the Emergence of Mexican-American Lawyering* (Houston: Arte Público, 2006); *A Class Apart: A Mexican American Civil Rights Story*, directed by Carlos Sandoval, produced by Carlos Sandoval and Peter Miller (New York: Camino Bluff Productions, 2006); and Ignacio M. García, *White But Not Equal: Mexican Americans, Jury Discrimination, and the Supreme Court* (Tucson: University of Arizona Press, 2009), the latter being the most scholarly historical analysis of the case, issues, and individuals involved.

51. Gustavo C. García, "An Informal Report to the People," in *A Cotton Picker Finds Justice! The Saga of the Hernández Case*, comp. Ruben Mungía (n.p., ca. 1954), folder 133.18, García Papers; *LULAC News*, June 1954, 19; García, *White But Not Equal*, 32–48, 45; and *American GI Forum News Bulletin*, November 1954, box 1, folder 3, Herrera Papers.

52. García, "An Informal Report to the People"; Maury Maverick, foreword to *A Cotton Picker Finds Justice!*; and Herrera interview, October 29, 1981. In subsequent years, I heard Herrera tell facets of the story of the *Hernández* case on numerous occasions. As a first-person participant, he was popularly viewed as the most articulate spokesperson regarding the case. For one of his later written descriptions, see John J. Herrera, letter to the editor, *Houston Post*, February 22, 1972, box 2, folder 24, Herrera Papers.

53. *LULAC News*, June 1954, 4, 17, 19–20. Gus García and Herrera taped a program for radio station KLVL, located in Pasadena, Texas (i.e., Houston), shortly after they argued the case, a session undoubtedly arranged by Herrera with the station's owners Félix and Angelina Morales. In the late 1940s, Herrera had served as local counsel for the Moraleses when they applied for the station's frequency with the Federal Communications Commission. As a LULAC official, John had spoken on KLVL many times. See García, *White But Not Equal*, 221n62, 145–46.

54. Herrera interviews, November 5, 1983, and October 29, 1981.

55. Herrera interview, February 29, 1984; Kreneck, *Mexican American Odyssey*, 101; and Ignacio M. García, telephone conversation with author, May 15, 2009.

56. De León, *Ethnicity in the Sunbelt*, 130–42; and Kreneck, *Mexican American Odyssey*, 99–105, 203–8.

57. Kreneck, *Mexican American Odyssey*, 203–8.

58. Ibid., 154, 309–10.

59. Herrera interview, February 29, 1984; and Herrera to George H. Templin, October 4, 1957, box 2, folder 20, Herrera Papers.

60. Herrera interviews, February 29, 1984, and October 29, 1981; Herrera resume, and Woodrow Seals and John H. Crooker, Jr. to Herrera, November 26, 1960, both in box 1, folder 3, Herrera Papers.

61. "Han Matado A Mi Presidente," box 3, folder 16, Herrera Papers; Herrera interview, February 29, 1984; Thomas H. Kreneck, *Del Pueblo: A Pictorial History of Houston's Hispanic Community* (Houston: Houston International University, 1989), 153, 170–71; John J. Herrera, "They've Killed My President," *Houston Chronicle*, November 18, 1983, box 12, folder 33, Herrera Papers; John J. Herrera, "Last Hours of J. F. K.," *LULAC News*, November–December 1963, 1–3; and photographs of LULAC reception for John F. Kennedy, Alex Arroyos / John F. Kennedy Collection, HMRC.

62. Herrera interview, February 29, 1984. The most poignant correspondence from Gus García to Herrera can be found in box 2, folder 20, Herrera Papers.

63. Christian, "Herrera, John J.," 575; "La Familia Herrera, Feliz!," *La Gráfica* (Houston), June 29, 1976, 5, box 1, folder 3, clippings, William (Canales) Gutierrez Collection, HMRC); Herrera resume; and "Rites Wednesday for John J. Herrera," *Houston Post*, October 14, 1986, n.p., box 1, folder 26, Herrera Papers.

64. Herrera interview, October 29, 1981; Romeo Vera, Sr. to Herrera, August 3, 1964, box 6, folder 18; Herrera to Dear Brother and Sister LULACs, April 21, 1977, box 7, folder 14; and John J. Herrera, "LULAC: The First 50 Years," speech, box 10, folder 36, all in Herrera Papers.

65. Christian, "Herrera, John J.," 575 and Guillermo Aguayo, "Johnny . . . My Friend," box 1, folder 26, Herrera Papers.

Figure 10.1. Newlyweds Vicente and Maria Ximenes, Floresville, Texas, ca. 1945. Vicente T. Ximenes Papers, Wilson County Historical Society, Floresville, Texas.

10

Vicente Ximenes and LBJ's Great Society

The Rhetorical Imagination of the American GI Forum[1]

MICHELLE HALL KELLS

The history of mid-twentieth-century civil rights reform reveals that social movements must become part of the sinew of governing organizations to affect enduring institutional change. They must shape and exercise the muscle and connective tissue of policy and practice from the inside out. It is not enough to stir a movement for social change. Activists must implement and administer institutional transformation. As the framers of the US Constitution realized early on, self-governance is a collective and generative endeavor. Democratization is a process of "progressive recognition and inclusion of different groups in the political life of society"[2] In *Doubt and the Demands of Democratic Citizenship*, David R. Hiley argues, "The legitimacy of democratic decision making depends on the political process being equally open to all citizen, or at least to legitimate representatives of all citizens."[3]

This chapter expands current research of post–World War II civil rights activism by examining the political history of Vicente Ximenes and his role as organizer and moderator of the historic 1967 Cabinet Committee Hearings on Mexican American Affairs in El Paso, Texas (also referred to as the White

DOI: 10.5876/9781607323372.c010

House Conference on Mexican American Affairs or the El Paso conference).[4] Ximenes holds a unique place in US civil rights history. He represents one of the few civil rights leaders who functioned as an activist, agitator, and mobilizer as well as operated as a national-level government representative, administrator, and policymaker. Few leaders in twentieth-century US history can claim this distinction. The Mexican American World War II generation signaled an unprecedented shift in civic participation. Maggie Rivas-Rodriguez argues in *Mexican Americans and World War II*, "It was not the actual battlefield experiences that set apart the Mexican American World War II experience, although Mexican Americans did have more Medals of Honor than any other ethnic group . . . What did separate the war-years experience for Mexican Americans, however, was that it would be the first time that they were participating fully in mainstream society, even working alongside Anglos as equals."[5]

Ximenes served as an Air Force major and was awarded two medals for combat duty in World War II. After his return from the battlefield, he emerged over the next twenty years as one of the highest ranking appointees in Lyndon B. Johnson's presidential administration and one of the most influential government representatives of Mexican American issues in post–World War II history. He served in the Johnson administration as the Commissioner of the Equal Employment Opportunity Commission (EEOC) (1967–1972) and the chairman of the president's Cabinet Committee on Mexican American Affairs (1967–1969). Ximenes also held the position of vice president for field operations under the National Urban Coalition (1972–1973).

Few leaders have had as far-reaching impact on the lives of Latinos in terms of equal opportunity in business, educational, and civic access. President Jimmy Carter appointed him to the Commission on White House Fellowships (1977–1981). He continues to serve as chairman of the New Mexico Youth Conservation Corps Commission, a position he held for nearly two decades, appointed by New Mexico's governor in 1991 and recently reappointed by Governor Bill Richardson in 2003. Ximenes was the recipient of the Common Cause Public Service Achievement Award (1982) and the New Mexico Distinguished Service Award (1981). He was awarded an honorary PhD in Humane Letters from the University of New Mexico in 2008 and currently lives in Albuquerque, New Mexico.

The rich rhetorical career of Vicente Ximenes spans nearly seven decades of human rights activism and leadership. He survives most of his World War II *compadres*, including his longtime Texas friends and cohorts, Dr. Héctor P. García and former President Johnson. Ximenes remains active in the Youth Conservation Corps, a program he instituted in New Mexico, as well as other human rights endeavors. Ximenes had spent many years caring for his ailing wife, María, who passed away on September 26, 2009. They celebrated over sixty-six years of marriage, sharing a devoted partnership that endured the challenges of military service, international assignments, civil rights organizing, and numerous White House appointments while sustaining a strong family life. The equity and mutuality that characterized their marriage inflected the activities and projects that distinguish Ximenes as one of the great Mexican American civil rights leaders of the twentieth century. The rhetorical presence, community engagement, social commitment, and spiritual generosity that informed his career found its source in the circle of relationships that shaped his life. "María was the thread that held everything together," friends reflected.[6]

Ximenes continues to mentor and invigorate community activism in Albuquerque, most recently by instituting the Vicente Ximenes Scholarship in Rhetoric and Community Literacy at the University of New Mexico (2005) to help stimulate a growing pool of research and knowledge in language and literacy that can be used to improve human relations across social groups in the state. Ximenes recognizes the necessity of cultivating skilled leaders to facilitate cultural, civic, educational, and economic development in New Mexico. His legacy evolves out of the critical historical moment of the World War II generation of Mexican American activists and extends to the landmark moment of the twenty-first-century Barack Obama–era generation of social reformers.

The first part of this chapter will provide an overview of Ximenes's political biography. The last part of this essay will examine his leadership role as chair of the 1967 Cabinet Committee Hearings on Mexican American Affairs, marking the inclusion of Mexican Americans in national civil rights reform.

Deliberative Democracy and Mexican American Civic Participation

As a World War II veteran, organizer of the American GI Forum (AGIF), educator, economist, political activist, government official, and social reformer, Ximenes successfully negotiated multiple roles and communities to institute and promote affirmative action policies on behalf of historically disenfranchised groups. In addition, he helped to launch bilingual education initiatives and fought for the inclusion of Hispanic-dominant areas in Johnson's urban renewal Model Cities Program. His legacy provides an important historical link in Mexican American civic engagement and represents one of the many influential strands of civil rights discourse of twentieth-century US history. Ximenes offers a particularly efficacious model of mid-twentieth century community organizing and deliberative democratic processes that evolved toward government institutionalization and civic inclusion for Mexican Americans. Ximenes's legacy maps the process from rhetorical imagination to rhetorical efficacy.

Social movements like Mexican American civil rights activism played a critical role in sustaining and invigorating postwar democracy. Founded by Dr. Héctor P. García in 1948, the AGIF represents a giant imaginative leap that moved Mexican American organizing from state- and regional-level mobilization into a national organization with far-reaching implications. Under García's leadership, Ximenes organized new chapters outside Texas and promoted public deliberation and engagement across the nation. He exercised rhetorical agency by articulating public problems and generating solutions for Mexican American communities and was a key player in the progression from Mexican American civic mobilization to civic inclusion.

The rhetorical impact of Ximenes's style of leadership resonated deeply with Mexican American communities and bridged the World War II–generation reformers of the 1950s with the Chicano activists of the 1960s. His political impulse and rhetorical imagination rested upon four dimensions of democratic practice, values inculcated throughout his youth growing up in South Texas and young adulthood serving in the US Air Force during World War II. Dissent, deliberation, dissonance, and disputation framed the discursive guideposts undergirding his earliest activist work as an organizer for the American GI Forum through his tenure as a commissioner on the EEOC, the chair of the Inter-Agency Committee on Mexican American Affairs, and the chair of the Cabinet Committee Hearings in El Paso. He represents one of the few leaders who successfully appealed to moderate reformers, as well as radical activists, through a deliberative approach to problem solving. Ximenes understood that viable democratic institutions most effectively practice civic participation and promote civic literacy when they permit and invite citizens into the democratic paradox of collective action and dissent, or what Hiley describes as "deep conviction and deep doubt."[7] Through his roles as a grassroots community activist as well as a national-ranking administrator, Ximenes cultivated opportunities locally and nationally to advance discursive democratic processes—most dramatically illustrated at the El Paso hearings. Moreover, the political career of Ximenes illustrates that the practice of deliberative democracy is a dynamic, generative, and pragmatic process of engaging disparate positions.

Whereas the grand narrative of twentieth-century civil rights reform traditionally focuses on African American civil rights activism, the examination of the deliberative rhetoric of Mexican American civil rights leaders such as Ximenes offers a relevant and timely heuristic of US civic activism. Johnson recognized the El Paso hearings as a significant moment in US civil rights history. Moreover, the history of Mexican American civil rights reform remains integral to the US democratic process of constituting what John S. Dryzek calls a "flourishing oppositional civil society"[8] The legacies of Ximenes, García, and the AGIF illustrate that the essence of discursive democracy is not only exercising the vote but participating in public deliberation. All three rallied together for over two decades for Mexican American access to the ballot as well as the political platform. Together they enacted a number of discursive democratic practices, acting on the conviction that deliberative processes allow citizens to discover their political interests, make sense of the issues that influence their lives, cultivate public opinions, and take positions on problems. Ximenes exercised these public rhetorical acts with diverse constituencies when he convened the 1967 El Paso hearings, which, as such, represent a landmark moment in national-level Mexican American civic participation.

Carlos Kevin Blanton argues in *The Strange Career of Bilingual Education in Texas, 1836–1981*, "Many scholars identify the El Paso Conference as the point from which the Chicano movement and the Chicano Generation of leadership emerged."[9] Unfortunately, the rhetorical import of the conference has been generally effaced from the narrative construction of the postwar civil rights movement and Chicano history. As I argued in *Héctor P. García: Everyday Rhetoric and Mexican American Civil Rights*, "The slow progression of American civil rights reform leading to the passage of the historic 1965 Civil Rights Act" and the eventual appointment of Ximenes to the EEOC and the El Paso hearings in 1967 was "teleologically linked to the relationships and issues articulated by Mexican-American activists" throughout the postwar era.[10] Ximenes directed the El Paso hearings, inviting Chicano nationalists into dialogue with members of Johnson's cabinet and postwar Mexican American reformers such as League of United Latin American Citizens (LULAC) leaders and the AGIF. It was the first and only moment in postwar history to successfully engage all of these different stakeholders across interest groups together in dialogue about Mexican American social and political concerns. The trajectory of Ximenes's political career began in the rural South Texas territory near the crossroads of San Antonio.

Ximenes Legacy: From Floresville, Texas, to Washington, DC

Vicente Ximenes was born in 1919 in Floresville, Texas, a town of about 2,000 divided strictly along ethnic and racial lines: *Mexicanos*, Polish, German, Anglos, and African Americans. He came from a family of Texas colonists who settled the area when it was still Mexican territory. His ancestors helped to build the town and held leadership positions in city government for generations. Vicente was one of eight children born to José Jesús Ximenes and Herlinda Treviño Ximenes. His father, a graduate of Draughon's Business College of San Antonio, maintained a strong commitment to education.[11] José ran his own general store for years before competition forced him out of business. Educated, articulate, and literate in Spanish and English, he was an important figure in his community.

As noted by Julie Leininger Pycior in *LBJ and Mexican Americans: The Paradox of Power*, José Ximenes was a political force in early twentieth-century South Texas. He had more formal education than most of the town leaders and held a distinguished role in Floresville.[12] José served as the court interpreter and became active in local politics. He provided both legal and business guidance for the citizens of Floresville, interpreting documents for those who could not speak English, bailing out those in trouble with the law, and extending credit to those who were struggling financially. José also served as the district clerk for adjoining counties. In many respects, he functioned as the political patron of Floresville, effectively negotiating between Anglo and Mexicano as well as state and local power structures. In addition, he maintained strong relations with Sam Fore, editor of the *Floresville Chronicle Journal* and chairman of the Texas Democratic Party. Likewise, Lyndon B. Johnson shared strong alliances with Fore as a personal friend, mentor, and political supporter.

The Johnson political network included other key players from South Texas. Vicente and his brother Edward attended high school with John Connally. Connally's lifelong association with Johnson, like Vicente's, would eventually lead to Cabinet-level appointments when Johnson finally occupied the White House. Vicente notes that soon after the Kennedy assassination, his father and Fore met personally with the newly inaugurated Johnson in Dallas to recommend Vicente for a position in Johnson's administration. Vicente remained unaware of the insider machinations at the time. But it wouldn't be the last time that his name would appear without his knowledge on Johnson's short list for administrative appointments.

"The economic and political climate in our community was similar to that of Johnson's in the hill country of Fredericksburg, Johnson City, Kerrville, and Luchenbach," Ximenes wrote. "I am told that there is a bar in Luchenbach that has a sign that reads, 'if you came here to forget, please pay in advance.' We were all just folks, poor and struggling to make a living from the land that was not particularly rich and bountiful. Our part of the county was mostly sand and Johnson's mostly oak trees. Elected positions in the counties and towns were fiercely sought after and politics was a way of life," he summarized.[13]

Johnson's long-term association with the Ximenes family began in the 1930s, when Johnson served as an aide to Congressman Richard Kleberg. José campaigned for political newcomer Johnson and drummed up votes for stalwart insider Richard M. Kleberg in these early years. Vicente recounts, "Representative Kleberg would come around every election year and ask for Dad's support in the primary."[14] Johnson and Kleberg regularly attended the barbecues and *matanzas* (pig roasts) held during election years to rally votes. Growing up at the nexus of this South Texas political network and joining forces with grassroots organizer García and the AGIF, Vicente was uniquely positioned for a leadership role in postwar Mexican American civil rights activism.

Edward Ximenes attended medical school at the University of Texas Medical Branch in Galveston with García (1936–1940). Both men were sons of poor but hardworking Mexicano merchant-class families and worked part time to put themselves through medical school. In the privileged sphere of the UT School of Medicine, they shared connections to a common culture, language, and socioeconomic condition. They both came from large, close-knit families whose educated fathers demanded more for their children than racist social configurations afforded them. During a visit to see his brother in Galveston, Vicente met García for the first time. They hit it off. Vicente confides, "He became my best friend outside my family."[15] García maintained a close association with the Ximenes family, visiting their home in Floresville on his way through South Texas. It would become a friendship and liaison with far-reaching implications.

After graduating from high school, Vicente joined the Civilian Conservation Corps in October 1939. The camp was located in Floresville and named the Richard Kleberg Conservation Camp, and Ximenes helped to clear mesquite trees and work the land. When he saw an opportunity for professional advancement, he taught himself typing and eventually landed a job as a company clerk, which he held for a year before enrolling at the University of Texas in 1940 for a degree in education. Like Johnson, Ximenes briefly served as the principal of a small South Texas school. As principal of a two-room schoolhouse for grades 1 through 6 in Picosa, about five miles from Floresville, Ximenes identified with the educational challenges facing the people of his community. He and one teacher ran the school for the children of the local Polish, German, and Mexican American farmers.

In December 1941, a week after the attack on Pearl Harbor, Ximenes joined the US Air Corps in San Antonio and served six years as a flying officer. He completed fifty combat missions in North Africa and Italy. His theater of military operations aligned closely with García, who served as a major in the Army Medical Corps in Europe. Both left the military as decorated officers. Ximenes was awarded the Distinguished Flying Cross and the Air Medal. García received the Bronze Star for service achievement while running operations across enemy lines. Through these familial, cultural, regional, and military connections, both men came to establish a personal partnership and political liaison that extended decades. Their association helped to forge the structure of the AGIF beyond its South Texas roots.

After the war, Ximenes moved to Albuquerque to finish his degree at the University of New Mexico. He reconnected with García in summer 1951 after completing his MA degree in economics. Ximenes was passing through Corpus Christi during a visit to see his family and called García, who invited him to drop by his medical office to chat. In quintessential García fashion, the good doctor did not inform Ximenes that he would be conducting an AGIF meeting at the same time. Ximenes remembers,

When I called to tell the doctor I was in town, I indicated that I just wanted to come by and say hello. I was in Corpus Christi to spend a couple of days at the beach and then return to Albuquerque, via Floresville. Discrimination, injustice, poverty, and the plight of the Mexican American were the furthest from my mind.

I noticed a large number of vehicles parked outside the doctor's office when I arrived and assumed someone was having a community health session. As I entered the office, Dr. García was addressing the group of persons who were obviously poor and from the barrio of Corpus Christi. The doctor introduced me as a friend who came all the way from Albuquerque to visit with him. The doctor then continued to address the group he called "GI Forum members." Most of his remarks were on the need to organize and bring new members into the GI Forum. Then he launched into the grievances the Mexican American had that in effect made us second-class citizens. We had fought for our country and deserved to be represented in local, state, and national government. He kept reminding everyone that organizing to demand our rights was the key to improving the condition of the Mexicano. The doctor was passionate in both English and Spanish and at first it appeared to me that he was talking radicalism, but as I listened to his plea it was a brand of non-violent action. He was exposing the discriminatory acts that took place daily in the lives of the Mexicano.

This meeting was the first time that I had heard a person speak publicly for everyone to hear the discrimination lodged against the Mexicano and then name the organizations or officials who discriminated against us. I had been in bull sessions that discussed all the facets of discrimination, but none that expressly opened up the avenues to eliminate the hurt being placed on the Mexicano. After the meeting the Dr. asked me to help him organize GI Forums in New Mexico. He gave me constitutions, by-laws, and other material and thus began our drive to expand the American GI Forum of Texas into the American GI Forum of the U.S. From that day forward I gave every ounce of energy outside my work to the development of the GI Forum and the fight to gain first class citizenship for the Hispanic and Mexican American.[16]

The AGIF was still a nascent veterans' organization when Ximenes attended his first meeting. It had been established only two years before and did not yet have chapters outside of Texas. García provided Ximenes with a copy of the AGIF constitution, bylaws, and other organizing material. As soon as he returned to New Mexico, Ximenes began mobilizing for the AGIF. It required eight people to charter a new chapter. His early attempts were frustrated by fear and racism. Points of resistance centered on arguments based on denial, fear of backlash, and provincialism. Albuquerque's established leaders argued, "New Mexico already had good race relations."[17]

The first AGIF meeting in New Mexico was held in 1951 in the basement of the Sacred Heart Catholic Church in the Albuquerque barrio of Barelas. Eight people joined Ximenes at that first meeting: a teacher, a lawyer, a law student, a union carpenter, a city worker, and three University of New Mexico students. After open discussion and debate, Ximenes was elected chairman of the first AGIF chapter in New Mexico. He staged their meetings at the Church of the Sacred Heart in an attempt to deflect attention of government officials, ever on the lookout for subversives and spies. Ximenes recalls, "The Catholic Church meeting place would give me cover from attacks on those who thought that any human rights organization, especially one made up of Mexican Americans must be by definition a subversive organization."[18] The strategy provided only limited protection. The word got out as the profile of the AGIF grew. Consistent with the red-baiting tactics of the period, Monsignor García, the pastor of the church, received a number of inquiries and complaints about providing space to the AGIF from the FBI.[19]

As a researcher for the University of New Mexico Bureau of Business and Economic Research, Ximenes reached out to college students, educated young professionals, and veterans who were willing to agitate to make visible the inequities within the community. They were the risk-takers and visionaries. The AGIF gathered political strength by taking on statewide discrimination issues as its first major project in 1951. Ximenes, acting on the group's behalf, aligned forces with the National Association for the Advancement of Colored People and the Anti-Defamation League in Albuquerque to draft legislation for the New Mexico Fair Employment Practices Commission. Ximenes took on the task of lobbying the House and Senate to adopt the new legislation. After heated debate, the vote tied in the Senate, and Lieutenant Governor Tibo Chávez cast the deciding vote to pass the first fair employment practices legislation in the state.

Over the next ten years, the profile of the AGIF in New Mexico enlarged and the reach of Ximenes's influence expanded: "Once I broke the ice in

Albuquerque, Hispanics from all parts of New Mexico, especially 'little Texas,' came to see me to get Forums organized in their communities."[20] Texas neighbor towns of New Mexico in communities like Clovis, Portales, and Hobbs struggled with the domination of Anglo political bosses and looked to the AGIF as a means of organized resistance. Ximenes took on other civil rights issues and won labor battles on behalf of city garbage workers. He helped to organize twenty-three chapters of the AGIF in New Mexico, a branch in Arizona, and three in Colorado as well as chapters in California, Kansas, Michigan, and Illinois.

By the mid-1960s, the American GI Forum had evolved into a national organization and claimed over 100,000 members.[21] The New Mexico AGIF, like the Texas AGIF, protested against police brutality and organized around the needs of the poor and the working class. As Carl Allsup notes in *The American G.I. Forum: Origins and Evolution*, Ximenes and the AGIF provided a watchful eye on incidents of discrimination and harassment in public and at workplaces.[22] The rise of the AGIF as a national organization foreshadowed the emerging presence of Mexican American leadership. The success of Ximenes's civil rights activism, however, would ultimately cost him his job at the University of New Mexico in 1961. Complaints about his work with the AGIF reached the president of the university and state Senator Clinton P. Anderson, and Ximenes was asked to leave his post. Nevertheless, the AGIF's role in the 1960 Viva Kennedy campaign had helped to put John F. Kennedy in the White House, and Ximenes received one of the few appointments afforded Mexican Americans as payback for bringing out the Spanish-speaking vote. As Ignacio M. García notes in *Viva Kennedy: Mexican Americans in Search of Camelot*, the success of the Viva Kennedy clubs was directly linked to their organizational style as grassroots, localized groups closely aligned with national AGIF chapters. Héctor García, Ximenes, and the AGIF demonstrated to the national Democratic Party that the Latino vote was a significant new political force.[23]

In 1961 Ximenes was appointed Program Officer and Economist to the US Agency for International Development (USAID) in Quito, Ecuador. The next ten years brought a whirlwind of administrative appointments for Ximenes, as García called in favors from the White House. Following in the wake of the Viva Kennedy clubs, Ximenes was appointed director of the Viva Johnson clubs in 1964: "I was in Ecuador and perfectly happy with the position. I was doing the job I had been trained to do at the University of New Mexico. My economic development and political science training made the assignment an enjoyable and productive one. The call for me to come to Washington came from the White House to the American Ambassador. I did not apply for the Viva-Johnson campaign directorship. Dr. García placed my name in nomination and worked to get the appointment."[24]

There were many others who applied and were recommended to direct Johnson's reelection campaign, but García wanted a Mexican American he knew and trusted in the position. President Johnson approved. Since his early days campaigning for Congress throughout South Texas, Johnson knew he could rely on Ximenes to secure the votes. The position would involve more than just nailing posters to mesquite trees this time around. In his role as director of the Viva Johnson clubs, Ximenes worked at the center of the national Democratic Party. His success would translate into the formation of the highest-level committee appointment for a Mexican American in the Johnson administration and implementation of the first Cabinet Committee Hearings on Mexican American Affairs in the US Southwest.

Mexican Americans and LBJ's Great Society

On April 4, 1967, Johnson called Ximenes from his current position as the deputy director of USAID in Panama and announced that he was putting forward Ximenes's nomination for the position of commissioner of the US Commission of Equal Employment. This nomination for this post came as no less a surprise to Ximenes than his 1964 nomination as director of the Viva Johnson clubs. The source, once again, was García. Ximenes recalls, "As it turned out two senators from New Mexico, Anderson and Montoya, had recommended other persons. And Senator Yarborough had recommended Dr. George Sánchez. It was Dr. García who had enough clout with the President that made it possible for me to get the appointment."[25] The appointment of Ximenes, while timely and significant, did not go uncontested.

In *The Civil Rights Era: Origins and Development of National Policy, 1960–1972*, Hugh Davis Graham argues that Johnson responded to "stirrings of discontent among the restive Hispanic leaders . . . voicing their resentment at being generally ignored" and addressed complaints that he had overlooked Mexican American leaders for high-level appointments in his administration.[26] In spring 1966, Mexican American leaders had conducted a vocal protest at an EEOC conference in Albuquerque and called for a White House conference on Mexican American issues similar to the African American civil rights conference convened earlier that year. Ximenes would ultimately replace Aileen Hernández, who resigned as commissioner of the EEOC. The selection of Ximenes addressed the complaints from Johnson's critics. But not everyone supported his choice.

Senator Clint Anderson from New Mexico was the most vociferous opponent to the Ximenes nomination, pointing to a large file of complaints surrounding Ximenes's AGIF activities in Albuquerque and his subsequent dismissal from the University of New Mexico in 1961. Ximenes's appointment as the commissioner of the EEOC went through nevertheless and was quickly followed by Johnson's surprising announcement of the formation of the Cabinet Committee on Mexican American Affairs and Ximenes's appointment as chair of this new White House committee. "When I returned to the Oval Office the President then called in [Joseph] Califano and asked him to draw up an executive order to create the Cabinet Committee and told him to place my name as chairman. I asked the President how was I going to get the Cabinet members to meet and he said hold your meetings here in the fish room next to my office and indicate that I will look into the progress of the committee."[27]

García had once again prevailed on Johnson to make good on his campaign promises to the Mexican American constituency. According to Ximenes, "On this appointment, Johnson went against tradition and Senator prerogatives. It was time to pay political debts owed to my father, Dr. Héctor García, the American GI Forum, the grassroots Hispanics, and myself as the director of the Viva Johnson campaign."[28] Johnson's June 9 memo to committee members Willard Wirtz (secretary of Labor), Orval Freeman (secretary of Agriculture), John Gardner (secretary of Health, Education, and Welfare), Robert Weaver (secretary of Housing and Urban Development), and Sargent Shriver (Office of Economic Opportunity) declared,

> Over the past three years, many members of my Administration have had discussions with Mexican American leaders and others interested in their problems. They have discussed the value of our programs to Mexican Americans in the search for equal opportunity and first-class American citizenship. The

time has come to focus our efforts more intensely on the Mexican Americans
of our nation . . .

The purpose of this committee is to: assure that the Federal programs are
reaching the Mexican Americans and providing the assistance they need and
seek out new programs that may be necessary to handle problems that are
unique to the Mexican American community.

I am also asking this committee to meet with Mexican Americans, to
review their problems and to hear from them what their needs are, and how
the Federal Government can best work with state and local governments,
with private industry and with the Mexican Americans themselves in solving
those problems.[29]

The formation of the Inter-Agency Committee on Mexican American
Affairs was a surprise to everyone present during the June 9 swearing-in ceremony, including Ximenes himself: "I believe the President kept it a secret
in order to avoid the criticism that might come from others who had been
asking for recognition. There is a possibility that if he had announced the
creation of the Committee at the same time as the EEOC appointment the
critics would have stopped the Committee appointment."[30]

In "The Genesis of a Rhetorical Commitment: Lyndon B. Johnson, Civil
Rights, and the Vice Presidency," Garth Pauley argues that Johnson's commitment to civil rights was strongly evidenced before his presidency. His
conflicted record on civil rights issues was resolved by 1963. An examination of Vice President Johnson's 1963 Memorial Day address at Gettysburg,
Pennsylvania, reveals that Johnson unequivocally proclaimed his conviction for equal rights and racial social justice.[31] What Pauley overlooks in his
analysis of Johnson's public rhetoric, however, is the strong alignment of
Johnson's civil rights agenda and progressive social programs with Mexican
American issues and his long-term alliance with Mexican American activists
such as García and Ximenes. Johnson's notion of the Great Society was constituted through the establishment of multiple federal initiatives and programs, including the formation of the Inter-Agency Committee on Mexican
American Affairs and poignantly enacted through the deliberations of 1967
El Paso hearings.

On June 9, 1967, the official appointment was made for Ximenes's joint
administrative positions, EEOC commissioner and chairman of the Cabinet

Committee. Johnson held a national-level ceremony with cabinet members, senators, congressmen, friends, family, and García all in attendance to celebrate Ximenes's appointment. Invoking the trope of the Great Society, Johnson's swearing-in ceremony remarks reflected on his past three years as president, declaring that America "is not great yet, but it has improved a lot . . . and it is going to improve a lot more."[32] Ximenes describes the ceremony as one of the most elaborate ceremonies ever conducted at the White House. Following the event, Johnson took Ximenes aside and reminded him that there wasn't much time left in his presidency and to make the most of his new appointments. According to Ximenes, rumors of Robert Kennedy's run for office were in circulation, and Johnson knew his White House days were numbered: "I had to dispense with celebrations and instead hit the ground running because the 1968 elections were just around the corner."[33]

Soon after Ximenes's appointment, Johnson asked him to suggest possible Hispanic nominations for high-level offices. In the wake of the landmark 1967 confirmation of Thurgood Marshall to the US Supreme Court, Johnson wanted to place a Mexican American on the federal bench. "Vicente," Johnson charged, "If you can find me somebody of the caliber of Thurgood Marshall, I will appoint him."[34] Unfortunately, Hispanics as a cohort had not reached equal national levels of professional or educational preparation. It would take over forty years until the presidency of Barack Obama before the name of a Hispanic leader would be put forward for US Supreme Court confirmation, an occasion celebrated heartily by a ninety-year-old Ximenes in his June 3, 2009 letter to the editor published in the *Albuquerque Journal*:

> I congratulate President Obama for his nomination of Sonia Sotomayor to the US Supreme Court . . . The journey to get a Hispanic on the Supreme Court began to intensify when President Kennedy was elected . . . In 1967, President Johnson appointed me to the federal Equal Employment Opportunity Commission and the Cabinet Committee on Mexican American Affairs. My job was to find qualified persons to serve in all aspects of the federal government . . . At that time there were only two Hispanic federal judges on the bench, but neither one had any civil rights experience that would qualify them to be a Supreme Court justice.[35]

The road to Hispanic political inclusion in US national governance branches from the historic 1967 El Paso hearings.

Making History: The 1967 Cabinet Committee Hearings on Mexican American Affairs

Ximenes details the sequence of events leading up to the El Paso hearings:

> One of the first assignments of the Committee was to organize a confer-
> ence of Hispanics similar to the ones known as White House Conferences.
> President Johnson had made a promise to Dr. García during the 1964 election
> to convene such a conference. Three years had elapsed when I was given the
> assignment and the Hispanics were disillusioned and disappointed that the
> blacks had a conference and there were no plans for a Hispanic conference.[36]

Ximenes contemplated how to go about organizing a White House conference and decided to plan a localized hearing instead of a Washington meeting
"where the usual results were some high sounding resolutions." He reflects,
"I wanted to bring the government to the people. A Washington conference
would have brought only a few grassroots people to attend. The hearing for-
mat, in contrast, would give a relatively large number of our most articulate grassroots people a chance to speak from conviction and not political
necessity."[37] He was also aware that he had to find a way to bring otherwise
disinterested Cabinet Committee members into the conversation: "I had five
Cabinet Committee members that I had to, not only educate, but to get the
message from the horse's mouth so to speak."[38] In sum, Ximenes believed
that the "best way to get them to listen to our cause was through a hearing from people most concerned with the Hispanic and Mexican-American
problems and solutions."[39] Ximenes sought to provide a forum that would
bring together a wide range of voices from Mexican American communities
throughout the nation, not just the privileged few who had White House
connections. The date for the meetings was set for October 1967.

In mid-September, Ximenes called a meeting with Johnson to make the
final decision about the location. Ximenes recounts, "The President said 'let's
go to El Paso.' You will get two Presidents to attend and address your conference since I will be meeting with President [Gustavo] Díaz Ordaz to sign a
treaty."[40] With little more than a month before the hearings were to be held,
Ximenes was very unsettled by Johnson's recommendation:

> I swallowed hard and said, "Mr. President, I have not even talked to the
> Mayor or made arrangements for the five major hotels we will need." The
> President said, "Pick up that White House phone and tell the Chamber of

Commerce we are coming to El Paso." I did and the Chamber of Commerce said something to the effect that if we don't have the hotels, we will build them. I then took a flight to El Paso to meet with the mayor. I explained our reason for the hearing to which the mayor replied, "Listen, I do not want the hearing in my town. You Mexicans will tear up El Paso." At the same time, the State Department was sending messages to our staff that they did not like the idea of a hearing on Mexican Americans since the Chamizal Treaty was going to be signed in El Paso. I reported both responses to the President and he just said, "Pay no attention. We are going to El Paso.[41]

Ximenes issued invitations to Mexican American leaders throughout the country. The Mexican American Youth Organization (MAYO), which had already been protesting on behalf of Mexican American youth in El Paso before the site for the cabinet hearings was announced, complained that they had been omitted from the guest list. Ximenes met with the MAYO delegation in El Paso in advance of the conference to hear their complaints and to offer them a place on the agenda. MAYO sent five delegates to the hearings. Ximenes reports, "They did well in their presentations and then they invited me to speak to them on the Sunday after the conference at the Sacred Heart Church hall. I did. This was the same place I heard that a demonstration was being held. I was the main speaker, but no one demonstrated."[42]

Other vocal activists who presented papers at the hearings included Ernesto Galaza, Ralph Guzmán, Albert Peña, Carlos Truan, and James DeAnda. Approximately 2,000 people attended the El Paso hearings and generated over 2,000 pages of testimony. The proceedings coalesced and published over fifty testimonies foregrounding labor, immigration, housing, education, and public access issues.[43] In his January 25, 1968, memo to Johnson, Ximenes delineated action items derived from the pages of testimony.[44] These action items were framed as suggested solutions in such areas as education, health and welfare, civil service problems, rural problems, manpower problems, and housing. All of the above were approved by committee members Freeman, Wirtz, Gardner, Weaver, and Shriver. Ximenes had achieved consensus among his initially reluctant committee members.

Who came to the El Paso hearings and who didn't? LULAC and the AGIF were represented. Although Ignacio M. García, in his book *Héctor P. García: In Relentless Pursuit of Justice*, charges that Héctor García did not attend, archival evidence and video footage of the hearings indicate that García was among the constituency present at the hearings. Roy Elizondo, representing the Political Association of Spanish-Speaking Organizations, a group of former Viva Kennedy organizers who established the nucleus of new national-level organization, gave testimony.[45] However, labor activist César Chávez declined attending. Chávez boycotted the event with these words, in a September 27, 1967, letter to Ximenes:

> Your and the President's concern for *most* Mexican-American problems is commendable. We have not participated in any such meetings and are reluctant to do so as we do not want to embarrass the administration. It is our considered opinion that the administration is not ready to deal with specific problems affecting farm workers.[46]

George I. Sánchez also declined an invitation to attend, saying, "I cannot accept the El Paso Conference as a sort of 'consolation prize,' with all due respect to the White House."[47] Other prominent Chicano activists such as Reies López Tijerina, who was under federal indictment for leading a raid on a New Mexico courthouse, were omitted from the guest list. According to Ximenes, "Tijerina was supposed to come with a caravan to demonstrate. Tijerina did not attend nor did he have a caravan."[48] Henry A. J. Ramos argues in his book, *The American GI Forum: In Pursuit of the Dream, 1948–1983,* that many of the Mexican American community's more militant leaders, such as Bert Corona, Rodolfo "Corky" Gonzales, and Galarza, boycotted the El Paso hearings and criticized Johnson administration policies, including US involvement in the Vietnam War.[49]

Current historical accounts of the El Paso hearings interpret the events quite differently. The rhetorical construction of the hearings appears to hinge on the question about whether this event represents a critical historical moment for the Mexican American civil rights movement. The stakeholders of Mexican American civil rights reform and the historical representation of postwar activists such as Ximenes and García continue to complicate the meta-narrative of Chicano history. Ignacio M. García reports in his book that the El Paso hearings failed for many reasons, not the least of which were the lack of representation of disenchanted youth leaders and the omission of Chicano counter-discourses.[50] Arguments about how to construct the discourses of history center on questions about the reproduction of power.

Was the El Paso conference as ineffectual as García asserts? Or was it a critical juncture for Mexican American civil rights reform, as Blanton argues? Tracing policy change—the recirculation of the discourses foregrounded at the hearings—represents one way to assess the outcome of the El Paso hearings. What was the trajectory of influence? Ximenes claims,

There were many accomplishments that can be attributed to the conference. John Gardner came away from the program determined to start a bilingual program in the US. It was John Gardner, a member of my committee, who came up with the money in his budget to start the programs . . . I can rightfully claim that as EEO Commissioner, affirmative action was made a part of the national agenda. I was the only Commissioner that fought and achieved the goal of affirmative action plans in the area of employment and the idea spread to almost every segment of our society.

Civil Service Commissioner John Macy, at my insistence and as a result of his attendance at the conference, started an affirmative action plan in the Civil Service. Willard Wirtz agreed to continue funding the SER Program. The Mexican American Legal Defense organization was funded by the Ford Foundation upon my recommendation to the Foundation representative who came to the conference to make a decision. Finally, Secretary Freeman started funding farm worker programs for health and housing.[51]

Other outcomes include the change in census-taking methods, the creation of bank charters for Latinos, and Hispanic inclusion in the Democratic National Committee.[52] In addition, during his administrative tenure as chair of the Inter-Agency Committee on Mexican American Affairs, Ximenes provided oversight for the appointment of over 4,000 Mexican Americans to federal positions.[53] If we consider the implementation of these aforementioned programs and policies, the El Paso hearings seeded exponential changes impacting not only Mexican Americans, but the entire nation.

Five years after the hearings, former President Johnson and Ximenes participated in the first civil rights symposium hosted by the newly established LBJ Presidential Library in Austin, Texas. On December 11, 1972, Johnson reflected on his role in US civil rights reform during his closing remarks for the event. Johnson reasserted his commitment to equal rights for all social groups, harkening back to his 1963 Gettysburg speech:

A decade ago, in the year 1963, we observed the 100th anniversary of the signing of the [Emancipation] Proclamation. On Memorial Day of that fateful year, I was called upon as Vice President to speak at Gettysburg Cemetery where, a century before, words had been spoken which all of us have long remembered. On that occasion, I said this: "Until justice is blind to color, until education is unaware of race, until opportunity is unconcerned with the color of men's skins, emancipation will be a proclamation but not a fact . . . When I spoke those words as Vice President, I could not know that the future would present me shortly with the opportunity and the responsibility to contribute toward fulfilling the fact of emancipation.[54]

Ximenes, likewise, played a role in this landmark event as a symposium speaker. He attended and delivered his panel address, extending the discussion to include the role of Mexican Americans in the civil rights movements of the postwar era. He admonished the exclusion of key Mexican American activists from the program and guest lists:

Yesterday, while we were reminiscing about the Civil Rights Movement, we left out a significant group of people. In the fifties and sixties in Texas, one of the panelists here today, Henry [B. González] was taking the lead in the Texas Legislature on the issue of civil rights for everyone. In New Mexico, it was Senator Chavez taking the lead on these issues. In Albuquerque—one of the first cities to pass the Public Accommodations Act and an FEPC—it was Senator Chavez and Senator Montoya. In California, it was Congressman Edward Roy Ball [sic]. There were others like Dr. Héctor P. García and the distinguished lawyer Gus García, who took his case on the jury discrimination, the *Hernandez* [sic] case, to the Supreme Court and won. Unfortunately, Gus was never recognized for his efforts: the Chicanos at the time did not understand what he had done and the rest of society hated him for it. These are some of the individuals in this part of the country that were part of the Civil Rights Movement, and they should be included in any symposium or panel or library that we may create throughout this Nation insofar as Civil Rights Movements are concerned.[55]

The problem of erasure and omission of Latinos from national deliberation and governance endures. As such, Ximenes's approach to the El Paso Cabinet Committee Hearings on Mexican American Affairs offers a valuable and effective model for negotiating national policymaking among US political structures. Moreover, the intricacies of the policy changes enacted by Ximenes in 1967 merit inclusion in the historical record of US civil rights moments. The political climate of the past twenty years, promoting the ongoing reversal of affirmative action policies in all facets of US society, including the erosion of bilingual education programs throughout the nation, challenges us to revisit the civil rights discourses and the political complexities surrounding the post-war Mexican American civil rights movement and the historic El Paso hearings. As Dryzek contends, authentic democracy can only exist "to the degree that reflective preferences influence collective outcomes."[56]

The success of social activists like Vicente Ximenes can be best measured by the effective and strategic placement of representatives within the larger social structure. Ximenes not only brought Mexican Americans to the White House, he brought the White House to Mexican Americans. He demonstrated that the American style of self-governance was not only redeemable but achievable. The rhetorical imagination of Vicente Ximenes, Héctor P. García, and the American GI Forum was capacious, synergistic, and pragmatic, grounded in an enduring sense of *phronesis* (practical wisdom). Why is this legacy important to us today? The current historical moment of healing national division and international polarization is dependent on discursive democratic processes. We need models of democratic practice and civic literacy that promote dissent, engage difference, cultivate debate, and negotiate the noise of disparate positions.

Notes

1. Segments of this chapter have been presented at the following conferences: 2006 Texas State Historical Association (Austin, TX); 2008 American GI Forum 60 Years of Activism Convention (Corpus Christi, TX); 2008 Rhetoric Society of America (Seattle, WA). This research has been generously supported by a University of New Mexico Faculty Research Grant and the LBJ Presidential Library Research Fellowship.

2. John S. Dryzek, *Deliberative Democracy and Beyond: Liberals, Critics, Contestations* (New York: Oxford University Press, 2000), 113–14.

3. David R. Hiley, *Doubt and the Demands of Democratic Citizenship* (New York: Cambridge University Press, 2006).

4. Michelle Hall Kells, *Héctor P. García: Everyday Rhetoric and Mexican American Civil Rights* (Carbondale: Southern Illinois University Press, 2006).

5. Maggie Rivas-Rodríguez, ed. *Mexican Americans and World War II* (Austin: University of Texas Press, 2005), xvii.

6. Lloyd Jojola, "María Ximenes: Wife Helped American GI Forum," *Albuquerque Journal*, October 17, 2009.

7. Hiley, *Doubt and the Demands*, 103.

8. Dryzek, *Deliberative Democracy and Beyond*, 113–14.

9. Carlos Kevin Blanton, *The Strange Career of Bilingual Education in Texas, 1836–1981* (College Station: Texas A&M University Press, 2004), 130.

10. Kells, *Héctor P. García*, 13.

11. Biography of José Jesús Ximenes, n.d., n.p., Vicente T. Ximenes Papers, Wilson County Historical Society, Floresville, TX (hereafter Ximenes Papers).

12. Julie Leininger Pycior, *LBJ and Mexican Americans: Paradox of Power* (Austin: University of Texas Press, 1997), 25.

13. Vicente Ximenes interview by author, January 31, 2005.

14. Vicente Ximenes interview by author, February 4, 2006.

15. Ibid.

16. Vicente Ximenes interview by author, February 6, 2006.

17. Ximenes interview, February 4, 2006.

18. Vicente Ximenes interview by author, February 8, 2006.

19. Ximenes interview, February 8, 2006.

20. Ximenes interview, February 4, 2006.

21. Henry A. J. Ramos, *The American GI Forum: In Pursuit of the Dream, 1948–1983* (Houston: Arte Público, 1998), 31.

22. Carl Allsup, *The American G.I. Forum: Origins and Evolution* (Austin: Center for Mexican American Studies, University of Texas at Austin, 1982), 68.

23. Ignacio M. García, *Viva Kennedy: Mexican Americans in Search of Camelot* (College Station: Texas A&M University Press, 2000).

24. Ximenes interview, February 6, 2006.

25. Vicente Ximenes, letter to author, May 31, 2003.

26. Hugh Davis Graham, *The Civil Rights Era: Origins and Development of National Policy, 1960–1972* (New York: Oxford University Press, 1990), 226.

27. Ximenes letter.

28. Ximenes interview, January 31, 2005.

29. Johnson quoted in "Inter-Agency Committee on Mexican American Affairs, 1967–1968," brochure, Ximenes Papers.

30. Vicente Ximenes, interview by author, February 19, 2006.

31. Garth Pauley, "The Genesis of Rhetorical Commitment: Lyndon B. Johnson, Civil Rights, and the Vice Presidency," in *Civil Rights Rhetoric and the American Presidency*, ed. James Arnt Aune and Enrique D. Rigsby (College Station: Texas A&M University Press, 2005).

32. "Remarks of the President at the Swearing-In Ceremony for Vicente T. Ximenes," June 9, 1967, box 95, folder 36, file 79, Dr. Héctor P. García Papers, Special Collections and Archives, Texas A&M University–Corpus Christi (hereafter García Papers).

33. Ximenes letter.

34. Ximenes quoted in Pycior, 202.

35. Vicente Ximenes, "Road to Sotomayor Started in 1961," *Albuquerque Journal*, June 3, 2009.

36. Ximenes letter.

37. Ximenes interview, February 19, 2006.

38. Ximenes interview, January 31, 2005.

39. Ximenes interview, February 19, 2006.

40. Ximenes letter.

41. Vicente Ximenes, interview by author, February 19, 2006.

42. Ximenes letter.

43. *Testimony Presented at the Cabinet Committee Hearings on Mexican American Affairs, El Paso, Texas, October 26–28, 1967*, Washington, DC: Inter-Agency Committee on Mexican American Affairs, n.d., Ximenes Papers.

44. Vicente Ximenes to Lyndon B. Johnson, memo, January 25, 1968, Ximenes Papers.

45. Ignacio M. García, *Héctor P. García: In Relentless Pursuit of Justice* (Houston: Arte Público, 2002). The Political Association of Spanish-Speaking Organizations was established March 26, 1961, in Phoenix, Arizona, during the National Political Leadership Conference of the Viva Kennedy club. The name of the new organization was passed by vote. The acronyms of PASSO and PASO are used interchangeably in the literature. "Narrative Report of National Political Leadership Conference, March 26, 1961, semi-processed file, García Papers.

46. Chávez quoted in Pycior, *LBJ and Mexican Americans*, 204.

47. Sánchez quoted in Pycior, *LBJ and Mexican Americans*, 203.

48. Ximenes letter.

49. Ramos, *American GI Forum: In Pursuit of the Dream*, 104.

50. García, *Héctor P. García: In Relentless Pursuit of Justice*, 273.

51. Ximenes letter.

52. Vicente Ximenes, interview by author, February 20, 2006.

53. Matt S. Meier and Margo Gutiérrez, eds. *Encyclopedia of the Mexican American Civil Rights Movement* (Westport, CT: Greenwood, 2000), 254.

54. Johnson quoted in Robert C. Rooney, ed., *Equal Opportunity in the United States: A Symposium on Civil Rights* (Austin: University of Texas Press, 1973), 163.

55. Ximenes quoted in Rooney, *Equal Opportunity in the United States*, 139.

56. Dryzek, *Deliberative Democracy and Beyond*, 2.

Figure 11.1. Leaders involved in civil rights litigation in Arizona at mid-century. Front row from left to right: Gus C. García, civil rights attorney from Texas; Rafael Estrada, attorney from Arizona; Jorge Ramírez of the University of Texas. Back row from left to right: Lauro R. Montaño from Los Angeles; Arturo Fuentes (president) and J. I. Gandarilla (vice-president) of the Alianza Hispano-Americana; and Fred Okrand, attorney from Los Angeles.

11

Ralph Estrada and the War against Racial Prejudice in Arizona

LAURA K. MUÑOZ

In 1999 the Arizona State University alumni association began a search for its earliest Mexican American graduates. Founded in 1885, the Tempe Normal School (TNS) graduated Mexican American women teachers as early as 1897, but 1923 yearbooks revealed that a young baseball captain named Ralph Carlos Estrada became the first Mexican American male graduate. Called "Güero" (fair-complexioned) by his classmates, the reddish-blond Estrada earned varsity letters in basketball, baseball, and football. A Tempe native, Estrada's success at the TNS made him a favorite on the field and in the classroom. His teammates elected him to the exclusive, all-male Letterman's Club, enhancing his personal and family reputation. His father and oldest siblings owned Estrada Brothers Grocery, only blocks from the campus. The Estradas banked on young Ralph's status as an athlete and a scholar, hoping that one day he would "become a person of influence and political stature."[1]

Estrada seared those aspirations into history in 1951 when he won the federal lawsuit *Gonzales v. Sheely*, ending the legal segregation of Mexican American children in Arizona schools before *Brown v. Board of Education of Topeka* (1954).

DOI: 10.5876/9781607323372.c011

Tolleson Elementary School District No. 17, a farming community just west of Phoenix, segregated white and Mexican American children into two different schools on the basis of race and ethnicity. Working with a team of lawyers, Estrada argued that separate Mexican schools violated the equal protection clause of the Fourteenth Amendment. While the scope of the case was limited to Tolleson, the victory created an opening for Mexican Americans and African Americans to challenge the constitutionality of race-based educational segregation across the state. The US District Court for the District of Arizona had followed precedence established by *Méndez v. Westminster School District* (1946), making *Gonzales* the first test case to uphold the *Westminster* rule. Arizonans felt the verdict's ramification quite swiftly, as Estrada won a second victory later that year in *Ortiz v. Jack* (1951) that desegregated Mexican schools in Glendale, another farming town north of Phoenix. By 1953 the Arizona State Board of Education issued an official policy of desegregation for all children. These victories became the hallmarks of Estrada's legal career and a confirmation of his status as a civil rights leader. The cases symbolized his lifelong mission to improve the Mexican American condition in Arizona and catapulted him into national and international politics.[2]

Within the context of the Mexican American generation, Estrada emerged as the most prominent Hispanic civil rights advocate in Arizona. He achieved recognition as an attorney representing indigent clients and class actions in Arizona and California throughout the era. He garnered statewide momentum for these legal challenges as supreme attorney and supreme president of the Alianza Hispano-Americana, the largest fraternal organization of Hispanics in the state at the time, which eagerly supported his campaign for equality. Yet from his early childhood, Estrada possessed a clear sense of himself as a US citizen. Born and raised into a middle-class family in Tempe, he engaged American society with gusto, excelling at school and building bicultural alliances with Anglos and Mexicans throughout the state. With a passion drawn from his family's aspirations, he fashioned himself into an All-American man who used both national and cultural allegiances as footholds for his personal achievement in education, law, and politics but also for extending the democratic promise to all Arizonans.

While historiography suggests that Arizona leadership was absent from the Mexican American civil rights struggle, Estrada, in fact, ranks among the few elite Hispanic leaders known nationally among mainstream politicians during the 1960s. Most historians' unfamiliarity with Arizona history and its emphasis on border politics and labor strife in the mining industry rendered Estrada and his contributions nearly invisible. Yet he was among the few Hispanic leaders of the era who had regular access to US presidents—most notably, John F. Kennedy, who appointed Estrada as an envoy to Nicaragua. He promoted Democratic Party politics among Arizona Hispanics as early as the 1930s, represented Arizona at national conventions, and built liaisons across the Southwest that took Alianza and Mexican American civil rights issues to the halls of Congress.[3]

Estrada's civil rights advocacy surfaced nationally when he chose to represent the plaintiffs in the *Gonzales* case. This is no coincidence. The case reflects quite well Estrada's perspective and history, which is the twentieth-century Mexican American experience in Arizona. According to Estrada's wife, Ruby López Estrada, "[e]ducation was one of the things that Ralph most treasured. He believed only through education could Mexican-Americans truly advance and fight for their rightful place in our country." The lawsuit brought the goals of justice, citizenship, and education together in a way that Estrada knew intimately in his journey through Arizona's public schools as student, teacher, and lawyer. He came to the *Gonzales* case with a civil rights agenda, borne from a history of racialization and personal experience negotiating the Anglo-American status quo in the Southwest. As a lawyer and later, as the Alianza president, Estrada dedicated his life to eliminating prejudice and encouraging Hispanics "to exercise the rights and privileges of good citizens by actively engaging in political life."[4]

Ralph Carlos Estrada learned this philosophy of citizenship at home from his ranch-hand father and immigrant mother, who worked hard to build a name for themselves in Arizona Territory. As a young girl, Estrada's mother, Rafaela Noriega, came north in a horse-drawn wagon from Pitiquito, Sonora, Mexico, a desert village southeast of Caborca. She was the youngest child in an extended family that settled in Tempe, a small ranching and farming community founded in 1887 on the banks of the Salt River. Mexican immigrants had moved into the region as early as the 1860s, supplying agriculture and irrigation labor to the new settlements and, in some instances, establishing their own homesteads. Rafaela met and married Rafael in 1889 at the nearby Sotelo Ranch, owned in part by his paternal aunt. Rafael was born in Florence, Arizona, fifty-five miles southeast of Tempe, but he came to live and work with his aunt when his father decided to return to Mexico's Central Plateau. The newlyweds moved to Tempe's Mexican settlement near the river base. Rafael worked for the Hayden Flour Mill, owned by Charles Trumbull Hayden, credited as being among the town's founders. Bilingual and endorsed by Anglos and Mexicans alike, Rafael was elected constable in 1896, a post that he held for two decades and that gave him the flexibility to begin several enterprises, including a grocery, restaurant, barbershop, and pool hall, which his oldest sons operated through the 1920s.[5]

Born on January 10, 1903, as the youngest son and the last of seven children, Ralph grew up fairly insulated from the hustle and bustle of the Estrada family businesses. He attended Tempe's public schools, beginning first grade in 1910. Tempe's population was near 1,000, and the city was progressive. Both Anglo and Mexican residents contributed financially to civic building. In 1885 twenty families, including husband and wife, James T. Priest and Mariana Gonzales, contributed $500 each to buy the land to build a state college, the Tempe Normal School. The Hayden family, who the Estradas regarded as friends, also deeded land for the modern, two-story brick school building in 1892. Ralph attended the stylish Eighth Street School through the eighth grade.[6]

However, in 1914, when Ralph was eleven, the Tempe Elementary School District No. 3 built a new school at Tenth Street and designated it for the "American children." Progressive social reform and its nativist hostility did not escape Tempe. The school board left the "Mexican children" at the old Eighth Street School. Mexican American parents responded with dismay, threatening to sue. Yet for unknown reasons, a lawsuit did not immediately materialize, and for the next ten years, the school district separated the children under a 1913 Arizona school code that allowed districts to segregate children for pedagogical needs. Whether Ralph managed to escape this de facto segregation through his father's connections is unknown.[7]

The Tempeñenos, as the local Mexican Americans called themselves, did challenge the steady growth of Jim Crow practices. In 1897 Mexican American businessmen, including Ralph's father, founded Tempe's Alianza Lodge No. 5. The lodge unified the Mexican American community by providing funeral insurance, social activities, and public defense through limited political activities, such as the formation of Tempe's volunteer firefighting team, Hose Company No. 1, which served the Hispanic neighborhoods. In 1914 Ralph's brother Ramón (Ray) helped organize a chapter of La Liga Protectora Latina (also called the Latin Protective League or LPL). With 115 members, the LPL publicized in the *Tempe Daily News* their activist platform "solely for the betterment of the condition of the Spanish-American citizens." Ramón was elected as a board trustee. The LPL possessed radical labor roots, having been established in Phoenix by Spanish-language newspaper owner Pedro G. de la Lama, specifically in response to the 1915 Claypool-Kinney Bill. This bill proposed by the Arizona Legislature intended to ban "non-English-speaking men from employment in hazardous occupations, an obvious threat to Mexicans who spoke only Spanish." While the legislature managed to defeat the bill, it too was a reaction to the San Francisco federal court's ruling on the original Kinney Bill, known as the 80 Percent Law. Arizona voters passed this anti-immigrant initiative in 1914, but it was struck down by the Ninth Circuit Court of Appeals. The bill intended to prevent businesses with at least five employees from hiring noncitizens. Eighty percent of an employers' workforce would have been reserved for "American" citizens.[8]

In this heightened anti-Mexican climate, young Ralph came of age, entering Tempe High School in 1918. While he enjoyed success as an athlete, his days were clouded by a political storm engulfing his father and, later, by his mother's death on his graduation day. Ralph's father resigned his post as constable to become the lead *enganchista* (labor contractor) for the Arizona Cotton Growers Association (ACGA) in 1916. With the advent of World War I, cotton boomed, and owners desperately needed workers to harvest "190,000 acres, three-fourths of the irrigated land in the valley." The ACGA paid $4 a head for each laborer recruited. For three years, Rafael traveled as far south as Mazatlán, Sinaloa, soliciting workers for the valley farms. In the East Valley, his eldest sons, Ramón and Pedro, oversaw the laborers in their father's absence and managed the Estrada Brothers Grocery that sold food and services to the laborers in exchange for their meager wages. According to de la Lama and the LPL, the Estradas appeared to be running a debt-peonage scam. De la Lama accused the Estradas of forcing the workers to live in unshaded camps during the summer and to buy overpriced goods from their store. Historian Herbert Peterson referred to Estrada as an "overseer" who took the workers' pay without consent directly from the ACGA in order to pay off their store debts. In May 1919 the LPL filed "a long list of complaints to Arizona Governor Thomas E. Campell, accusing Rafael Estrada and the ACGA of gross discrimination and exploitation of the contracted Mexican laborers."[9]

The accusations split the Mexican American community and tested Anglo-Mexican alliances as well as US-Mexico relations. The ACGA, the US Army, immigration officials, and the Phoenix Mexican consul defended the elder Estrada after an "inspection tour" of the workers' camp. W. H. Knox of the ACGA called de la Lama's accusations a "political vendetta." According to Peterson, Estrada's son Pedro and cousin Juana Peralta Estrada attributed the complaints to "malcontents" or "broncos" deported by the ACGA. The incident raised so much suspicion about immigrant labor that it provoked concern from the US Department of Labor and the American Federation of Labor. But as soon as the case gained national interest, the cotton boom busted. By 1921 the ACGA abandoned an estimated 15,000 to 20,000 Mexican laborers across the state. Historian Bradford Luckingham wrote that Mexican newspapers reported "hunger in Phoenix" and "charged that the ACGA treated Mexican workers 'worse than Negroes.'" When the ACGA failed to rescue the workers, Mexican President Álvaro Obregón interceded and repatriated many of them. The Estrada men, whose small farm also failed, left Arizona temporarily, entrusting their businesses to extended family, and for protection sent young Ralph to his oldest sister, Leona Estrada Valenzuela Taylor, who lived across the Salt River.[10]

Amidst this tragedy, he stayed true to the goals his father had imagined for him. Following in the footsteps of his sister Isabel, Estrada entered the Normal School in Tempe, the state's premier teacher-training institution, in 1921. At TNS, he found himself among a cross section of students from Arizona and other western states. He also joined a small minority of Mexican American students whose parents comprised a burgeoning middle class. Many of these students' parents were members of the Alianza, the LPL, and other ethnic social organizations. The Mexican American students regularly came together as members of the Spanish Club, then called Los Hidalgos del Desierto, which Estrada also joined.

But Estrada found his true passion at TNS in sports, and he used his athletic prowess to cultivate a leadership role he had established in high school. Perhaps this was his way of remaking his family's reputation. Estrada had held local favor as a champion of the Tempe High School football team. His "eagle eye for baskets" and "his good work with the stick" escalated his popularity among his TNS classmates. Though stockier and shorter than most of his teammates by a head, his perseverance resonated in his nickname—"Wheto"—which the yearbook staff translated as "fighter." If pronounced in Spanish, this nickname sounds more like Güero, which was his father's nickname. Nonetheless, Estrada's classmates considered him a prominent campus man, featuring his photograph in a special section called "Those Familiar Faces." The yearbook staff wrote him up in the football, basketball, and baseball sections and devoted a whole page to "Captain Estrada," featuring the "three Major Sports man" in a full-length body shot, wearing his Lettermen's sweater, sports pants, and cleats. Clearly, a hero, Wheto kindly autographed his portrait for friends and fans alike. His success, according to his widow, Ruby, stemmed from his determination off the field as a man clearly aware of his ethnic identity: "His accomplishments were rare for a Mexican-American in the 1920s, and he was respected by his peers because he demanded respect for himself and his heritage."[11]

Estrada's success at the TNS was in fact quite rare, as he became the first Mexican American man to complete the two-year degree and graduate with a diploma, a credential that certified him to teach in any public school in Arizona. He immediately acquired a teaching and coaching job in Winslow, Arizona. Three hours northeast of Tempe, in Navajo County, Winslow was created in 1882 as a terminal for the Santa Fe Railway; its population and politics reflected the state's diversity. Estrada taught at the South Side School for Mexican children. Arizona's school curriculum emphasized Americanization, and during American Education Week in November 1923, Estrada hosted an evening symposium "especially for Mexican parents." Three hundred parents attended to hear their children sing "patriotic songs" and recite the "American Creed." The children also reenacted the signing of the Declaration of Independence and then hosted a reception in the "Domestic Science" room. At the end of the week, Estrada's students joined in a town parade, carrying a banner that read "Every Day in Every Way We Are Learning English Better and Better." Estrada remained in Winslow for two years before venturing to Greeley, Colorado; Los Angeles; and San Diego, where he supported himself as a teacher and continued taking college courses to complete his baccalaureate.[12]

Two significant events occurred early in Estrada's teaching career that would shape his professional development as an educator and his perspective about civil rights. First, in 1923 he met an important mentor, Grady Gammage, the Winslow school superintendent. Known for being supportive of Mexican American education, Gammage introduced Estrada to Winslow society and sponsored his membership in Winslow Lodge No. 13 of Free and Accepted Masons, a membership that he would retain throughout his life. In 1925 Gammage left Winslow to accept the vice presidency of the Northern Arizona State Teacher's College, and in 1928 he moved to Tempe to become president of the TNS, Estrada's alma mater. A self-made man from Arkansas, Gammage no doubt encouraged Estrada to continue his education, and the two remained friends throughout their lives. This friendship became prophetic in 1952 when attorney Estrada sued members of the Arizona State Board of Education, including Gammage, in *Ortiz v. Jack*, a school desegregation lawsuit that Estrada settled out of court in favor of his plaintiffs.[13]

Second, in 1925 Estrada must have learned about the *Romo v. Laird* school desegregation lawsuit filed by Mexican American parents in his hometown. *Romo* is the earliest known Mexican American school desegregation case. By this time, Estrada's brother Pete, who was active in the Democratic Party, had been appointed as court interpreter of the Maricopa County Superior Court. So Pete could have relayed firsthand knowledge of the *Romo* case to his brother. According to court records, Adolfo Romo, whose four children attended the Eighth Street School for "Mexican children," sued Tempe Elementary School District No. 3 and its school board for racial segregation. Romo wanted his four children to attend the Tenth Street School designated for "American children." The lawsuit, which Tempeñenos had considered for nearly a decade, became reality when they discovered that the district had negotiated with the TNS to turn the Eighth Street School into a "Mexican Training School" for college students. In the agreement, the college assumed the school operations and college students, not certified teachers, taught the classes. Superior Court Judge Joseph S. Jenckes ruled in favor of Romo, arguing that the *Plessy v. Ferguson* rule of "separate but equal" had not been met. The district did not hire certified teachers for the Eighth Street School as it did for the Tenth Street School, therefore, the Romo children could not receive an equal education. As a result, they gained admittance to the Tenth Street School, but the college regained control of the Mexican Training School by hiring certified teachers to oversee the practicing teachers. Mexican American parents, then "chose" to send their children to either school. Segregation remained in place until 1945.[14]

As *Romo* unfolded, Estrada traveled throughout the Southwest and matured into manhood. From 1926 to 1931, he taught school and attended universities in Colorado and California. He returned to Phoenix in 1931 and resumed teaching. He joined his brother Pete in the Democratic Party and focused on building political alliances to improve the Mexican American condition. In 1932 he helped found the Latin American Club with a group of affluent and politically savvy Mexican American men, including criminal defense attorney Gregorio "Greg" García and Southern Pacific boilermaker Luis Córdova, both known for their community engagement. The Latin American Club pursued a platform dedicated to equal education and political access. The club endorsed Democratic Party candidates sympathetic to Mexican American concerns and sponsored voter registration drives. Estrada served as its president and magazine editor. In 1933 he joined the founding membership of the Arizona Young Democrats and was elected vice president. During these early years of the Great Depression, Estrada also met his wife, Ruby, a college student in Tempe who was eight years his junior. They wed after a two-year courtship, and by 1935 the young couple moved to Tucson so that Estrada could pursue a law degree at the University of Arizona. Ruby cared for their growing family (three children at the time) while her husband worked part time and attended school full time. He completed his bachelor's degree and entered the James E. Rogers College of Law in 1936. He passed the Arizona bar exam in 1939 and the Estradas returned, once again, to Phoenix.[15]

While available sources do not reveal why Estrada became a lawyer, in all likelihood he based the decision on his developing political consciousness and, perhaps, on the implicit promise to fulfill his father's aspirations. As soon as he returned to Maricopa County, Estrada opened his legal practice and won an appointment as a Phoenix city magistrate. He resumed his activism with the Arizona Democratic Party and joined the political leadership of the Alianza. His practice grew steadily, and he often worked as co-counsel with attorneys García and Harry J. Valentine. In 1942 Estrada and García joined Fred Fickett and William Misbaugh of Tucson, in defense of the Alianza. The Arizona Corporation Commission sued the Alianza for receivership, alleging that the fraternal insurance society was not solvent, as required by the 1939 Arizona Code. According to historian Lynn Briegel, the Alianza had a deficit of $54,000, which resulted from investment losses during the Great Depression, membership turnover, and increased claims for funeral expenses.

The success of the new government-sponsored Social Security system, which also provided insurance to families and dependent children, also decreased Alianza subscriptions and revenue. The Alianza legal team, however, convinced the Pima County Court and, on appeal, the Arizona Supreme Court, that property investments could cover the deficits and that new leadership could maintain 100 percent solvency, an issue that would later result in the Alianza's demise. The case, however, brought Estrada and García together as Alianza's legal team, and by 1950 they assumed its national leadership— García as supreme president and Estrada as supreme attorney. The lawyers now envisioned a new civil rights agenda called the *"Guerra al Prejucio Racial"* (the War Against Racial Prejudice).[16]

Estrada and García introduced modern Mexican American civil rights litigation to Arizona. Their legal strategy centered on due process and focused on both civil and criminal matters affecting Mexican Americans. They tackled cases that ranged from commuting death sentences to desegregating schools and swimming pools. This counteroffensive on racial prejudice began in earnest in 1950 with the decision to file *Gonzales v. Sheely* in the US District Court in Phoenix. Prior to this class action, the Alianza typically defended itself in legal matters or wrote amicus curiae (friend of the court) briefs on behalf of individuals or other civil rights organizations. In *Gonzales*, Estrada and García represented the Comité Movimiento Unido Mexicano Contra la Discriminación, a group of parents and children led by Porfirio Gonzales and Faustino Curiel, who had challenged segregation in Tolleson Elementary School District No. 17. Prior to seeking legal assistance, Mexican American parents held numerous meetings with Superintendent Kenneth Dyer and the school board hoping to negotiate integration. They also petitioned Arizona Senator Carl Hayden to no avail. Racial segregation in Tolleson resembled the kind of segregation Estrada had witnessed as a child in Tempe and as a teacher in Winslow. Initially, the Tolleson district taught white and Mexican American children in the same building, although in different classrooms. When a second school opened, the white children attended the new school, and only a few Mexican American children who could "speak English" were allowed to join them. The majority of the Mexican American children remained in the old building.[17]

Following the reasoning of *Méndez*, Estrada and García argued that Tolleson's policy of Mexican American segregation violated the equal protection clause of the Fourteenth Amendment. Separating Mexican American children based on race or national origin, language, or intelligence was unconstitutional. Arizona law did not mandate Mexican American segregation and, further, the state code deemed Mexican Americans as white. In both *Gonzales* and *Méndez*, the school districts argued that the children's English language deficiencies necessitated their segregation. But Judge David W. Ling found that Tolleson inadequately tested the children's language abilities and relied instead on surnames to separate them. He carefully pointed out that the district could not segregate an entire group of students on the basis of a few students' language inabilities, nor could they do so on the basis of lineage. Separating the Spanish-speaking children hindered their ability to acquire English, which diminished their socialization with white children and heightened antagonisms between them. Ling emphasized "social equality" as "paramount" to public education as the "commingling of the entire student body instills and develops a common cultural attitude among the school children which is imperative for the perpetuation of American institutions and ideals." Ling ruled Tolleson's actions discriminatory and in violation of the US Constitution.[18]

The decision to employ the *Méndez* framework stemmed from alliances Estrada and García had negotiated with civil rights attorneys working on similar cases throughout the Southwest. Attorney A. L. Wirin of the American Civil Liberties Union (ACLU), Southern California division, joined *Gonzales* as official co-counsel only a week prior to the initial hearing. Wirin served as co-counsel on *Méndez* and with Texas attorney Gus García on *Delgado et al. v. Bastrop Independent School District of Bastrop County, et al.* (1948), where they tested the equal protection promise of the Fourteenth Amendment. After the *Méndez* win, Wirin and Dr. George I. Sánchez from the University of Texas coordinated a series of lawsuits "to challenge the de facto segregation of Mexican-American students in Texas, Arizona, and California." The *Gonzales* win in March 1951 became the first of these Arizona cases. In May 1951, Estrada formally aligned the Alianza with the American Council of Spanish Speaking People (ACSSP), a regional effort spearheaded by Sánchez and funded by the Robert C. Marshall Trust Fund (called the Marshall Fund). Uniting the Alianza, the League of United Latin American Citizens (LULAC), the American GI Forum, and the Los Angeles–based Community Service Organization, the ACSSP sought to eliminate Mexican American segregation in all aspects of public life through litigation. Estrada received grants from the ACSSP to pay for a series of desegregation cases, including *Ortiz v. Jack* (1951), *Baca v. Winslow* (1955), and, in El Centro, California, *Romero v. Weakley* (1955).[19]

Ortiz v. Jack became the death knell of de facto Mexican American school segregation in Arizona. In *Gonzales*, the judgment was limited only to the Tolleson Elementary School District. In *Ortiz*, however, Estrada and Wirin sought a ruling that would challenge the constitutionality of Arizona's school code and eliminate Mexican American segregation permanently. Acting on behalf of the Alianza and parents Ricardo Ortiz and Mrs. Jessie G. Leyva, Estrada and Wirin sued the school board and the superintendent of Glendale Elementary School District No. 40 and the State Board of Education, including Governor Howard Pyle. The attorneys intentionally named the board of education to broaden the scope of the case to include all "Mexican schools." In Glendale, just northwest of Phoenix, 300 Mexican-descent children exclusively attended the Mexican School No. 2. Yet the Alianza also documented school segregation in other cities, such as Winslow and the central mining communities of Douglas (Seventh Street and Pirtleville Schools) and Miami (the Bullion Plaza School). With the ACSSP's financial support, Estrada and Wirin brought attorneys Gus García of San Antonio and Fred Okrand of the ACLU to Phoenix to help try the case. On March 24, 1952, the county prosecutor filed a motion to throw out the case, but Judge Ling, who ruled in *Gonzales*, refused. He learned that Glendale had begun plans to build a new school to accommodate both Mexican and white children. He left the case pending, but it was never tried. Estrada, Wirin, García, and Okrand may have felt disappointed in losing the chance to gain the federal ruling, but the Alianza called the settlement a triumph (*un truinfo*). *Ortiz v. Jack* integrated the Glendale schools, and the county prosecutor's decision to withdraw from the legal challenge sent a clear message that the state would no longer defend school segregation.[20]

In the midst of the desegregation cases, however, Estrada confronted a series of personal and political battles within the Alianza. Just prior to *Gonzales*, Estrada's co-counsel, Gregorio García, lost his bid for Alianza's supreme presidency. García ran against incumbent Candelario Sedillo. García had served as supreme attorney under Sedillo for nearly a decade, and both Estrada and García defended Sedillo during the attempted takeover by the

Arizona Corporation Commission in 1942. When García challenged Sedillo for the supreme presidency at the 1948 national convention in Tucson, Sedillo rigged the election, claiming victory. Unable to resolve the issue internally (police broke up a fight at the convention), García sued Sedillo in the Maricopa County Superior Court and lost. The court ruled that it was a fair election. However, in 1950 Estrada appealed García's case to the Arizona Supreme Court and won by claiming that Sedillo and other Alianza members conspired to control the vote count. García was installed as the new Alianza supreme president and Estrada as the new supreme attorney. The case, however, destroyed García's presidency and the Alianza's financial solvency, as the organization had spent its funds to defend the incumbent president. In deficit, the Alianza and its supreme executive council refused to support García's efforts to refinance the organization's debt. In frustration, García quit. Without the financial support of the Alianza, Estrada paid the court costs for *Gonzales* and the new Alianza president, Arturo Fuentes, reappointed him as supreme attorney. García and Estrada continued to work together on desegregation cases until García's untimely death on September 8, 1953. He died in his law office from a heart attack. He was sixty years old.[21]

Despite this tragedy, Estrada continued to push forward the civil rights agenda he and García had imagined. From 1954 to 1962, Estrada assumed the Alianza's supreme presidency and established a new Civil Rights Department and a Civil Liberties Program. The program educated Mexican Americans about their constitutional rights through bilingual media, including a radio show, news service, and speakers' bureau. Meanwhile, the department launched offices in Tucson and Los Angeles, where attorney Ralph Guzmán tracked civil rights violations and helped clients find legal representation. The department immediately took on cases in both states related to segregation and equal protection of Mexican Americans. In 1954 Estrada returned to the city of Winslow, where the plaintiffs from the Alianza Lodge No. 56 sought access to the town's swimming pool. Winslow only allowed Mexican Americans to swim in the pool on Wednesdays, the day before it was drained. Estrada filed *Baca v. Winslow* in the US District Court in Phoenix but settled the case when the city agreed to change its discrimination policy and open the pool to everyone.[22]

In El Centro, California, another school desegregation challenge emerged in *Romero v. Weakley*. In this 1955 case, the Alianza joined with the National

Association for the Advancement of Colored People (NAACP) to challenge the race-based segregation of black and Mexican American youth at the El Centro School District and the Central Union High School District in Imperial County, just south of Los Angeles. In El Centro, the school district allowed white parents to select their children's elementary schools but forced black and Mexican American parents to send their children to two designated neighborhood schools, Douglas and Washington, with all-black faculties "except for one white principal." Further, while the high school integrated students, it did not hire any black teachers. When parents of color challenged both of these scenarios with the help of the NAACP, the two school districts encouraged white families to transfer their children to other school districts within the county but refused to approve similar transfers for black and Mexican American families. The Imperial County Board of Supervisors and the county superintendent of schools endorsed this plan as well. At this point, the NAACP and the Alianza convinced the parents to take legal action. Estrada's decision to unite the Alianza and the NAACP in *Romero* demonstrated racial cooperation and a rare progressivism absent among other Mexican American organizations—most notably, LULAC, led in 1957 by national president Félix Tijerina, a Houstonian who unabashedly refused to work with African Americans on school desegregation.[23]

The final verdict in *Romero v. Weakley* generated an important legal clarification in the filing of federal class action school desegregation cases. Originally, the attorneys filed the suit in San Diego at the US District Court for the Southern District of California, Central Division; however, Judge Pierson M. Hall "stayed the proceedings pending a determination in the state court." Hall argued that the case would be more appropriately resolved at the local level in the Superior Court, Imperial County, and he did not want to "remove the conduct of schools from the locally elected representatives." The seven attorneys for the plaintiffs, including Estrada and Wirin, filed an immediate appeal to the Ninth Circuit Court of Appeals in San Francisco, arguing for the right to "direct access" to the federal courts. The Ninth Circuit immediately reversed the district court's decision and remanded it for resolution. In the opinion, Chief Judge William Denman sardonically wrote that it would be highly questionable to ask the same voters who elected the Imperial County court, the grand jury, the school boards, and county board of supervisors to decide on the alleged discrimination. "The appellants well could have concluded that there was a greater assurance of a just consideration of their complaints in the District Court of the United States than in the Superior Court of Imperial County." Estrada's legal team eventually won their suit and the right to a federal trial. In lieu of another appeal, however, the El Centro school board settled the integration arrangements out of court, lifting the bans on "race, color, religious creed or national origin" in the school assignments of its students and teachers.[24]

While the Alianza's class action desegregation cases brought considerable attention and relief to Mexican Americans in Arizona and California, Estrada and Guzmán also pursued individual civil and criminal cases with the help of other attorneys, especially Wirin and Okrand at the Southern California ACLU. Two cases, in particular, *The People v. Manuel Mata et al.* (1955), a criminal charge for murder against three Mexican American youths, and *Gonzales v. Landon* (1955), an immigration deportation case involving a US citizen, represent the scope of these challenges. In *Gonzales*, Wirin won a Supreme Court verdict reinstating the citizenship of Daniel Castañeda Gonzales. The US Immigration and Naturalization Service attempted to deport Gonzales because he did not enlist in the Armed Forces during World War II. Gonzales, who was born in New Mexico but lived in Chihuahua until 1946, did not realize he had a military obligation. In *Mata*, the Alianza wrote an amicus brief appealing the manslaughter convictions of three Mexican American youth, Manuel Mata, Robert Márquez, and Richard Venegas. The Los Angeles Superior Court charged the three men with the death of William D. Cluff, a bystander who attempted to break up a fight between them and US Marine Corps Private John W. Moore in downtown Los Angeles on December 6, 1953. Estrada and Wirin challenged the convictions on the basis of unfair jury selection, potential juror bias due to newspaper publicity surrounding the case, and the court's denial of a change of venue. In 1955 the ACLU won the appeal and retrial, but the L.A. district attorney withdrew the case freeing the young men. Both *Mata* and *Gonzales* proved to be life-changing victories for the Mexican American defendants.[25]

Estrada's legal work on behalf the Alianza drew him into national networks of mainstream politics and civil rights advocacy. In the eight years of his supreme presidency, from 1954 to 1962, he broadened and emphasized the fraternity's *mutualista* heritage by asserting its political goals in defense of Mexican Americans. At the beginning of 1959 he wrote to his membership,

"Our efforts in the field of Civil Rights and in promoting needed legislation for the elimination of discrimination in housing, employment, and public accommodations have remained vigorous and shall continue to be until prejudice is a thing of the past." Estrada took these words seriously and literally, steering the Alianza deep into Democratic Party politics and straight into the pocket of President Kennedy.[26]

Estrada was instrumental in shaping the Viva Kennedy clubs. His son-in-law, James Carlos McCormick, was the national campaign organizer for the clubs. Long active in the Arizona Democratic Party, Estrada had earned a delegate seat at the 1956 Democratic National Convention. At Estrada's request, Senator Carl Hayden (D-Arizona), an old family friend (their families had lived and worked together in Tempe for two generations), arranged a job for McCormick on the Capitol Police Force in 1958. A law student at George Washington University, McCormick managed to introduce himself to Senator Kennedy's presidential campaign by offering to translate press releases into Spanish. Winning Robert Kennedy's confidence, McCormick joined a February 1959 campaign stop in Arizona, where he personally introduced his father-in-law to the Kennedy brothers. As McCormick began establishing a national board and state program directors for the Viva Kennedy clubs, he turned to Estrada's civil rights networks in the Alianza and the ACSSP. Kennedy also began consulting Estrada on Mexican American issues. In October 1960, Kennedy invited Estrada along with other Viva Kennedy leaders such as Dr. Héctor P. García of the American GI Forum (AGIF) and New York Puerto Rican Assemblymen Felipe Torres and José Ramos López to a national conference on constitutional rights in Boston. It appeared to be the first time that Hispanic leadership was consulted and invited to a national dialogue.[27]

Through his initial entrée into the ACSSP and later, in his work with the Viva Kennedy clubs, Estrada connected himself and the Alianza to a national civil rights advocacy network of religious, ethnic, and racial organizations. For example, in January 1959 he joined George I. Sánchez, a Mexican American education expert and civil rights leader, and Carey McWilliams, an investigative journalist and immigration authority, in Austin to give expert testimony to the Division of Racial Minorities of the National Council of the Episcopal Church. Estrada's talk focused on the "social and civil inequalities experienced by the Latin Americans." His racial and social justice agenda reflected a spectrum of organizational efforts that promoted the "rights and privileges of good citizens," ideals that he hoped would be extended to and practiced by Mexican Americans. Over the course of this life, Estrada held memberships in the AGIF; LULAC; the NAACP; the National Conference of Christians and Jews, where he was a national board member; the Anti-Defamation League of B'nai B'rith; the Arizona Council for Civic Unity; the Elks; and the Order of Free and Accepted Masons, in addition to state, national, and international bar associations and other social clubs.[28]

These organizational connections, specifically the Viva Kennedy campaign, earned Estrada recognition as a national Mexican American leader in the mid-twentieth century. Even though President Kennedy appeared reticent to appoint Hispanic leadership to national and international posts after his election, Estrada, along with Héctor García, was among the handful of Hispanics within Kennedy's circle. When García challenged the president to meet his campaign promise to appoint Spanish-speaking leaders to his administration, García nominated Estrada as a potential ambassador to a Latin American country. McCormick, who garnered an assistantship for a deputy assistant secretary of state for Inter-American Affairs at the State Department and later joined the Democratic National Committee, also echoed García's pleas advancing his father-in-law's credentials. Finally, in 1962 Kennedy appointed several Hispanics to the US Agency for International Development (USAID), the State Department, and the Peace Corps as liaisons to Latin American countries. Kennedy named Estrada as USAID director of operations in Nicaragua, a post he held for two years. Ralph Guzmán, the Alianza co-counsel from Los Angeles, also garnered a Peace Corps post in Venezuela.[29]

With the international assignment, Estrada relinquished his Alianza presidency to its vice president, Carlos McCormick, who returned to Tucson in 1962 to manage the dwindling organization. With the changing tenor of civil rights politics and its growing appeal among Chicano youth, the Alianza lost membership steadily after World War II—from an all-time high of 17,366 in 1939 to 6,147 in 1961. Estrada's and Guzmán's departures also ended the Alianza's civil rights litigation, further limiting the organization's appeal. McCormick attempted to shift the Alianza's priorities to spur membership among the younger generation. He invested Alianza funds in a miscalculated radio station venture that resulted in significant financial losses and several lawsuits over his management. Unable to recover from these shortfalls, the

Alianza fell into receivership and ceased to exist as an organization. It sold its assets and paid out existing death benefit claims through the 1970s.[30]

Estrada returned to Phoenix in 1964 but stepped away from Alianza politics to focus on his legal career. He continued his membership in the Democratic Party and pursued civil, criminal, and appellate cases as late as 1975. He worked as a partner for several Phoenix firms, including Peterson, Estrada & Matz and later, with his sons, at Estrada & Estrada. Ralph Estrada died on October 3, 1979, from a heart attack at the age of seventy-six. On the day he was buried, he was scheduled to have met with Catholic Pope John Paul II. President Jimmy Carter had invited Estrada to a private White House reception to receive the pope on his first papal visit to the United States. Even in death, Estrada remained at the center of national Hispanic politics.[31]

Ralph Carlos Estrada's standing among Mexican American leaders of the twentieth century demonstrates that Arizonans decisively contributed to a political ethos that brought Hispanics into the American consciousness. His legal work helped change national impressions of Mexicans as immigrants and laborers into Mexican American citizens and voters. Working early in his career with veteran attorney Greg García and the Alianza Hispano-Americana, Estrada helped cultivate modern civil rights and Mexican American legal defense in Arizona and California. Their school desegregation victory in *Gonzales v. Sheely* allied them with similarly motivated activists, lawyers, and scholars across the Southwest who joined together in a revitalized equality project. Estrada's coalition efforts further aligned the Alianza with national networks—from the ACLU to the AGIF—that challenged the status quo and second-class treatment of ethnic minorities and demanded full citizenship and equal protection under the law for all Americans.

Estrada's savoir faire and ability to cultivate strategic alliances within the Democratic Party also was critical to the establishment of the Viva Kennedy clubs and the notion of a national Hispanic voting bloc. His ability to sustain his membership and reputation within the Arizona Democratic Party for over four decades ultimately created the opportunity for Carlos McCormick to coordinate the Viva Kennedy movement. Estrada's entrée into presidential politics helped establish a new Hispanic unity between Mexican Americans and Puerto Ricans who supported the campaign. Later he applied similar skills to build Pan-American allegiances as a John F. Kennedy envoy to Latin America. In 1962, at the height of his political activism, Estrada had finally accomplished his family's ambition. He not only established himself as a man of power but also influenced a generation to reshape American society.

Notes

1. Bob Jacobsen, "ASU Tradition: Mexican-Americans Define the Student Body for Nearly a Century," *ASU Vision*, Spring 1999, 8–9, 34–35; Barry Edward Lamb, "The Making of a Chicano Civil Rights Activist: Ralph Estrada of Arizona" (master's thesis, Arizona State University, 1988), 44; and Laura K. Muñoz, "Desert Dreams: Mexican American Education in Arizona, 1870–1930" (PhD diss., Arizona State University, 2006), 223, 234–35.

2. *Brown v. Board of Education of Topeka*, 347 US 483 (1954); *Gonzales v. Sheely*, 96 F. Supp. 1004 (D. Ariz., 1951); *Méndez v. Westminster School District of Orange County*, 64 F. Supp. 544 (S.D. Cal. 1946); and *Westminster School District of Orange County v. Méndez*, 161 F.2d 774 (9th Cir. 1947). The Alianza Hispano-Americana documented school segregation in the Arizona communities of Douglas, Glendale, Miami, and Winslow, among others. See "Lucha Contra La Segregación," *Alianza Magazine* 45, no. 3 (1952), 3, 18. For Arizona desegregation law, including actions of the State Board of Education, see Terry Goddard, "The Promise of *Brown v. Board of Education*: A Monograph" (Phoenix: Arizona Attorney General's Office, 2005), accessible online at http://azmemory.azlibrary.gov/cdm/ref/collection/statepubs/id/21093.

3. Historians of Mexican American generation leadership have emphasized Texas and California as the centers of civil rights activism, leaving Arizona's history incomplete, even though Mexican Americans in the state created and held memberships in the major civil rights, labor, and political organizations formed between 1930 and 1970. Part of this absence was due in part to unprocessed collections such as the Alianza Hispano Americana Records at the Arizona State University Chicano/a Research Collection. Historians Christine Marin, Julie Leininger Pycior, and myself successfully pushed for grant funding to process these records, so they are now accessible to scholars.

4. Ralph Estrada, "Fraternally Yours," *Alianza Magazine* 52, no. 1 (1959): 5 and Ruby Estrada, "She Remembers," *ASU Vision*, Spring 1999, 35.

5. Family Tree Poster, Estrada Family File, Tempe Historical Society, Tempe, Arizona; Lorine Morris, "Pete Estrada Numbered Among Deans of Native Tempeans Still Alive; Ex-Librarian," *Tempe Daily News*, April 26, 1971, and "Rites for Ralph Estrada, Noted Tempe Native, Held," *Tempe Daily News*, October 6, 1979, both in THS; and Lamb, "Chicano Civil Rights Activist," 44–45.

6. Muñoz, "Desert Dreams," 197–98.

7. Tempe Elementary School District Centennial History, March 1, 1977, CE Ephemera E–10, Arizona Collection, Archives and Special Collections, Arizona State University and *Tempe Daily News*, July 9, 1915.

8. *Tempe Daily News*, July 2, 1914; Scott W. Solliday, "The Journey to Rio Salado: Hispanic Migrations to Tempe, Arizona" (PhD diss., Arizona State University, 1993), 100; Bradford Luckingham, *Minorities in Phoenix: A Profile of Mexican American, Chinese American, and African American Communities, 1860–1992* (Tucson: University of Arizona Press), 29; and Scott Solliday, "The Journey to Rio Salado: Hispanic Migrations to Tempe, Arizona" (master's thesis, Arizona State University, 1993), 104–6.

9. "Biografias Breves: Rafael Estrada," *Alianza Magazine* 47, no. 7 (1954), 3–4, 17; Lamb, "Chicano Civil Rights Activist," 44–51; Morris, *Tempe Daily News*, 1971; Luckingham, *Minorities in Phoenix*, 32–34; Bradford Luckingham, *Phoenix: The History of a Southwestern Metropolis* (Tucson: University of Arizona Press, 1989), 76; Eric V. Meeks, *Border Citizens: The Making of Indians, Mexicans, and Anglos in Arizona* (Austin: University of Texas Press, 2007), 95–96; Herbert B. Peterson, "A Twentieth Century Journey to Cíbola: Tragedy of the Bracero in Maricopa County, Arizona, 1917–21" (master's thesis, Arizona State University, 1975); and Herbert B. Peterson, "Twentieth-Century Search for Cibola: Post-World War I Mexican Labor Exploitation in Arizona," in *An Awakened Minority: The Mexican-Americans*, ed. Manuel P. Servín (Beverly Hills, CA: Glencoe, 1974), 117.

10. Lamb, "Chicano Civil Rights Activist," 44–51; Luckingham, *Minorities in Phoenix*, 32–34; Luckingham, *Phoenix*, 76; Meeks, *Border Citizens*, 95–96; Peterson, "A Twentieth Century Journey to Cíbola"; and Peterson, "Twentieth-Century Search for Cibola," 117.

11. Muñoz, "Desert Dreams," 223, 229–30, 338.

12. Estrada graduated in 1923 with Benton James, who was the first African American graduate of the TNS. Prior to Estrada, estimates suggest that at least twenty-two other Mexican American had attended the college between 1886 and 1923. See Muñoz, "Desert Dreams," 223 and Alfred Thomas, Jr., "Arizona State University: A Documentary History of the First Seventy-Five Years, 1885–1960," vol. 3 (Tempe: Alfred Thomas, 1960), 60–64.

13. Lamb, "Chicano Civil Rights Activist," 53, 181; and *Ortiz v. Jack*, no. 1723 (D. Ariz. 1951).

14. *Adolpho Romo v. William E. Laird, et. al.*, no. 21617 (Maricopa County Superior Court, 1925); Morris, *Tempe Daily News*, 1971; Laura K. Muñoz, "Separate But Equal? A Case Study of *Romo v. Laird* and Mexican American Education," *OAH Magazine of History* 15 (Winter 2001): 28–35; Muñoz, "Desert Dreams," 134–86; *Plessy v.*

Ferguson, 163 US 537 (1896); and Richard R. Valencia, *Chicano Students and the Courts: The Mexican American Legal Struggle for Educational Equality* (New York: New York University Press, 2008), 13–15. The TNS, as the college was known locally, changed its name three times in the 1920s. When Estrada graduated in 1923 it was called the Tempe Normal School; in 1925 the Arizona legislature made it a four-year college, changing its name to the Tempe State Teachers' College (the name used in the *Romo* lawsuit). When Grady Gammage took over the college presidency, the TNS became the Arizona State Teachers College.

15. Estrada earned his teaching credentials at the Tempe Normal School but had to complete the Bachelor of Arts degree at the University of Arizona before entering law school. "Biografías Breves," 3; R. Estrada, "She Remembers," 35; Ruby Estrada, interview by María Hernández, August 4, 1981; Lives of Arizona Women Collection, transcript, Archives and Special Collections, Arizona State University; Lamb, "Chicano Civil Rights Activist," 67–69; F. Arturo Rosales, "Latin American Club, Arizona, Inc.," in *Dictionary of Latino Civil Rights History* (Houston: Arte Público, 2007), 246; David R. Dean, "Hispanic Historic Property Survey: Final Report" (Phoenix: Athanaeum Public History Group, 2006), 52; and Luckingham, *Minorities in Phoenix*, 46.

16. In 1952 *Alianza Magazine* published a photo titled "Guerra al Prejucio Racial," featuring Estrada with Texas attorney Gus García; University of Texas professor Jorge Ramírez; Lauro Montaño of Alianza Lodge No. 52 Los Angeles; Arturo Fuentes, Alianza supreme president; J. I. Gandarilla, Alianza supreme vice president; and Fred Okrand, an ACLU attorney from Los Angeles. Kaye Lynn Briegel, "Alianza Hispano-Americana, 1894–1965: A Mexican American Fraternal Insurance Society" (PhD diss., University of Southern California, 1974), 140–67; "Guerra al Prejucio Racial," *Alianza Magazine* 45, no. 4 (1952), 5; *State. v. Alianza Hispano-Americana*, no. 4504 (Sup. Ct. Ariz. 1942), affirmed 60 AZ 1 (130 P.2d 910); and Jeanne M. Powers and Lirio Patton, "Between *Méndez* and *Brown: Gonzales v. Sheely* and the Legal Campaign Against Segregation," *Law and Social Inquiry* 33 (Winter 2008): 152–53.

17. Scholars have called the Comité Movimiento Unido Mexicano Contra la Discriminación by other names, including the Committee for Better Citizenship and the Committee for Better Americanism. According to Jeanne M. Powers and Lirio Patton, in 1950 Tolleson School District No. 17 had 839 students; of those, 360 were identified as being of Mexican descent and sent to the segregated Unit 2. Based on teacher assessments of language proficiency, another 10 Mexican American students were sent to Unit 1. In the court testimony, attorneys Estrada and Wirin challenged Superintendent Dyer on the teacher assessments, achievement testing, and student learning patterns. See *Gonzales v. Sheely* (1951); Goddard, "The Promise

of *Brown*," 4; Lamb, "Chicano Civil Rights Activist," 121; and Powers and Patton, "Between *Méndez* and *Brown*," 152–55.

18. *Gonzales v. Sheely* (1951); Powers and Patton, "Between *Méndez* and *Brown*," 161–62; and Valencia, *Chicano Students and the Courts*, 53–54.

19. *Delgado v. Balstrop Independent School District*, Civ. No. 388 (W.D. Tex., June 15, 1948); *Baca v. Winslow*, Civ. No. 394-Pct A. (D. Ariz. 1955); *Gonzales v. Sheely* (1951); *Romero v. Weakley*, 131 F. Supp. 818 (S.D. Cal. 1955); *Ortiz v. Jack* (1951); Briegel, "Alianza Hispano-Americana," 172; Lamb, "Chicano Civil Rights Activist," 82–120; Luckingham, *Minorities in Phoenix*, 49–50; and Powers and Patton, "Between *Méndez* and *Brown*," 148.

20. "Lucha Contra La Segregación," 3, 18; "Un Triunfo Más de la Alianza" and "Guerra al Prejuicio Racial," both in *Alianza Magazine* 45, no. 4 (1952), 5; "Bullion Plaza School," National Register of Historic Places, accessed September 15, 2009, http://www.nps.gov/history/nr/feature/hispanic/2008/bullion_plaza_school.htm; Briegel, "Alianza Hispano-Americana," 174; Luckingham, *Minorities in Phoenix*, 50; and *Ortiz v. Jack* (1951).

21. *García v. Sedillo*, no. 5247, 70 Ariz. 192 (1950), reversed 218 P.2d 721; Greg García, certificate of death, state file no. 5531, Office of Vital Records (Arizona Department of Health Services, Phoenix); Stan Watt, *A Legal History of Maricopa County* (Charleston, SC: Arcadia, 2007), 35; "Murió el Ex-Presidente Supremo, Hno. García," *Alianza Magazine* 46, no. 10 (1953), 9; Briegel, "Alianza Hispano-Americana," 155–62, 167–68; and Lamb, "Chicano Civil Rights Activist," 100, 124.

22. *Baca v. Winslow* (1955); "Nuestro Presidente Supremo Visita Algunas Logias del Norte de Arizona," *Alianza Magazine* 46, no. 11 (1953), 5; "Discrimen Racial en Winslow, Ariz.," *Alianza Magazine* 47, no. 1 (1954): 3; and Briegel, "Alianza Hispano-Americana," 175–80.

23. *Romero v. Weakley* (1955); "Nuestro Presidente Supremo," *Alianza Magazine*, 5; Thomas H. Kreneck, *Mexican American Odyssey: Félix Tijerina, Entrepreneur and Civic Leader, 1905–1965* (College Station: Texas A&M University Press, 2001), 205–7; Briegel, "Alianza Hispano-Americana," 175–80; and Valencia, *Chicano Students and the Courts*, 55–56.

24. *Romero v. Weakley* (1955); *Romero v. Weakley*, 226 F.2d 399 (9th Cir. 1955); "Triunfo de la ALIANZA en los tribunals; obtuvo que se oigan sus quejas; la corte federal oirá de caso el la segregación," *La Opinion* (Los Angeles), October 16, 1955; and Briegel, "Alianza Hispano-Americana," 179–80.

25. *Gonzales v. Landon*, 350 U.S. 920 (1955); *The People v. Manuel Mata et al.*, Crim. No. 5273, 283 P.2d 372 (1955), reversed with directions 133 Cal. App. 2d 18; Briegel, "Alianza Hispano-Americana," 180–83; and Lamb, "Chicano Civil Rights Activist," appendix D, 183. *Gonzales* has become a notable precedent in similar cases involving

evidentiary standards of expatriation proceedings, such as *Nishikawa v. Dulles* (356 US 129 [1958]), which involved a Japanese American man faced with dual citizenship obligations to serve in World War II.

26. Ralph Estrada, "Fraternally Yours," *Alianza Magazine* 52, no. 1 (1969), 5.

27. Kenneth C. Burt, *The Search for a Civic Voice: California Latino Politics* (Claremont, CA: Regina Books, 2007), 186; Ignacio M. García, *Viva Kennedy: Mexican Americans in Search of Camelot* (College Station: Texas A&M University Press, 2000), 44–59; and Lamb, "Chicano Civil Rights Activist," 133. On April 9, 1960, Senator Kennedy campaigned at a Democratic luncheon in Tucson and gave an evening speech in Phoenix; in all likelihood he met Estrada at one or both of these events. Copies of the speeches for both events are located at www.jfklibrary.org. Also, for an amazing image of Kennedy with Estrada, Felipe N. Torres, Henry B. González, Héctor García, Henry López, and José Ramón López, see Julie Leininger Pycior, *LBJ and Mexican Americans: The Paradox of Power* (Austin: University of Texas Press, 1997), 162. The same image also appears in García's *Viva Kennedy*.

28. "Ralph Estrada Speaker at Conference" and "Message," *Alianza Magazine* 52, no. 1 (1959), 16–17; and "Lawyer Ralph Estrada Dies at 76; Fought for Civil Rights of Hispanics," *Arizona Republic*, October 5, 1979. For more on Sánchez, see the George I. Sánchez Papers, Benson Latin American Collection, University of Texas at Austin. For more information on Carey McWilliams, see the new edition of his book *North From Mexico: The Spanish-Speaking People of the United States*, updated by Matt S. Meier (Westport, CT: Greenwood, 1990).

29. Michelle Hall Kells, *Héctor P. García: Everyday Rhetoric and Mexican American Civil Rights* (Carbondale: Southern Illinois Press, 2006), 189; Craig A. Kaplowitz, *LULAC: Mexican Americans and National Policy* (College Station: Texas A&M University Press, 2005), 76, 82; and Burt, *Search for a Civic Voice*, 186.

30. In 1942 the Alianza claimed 372 lodges in California, Colorado, New Mexico, and Texas. In the 1920s the Alianza also had 1 chapter in Chicago and 44 chapters spread throughout Mexico in Baja California, Chihuahua, Coahuila, Guanajuato, Nuevo Leon, Sinaloa, Sonora, and the Distrito Federal. See Briegel, "Alianza Hispano-Americana," 100–2, 128–34, 203–8, 214–15; and Lamb, "Chicano Civil Rights Activist," 135–40.

31. "Lawyer Ralph Estrada Dies"; "Rites for Ralph Estrada, Noted Tempe Native, Held," *Tempe Daily News*, October 6, 1979; "Services for Early Crusader Estrada," *Tucson Citizen*, October 5, 1979; *Robayo v. Robayo*, 416 P. 2d 198 (1966); and *Olson v. Staggs-Bilt Homes Inc.* 534 P.2d 1073 (1975).

Figure 12.1. Ernesto Galarza in the 1950s. Occidental College Library, "The Life of Ernesto Galarza," file:///var/folders/89/61sl8vy97n7d10j08q8k7z700000gn/T/com.apple.iChat/Messages/Transfers/IMG_2493.JPG.jpeg.

12

"Vale más la revolución que viene"[1]

Ernesto Galarza and Transnational Scholar Activism

JULIE LEININGER PYCIOR

A leading member of his generation of Mexican American activists, Ernesto Galarza worked for civil rights and, in particular, for worker rights. He did so with a strong trans-border perspective, and as such, his trailblazing publications, Congressional testimony, and transnational unionization efforts matter more than ever in this era of globalization. "Ernesto Galarza was an oracle and a visionary," notes historian Stephen J. Pitti, "an immigrant himself, who appealed to his co-ethnics' trans-national sensibilities and to their involvement in community organizations, becoming, in the process, an activist of national and international prominence."[2]

A scrupulous researcher, Galarza conducted careful, thoughtful studies that hold up well today. The sole exception—an exception that proves the rule—serves to illustrate the one handicap to scholar activism: the possibility that deep engagement with a controversy of the moment may unduly influence one's perspective on it. Galarza mostly navigated successfully between activism and research, however, using the two to inform each other in path-breaking ways. Besides, researchers holed up in offices far from the fray are

DOI: 10.5876/9781607323372.c012

by no means unbiased, with history providing many cautionary examples of pseudo-objectivity—as with research that supported the theory of eugenics, for instance. At any rate, as a scholar-activist with trailblazing insights, Ernesto Galarza set the example for applying one's talents in the making of a better world.

"Unlike people who are born in hospitals . . . I showed up in an adobe cottage with a thatched roof . . . in the wild, majestic mountains of the Sierra Madre de Nayarit." So begins *Barrio Boy*, Galarza's evocative, widely anthologized memoir. His mountain village was so remote that "even if you lived there, arriving . . . was always a surprise," he noted of its hidden location, explaining that "Jalcocotán was meant to give protection against outsiders . . . The first settlers were refugees" from the coast, where "the Spaniards had come, killing the Indians with the guns and running them down with their hunting dogs." As in so many villages from time immemorial, activity in Jalcocotán followed the sun. Thus, young Ernesto could hear the quiet voices of the adults talking outside as night enveloped them, and in the morning he could make out the lines left in the dirt by their machetes.[3]

But those machete marks also represented a rupture with traditional ways, for the villagers were discussing their roles in the world's first modern revolution. Galarza would make this point in a 1965 policy address that took aim at the notion of Mexicans as somehow apathetic. "It was in these little Mexican villages that one of the most portentous events in the twentieth century history of the Americas got started," he said. The people of Jalcocotán were defending themselves against the hated *rurales* (storm troops loyal to the local landlords and to Díaz) associated with longtime dictator Porfirio Díaz. "Toward noon the *rurales* rode out of Jalco" after vainly searching for booty and draftees, Galarza recalled. "'Malditos,' my mother said that night at supper." She took matters into her own hands, and the family left for Mazatlán. There she soon discovered that they were under suspicion by one of Díaz's men after her brother had complained about the working conditions. "He knows what we know," she warned, concluding, "It is better that we leave," so they headed for the United States.[4]

They entered at Nogales, Arizona, eventually ending up in Sacramento, California. There Galarza's elders spent their days scraping out a living, but his jobs were limited to after-school hours, for his mother valued education. "My mother used to read to me in Spanish . . . She read beautifully, very expressively," he noted, adding that she had him read particularly evocative paragraphs back to her. Several of the boy's Sacramento teachers noticed his keen interest in books and took him under their wing. He recalled that the most effective of these educators tried to use Spanish with him and encouraged reports on his own cultural heritage. As such, they prefigured the bilingual education approach—in sharp contrast to the segregation of ethnic Mexicans, then the rule in many school districts from California to Texas.[5]

Tellingly, *Barrio Boy* ends just before the death of his mother and a beloved uncle in the influenza epidemic of World War I—a tragedy so profound that it must have been too painful to commit to paper. Meanwhile, Galarza had advanced to after-school jobs that included interpreting for the local courts. Similarly, his summers as a laborer in the vast, sun-scorched fields were punctuated by serving as the farmworkers' voice to a wider world, as when he reported their grievances to a Sacramento journalist. Nonetheless, his horizon remained limited. "During the last weeks of my senior year in high school I was already shopping around for a job in the canneries," he explained years later to a group of Chicano/a students. "I had a tentative offer lined up . . . to start that July. That was going to be my life." But a dedicated teacher intervened, saying,

> "Why don't you consider going on to college?" which was an amazing idea to me.
>
> I said, "I don't have the money and I don't know anybody. I don't know anyone at college. I have no friend anywhere."
>
> So he said, "Well, don't go to work in the cannery for keeps. Take a summer job, but don't plan to stay there."
>
> In the summertime this man got busy. He wrote to some people down in Occidental College; and one thing and another, I was in Occidental that fall.[6]

Galarza thrived there, working on the college paper, joining the debate team, earning election to Phi Beta Kappa. At the same time he kept one eye on his native land via a senior thesis that included field research in Mexico. The Catholic Cristero revolt was challenging the post-revolutionary government of Plutarco Elías Calles, and Galarza's critical analysis of the historical context, *The Roman Catholic Church as a Factor in the Political and Social History of Mexico*, was published in 1928. By that time he was studying at Stanford University, where he wrote the thesis "Mexico in the World War" and received an MA in 1929.[7]

That same June, Galarza addressed the National Conference of Social Work in San Francisco on "Life in the United States for Mexican People: Out of the Experience of a Mexican." Undaunted by a profession that included eugenicists calling for restriction of Mexican immigration on racist grounds, this young man from the Sacramento barrio told the audience,

> The Mexican immigrant feels the burden of old prejudices . . . that he is unclean, improvident, intolerant, and innately dull. Add to this the suspicion that he constitutes a peril to the American worker's wage scale and you have a situation with which no average Mexican can cope.

He then proceeded to tick off his proposals:

> First, that some order be should brought out of the seasonal labor supply by state initiative . . . Second, that a bilateral accord with the Mexican government should be sought to iron out the immigration issue. Third, wherever feasible, that social service agents working with Mexican groups should use workers of Mexican extraction to make the firsthand contacts. Fourth, there should be more real understanding of the adjustment which the Mexican is making to his American environment . . . Last, I should ask for recognition of the Mexican's contribution to the agricultural and industrial expansion of [the] western United States.[8]

Back in Sacramento, Galarza fell in love with his younger sister's teacher, Mae Taylor. They married in 1928 and then headed for the East Coast. Galarza made Ivy League history as the first Mexican American to enroll in the doctoral program at Columbia University. He studied history while Mae evidently attended Columbia University Teachers College, famous for John Dewey and progressive education. Indeed, in later years she recalled that her husband was introduced to this theory at Columbia, adding that "in New York there were many progressive schools" implementing that philosophy in elementary classrooms.

As the nation plunged into economic depression, a Teachers College professor, George S. Counts, challenged educators to respond boldly to the crisis in a series of highly publicized lectures titled *Dare the School Build a New Social Order?*[9] The Galarzas did dare; they codirected the Year-Long School, with an innovative multicultural curriculum and public discussions about social change, such as a series on progressive education that was publicized in *The*

New York Times.[10] Decades later, citing this pioneering progressivism, activist Polly Baca would call on Chicanas to follow "in the footsteps on Ernesto and Mae Galarza, to take this example and challenge those who would inflict the pain of sexism on others."[11] Indeed, side-by-side, these men and women championed human rights and economic justice in the educational curriculum, but they did not trumpet gender rights per se. After all, it would be decades before any major sector of society would directly address that concern.

In New York, Galarza also worked as a research associate for the Foreign Policy Association, which published his reports on upheavals in Argentina, Bolivia, and Peru. For its part, *The New York Times* circulated them as articles under his own byline. He even tried his hand at poetry, publishing the volume *Thirty Poems* in 1935.[12] The following year, General Francisco Franco's attack on the democratically elected government of Spain prompted Galarza to join those giving fund-raising talks on behalf of the loyalist cause. With Fascism on the rise in Spain, Germany, and Japan, he decided to work full time in the international arena, at the Pan American Union (PAU) in Washington, DC.

Evidently he invited another trailblazer to join the PAU: Luisa Moreno. Galarza may have met Moreno in New York City, where she was an organizer for the giant progressive union, the Congress of Industrial Organizations (CIO); at the time he had been coediting an issue of the CIO-affiliated magazine *Photo-History*. Moreno soon left the PAU, however, in favor of the (Popular Front) Congress of Spanish-Speaking Peoples and the CIO. With these two organizations she pioneered the national mobilization of Latino/a workers.[13] For his part, Galarza became concerned about what he saw as the PAU's unduly close ties to US business interests in Latin America. Originally hired as a researcher of Latin American educational policy, he published several important studies on the subject, but now he convinced the PAU to establish a Division of Labor and Social Research, of which he became the director.[14]

Galarza's interest in the pressing issues of the day was also reflected in the fact that he changed his doctoral focus from history to politics/public policy. In 1940 the Galarzas and their two daughters traveled to Mexico, where Ernesto conducted research for a dissertation about that nation's electrical system. The study was published in Mexico the following year, with Galarza receiving his PhD from Columbia in 1944.[15] Of that Mexican trip, Mae recalled, "We travelled rolling hills: beautifully unspoiled, sparsely populated, with hamlets and churches." They couldn't help noticing the "many signs painted on roadsides, walls, bridges and markets. Every sign carried this word: Revolución—even those near religious saints tucked in the crevices of rock embankments." Back home, Mae and Ernesto had to be so careful. "I had thought of it as an underground word," she said. "People would think that you were a communist." They believed in a revolution of the community-based sort that they had intimated in those signs. As Ernesto put it, "Más vale la revolución que viene que la que fue." Or as Mae explained, that "means change, advance, progression in the way the less advantaged earn a living in an environment of much hostility."[16]

Less than a month after the Nazis took Paris, Galarza issued a warning, according to the Associated Press news agency, that "unless the United States takes immediate steps to aid Latin-American countries, assuring democracy and opportunity where there is none now, a new dark age of domination by a Greater Germany will descend upon the Americas."[17] He watched with alarm as US entry into the war instead reinforced the nation's ties to Latin American regimes manifestly unpopular with their own people. In December 1942, Galarza accused the US ambassador to Bolivia of pressuring that country's president not to implement the new labor code in the crucial tin industry, even as later that month union leaders charged the dictatorship with having massacred striking miners. National news outlets reported Galarza's charges, prompting the State Department to issue a statement denying his accusations. That, in turn, prompted him to quit the PAU in protest, which triggered even more publicity, as with *Time*'s profile, "Man against Tin":

> In his cluttered office on the ground floor of the Pan American Union's exotic building in Washington, shock-haired Ernesto Galarza gazed thoughtfully through a dirt-dimmed window at the sunken gardens below. What he would do next, now that he had quit his job as Chief of the Union's Division of Labor & Social Information, he did not know. Nor did he care. He had made his point.[18]

The White House responded with a fact-finding commission that, in addition to businessmen and the government's Coordinator of Inter-American Affairs, included representatives of organized labor. *The New York Times* reported, "It is believed that the designation of the commission is at least in part a sequel to the charges of Ernesto Galarza." For its part, *The Nation* called for Franklin Roosevelt to "ask the Pan American Union to reinstate

Ernesto Galarza as chief of its Labor and Social Information Division."[19] Galarza did return, but three years later he quit for good, saying, "the ineffectiveness of the Division of Labor and Social Information culminated in its practical absorption by the more aggressive elements of the [Pan American] Union representing business, industry and finance."[20] He noted bitterly,

> Latin American liberals, democrats and workers are also coming to the conclusion . . . that the declarations of the United States with respect to the principles of honest and democratic dealing do not apply to Latin America . . . The door to reform has been slammed shut.[21]

Henceforth, Galarza would engage the government from the outside. As historian David Green writes,

> In 1947, former Pan American Union official Ernesto Galarza told the House Foreign Affairs Committee that in a number of Latin American countries, parades and peaceful demonstrations against economic privation were already being broken up by government troops using weapons obtained from the United States . . . The proposed armaments programs would only intensify such developments, Galarza warned.

Although US officials ignored his advice, he reported on the situation for the Bolivian government in 1949, and seven years later, that appreciative nation bestowed on him its highest award: the Order of the Condor.[22]

By that time Galarza was busy organizing farmworkers in California. It must have shocked his Washington colleagues to hear that this sophisticated power player had forsaken the national stage—and that despite his Columbia PhD he had turned his back on academe as well—to join the fledgling National Farm Labor Union (NFLU). To Galarza, laborers contributed the most wealth to the economy while economic justice constituted the lifeblood of democracy. Moreover, he saw international and domestic issues as intertwined. Thus, at the PAU he had decried as "race warfare" attacks by US sailors on Mexican American zoot-suiters and had provided information to the Fair Employment Practices Commission (FEPC). He had testified before Congress on behalf an even stronger FEPC, providing evidence of continuing, pervasive job discrimination against ethnic Mexicans, even as he reminded the committee that they were essential to the war effort.[23]

Now, with the founding of the NFLU, Galarza saw an opportunity to make a difference in the harsh world of field work that he knew all too well—and with a union that stemmed from the bravely progressive, biracial Southern Tenant Farmers' Union (STFU). The STFU was fading, however, so the NFLU joined the nation's oldest, most powerful labor organization, the American Federation of Labor (AFL), with its large strike fund. Moreover, the AFL, with its staunch anti-Communist reputation, seemed to promise some measure of protection from the harassment that befell both the STFU and the most successful union among California agricultural laborers, the United Cannery, Agricultural, Packing, and Allied Workers of America (UCAPAWA). Many of UCAPAWA's leaders, including Luisa Moreno, were being hauled before the House Un-American Activities Committee and summarily jailed and/or deported as "subversive."[24]

For over a decade Galarza threw himself into farmworker organizing. In taking on the DiGiorgio Fruit Corporation, the union was up against, in Galarza's words, "the keystone" of California's main economic sector—agriculture, as DiGiorgio lead the world in pear, plum, and grape production. Galarza makes this clear in his book chronicling the protracted battle:

> It was not a strike against a ranch, but against an economic empire.
> Agribusiness had stabilized social relations in rural California and collective bargaining had no place in them. To accept it would have strained DiGiorgio's connections with those who controlled banking, transportation, marketing, and political sectors, from the local sheriff's office to the halls of Congress in Washington, D.C.[25]

Despite the odds—and indeed, with a sense of indignation at the power imbalance—the NFLU membership voted for a strike in September 1947 "in a protest against a wage reduction of about $1 a day," as noted by *The New York Times*. According to Galarza, when Joseph DiGiorgio was informed that a majority of his workers had signed union membership cards, he made no reply, instead applying to the government for braceros from Mexico to use as strikebreakers. NFLU officials cried foul, given that such an action was prohibited by the Bracero program. "When pressed by [the] union for explanations, the Department of Agriculture . . . relied necessarily on information that could have been supplied only by the corporation and the sheriff," stated Galarza. He charged that Washington took the growers' version of the strike at face value, even when "contradicted by information possessed by the union."[26]

Galarza was citing a program on which he was an expert. In 1942 he had commissioned a study of the new program, and three years later his division of the PAU published the results: Robert C. Jones's *Mexican War Workers in the United States*, with an introduction by Galarza. It explained that the program was a response to the emergency labor shortage. The AFL had opposed it outright, in keeping with its historic policy against any contract labor agreements. As historian Mae M. Ngai writes, "The decision to use foreign contract labor was a momentous break with past policy and practice . . . Since the time of the Civil War Americans had believed that contract labor, like slavery, was the antithesis of free labor, upon which democracy depended."[27] At the same time, as she also notes, the AFL had always been a leading voice for immigrant exclusion, a position taken out of concern for jobs but also highly steeped in nativism. In contrast, Galarza, as an immigrant himself, came to oppose the program due to circumstances on the ground: the end of the wartime labor shortage and, especially, in the face of the government's failure to enforce provisions meant to protect the contract workers themselves.

In 1950 the NFLU, at his initiative, passed a resolution charging the government with complicity in the "exploitation of both the American and national Mexican farm workers," according to *The New York Times*.[28] The trans-border nature of this statement was also reflected in Galarza's trailblazing recruitment efforts among ethnic Mexicans, broadly defined, regardless of citizenship or immigration status. As such, Galarza bilingually touted the benefits of unionization while flanked by US and Mexican flags. "Galarza's union allowed Mexican people to be very Mexican," a union member recalled to Pitti years later, adding, "It gave everybody the sense that we could be Mexicanos and demand our rights as residents of California." Pitti notes, "Galarza followed UCAPAWA's example by linking Mexicanidad and unionization." Thus, these "Mexican organizing committees," as he called them, organized among all farmworkers, whether a native-born person, a temporary contract worker, or someone who had come to the United States through the traditional immigrant route.[29]

Galarza tried to build solidarity between braceros and the other workers, even to the point of breaking up fights between the two groups—not for him the cozy, book-lined world of a professor. He also endeavored to link up with the bracero union based in Mexico, but its leaders told him that organizing was stymied by contract laborers' fear of being fired and summarily deported. Meanwhile, he knew that among those who had immigrated in the traditional manner were people who had entered without official papers, and his meetings welcomed them as well. He realized that anyone who immigrated at some remote spot along the border obviously had no documentation, even in this period before the government instituted a numerical ceiling on Mexican immigration (i.e., at a time when almost anyone crossing at the formal immigration entrepots could enter legally). After all, if the Galarzas had entered the United States at some rural Arizona crossroads rather than at Nogales, he himself would not have come over "legally."

Meanwhile, Galarza knew that the AFL directors understood none of this, and that in fact the union's longtime, fierce opposition to contract foreign labor and illegal immigration was tinged with prejudice: "historic racial policies," Galarza called it.[30] Moreover, neither the AFL nor the unions in Mexico supported his attempt to organize farmworkers in both countries without regard to their status. Then there was the fact that the AFL studiously ignored his economic critiques, as in a 1949 magazine article arguing that the Mexican immigrant "is forced to seek better conditions north of the border by the slow but relentless pressure of the United States' agricultural, financial and oil corporate interests on the entire economic and social evolution of the Mexican nation."[31] At the same time, he was keenly aware that virtually the only voices calling for leniency in immigration enforcement were the growers, now that the Red Scare had effectively silenced the voices that heretofore had most strongly defended undocumented immigrants themselves, such as Luisa Moreno.

His options thus circumscribed, Galarza joined the chorus calling for termination of the Bracero program and enforcement of immigration laws—a chorus that included major Mexican American civil rights leaders. Moreover, as historian Carlos Kevin Blanton has noted, "This perspective was part of the liberal mainstream . . . the National Association for the Advancement of Colored People, the National Coalition of American Indians, the National Consumers League, the National Educational Association."[32] Cold War labor/liberals even voiced support for the Dwight Eisenhower administration's Operation Wetback, the infamous immigration dragnet that swept through communities across the Southwest in 1954. Here is the one time when the activist approach to research may have not served Galarza well (i.e., to the extent that understandable opposition to the power of agribusiness made it difficult for him to question Cold War liberals' immigration restriction views).

At the same time, in contrast to the AFL, Mexican American activists had long considered the idea of a Mexican quota a discriminatory policy.[33] Meanwhile, the NFLU's decision to affiliate with the famously anti-Communist AFL did not keep the fledgling union from being subjected, early on, to an anti-Communist investigation by a committee of the California State Senate. No Communist affiliations were proven, but that same month, five union pickets were attacked by men who emerged, according to Galarza, "from inside the ranch, armed with chains and irons." Three months later, in May 1948, shots rang out in the darkness during an evening labor meeting, injuring labor official James Price in the head. Although three NFLU people had to be hospitalized, local officials came up with nothing. Next came Congressional hearings, during which attorneys for growers filed a libel suit against the NFLA over the film *Poverty in the Land of Plenty.* The AFL pressured the NFLA to settle with DiGiorgio; the grower was to pay the union damages of one dollar and the film was to be destroyed. After thirty long months, the strike was over.[34]

Undaunted, within a few years Galarza was laying out the ambitious goal of 200,000 members nationwide. "Galarza and the union were entangled in libel suits and countersuits with DiGiorgio for more than fifteen years," notes the Ernesto Galarza Papers. Galarza's 1956 chronicle of the saga received wide attention. Titled *Strangers in Our Fields*, it charged that these farm laborers who contributed so much to the national economy were treated as strangers by a US government policy that refused to let them be permanent residents, let alone citizens.[35]

By the late 1950s, the NFLU was experiencing declining support from the AFL. After Galarza's union was renamed and then was merged with the Amalgamated Meat Cutters and Butcher Workmen of North America, he quit in 1960.[36] He focused again on activist research. His 1963 report to the House Committee on Education and Labor constituted a devastating exposé of the criminal neglect that had contributed to the accident at a railroad crossing involving the deaths of thirty-two braceros. This was followed by his landmark history of the Bracero program, *Merchants of Labor*, published in 1964, the same year that bracero authorization was terminated by Congress. Galarza went on to chronicle the history of farmworker struggle in a number of important books.[37]

The timing was right, for the cause was gaining national attention through the United Farm Workers Union (UFW) of Cesar Chavez. As a young man, Chavez had participated in some of the NFLU's first strikes. As noted in a Chavez biography, his innovative style—drawing support from the public at large—was "foreshadowed" by Galarza, that the older activist had initiated the "consumer boycott against DiGiorgio table grapes" later made famous by Chavez's UFW.[38] Along with Galarza, another important adviser to Chavez was Bert Corona, the pioneering postwar community organizer. Corona was a longtime ally of Galarza's, with the two men's common vision dating from the 1930s, when Corona in California, like Galarza in Washington, supported Luisa Moreno's organizing efforts.[39]

Thus, the two veteran activists thought that both a Mexican immigration quota and a bracero recruitment program were bad ideas. At the same time, Corona never supported immigrant roundups. In fact he would cofound a pioneering immigrant rights self-help group with particular concern for the undocumented. This was in 1968—and perhaps not incidentally—the year the first-ever numerical ceiling on Western Hemisphere immigration went into effect. And while Galarza and his colleagues in the two main Mexican American civil rights groups did not yet stand with Corona on the undocumented issue, they opposed the immigration ceiling proposal, warning the administration of Lyndon Johnson that it would be manifestly unworkable.

Moreover, along with Corona, Galarza continued to lead the way on the issue of transnational worker activism, as when he criticized the Johnson administration's new Border Commission, demanding that it include labor representatives from both sides of the border, "to raise Mexican levels of income to American standards . . . not . . . lowering American to present Mexican levels." He warned, "Otherwise, goods will be manufactured at Mexican wages and re-imported for sale at American prices." Thus, he anticipated questions of economic fairness raised twenty-five years later in connection with the North American Free Trade Agreement of 1993. Meanwhile, Corona and many in the rising Chicano movement argued with increasing effectiveness that employer sanctions would escalate prejudicial hiring policies.[40]

Galarza was recalibrating his stance, but he was fading from the scene and would pass away in 1984. At the same time, Chavez, whose UFW had worked for termination of the Bracero program in 1964, shifted in subsequent decades to such an extent that the union signed the first nationwide contract with braceros (or *guest workers*, in the current lingo) in 2006. This nationwide contract made history while two years earlier the first-ever guest worker union contract, signed with a North Carolina grower, had been won by Chavez protégé Baldemar Velásquez and his Farm Labor Organizing Committee (FLOC). For his part, Velásquez has invoked Galarza, as in a 2009 interview with a leading Mexican newspaper. In fact, Velásquez champions the kind of transnational organizing that Galarza always envisioned, with the Ohio-based FLOC having established worker centers in Mexico.[41]

But the issue of Mexican immigration remained mostly on the back burner in the 1960s in comparison to such new initiatives as the Johnson administration's War on Poverty program (officially known as the Office of Economic Opportunity, or OEO). Galarza signed on to the OEO as a program analyst for its Economic and Youth Opportunity Agency, explaining,

> There are things to be done in East Los Angeles that have been crying to be done for fifty years, and here we have a law, the Economic Opportunities Act, that is based on a tremendous concept. They tell us to go out and organize the poor in the neighborhoods—teach them, help them elect their representatives, and lead them to the point that they can run their own program.[42]

Nevertheless, as he told a liberal think tank,

> In my judgment the War on Poverty at this stage is a mere skirmish. I don't think it's going to become a war until the amount of money appropriated by Congress enables us to mount a massive attack on the problem of unemployment. I mean by that not just the problem of creating jobs, I mean the basic decisions that our society is continuously making; such as, for instance, the allocation of resources: where money in vast quantities shall be invested, and how it shall be spent. This is what creates jobs.[43]

He added, tellingly, "To those decisions the poor are not parties." Or as he put it in an address to Mexican American activists, "I wish I could tell you how difficult this is inside the bureaucracy. I don't know how long I'm going to last."[44]

Indeed, soon he was spending more and more of his time advising Chicano/a college students, encouraging them in their inclination to forge ties to the farmworker movement and to grassroots barrio initiatives. In San José this bore fruit with the establishment of the Mexican American Community Services Agency—to this day an important local resource and leadership laboratory.[45] Moreover, the progressive educational values pioneered by the Galarzas found a kind of rebirth with the Chicano movement's emphasis on bicultural pride. Mae Galarza steeped herself in the bilingual methodology and encouraged Ernesto to write "mini-libros" in the spirit of his pathbreaking 1944 children's book *Rimas Tontas*.[46]

But increasingly, the War on Poverty was colliding with a real war: the escalating war in Vietnam. As Galarza was quick to point out, "Mexican Americans and all our children will suffer." The climax came in October 1967 at the White House Conference on Mexican American Affairs in El Paso, Texas. An unprecedented panoply of top officials—the president, the vice president, the governor of Texas, White House cabinet heads—all came to El Paso expressly to hear the concerns of Mexican American community representatives. But Galarza was not impressed, declaring,

> We, who for thirty years, have seen the government stand by, sometimes connive, while farm labor unions were destroyed by agribusiness . . . We who have seen the Office of Economic Opportunity retreat with its shield, not on it, after calling on the Mexican poor to do battle for maximum feasible participation . . . We remain profoundly skeptical.[47]

At an opening ceremony featuring the presidents of Mexico and the United States, Chicano activists booed both chief executives. Then outside the conference hotel, protestors demonstrated, demanding sessions on the Vietnam War and farm labor rights. They marched from the conference headquarters to the El Segundo barrio, where a rump meeting was presided over by Galarza. He read a message from Chavez, who sent prayers and congratulations to La Raza in their "social revolution" against "pretty, perfumed sellouts." The assembly dubbed itself "La Raza Unida," from the barrio connotation of *la raza*, meaning "our folks / our people." Indications are that Galarza suggested the name. The Plan de La Raza Unida, while echoing many of the suggestions at the official conference, placed special emphasis on government support of farmworker rights, recognition of land grant rights under the 1848 Treaty of Guadalupe Hidalgo, and an end to the Vietnam War.[48]

The plan also challenged those present to organize in their home communities for social change. To this end a follow-up conference was scheduled for San Antonio a few months later. Once again Galarza presided, and again the mood was electric. With a steely intensity honed by decades of organizing against the odds, with an eloquence borne of a lifetime with words, this *Mexicano* with the shock of salt-and-pepper hair inspired the crowd even as he drew energy from them. "This is the dawn of a new era for the Mexican American," he declared. Indeed, one of the results was the founding of the Mexican American Legal Defense and Educational Fund, on whose board he served.[49]

Still, Galarza and other veteran activists such as Herman Gallegos and Julian Samora recognized that the Chicano leadership had its elements of hyperbole and posturing and that the yeasty grassroots initiatives then aborning needed to be linked together as a national advocacy network. The three men had conducted a groundbreaking study for the Ford Foundation in 1966, "The Mexican-American People: The Nation's Second-Largest Minority"; with seed money from that foundation, as well as from the National Council of Churches and the United Auto Workers union, they established the Southwest Council of La Raza (SWCLR). The SWCLR soon became the National Council of La Raza (NCLR), bringing together thousands of local initiatives into one organization, with the potential to help shape the national debate itself.[50]

This dream came to realization in large part through the leadership of NCLR founder Raúl Yzaguirre, and today NCLR is arguably the nation's most influential Latino/a organization. Thus, at NCLR's fortieth anniversary convention in July 2008, presidential candidates John McCain and Barack Obama both gave major addresses.[51] Doubtless, Galarza would applaud the NCLR's organizational savvy, its defense of La Raza at the highest levels of the power structure, and its strong civil rights advocacy. For its part, the organization calls its $500–$999 donor level the "The Ernesto Galarza Circle"—the only donor level named for any individual. (At the same time, Galarza might question the NCLR showcasing so many corporate sponsors, from Citi to Walmart while making virtually no mention of organized labor.)[52]

In his last decade Galarza held a number of visiting professorships while today his name graces research centers and public lectures. The city of San

José even raised a statue of him. The memorial that would please him most, though, would be the scholarship programs in his honor—or simply any young person curled up with a mini-libro or *Barrio Boy*. At the Fourteenth Annual Dr. Ernesto Galarza Symposium, his friend Dr. José D. Villa captured something of his legacy:

> Dr. Ernesto Galarza was the solitary sentinel standing before the portals of institutional injustices. His message to us is that so long as there is one lonely picket on duty, there is still hope for justice. He was telling us that we must be constant in our vigilance and see to it that our children, our families, and our communities [are] respected and well served. He is also telling us to be well prepared to serve others. He was telling us to learn from our past experiences, to hold onto those values which give meaning to our lives, and to be diligent in our efforts to forge our character on what is right and just.[53]

Or as Mae Galarza put it at that same symposium, quoting a saying associated with her beloved life partner, "Vale más la revolución que viene que la que se fue."[54]

Notes

1. This article's title is referenced in part by Mae Galarza, "Vale Más La Revolución Que Viene" in *Man of Fire: Selected Writings—Ernesto Glarza*, ed. Armando Ibarra and Rodolfo D. Torres (Urbana: University of Illinois Press, 2013), 279–82. I was present in 1970 when Galarza gave the keynote address at the first Midwest Conference of La Raza, held at the University of Notre Dame, at which he decried the near-total denial of the crucial role of Mexican Americans in US history. I wish to thank Anthony Quiroz, Carmen Samora, and Barbara Driscoll de Alvarado for their encouragement and suggestions and to dedicate this essay to the memory of Ernesto Galarza, who exactly forty years ago inspired me to pursue research in Mexican American history.

2. Stephen J. Pitti, *The Devil in Silicon Valley: Northern California, Race, and Mexican Americans* (Princeton: Princeton University Press, 2003), 137.

3. Ernesto Galarza, *Barrio Boy* (Notre Dame, IN: University of Notre Dame Press, 1973), 3, 5.

4. Ernesto Galarza, "The Burning Light: Action and Organizing in the Mexican Community in California," interviews by Gabrielle Morris and Timothy Beard, 1977, 1978, and 1981, Regional Oral History Office, Bancroft Library, University of

California, Berkeley, accessed December 30, 2009, http://content.cdlib.org/view?d ocId=hb7g50084v&doc.view=frames&chunk.id=div00006&toc.depth=1&toc.id =div00006&brand=calisphere.

5. Galarza, "Burning Light," 132; and Galarza, *Barrio Boy*, 257–61 and part 4.

6. Ernesto Galarza, talk to Chicano studies students, April 20, 1977, University of California, Berkeley, accessed December 30, 2009, http://content.cdlib.org/view? docId=hb7g50084v&doc.view=frames&chunk.id=div00018&toc.depth=1&toc.id= div00018&brand=calisphere&query=community%20action.

7. Galarza talk; Ernesto Galarza, *The Roman Catholic Church as a Factor in the Political and Social History of Mexico* (Sacramento: Capital Press, 1928); Alicia Schmidt Camacho, *Migrant Imaginaries: Latino Cultural Politics in the U.S.-Mexico Borderlands* (New York: New York University Press, 2008), 84–86; and "Biography," Ernesto Galarza Papers, 1936–1984, Special Collections M0224, Stanford University, accessed December 30, 2009, http://content.cdlib.org/view?docId=tf2290026t &chunk.id=bioghist-1.8.3&brand=oac (hereafter Galarza biography).

8. Ernesto Galarza, "Life in the United States for Mexican People: Out of the Experience of a Mexican," in *Man of Fire: Selected Writings—Ernesto Glarza*, ed. Armando Ibarra and Rodolfo D. Torres (Urbana: University of Illinois Press, 2013), 27–31; and Michael C. LeMay, *Guarding the Gates: Immigration and National Security* (New York: Praeger, 2006), 131–32.

9. Carlos Muñoz, Jr., "Galarza: Scholar on the Ramparts," foreword to Inaugural Ernesto Galarza Commemorative Lecture, Stanford University, 1986, http://chs .stanford.edu/pdfs/1st_Annual_Lecture_1986.pdf; George S. Counts, *Dare the School Build a New Social Order?"* (New York: John Day, 1932), 40–47, 50–58.

10. "Burning Light"; and "Notes of the New York Schools," *New York Times*, March 17, 1935.

11. Polly B. Baca, "Silent No More: A Chicana's Vision for Leadership" (speech, Sixth Annual Ernesto Galarza Commemorative Lecture, Stanford University, 1991), accessed December 30, 2009, http://chs.stanford.edu/pdfs/6th_Annual_Lecture _1991.pdf.

12. Ernesto Galarza, *Argentina's Revolution and Its Aftermath* (New York: Foreign Policy Association, 1931); Ernest [sic] Galarza, *Debts, Dictatorship and Revolution in Bolivia and Peru* (New York: Foreign Policy Association, 1931); Ernest Galarza, "Bolivia's Revolt a Popular Rising," *New York Times*, July 6, 1930; Ernest Galarza, "Peru's Old Quarrels Form Background of Revolution," *New York Times*, August 31, 1930; and Ernest Galarza, "Finances Critical in Bolivia and Peru," *New York Times*, May 18, 1931.

13. Galarza's second poetry volume would not come until the 1980s and would constitute the final book of his life. Ernesto Galarza, *Thirty Poems* (Jamaica, NY:

Yearlong School, 1935); Ernesto Galarza, *Kodachromes in Rhyme: Poems* (Notre Dame, IN: University of Notre Dame Press, 1982); Camacho, *Migrant Imaginaries,* 65–66; Muñoz, "Galarza: Scholar on the Ramparts"; Richard Storrs Childs, Ernest Galarza, and Sidney Pollatsek, eds., "Labor's Challenge," in *Photo-History* 1, no. 2 (1937); Ernesto Galarza and Francisco S. Céspedes, *Educational Trends in Latin America* (Washington, DC: Pan American Union, 1936); Ernesto Galarza, "Educational Research in Latin America," *Review of Educational Research* 9 (October 1939): 368–71, 427–28; Mario T. García, *Memories of Chicano History: The Life and Narrative of Bert Corona* (Berkeley: University of California Press, 1994), 117; and Vicki L. Ruiz, *Cannery Women, Cannery Lives: Mexican Women, Unionization, and the California Food Processing Industry, 1930–1950* (Albuquerque: University of New Mexico Press, 1987), 45–46.

14. Ernesto Galarza, "Crisis of the Pan American Union" *Inter-American Reports,* no. 5 (1949): 5–6, 36.

15. Most sources indicate that his doctorate was in economics. A few say it was in history, but Galarza told a group of Chicano students in 1977 that at Columbia he studied history, political science, and public law. Maria Montes de Oca Ricks, "Ernesto Galarza," in *Chicano Writers: Second Series, Dictionary of Literary Biography* 122, ed. Francisco Lomeli and Carol R. Shirley (Detroit: Gale Research, 1992); Arturo de la Madrid, conversation with author, April 11, 2009; and Galarza talk.

16. M. Galarza, "Vale más la revolución que viene."

17. Organization of American States, "OAS History at a Glance," accessed December 30, 2009, http://www.oas.org/en/about/our_history.asp; and "Warns of Nazi Inroads: Pan-American Official in Talk in Pittsburgh Urges Action," *New York Times,* July 12, 1940. The article referred to him as "Dr. Galarza," although he had yet to obtain that degree.

18. "The Americas: Castles of Tin," *Time,* December 28, 1942; and "Bolivia: Man against Tin," *Time,* January 25, 1943.

19. "Hull Clears Boal of Union's Charges: Denies Ambassador to Bolivia Took Part in Labor Law," *New York Times,* December 29, 1942; "U.S. To Investigate Bolivian Tin Problems," *New York Times,* January 12, 1943; "The Americas: Castles of Tin"; Bolivia: Man against Tin"; Robert Jackson Alexander and Eldon M. Parker, *A History of Organized Labor in Bolivia* (New York: Praeger, 2005), 45–48; Rafael Menjívar, *Reforma agraria: Guatemala, Bolivia, Cuba* (San Salvador: Editorial Universitaria de El Salvador, 1969), 217; and "Good Neighbor Daydream," *The Nation* (January 16, 1943), 77.

20. Ernesto Galarza, "The Crisis of the Pan American Union," 5–6, 36; William Becker, interview by Gabrielle Morris, Governmental History Documentation

Project, Regional Oral History Project, Bancroft Library, University of California, Berkeley, 1981, accessed December 30, 2009.

21. Organization of American States, "Staff Association," accessed December 30, 2009, http://www.oas.org/columbus/staffassociation.asp; and Ernesto Galarza, "Standardization of Armaments in the Western Hemisphere," *Inter-American Reports*, no. 1 (October 1947).

22. David Green, "The Cold War Comes to Latin America," in *Politics and Policies of the Truman Administration*, ed. Barton Bernstein (Chicago: Quadrangle, 1972), 184; and "The Life of Ernesto Galarza: Social Activist and Educator," Special Collections and College Archives, Occidental College, accessed December 30, 2009, http://sites .oxy.edu/special-collections/galarza/timeline.htm.

23. Zaragoza Vargas, "Citizens, Immigrants, and Foreign Wage Workers: The Chicana/o Labor Refrain in U.S. Labor Historiography," Julián Samora Research Institute Occasional Paper No. 19, June 1997, accessed December 30, 2009, http:// jsri.msu.edu/upload/occasional-papers/oc19.pdf; Clete Daniel, *Chicano Workers and the Politics of Fairness: The FEPC in the Southwest, 1941–1945* (Austin: University of Texas Press, 1991), 4–5, 193; "First Lady Urges Facing Race Bias," *New York Times*, February 12, 1944; and A. Bruce Hunt, "The Proposed Fair Employment Practice Act: Facts and Fallacies," *Virginia Law Review* 32 (December 1945): 34.

24. William H. Cobb, "Southern Tenant Farmers' Union," *Encyclopedia of Arkansas History and Culture*, accessed December 30, 2009, http://www.encyclopediaof arkansas.net/encyclopedia/entry-detail.aspx?entryID=35; Pitti, *Devil in Silicon Valley*, 136–37; Ernesto Galarza, introduction to *Farm Workers and Agri-Business in California, 1947–1960* (Notre Dame, IN: University of Notre Dame Press, 1977); Ernesto Galarza, *Merchants of Labor: The Mexican Bracero Story* (Charlotte: McNally & Loftin, 1964); and Ernesto Galarza, *Spiders in the House and Workers in the Fields* (Notre Dame, IN: University of Notre Dame Press, 1970).

25. Galarza, *Farm Workers and Agri-Business*, 114; Funding Universe, "The DiGiorgio Corporation," accessed December 30, 2009, http://www.fundinguniverse.com /company-histories/di-giorgio-corp-history/; and Ruiz, *Cannery Women, Cannery Lives*, 45–46, 100–1, 116.

26. *New York Times*, September 27, 1949; and Galarza, *Farm Workers and Agri-Business*, 98–105.

27. Barbara A. Driscoll, *The Tracks North: The Railroad Bracero Program of World War II* (Austin: Center for Mexican American Studies, University of Texas at Austin, 1999), xii; and Robert C. Jones, *Mexican War Workers in the United States* (Washington, DC: Pan American Union, Division of Labor and Social Information, 1945), title page; and Mae M. Ngai, "The Lost Immigration Debate," *Boston Review*,

September/October 2006, accessed December 30, 2009, http://bostonreview.net/mae-m-ngai-the-lost-immigration-debate-border-control.

28. Galarza, "The Crisis of the Pan American Union," 9n15; Lawrence E. Davies, "Farm Union Urges Government Deal End," *New York Times*, January 15, 1950, 44; Christian Joppke, *Selected by Origin: Ethnic Migration in the Liberal State* (Cambridge: Harvard University Press, 2005), 58; Mraz, Storey, and Storey, *Uprooted: Braceros in the Hermanos Mayo Lens* (Arte Público, 1996) 45–46; Matt S. Meier and Feliciano Rivera, *Dictionary of Mexican American History* (Westport, CT: Greenwood, 1977), 55–57; and Funding Universe, "DiGiorgio Corporation."

29. Pitti, *Devil in Silicon Valley*, 139–47, 240n32; and Camacho, *Migrant Imaginaries*, 84–88.

30. Gilbert G. González and Raúl Fernández, *Pacific Historical Review* 71 (February 2002): 19; and Funding Universe, "DiGiorgio Corporation."

31. Ernesto Galarza, "Program for Action," *Common Ground*, no. 10 (1949), cited in "Empire and the Origins of Twentieth-Century Migration from Mexico to the United States"; Ngai, "Lost Immigration Debate."

32. Carlos Kevin Blanton, "The Citizenship Sacrifice: Mexican Americans, the Saunders-Leonard Report, and the Politics of Immigration, 1951–1952," *Western Historical Quarterly* 40 (Autumn 2009): 308.

33. Galarza, *Spiders in the House*, 13; Dino Cinel, *From Italy to San Francisco: The Immigrant Experience* (Stanford: Stanford University Press, 1982), 232; Vargas, "Citizens, Immigrants, and Foreign Wage Workers"; "Labor History Timeline," accessed December 30, 2009, http://www.aflcio.org/About/Our-History/Labor-History-Timeline; and Julie Leininger Pycior, "The Johnson Administration and Mexican Immigration Policy" (paper presented at the Texas State Historical Association Annual Meeting, Corpus Christi, TX, March 5–8, 2008).

34. Evidently the film was not destroyed, for it was reportedly shown in Los Angeles as recently as 2001. LAUC Diversity Committees, "Annual Report: 2001 Activities," accessed December 30, 2009, http://unitproj.library.ucla.edu/laucla/members/committees/reports/01reports/files/lauc2001diversitydivisionreports.doc; Galarza, *Farm Workers and Agri-Business*, 109–16; *New York Times*, September 15, 1951; and "Strikers on Coast Arrest 'Wetbacks,'" *New York Times*, May 31, 1951.

35. Galarza biography; Ernesto Galarza, *Strangers in Our Fields* (Washington, DC: US Section, Joint United States-Mexico Trade Union Committee, 1956); and *New York Times*, July 29, 1956 .

36. Galarza, *Farm Workers and Agri-business in California, 1947–1960* (Notre Dame: University of Notre Dame Press, 1977), 109–116; 330–332.

37. *Merchants of Labor* echoed the Woody Guthrie song of a plane crash in which numerous braceros died, concluding,

Is this the best way we can grow our big orchards?
Is this the best way we can grow our good fruit?
To fall like dry leaves to rot on my topsoil?
And be called by no name except "deportees"?

"Plane Wreck at Los Gatos (Deportee)," (Woody Guthrie Publications, Inc., 1961), accessed December 30, 2009, http://www.woodyguthrie.org/Lyrics/Plane_Wreck_At_Los_Gatos.htm; H. Comm. on Education and Labor, 88th Cong., 2d Sess. "Report on the Farm Labor Transportation Accident at Chualar, California on September 17, 1963," published as Ernesto Galarza, *Tragedy at Chualar: El crucero de las treinta y dos cruces* (Santa Barbara: McNally & Loftin, 1977); Galarza, *Merchants of Labor*; Michael Denning, *The Cultural Front: The Laboring of the American Culture in the Twentieth Century* (London: Verso, 1997), 280; and "List of Works" Special Collections and College Archives, Occidental College, accessed December 30, 2009, http://sites.oxy.edu/special-collections/galarza/list%20of%20works.htm.

38. Richard Griswold del Castillo and Richard A. Garcia, *César Chávez: A Triumph of Spirit* (Norman: University of Oklahoma Press, 1997), 16; and Roger Bruns, *Cesar Chavez: A Biography* (Westport, CT: Greenwood, 2005), 10–11, 55.

39. García, *Memories of Chicano History*, 117; and Carlos Larralde and Richard Griswold del Castillo, "Luisa Moreno: A Hispanic Civil Rights Leader in San Diego," *Journal of San Diego History* 41 (Fall 1995): 284–310.

40. The Immigration and Nationality Act of 1965 is best known for having overturned discriminatory quotas aimed at southern and eastern Europeans, but especially at Asians. But the non-discriminatory quotas that the new law instituted globally included the first-ever quota on Western Hemisphere immigration. Julie Leininger Pycior, "Ahead of Their Time to No Avail: The American GI Forum and the Immigration Reform Act of 1965" paper presented at American GI Forum 60th Anniversary Symposium, Corpus Christi, TX, March 27, 2008; David Bacon, "El Valiente Chicano," *In These Times*, August 12, 2009; David G. Gutiérrez, *Walls and Mirrors: Mexican Americans, Mexican Immigrants, and the Politics of Ethnicity* (Berkeley: University of California Press, 1995), 160, 190–93; and Julie Leininger Pycior, letter to the editor, *New York Times*, November 12, 1993.

41. Steven Greenhouse, "Farmworkers' Union Is Set to Announce First National Contract for Guest Workers," *New York Times*, April 11, 2006, accessed December 30, 2009, http://www.nytimes.com/2006/04/11/us/11union.html?scp=26&sq=%22steven+greenhouse%22+immigration&st=nyt; Steven Greenhouse, "Growers' Group Signs the First Union Contract for Guest Workers," *New York Times*, September 17, 2004, accessed December 30, 2009, http://www.nytimes.com/2004/09/17/national/17labor.html?scp=53&sq=%22steven+greenhouse%22+immigration&st=nyt;

and Arturo Cano, "Organizar esclavos en EU, principal tarea de Baldemar Velásquez," *La Jornada*, January 12, 2009.

42. Ernesto Galarza quoted in Lino M. Lopez, Juan Acevedo, et al., "Proceedings of the Mexican-American Adult Leadership Conference: May 14–16, 1965, Camp Max Strauss, Glendale, California" (San Jose, CA: Mexican-American Community Services Project, 1965), 20–22.

43. Ernesto Galarza, "The Mexican Americans" (excerpts from a conference talk at the Center for the Study of Democratic Institutions, Santa Barbara, labeled ca. 1959–1960 but evidently delivered after November 1963, as the talk makes reference to Johnson administration programs), accessed December 30, 2009, http://content .cdlib.org/view?docId=hb7g50084v&doc.view=frames&chunk.id=div00006&toc .depth=1&toc.id=div00006&brand=calisphere&query=eyoa.

44. Galarza, "The Mexican Americans."

45. Pitti, *Devil in Silicon Valley*, 187–88.

46. Galarza biography; Galarza, "Mexican Americans"; and Pitti, *Devil in Silicon Valley*, 187–88.

47. Ernesto Galarza, "The Mexican American: A National Concern—Program for Action," *Common Ground* 9, no. 4 (1949); 29–38; and Galarza, "Burning Light."

48. Pitti, *Devil in Silicon Valley*, 183; and Julie Leininger Pycior, "Climax," in *LBJ and Mexican Americans: The Paradox of Power* (Austin: University of Texas Press, 1997), chapter 9.

49. Armando Navarro, *La Raza Unida Party: A Chicano Challenge to the U.S. Two-Party Dictatorship* (Philadelphia: Temple University Press, 2000), 25; Pycior, "Climax"; Pitti, *Devil in Silicon Valley*, 185–86; and Galarza, "Burning Light."

50. National Council of La Raza, accessed December 30, 2009, http://nclr.org; National Council of La Raza, "Formation of SWCLR," http://nclr.org/section /about/history/history_formation_swclr, accessed December 30, 2009; and Jake Tapper, "The McCain-Obama Immigration Wars," *Political Punch* (blog), *ABC News*, July 14, 2008, accessed December 30, 2009, http://blogs.abcnews.com/political punch/2008/07/the-mccain-obam.html.

51. National Council of La Raza, "Institutional Corporate Sponsors," accessed December 30, 2009; National Council of La Raza, "NCLR Affiliates Network," accessed December 30, 2009; National Council of La Raza, "Donor Benefits," accessed December 30, 2009; Pycior, "Climax"; and Jorge Mariscal, "Which Way for Latinos: Dr. Galarza v. Alberto Gonzalez," January 12, 2005, accessed December 30, 2009, http://www.counterpunch.org/mariscal01132005.html.

52. At the same time, doubtless Galarza would have led the chorus decrying the bowlderized/"sanitized" *Barrio Boy* excerpt that New York State used in its Regents High School Exam—that is, until a sharp-eyed Brooklyn mom flagged it. The exam

even misspelled Galarza's name as "Galarzo." N. R. Kleinfield, "Elderly Man and the Sea? Test Sanitizes Literary Texts," *New York Times*, June 2, 2002.

53. José D. Villa, "Ernesto Galarza, Mentor and Friend" (speech at Fourteenth Annual Dr. Ernesto Galarza Scholarship Symposium, San José State University, San José, CA, September 16, 1998).

54. M. Galarza, "Vale más la revolución que viene."

Figure 13.1. Los Angeles City Councilmember Edward R. Roybal meets with President John F. Kennedy at the White House for an issues briefing prior to the start of the fall 1962 congressional campaign. Edward R. Roybal Papers, UCLA Chicano Studies Research Center, University of California, Los Angeles. Photo courtesy of the UCLA Chicano Studies Research Center and the Roybal family.

13

Edward R. Roybal

Latino Political Pioneer and Coalition Builder

KENNETH C. BURT

The Great Depression, the rise of the industrial labor movement, and World War II shaped Edward R. Roybal, as did growing up in a multiethnic neighborhood that served as the cauldron of radical politics in 1930s Los Angeles. The most liberal of the three Mexican American congressmen serving during the 1960s and the most accommodating to the Chicano movement, Roybal is best remembered as the founder of two of the nation's most enduring institutions: the Congressional Hispanic Caucus (CHC) and the National Association of Latino Elected and Appointed Officials (NALEO). But he also helped found two organizations central to Mexican American political development in California. The Community Service Organization (CSO) registered 440,000 new voters between its inception in 1947 and 1960, the year Roybal became founding president of the Mexican American Political Association (MAPA). Roybal is rightly remembered as a pioneering Latino leader; less recognized is his role as a master coalition builder, the forerunner to Los Angeles Mayor Antonio Villaraigosa.[1]

DOI: 10.5876/9781607323372.c013

Edward Ross Roybal was born in Albuquerque, New Mexico, on February 10, 1916, to a working-class family that traced its roots in the New World back some four hundred years. Roybal's father moved the family to Los Angeles after a failed railroad strike in 1922. Like other transplants from New Mexico, Roybal remained proud of his Spanish heritage but assumed the Mexican American moniker more common to the Spanish speakers in California, where most adults his parents' age were refugees from the violence of the Mexican Revolution (1910–1917). In 1934 Roybal graduated from Roosevelt High School and joined the Civilian Conservation Corps. He left after a year to pursue his education. He studied at UCLA and Southwestern University and worked at a number of odd jobs. Roybal joined the Los Angeles County Tuberculosis and Health Association in 1942 and served in World War II from April 1944 to December 1945. He remained in Los Angeles and managed to increase his civic engagement. He was elected to a two-year term on the Los Angeles County Democratic Central Committee in June 1944 and was an honored guest at the October 1944 Franklin Roosevelt Good Neighbor rally that featured US Senator Dennis Chávez (D-New Mexico).[2]

In the postwar years, Roybal was more established in the community and in his family life than most other World War II veterans, who were getting married and starting families or using the GI Bill to attend college or launch a business. He returned to his prewar employer, the Los Angeles County Tuberculosis and Health Association. As a health educator, he was responsible for working with the Mexican American community to reduce the incidence of tuberculosis. This cemented a lifetime interest in public health. It also increased his visibility, as the position required him to speak before large groups as well as to advise individuals, further expanding his growing personal network.

Then in 1947, Roybal, thirty-one, ran for a seat on the Los Angeles City Council. Each morning he boarded the streetcar that took people from their homes in Boyle Heights to the factories and offices downtown. Wearing a red, white, and blue campaign button, he shook hands and distributed union-printed palm cards. The cards stressed Roybal's name and the words *veteran* and *progressive*. According to Roger Johnson, his campaign manager, "We carried on a campaign of not very great intelligence. It was basically, 'We need better street cleaning,' 'We need better street lights,' 'We need protection from police brutality,' and that type of thing, rather than anything very lofty."[3]

After a distant third-place finish, Roybal met a group of his supporters at the Carioca Café, a popular area restaurant. They decided to stay together, forming the Community Political Organization, with Roybal as president. It would likely have developed like previous political organizations—providing a needed voice but achieving limited results. Instead, a confluence of interests developed that would transform the community. Fred Ross, who was organizing Mexicans Americans into Civic Unity Leagues in nearby cities, was seeking a full-time organizing job. Saul Alinsky, head of the Chicago-based Industrial Areas Foundation (IAF), met Ross on a trip to Los Angeles, where he also toured blighted Mexican American neighborhoods. Roybal and friends ultimately agreed to rename their group the Community Service Organization so as to be eligible for funding from Alinsky's nonprofit. They also accepted Ross as the organizer, and Alinsky agreed to pay Ross's salary.

Within a year, the Roybal-led organization had 1,000 members, had registered some 10,000 new voters, and was enjoying institutional ties to the Roman Catholic Church, the International Ladies Garment Workers Union, and the United Steel Workers of America—three groups with large Mexican American memberships. It had also established ties to Yiddish-speaking Jews—the largest group in Boyle Heights and the heart of the polyglot city council district—and to smaller numbers of African Americans, Japanese Americans, Irish Americans, and other white ethnics.[4]

In January 1949, Roybal again declared to run for the city council and set about building a new coalition. This time the Jewish community decided not to run one of their own against Anglo incumbent Parley P. Christensen, making it easier for their members to back Roybal. Beyond the Jewish community, Roybal reached out to a plethora of minority group leaders, including African Americans, who accounted for 15 percent of the district and were concentrated around Central Avenue, south of downtown. When asked why they should support him, Roybal said, "Our skin is brown—our battle is the same. Our victory cannot but be a victory for you, too."[5] The two big labor bodies split in the heavily unionized, working-class district. The Central Labor Council of the American Federation of Labor (AFL) endorsed the incumbent; the Los Angeles Congress of Industrial Organizations (CIO) Council backed Roybal.

Pleased to get CIO support, Roybal had never trusted the motives of its Communist leader, Philip Connelly. "Connelly and company" joined the campaign only after Monsignor Thomas O'Dwyer and "everybody else was in there," emphasized Roybal.[6]

Roybal and his allies mobilized hundreds of volunteers who campaigned door-to-door—as did the candidate—and targeted Temple Street, an area of downtown dominated by long-time residents down on their luck and new arrivals en route to a nicer area. "We were all children of immigrants—whether Latino, Japanese, Jewish, whatever—and everyone was struggling," stated Rebecca Tuck, then a Belmont High School student living with her family in the back of a small grocery store. "[Roybal] came around to every person's door and talked to us," she said, adding that her family "voted for him and we loved him" because of his desire to help all people, regardless of race or creed.[7]

On Election Day, with emotions among Latinos in Boyle Heights hitting a fever pitch, the Roybal campaign worked to get every identified supporter to the polls. The CSO focused its organizational efforts on turning out newly registered Latinos. Paired volunteers knocked on their neighbors' doors with the simple message that "today is the day." Through voting, residents could achieve a new level of dignity while improving their lives materially. The message was clear, and it was delivered again and again.

When the polls closed and the votes were counted, the extent of the CSO's operation and the larger Roybal campaign became clear for all to see. Winning election to city council, Roybal received more than 20,000 votes, twice his primary total and more than double the total votes cast in the entire 1947 election. His margins were greatest in the Latino and Jewish sections of Boyle Heights. According to the CSO, the newly registered voters had turned out at the unbelievably high rate of 87 percent. It was a harbinger of future coalitions.[8]

Voters in Los Angeles had elected the first Mexican American councilman since 1881. This was the result of Roybal and the CSO having created a social movement to bring new voters to the polls and to realign existing voter blocs. It also represented a fulfillment of New Deal yearning and relationships that grew out of the coalition that had rallied around President Roosevelt. On another level, the Roybal election served as the political coming-of-age of the Mexican American generation in Los Angeles, the city with the largest Latino community in the United States.[9]

Being the lone minority on a council that included thirteen white Protestants and an Irish American, Roybal continued the role he had created during the campaign as a champion for all unrepresented groups. He used these relationships to assist the larger community, whether it was advocating for fair employment and housing laws, ending police brutality, or defending the rights of political minorities.

Upon taking office, Roybal introduced a fair employment ordinance, and the city's labor and minority organizations organized lobbying efforts in every city council district. The liberal-led groups refused to allow radicals to join the new civil rights coalition, the Council for Equality in Employment (CCE). Many of the affiliated groups were actively engaged in purging Communists from their own ranks; Philip Connelly, who had led the CIO and the left in support of Roybal, had been forced to resign as the head of the Los Angeles CIO Council (he became editor of the Communist West Coast daily, *People's World*). Roybal and the CSO participated in the CCE but also created a separate coalition in Roybal's council district that brought together a unified liberal left. Despite all of the organizing and the effort to associate fair employment with the highest American values, it failed by one vote—the same result as a similar measure the year before.[10]

In the developing Cold War context, Roybal stood alone on the Los Angeles City Council in voting against a council measure requiring Communists to register with the city. This won him accolades from civil libertarians and the respect of the left, which remained a powerful force in his district. Roybal also stood out as the first councilman to publicly accuse the Los Angeles Police Department of brutality after officers beat up CSO president Tony Ríos, which followed another, subsequently more infamous event.

On Christmas Eve 1951, a coterie of friends left a family gathering in Boyle Heights seeking a nightcap at the Wagon Wheel, a nearby bar. The police arrested seven young men—four Latinos and three Anglos—for disturbing the peace. While at the jail, the police officers, drunk from their own holiday revelry, responded to a false rumor that the men had killed a cop by taking turns mercilessly beating the men. The Bloody Christmas police beating was later immortalized in the movie *L.A. Confidential*. The CSO urged the men to shine a spotlight on the abuse. They declined, figuring it would only antagonize law enforcement and lead to a longer sentence.

In an unrelated incident, the police had arrested CSO president Ríos at the Carioca Café, where he had gone to pick up funds raised by the owner from selling raffle tickets. While there he intervened when two drunken patrons attacked another man. The inebriated men turned out to be undercover police officers. They arrested the thirty-nine-year-old Ríos and another man. At the police station, the two men were stripped and beaten. Only a call to the station by an alerted Councilman Roybal stopped the beating.

The CSO knew they had a historic opportunity to address the problem of police brutality because Ríos was a well-known civic leader. In addition to heading the CSO, he was active in the Catholic Church, the CIO Council, and the Democratic Party. William Barry, the Roman Catholic priest who had served on the CSO board during its formative years, said, "They beat up the wrong guy, because Ríos was a real good guy and a well known guy."[11] This emboldened Roybal to talk about the Ríos beating at an open city council meeting—a breach of unwritten rules that infuriated law enforcement, who threatened to either catch Roybal in a compromising position or otherwise "get" him. Undeterred, the CSO mobilized labor, Catholic, Jewish, and black allies who forced a grand jury to investigate and angry crowds filled the city hall chambers. Then an all-Anglo jury did the unexpected: they sided with Ríos against the police department, which had accused him of interfering with a police officer in the line of duty. This surprising victory gave the Bloody Christmas defendants—on trial in the same courthouse—new faith in the judicial system, and they talked about their own beating.[12]

Roybal's progressive and politically courageous stands infuriated conservative business interests such as the apartment owners who declared their intent to block his reelection to what were then two-year terms. The anti-Roybal forces sought to fragment the multiracial coalition and portray the councilman as not fully American because he was a minority who worked with leftists at a time the United States was battling Communists in Korea. They failed to recruit either a black or an Asian challenger but did convince Irving Rael, the popular proprietor of the Great Western Furniture Store, to run. This threatened to divide the Latino-Jewish coalition at the core of Roybal's political base.

For his part, Roybal won the backing of the AFL, which rewarded supportive incumbents, as well as the CIO, whose new Latino political director, Henry Santiestevan, shared his progressive politics. The Roybal campaign focused first on uniting the multiethnic, liberal left. The independent Citizens Committee to Re-Elect Roybal sponsored a campaign kickoff at the San Kwo Low restaurant in Little Tokyo that was attended by more than 200 people.

Bill Phillips presided. The proprietor of the music store in Boyle Heights also served as the vice president of the Soto-Michigan Jewish Community Center that offered multicultural programs and had become controversial in the larger city because it reflected the Eastside's radical political tradition. It worked, for example, with Roybal and both the CSO and the National Association of Mexican Americans, founded by leftists who had backed Henry Wallace against President Harry Truman in 1948.[13] Dr. E. I. Robinson, chair of the Central Los Angeles–based National Association for the Advancement of Colored People (NAACP), served as the master of ceremonies. The event attracted both liberals and leftists from all racial and ethnic and religious groups, including iconic figures such as Carey McWilliams.[14]

The formal Roybal campaign, the Committee to Re-Elect Councilman Roybal, mailed an issue-oriented pamphlet that served as an anchor for his reelection. Titled "Get Things Done in '51!," it stressed, "Vote For Roybal— He Votes For You!" It listed "20 Reasons Why You Should Keep Roybal," an impressive list of achievements, including "22 new traffic signals, 23 new pedestrian crosswalks, and 18 boulevard stops." The mailer also stressed Roybal's work to open public libraries, increase the number of streetcars, and fight for rent control and public housing. The mailer included the tagline "Councilman Roybal says: 'To drive out Communism, we must strike at the conditions which foster its growth.'" This slogan sought to place liberalism in a patriotic context; it also appears on the cover of the CSO's biographical publication *Across The River*.[15]

For the purpose of its diversified mail program, the Roybal campaign helped create yet another group, the Non-Partisan Committee to Re-Elect Ed Roybal. It reinforced the twenty reasons to support Roybal and the afore-mentioned tagline in a piece that sought to demonstrate the breadth of his coalition. The mailer featured a letter by African American Assemblyman (and later Roybal ally in Congress) Augustus Hawkins and listed Jewish, Latino, and ethnic Catholics as endorsers, including religious leaders such as Monsignor O'Dwyer. The group's focus, however, was placed on labor unions, which cut across ethnic lines, and the smaller minority groups within the district, including Armenians and Chinese.[16]

As Election Day approached, the liberal *Los Angeles Daily News* endorsed Roybal, calling him "our favorite councilman." The paper gushed, "Roybal has demonstrated not only great ability and deep sympathy with the needs of the people but he has proved his courage on many occasions by standing for principle when it was unpopular and politically dangerous."[17] So too did all four of the state assemblymen whose districts overlapped the council district. The four—two Anglos, a black, and a Jew—shared a commitment to liberalism and had similar individual and institutional supporters.[18] The conservative *Los Angeles Times* remained neutral.[19]

On Election Day, Roybal achieved a landslide reelection unparalleled in the history of the cosmopolitan district, besting his opponent by more than 3:1. Roybal received 17,967 votes to Rael's 5,864. Through his leadership as a councilman and a candidate, Roybal had once again demonstrated the power of coalition politics. As a result, he won over a larger share of the voting electorate, including overwhelming support in the Jewish precincts—despite having a Jewish opponent. His position on the city council was now secure; he would never again face a serious opponent for city council.[20]

The organizational growth in the Mexican American community in California and throughout the Southwest led to the formation of the liberal American Council of Spanish-Speaking People in 1951. While short lived, the umbrella body served to network emerging leaders, connecting Councilman Roybal and the CSO to Ralph Estrada of the Alianza Hispano-America in Arizona and to Dr. Héctor P. García and Gus García of the American GI Forum (AGIF) in Texas. Roybal also worked with Ernesto Galarza, who had left the Washington, DC–based Pan-American Union to organize farmworkers in California.[21] As the highest-ranking Mexican American in California, Roybal was part of two multicultural organizations formed in 1953. The California Democratic Council (CDC) dedicated itself to uniting Democrats in electing state officials.[22] The California Committee for Fair Employment Practice made Roybal a cochair and lobbied for passage of a fair employment ordinance in every session of the state legislature until its passage in 1959.[23]

Roybal used his position as the CSO's founding president to assist the growing organization that by 1955 would have fifteen chapters in California; CSO organizer Fred Ross recruited and trained talented young leaders like Dolores Huerta in Stockton and César Chávez in San Jose. Chávez recalled their first meeting: "I didn't know what CSO was, or who this guy Fred Ross was, but I knew about the bloody Christmas case, and so did everybody in the room. Five cops actually had been jailed for brutality. And that miracle was the result of CSO."[24] The group built power by sponsoring voter registration drives and citizenship classes across the state. CSO differed from other groups in their outreach to citizens and noncitizens alike. "We are endeavoring to have these potential citizens participate actively on our many committees," stated Roybal in 1953. "This, we think, will give them firsthand knowledge of the many civic problems that confront the [city council] district and will help them become better Americans."[25]

In 1954 the CDC endorsed Roybal for lieutenant governor in the June primary, which he won. Roybal agreed to undertake the uphill effort in part because he did not need to give up his council seat. Ross, now the IAF's West Coast director, was among those most excited by the prospect of the Roybal candidacy. "I don't have to draw a picture for you of the importance of this decision both with regard to the morale-heightening effect it will have on the Spanish-speaking people of California [and] facilitation of CSO's program of voter registration and membership," stated the legendary organizer.[26]

For the November 1954 election, Roybal traversed the state by automobile, campaigning before a variety of audiences, including Mexican Americans. In San Diego Roybal was "very strongly supported by the community," said educator Armando Rodríguez.[27] The excitement over having a Mexican American on the ballot likewise reached into the Central Valley, according to Richard Chávez, who helped organize the CSO in Kern County.[28] Alvina Carrillo and other Latinas in the CSO provided much of the clerical support in Roybal's Los Angeles headquarters.[29]

Despite their best efforts, Democrats lost all but one statewide election; the lone winner being Attorney General Pat Brown, who was reelected. Republicans also maintained control of the state legislature. In losing, Roybal emerged with enhanced stature because of his energetic campaigning and his receiving more votes than Richard Graves, the party's gubernatorial candidate.[30]

Roybal remained the titular head of the CSO. He attended the 1957 national CSO convention in Fresno, along with Alinsky and Franklin Williams, West Coast regional counsel to the NAACP. Roybal told the 200 delegates that Mexican Americans were progressing politically: "The sleeping giant is beginning to awaken, and it will not be long before his strength begins to be felt in the state and local elections."[31]

In 1958 Roybal ran for an open seat on the Los Angeles County Board of Supervisors with the active support of John Anson Ford, the outgoing incumbent. "He, like myself, can be described as a progressive," announced

Ford.[32] The campaign represented a bitter intraparty fight among Democrats. Roybal had the progressive Jews and the African Americans and more liberal unions such as the garment workers, auto workers, and steel workers. His opponent, liberal Councilman Ernest Debs had more moderate minorities, much of the AFL and the construction trades, and the building industry.

The November 1958 campaign concluded for Roybal (and Henry P. López, the Democratic candidate for secretary of state) in a grand, open-air rally at the corner of Brooklyn and Breed Streets in Boyle Heights, birthplace of the state's modern Latino politics. Supporters held a get-out-the-vote rally billed as a celebration of the "East Side's Favorite Sons." Grace Montañez Davis, an early CSO leader who oversaw the Roybal headquarters in her part of the city for the runoff, stated that she was "very optimistic, we felt like we had a good chance . . . [and] we worked hard to get people out. There was just an incredible amount of response in terms of volunteers."[33]

On election night, Roybal trailed ever so narrowly, with additional absentee ballots yet uncounted. Election officials ordered a recount of the hand-calculated results. On Thursday, two days after the election, the Los Angeles County Registrar of Voters announced that Roybal had won by 393 votes— 139,800 to 139,407. Then something happened. That night the county registrar discovered boxes of previously uncounted votes. These newly located ballots gave Debs a 12,000-vote margin. Friday morning, Roybal supporters protested the results, complaining about election irregularities, but no new election was called. A disheartened Roybal accepted the official results, although he and his supporters believed that he had been robbed of an important election victory.[34]

This was a difficult time for Roybal and his supporters. The frustration came to a boiling point at the CDC convention in March 1959 in Fresno. "I called a meeting of all the Hispanic delegates and talked to them about organizing a political organization," stated Roybal. "We came to the conclusion that . . . Governor Brown and those on the ticket, did not fully support [López]," the only statewide Democratic candidate to lose in a historic sweep that also saw the party of Roosevelt win control of the state legislature.[35] As a result, the forty-seven-year-old councilman was still the only Mexican American to occupy any of the top 300 elected positions in California.[36] Juan Acevedo, the group's organizing secretary, explained, "Roybal's job is to be the Godfather or Elder Statesman."[37] This led to the formation of MAPA at a founding convention in Fresno, April 22–24, 1960. The group elected Roybal as president by acclamation.

The 1960 presidential campaign presented an opportunity for Roybal to demonstrate the growing importance of the Mexican American vote. He attended the Democratic National Convention as a delegate supportive of Senator Adlai Stevenson. When Senator John F. Kennedy won the nomination, Roybal signed on to head a new group, Viva Kennedy, in California. Carlos McCormick led the national organization and had ties to three major organizations. McCormick had married the daughter of Ralph Estrada, the head of the Arizona-based Alianza Hispano-Americana; he had become the AGIF's chief contact in Washington, DC; and his Mexican American mother was a member of the CSO in Santa Barbara, California, through whom he met CSO executive director César Chávez, who helped register 140,000 new voters for the 1960 election.

Roybal and other Viva Kennedy leaders in the Southwest looked to President Kennedy to reward Mexican Americans with a number of high-level federal appointments. Roybal was one of three major contenders for deputy assistant secretary of state for Inter-American Affairs. Senator Dennis Chávez and McCormick supported Roybal's candidacy, but the State Department decided to select a person with diplomatic experience: Arturo Morales-Carrión, who had served as secretary of state for Puerto Rico.[38] Unmet expectations led Roybal to express frustration with Kennedy and served as an impetus for a radicalized Chicano movement, important elements of which rejected the Democratic Party and existing middle-class organizations.[39]

The 1961 reapportionment of congressional districts, combined with the state's ever-growing population, presented an opportunity to elect Mexican Americans to office. The state legislature turned down Roybal's request to design majority Latino legislative and congressional districts. Instead, they drew several districts Roybal or other Mexican Americans could win. Roybal recognized that he could get elected to Congress if he followed the model he successfully employed thirteen years earlier to win the city council seat: build a multiracial, working-class coalition. He set his sights on a new Democratic-leaning district that started in Boyle Heights and moved westward across downtown to Hollywood. His toughest possible opponent, Judge William Rosenthal—formerly the assemblyman from Boyle Heights—agreed not to run, making it possible for Roybal to reassemble his important Latino-Jewish alliance.

Assemblyman Jesse Unruh, a Kennedy ally and longtime rival of CDC-affiliated liberals, backed one of Roybal's primary opponents, William Fitzgerald, a professor at Loyola Marymount University. Unruh's actions dismayed Mexican American leaders. So severe were the differences within the Democratic coalition that McCormick flew to California in an effort to mitigate the damage. In a meeting with the MAPA board of directors, McCormick, then assistant to the chairman of the Democratic National Committee, reiterated the White House's commitment to Mexican Americans. He likewise made it clear to Democratic Party leaders that the president would be pleased to see California send a Latino to Congress.[40]

Roybal won the primary election easily; his fall 1962 campaign emphasized his support for Kennedy and the president's domestic agenda. The Kennedy administration aided Roybal and a number of other Democratic congressional candidates by inviting them to the White House for a series of policy briefings and to have their photos taken with the president. Roybal mailers featured the councilman interacting with Abraham Ribicoff, the Jewish Secretary of Health, Education and Welfare; Robert Weaver, the African American head of the federal Housing and Home Finance Agency; and former first lady and liberal icon Eleanor Roosevelt. Roybal spoke to a myriad of groups and hundreds of volunteers walked door-to-door on his behalf.[41]

The hoped-for highlight of the fall campaign—a personal visit to the congressional district by President Kennedy planned for October 27—never happened, owing to the Cuban Missile Crisis. But the White House did issue a letter endorsing Roybal, which he used in a mailer.[42] His liberal coalition was augmented by the Democratic Party's get-out-the-vote drive paid for in part by Kennedy. As a result, Roybal won 56 percent of the vote in the racially and ethnically diverse district. Mexican Americans likewise won two state assembly seats. He was the first Latino to represent the state in Congress since 1883.

Congressman Roybal marched for civil rights, backed an end to the Bracero program (whereby Mexican nationals worked in US agriculture), and supported President Lyndon Johnson's War on Poverty programs to benefit his low-income constituents. Anger grew within the Mexican American community that African Americans were getting a disproportionate amount of federal largess. Roybal used his office to lobby for Mexican American–oriented programs and appointments. He sent the names of "qualified Spanish-speaking individuals" to federal agency heads.[43]

Roybal joined Mexican American organizational leaders in June 1965 at the Mayflower Hotel in Washington, DC, for a Great Society conference, under the aegis of the Democratic National Committee. Johnson hosted the group that evening at the White House. When Johnson failed to follow up on his promise to sponsor a White House conference, anger grew among middle-class activists. Roybal sought to remain close to activist groups while nudging a recalcitrant White House ever more forcibly. To ratchet up the pressure, Roybal convinced the California Democratic Congressional Delegation to approve a resolution calling on Johnson to address Mexican American concerns. The message was unambiguous. An internal White House memorandum stressed that Roybal and colleague George Brown "are increasingly concerned about themselves, and incidentally the President." Soon thereafter, Johnson invited Roybal and other dignitaries to the White House when he signed an executive order creating a cabinet-level Inter-Agency Committee on Mexican American Affairs.[44]

Roybal's chief legislative achievement during this period was passage of the nation's first bilingual education bill. It was formally an amendment to the Elementary and Secondary Education Act of 1967. Johnson pledged to sign the bill while he and Roybal were riding on Air Force One. The president memorialized the agreement with a photo of the two men flying on the presidential plane.[45]

Other images from 1968 show Roybal meeting with predominately Mexican American high school students in Los Angeles after they walked out of classes under the banner of the United Mexican American Students. Congressman Roybal and Los Angeles School Board of Education member Julián Nava mediated between administrators and students. Roybal expressed his support for "constructive educational objectives of the majority of student protestors."[46]

On the issue of Vietnam, Roybal was always more antiwar than the other Mexican Americans in Congress. Roybal and twenty-nine other congressmen announced their opposition to Johnson's bombing of North Vietnam in 1967, and he was one of sixty-seven to ask Johnson to request United Nations mediation. As an indication of the growing antiwar sentiment in California, MAPA voted in mid-1968 to oppose the Vietnam War. In 1970 Roybal endorsed the Chicano Moratorium in East Los Angeles.[47]

Roybal founded the Congressional Hispanic Caucus in 1976 to unite Mexican Americans and Puerto Ricans in order to magnify the Latino voice in civic debate. He founded the National Association of Latino Elected and Appointed Officials to bring together officials at federal, state, and local levels. He supported Tom Bradley's election as Los Angeles's first African American mayor; the 1949 "Roybal coalition" provided a template for Bradley's multiracial alliances.[48] Roybal's inclusive approach also served the interest of the Latino community, which itself grew increasing diverse. The dramatic increase in Latino voters has increased their geographic, ethnic, and ideological differences as well as the growth in the number of female and openly gay Latino elected officials.

In 1982, at age sixty-six, after serving two decades in Congress, Roybal assumed the chair of the House Select Committee on Aging. He served as its chair until his retirement in 1993. He exercised influence as a member of the Appropriations Committee and chair of the Appropriations Subcommittee on Treasury, Postal Service, and General Government. He obtained funding for a host of worthwhile causes, such as fighting HIV / AIDS. In 2001 President Bill Clinton awarded an ailing Roybal the prestigious Presidential Medal of Honor. He passed away four years later, at age eighty-nine.[49]

"The sleeping giant," that Roybal said in 1957 was "beginning to awaken" is now fully alert and active beyond what most of that generation of activists could have imagined. This is due in part because of the voter registration drives that he encouraged, starting in 1948, and the subsequent arrival of millions of Mexicans and Central Americans—and their offspring—who have become part of the state's economic, cultural, and civic life. These new voters have provided the political base to elect thousands of Spanish-speaking elected officials at all levels of government. Within the state legislature, the Latino Caucus holds great sway; this, and a recognition of intergroup relations, has resulted in four of the last eight Assembly speakers being Latino (along with two African Americans, an Anglo lesbian, and a Jewish man married to a Latina).

This coalition building among political elites and voters is an important and sometimes overlooked aspect of the Roybal legacy. Roybal, like a substantial number of the state's Latino Legislative Caucus, was elected from districts without a majority of Latino voters. Roybal's three key victories— for city council in 1949 and 1951 and for Congress in 1962—were based on progressive coalitions that included Jews, African Americans, Asians, ethnic Catholics, labor, and the liberal left. This core Roybal support was likewise present in his campaigns for lieutenant governor and county supervisor. In these cases it was sufficient to come in first in the primary or initial election but insufficient in the runoff or general election. This is not a repudiation of coalition politics but a reflection of partisan trends in 1954 and being either out-organized or defrauded in 1958.

Congresswoman Lucille Roybal-Allard, his daughter, and other officials at the dedication of the Los Angeles Unified School District's Edward R. Roybal Learning Center in 2008 stressed ethnic empowerment and pointed to Roybal as a Latino political pioneer. Mayor Villaraigosa articulated that the late congressman represented a Latino first but also was the architect for coalition politics. This reflected both an understanding of history and his experiences as a former Assembly speaker and the first Latino mayor of Los Angeles. For while the growth in the number of Latino politicians and voters has forever changed the political dynamic within the state and nation, the Roybal model of coalition politics has proved to have enduring value in an increasingly multicultural society.

Notes

1. The Roybal story is central to Kenneth C. Burt's *The Search for a Civic Voice: California Latino Politics* (Claremont, CA: Regina Books, 2007). For insights on his electoral coalitions, see Katherine Underwood, "Process and Politics: Multiracial Electoral Coalition Building and Representation in Los Angeles' Ninth District, 1949–1962" (PhD diss., University of California, San Diego, 1992). For biographical material, see Himilce Novas, *The Hispanic 100: A Ranking of the Latino Men and Women Who Have Most Influenced American Thought and Culture* (New York: Citadel, 1995), 81–85.

2. Members of County Central Committees, May 1944, Los Angeles County Registrar of Voters and Roosevelt Good Neighbor rally program, box 2, folder 3, Eduardo Quevedo Papers, Department of Special Collections and University Archives, Stanford University.

3. Roger Johnson, interview by author, December 19, 1981; and Edward Roybal, interview by author, March 10, 1995.

4. Juan Gómez-Quiñones, *Chicano Politics: Reality and Promise, 1940–1990* (Albuquerque: University of New Mexico Press, 1990), 53–54; Robert Gottlieb et al., *The Next Los Angeles: The Struggle for a Livable City* (Berkeley: University of California Press, 2005), 31; and Sanford D. Horwitt, *Let Them Call Me Rebel: Saul Alinsky, His Life and Legacy* (New York: Knopf, 1989), 227–35.

5. Josh Sides, *L.A. City Limits: African American Los Angeles from the Great Depression to the Present* (Berkeley: University of California Press, 2004), 153.

6. Edward Roybal, interview by author, March 20, 2001.

7. Rebecca Tuck interview by author, Los Angeles, September 27, 1997.

8. Many of the CSO-registered voters were not in the council district; the largest concentrations of Mexican American voters were in the unincorporated areas of East Los Angeles. This reinforced the need for an electoral alliance. Kenneth C. Burt, "The Power of a Mobilized Citizenry and Coalition Politics: The 1949 Election of Edward R. Roybal to the Los Angeles City Council," *Southern California Quarterly* 85 (Winter 2003): 413–38; and Underwood, "Process and Politics," 92–114.

9. George J. Sánchez, *Becoming Mexican American: Ethnicity, Culture and Identity in Chicano Los Angeles* (New York: Oxford University Press, 1993), 250; and Zaragosa Vargas, *Labor Rights Are Civil Rights: Mexican American Workers in Twentieth-Century America* (Princeton: Princeton University Press, 2005), 275.

10. For a discussion of the changing civil rights coalitions during the Cold War, see Kenneth C. Burt, "The Fight for Fair Employment and the Shifting Alliances among Latinos and Labor in Cold War Los Angeles," in *Labor's Cold War: Local Politics in a Global Context*, ed. Shelton Stromquist (Urbana: University of Illinois Press, 2008), 79–109.

11. William Barry, interview by author, November 2, 1994.

12. Kenneth C. Burt, "Tony Rios and Bloody Christmas: A Turning Point Between the Los Angeles Police Department and the Latino Community," *Western Legal History* 14 (Summer/Fall 2001): 159–92; and Edward J. Escobar, "Bloody Christmas and the Irony of Police Professionalism: The Los Angeles Police Department, Mexican Americans, and Police Reform in the 1950s," *Pacific Historical Review* 72 (May 2003): 171–99.

13. Rodolfo Acuña, *Occupied America: A History of Chicanos*, 3rd ed. (New York: HarperCollins, 1988), 294; and George J. Sánchez, "'What's Good for Boyle Heights Is Good for the Jews': Creating Multiracialism on the Eastside during the 1950s," *American Quarterly* 56 (September 2004): 633–61.

14. This led the Communist Party's *People's World* to call the committee the "broadest that has been seen in many a political moon" and resulted in the FBI monitoring the fundraiser. "Reaction Begins Its Drive Against Edward Roybal," *People's World*, February 19, 1951, 5 and memo, March 21, 1951, CSO FOIA FBI File, in author's possession.

15. CSO, *Across The River*, box 4, folder 31, United Steelworkers of America (USWA), District 38 Records, Historical Collections and Labor Archives, Special Collections Library, Penn State University and "Get Things Done in 51!," pamphlet, in author's possession. Shanna Bernstein cites the anti-Communist phrase in her CSO

case study to examine "the way civil rights groups looked to each other for strength and support as they struggled to establish their moderate stance and legitimacy in this conservative climate." "Building Bridges at Home in a Time of Global Conflict: Interracial Cooperation and the Fight for Civil Rights in Los Angeles, 1933–1954" (PhD diss., Stanford University, 2004), 221.

16. "Non-Partisan Committee to Re-Elect Ed Roybal," brochure, box 9, folder LA CIO Council Committees: PAC Corres., Jan. 1951–Apr. 1951, Los Angeles County Federation of Labor Collection, 1937–1975, Special Collections and Archives, Oviatt Library, California State University Northridge.

17. "As the Daily News Sees Council Race," *Los Angeles Daily News*, March 13, 1951.

18. "Assemblymen Back Ed Roybal for Reelection," *Los Angeles Citizen*, March 23, 1951.

19. "The Contests for Council," *Los Angeles Times*, March 31, 1951.

20. Election results, 1951, Los Angeles City Archives and Underwood, "Process and Politics," 125.

21. *Civil Liberties Newsletter*, 1951–1953, box 13, folder 1, Ernesto Galarza Papers, Department of Special Collections and University Archives, Stanford University.

22. Henry P. López, interview by author, January 4, 1982; and Frederick B. Tuttle, Jr., "The California Democrats: 1953–1966" (PhD diss., UCLA, 1975), 57.

23. Burt, "Fight for Fair Employment," 79–109.

24. Jacques Levy, *César Chávez: Autobiography of La Causa* (New York: W.W. Norton, 1975), 98.

25. David G. Gutiérrez, *Walls and Mirrors: Mexican Americans, Mexican Immigrants, and the Politics of Ethnicity* (Berkeley: University of California Press, 1995), 171.

26. Fred Ross to Edward Roybal, February 16, 1954, box 9, folder CSO–2, Edward C. Roybal Papers, Chicano Studies Research Center, University of California, Los Angeles (hereafter Roybal Papers).

27. Armando Rodríguez, interview by author, April 5, 2003.

28. Richard Chávez, interview by author, April 16, 2005.

29. Charlotte Negrete White, "Women in the Political Process: The Community Service Organization of East Los Angeles" (classroom paper written at Claremont College, December 5, 1994).

30. "GOP Knight, Dem Roybal Strong Men," *Daily Mirror* (Los Angeles), November 4, 1954.

31. "NAACP Aide Says State Lacks Minority Rights," *Fresno Bee*, March 24, 1957; and other items in box Newspaper Clippings, folder 1957, Roybal Papers.

32. "Ford Names Roybal As Choice For His Job," *Roybal Newsletter*, Spring 1958, box 132, folder 18, 1, Roybal Papers.

33. Katherine Underwood, "Pioneering Minority Representation: Edward Roybal and the Los Angeles City Council, 1949–1962," *Pacific Historical Review* 66 (August 1997): 420.

34. "Complete L.A. Vote Returns: 10,000-Vote-Error; Roybal Upsets Debs," *Los Angeles Evening Herald and Express*, November 6, 1958, 1; "Es Posible Que Se Investigue el Caso Debs-Roybal," *La Opinión*, November 7, 1958, 1; Johnson interview; and Hope Mendoza Schechter, interview by author, September 3, 1994.

35. Roybal interview. See also Ralph C. Guzmán, *The Political Socialization of the Mexican American People* (New York: Arno, 1976), 143–44.

36. Fernando J. Guerra, "The Emergence of Ethnic Officeholders in California," in *Racial and Ethnic Politics in California*, ed. Michael B. Preston, Bruce Cain, and Sandra Bass (Berkeley: Institute of Governmental Studies Press, 1998), 2:117–32.

37. Juan Acevedo, interview by author, November 3, 1981.

38. Carlos McCormick, telephone interviews by author, April 3, 1984 and June 1984.

39. Carlos Muñoz, Jr., *Youth, Identity, Power: The Chicano Movement*, revised edition (New York: Verso, 2007), 61–76.

40. McCormick interview, April 4, 1984.

41. Box Newspaper Clippings, folder 1962, Roybal Papers.

42. "Presidential Tour Slated for District," *30th CD Demo* and campaign mailer of White House letter, October 23, 1962, box Newspaper Clippings, folder 1962, Roybal Papers.

43. Box 177, folder "Recommendations—Mexican-Americans, 1963–1969," Misc. docs., box 177, Roybal Papers and Julie Leininger Pycior, *LBJ and Mexican Americans: The Paradox of Power* (Austin: University of Texas Press, 1997), 154–55.

44. Box 177, folder "Mexican-American White House Conference," Misc. docs., Roybal Papers; Irv Sprague to Joe Califano, quote from memo, March 1, 1967, in folder "Mexican American Conference (2)," Office Files of Irvine Sprague, container 7, LBJ Library.

45. Roybal interview. The photo was on display in Roybal's office at California State University, Los Angeles during this period.

46. "Roybal Supports Objectives of Student Protest," *Eastside Sun*, March 14, 1968, Newspaper Clippings, Roybal Papers.

47. "30 Congressmen Ask LBJ to Halt Bombing," *Herald Examiner*, October 13, 1967; and Lorena Oropeza, *¡Raza Sí! ¡Guerra No! Chicano Protest and Patriotism During the Viet Nam War Era* (Berkeley and Los Angeles: University of California Press, 2005), 66–67, 152.

48. Raphael J. Sonenshein, *Politics in Black and White: Race and Power in Los Angeles* (Princeton, Princeton University Press, 1994); and Raphael J. Sonenshein,

"Coalition Building in Los Angeles: The Bradley Years and Beyond," in *Seeking El Dorado: African Americans in California*, ed. Lawrence B. de Graaf, Kevin Mulloy, and Quintard Taylor (Los Angeles: Autry Museum of Western Heritage, 2001), 450–72.

49. "Edward R. Roybal Legacy Gala," www.naleo.org/aboutroybal.html.

Conclusion

Anthony Quiroz

This collection shares the accomplishments of a salient portion of what historians refer to as the Mexican American generation. Struggling for change on numerous fronts, including equal access to public schools, the right to a jury of their peers, and fair treatment for workers, they sought a better place in American society for themselves and their brethren from all walks of life. To be sure, most of these figures had undergraduate, if not graduate degrees. Certainly some of them were active in LULAC, an organization deemed to have been solidly middle class. But once one digs beneath the surface, the nature of all these individuals emerges as one dedicated to the resistance of the oppressive status quo for all Mexican Americans.

So I have made it a point to include people who operated in a variety of venues. Luisa Moreno and Ernesto Galarza, for example, indicate that this was a complex generation that cannot be homogenized. These two individuals worked very closely with workers and their organizations seeking fair wages and decent working conditions. They disagreed with other members of this generation, but I pose that, similar to the Progressive Era—a time

DOI: 10.5876/9781607323372.c014

in American history that was marked by a zeitgeist for change but which manifested itself in different, often contradictory ways—so too did this generation move for change, but in separate ways. Yet underneath the surface was always a dedication to Mexican culture and traditions and a belief in the promise, if not the reality, of American society.

As I mentioned in the introduction, the generational model of historical interpretation can tell us a lot about the trajectory of Mexican American identity formation. Each generation left its own imprimatur. For the Mexican American generation, the legacy was a bicultural identity and being rooted in American society. The years between 1920 and 1960 were crucial to forming Mexican American identity and defining the shape of the civil rights struggle. A small but dynamic middle class of attorneys, teachers, professors, and doctors led the fight for equality among Mexican Americans. These professionals embraced a set of commonly accepted ideals that defined American citizenship, such as patriotism to the United States, and an acceptance of the values, practices, traits, and beliefs that defined the daily stuff of citizenship. As such, they promoted equality, political action, and hard work—all central ingredients required of Americans. This clearly American identity also shaped the parameters of the ensuing civil rights struggle. Due to their deeply held loyalty to the nation, much of this group of activists embraced the weapons of the citizenry: union organization, the ballot box, and the lawsuit.

In defense of the generational model, I argue that the generational boundaries we have created make sense. Yet it is important to remain sensitive to the nuances of such structures. Many participants of the Mexican American generation were active well after 1960. Evidence in these biographies indicates the ways in which the generation had its roots in events prior to 1920 and certainly had an impact well after the onset of the Chicano movement, which began in the early 1960s with Cesar Chavez's actions in California and Reies López Tijerina's land reclamation movement in New Mexico. Ana Luisa Martinez-Catsam has demonstrated the ways in which *El Regidor* proclaimed a bicultural identity as early as the 1880s. Similarly, Tijerina (one of four central figures in the Chicano movement) was active in the late 1950s. In 1962 he created La Alianza Federal de Mercedes, which later helped lead the land reclamation movement in New Mexico and which was involved in several "radical" acts such as the occupation of federal lands at Carson National Forest and the shootout at the Tierra Amarilla courthouse. Chavez developed the National Farm Workers Association in 1962 but had been an organizer for the Community Service Organization since the 1950s.

From these essays, we see the emergence of the two earliest national civil rights organizations: the League of United Latin American Citizens and the American GI Forum. And out of this period of activism grew the Mexican American Legal Defense and Educational Fund, the Congressional Hispanic Caucus, and the National Council of La Raza. The continued existence of these organizations into the present day indicates the legacy of this generation. While the Chicano movement offered other new institutions such as Movimiento Estudiantil Chicano de Aztlán and Chicano studies departments, which helped begin to ensconce Mexican American history in academe, these new and important contributions did not replace these other groups. Indeed, as the Hispanic generation emerged, the traditional view of this generation still holds sway in many parts of the country, attesting to the lasting value of the idea and actions of the Mexican American generation.

Scholars, including myself, have struggled to build gender into their narratives—not as a sidelight but as Linda Kerber once reminded me, as a foundational principle. While I could not impose gendered structures on the individual contributions to this volume, I tried very hard to include the stories of women. And because of the tendency to marginalize women away from the "real story," I have chosen to not have a separate segment for the few women who appear here. Indeed, I suggest that we all need to integrate women more richly into the fabric of our analyses, just as we wish to see Mexican Americans more deeply enveloped in the larger narrative of American history.

This diversity of experience and the resultant attitudes drive this work. Previous authors had tended to homogenize this generation as middle-class people who pursued whiteness and who were willing to sell out their *Mexicanidad* in order to secure a richer place in society. The authors included in this collection, however, challenge those notions and offer us a new way to think about this generation and its leaders. Thus, this work stands as a piece of revisionist history as it attempts to place these actors in a new light.

I would like to use this opportunity to issue a call for more biographical scholarship on all generations of Mexican American history. Other important leaders such as George I. Sánchez and Bob Sánchez were not addressed in this work but need to be. Certainly a biographical collection of leaders such as José Ángel Gutiérrez, Reies López Tijerina, Mario Compeán, Rodolfo

"Corky" Gonzales, and others would be of tremendous value to the field. This is particularly true at a time when places such as the state of Texas are trying to encourage the development of Mexican American studies at community colleges and universities. As the Mexican American population grows in size, its impact will only grow. That growth can be channeled into a positive direction through adequate education in all areas. The continued presence of this population can be better understood through a deeper understanding of our past and our struggles for inclusion.

Contributors

Carl Allsup holds a PhD in history from the University of Texas at Austin. He taught at the University of Wisconsin–Platteville for several decades, where he also served as chair of the Ethnic Studies Department. He is author of *The American GI Forum: Origins and Evolution* (Austin: Center for Mexican American Studies, University of Texas at Austin, 1982).

Kenneth C. Burt is the political director of the California Federation of Teachers and the author of *The Search for a Civic Voice: California Latino Politics* (Claremont, CA: Regina Books, 2007). A longtime visiting scholar at the University of California, Berkeley, Burt graduated from Berkeley and Harvard University. He has chapters in numerous anthologies relating to Latinos and politics, labor, and the Cold War. His book, *The Search for a Civic Voice*, has received accolades within academic circles and in the press.

Patrick J. ("Pat") Carroll is a professor of history at Texas A&M University–Corpus Christi. He is the author of two books: *Blacks in Colonial Veracruz: Race, Ethnicity, and Regional Development* (Austin: University of Texas Press, 1991) and *Felix Longoria's*

Wake: Bereavement, Racism, and the Rise of Mexican American Activism (Austin: University of Texas Press, 2003), winner of the Tullis Memorial Prize in Texas history. He is a former department chair and has published numerous book chapters and peer-reviewed articles in a range of publications. He is frequently invited to give talks on his areas of specialization at academic venues around the nation.

María Eugenia Cotera teaches at the University of Michigan in the Departments of American Culture and Women's Studies and in the Latino/Latina Studies Program (of which she is a past chair). She has edited two volumes: *Caballero: A Historical Novel* (College Station: Texas A&M University Press, 1996) (with José E. Limón) and *Life along the Border: A Landmark Tejana Thesis*, by Jovita González (College Station: Texas A&M University Press, 2006). She has also published several articles and essays in various collections and peer-reviewed publications.

Richard A. Garcia is a professor in the History Department at California State University, East Bay. He is an American intellectual and cultural historian with a teaching and publishing emphasis on Mexican American history and Mexican American / Latino cultural studies. His other areas of interest are ethnic history, Southwest and California history, history and theory, biography, and American cultural studies. Garcia is the author of numerous books, including *The Chicanos in America, 1540–1974: A Chronology and Fact Book* (Dobbs Ferry, NY: Oceana, 1977); *Political Ideology: A Comparative Study of Three Chicano Youth Organizations* (San Francisco: R and E Research Associates, 1977); *Rise of the Mexican American Middle Class: San Antonio, 1929–1941* (College Station: Texas A&M University Press, 1991); the award-winning *César Chávez: A Triumph of Spirit* (Norman: University of Oklahoma Press, 1995) (with Richard Griswold del Castillo); *Notable Latino Americans: A Biographical Dictionary* (Westport, CT: Greenwood, 1997) (with Matt S. Meier and Conchita Franco Serri), which won a CHOICE outstanding book award for 1997; *Ethnic Community Builders: Mexican Americans in Search of Justice and Power* (Lanham, MD: Altamira, 2007) (with Francisco Jiménez and Alma M. García); and the soon-to-be-published *Mexican Americans: Essays of History, Culture, and Thought*. He also was the coeditor of *Race and Class* (2001) and the consulting editor for a 1995 special issue on Mexican Americans in California in *California History*. He is also the author of several articles, including "Religion as Language, Church as Culture: Changing Chicano Historiography" in *Reviews in American History* 34 (December 2006), and has presented research at numerous professional conferences in several countries.

Michelle Hall Kells is an associate professor in the Department of English at the University of New Mexico, where she teaches graduate and undergraduate classes in twentieth-century civil rights rhetoric, contemporary and classical rhetoric, writing and cultural studies, and discourse studies. She serves as Special Assistant to the Dean of the College of Arts and Sciences and program chair of the Writing Across Communities initiative at UNM. Kells received the LBJ Presidential Library Research Fellowship in 2008. She is a Senior Fellow at the Robert Wood Johnson Foundation Center for Health Policy at UNM. Kells's research interests include civil rights rhetorics, sociolinguistics, and composition/literacy studies. Kells is coeditor (with Valerie M. Balester) of *Attending to the Margins: Writing, Researching, and Teaching on the Front Lines* (Portsmouth, NH: Heinemann, 1999) and coeditor (with Valerie M. Balester and Victor Villanueva) of *Latino/a Discourses: On Language, Identity, and Literacy Education* (Portsmouth, NH: Heinemann, 2004). Her work has been featured in the journals *JAC, Written Communication, Reflections*, and *Rhetoric and Public Affairs*, as well as in a number of edited books, including *Cross-Language Relations in Composition; Dialects, Englishes, Creoles, and Education;* and *Who Belongs in America? Presidents, Rhetoric, and Immigration*. Kells is the author of *Héctor P. García: Everyday Rhetoric and Mexican American Civil Rights* (Carbondale: Southern Illinois University Press, 2006). Her current book project is *Vicente Ximenes and LBJ's "Great Society": The Rhetoric of Mexican American Civil Rights Reform*.

Thomas H. Kreneck served as Associate Director for Special Collections and Archives and was the Joe B. Frantz Lecturer in Public History at Texas A&M University–Corpus Christi. Prior to coming to Texas A&M University–Corpus Christi in 1990, he was assistant manager of the Houston Metropolitan Research Center. He specialized in the development of research resources on the Mexican American experience and was a 2006 Fellow of the Texas State Historical Association. He has authored, edited, and coedited nine books, including *Mexican American Odyssey: Felix Tijerina, Entrepreneur and Civic Leader, 1905–1965* (College Station: Texas A&M University Press, 2001).

Laura K. Muñoz is an associate professor of history at Texas A&M University–Corpus Christi. She has published numerous pieces for works such as *The Oxford Encyclopedia of Women in World History*, ed. Bonnie G. Smith (New York: Oxford University Press, 2007) and *Latinas in the United States: A Historical Encyclopedia*, ed. Vicki L. Ruiz and Virgina Sánchez Korrol (Bloomington: Indiana University Press, 2006). She has also published (with Julio Noboa) "Hijacks and Hijinks on the US History Review

Committee," in *Politics and the History Curriculum: The Struggle over Standards in Texas and the Nation*, ed. Keith Ereckson (New York: Palgrave MacMillan, 2012). Further, she won the Claude A. Eggertsen Dissertation Prize from the History of Education Society in 2007 and received a National Academy of Education/Spencer Postdoctoral Fellowship in 2011.

Cynthia E. Orozco earned her BA from the University of Texas at Austin and her MA and PhD from UCLA. She has taught at the University of Texas at San Antonio and the University of New Mexico. She currently teaches at Eastern New Mexico University in Ruidoso. She served as a research associate at the Texas State Historical Association, where she contributed eighty short essays on various aspects of Texas history. The TSHA subsequently named her a fellow in 2012. She was also appointed by the governor of New Mexico to the New Mexico Humanities Council. She is a coeditor (with Emilio Zamora and Rodolfo Rocha) of *Mexican Americans in Texas History* (Austin: Texas State Historical Association, 2000) and an associate editor of *Latinas in the United States: A Historical Encylopedia* (Bloomington: Indiana University Press, 2006). She has authored *No Mexicans, Women, or Dogs Allowed: The Rise of the Mexican American Civil Rights Movement* (Austin: University of Texas Press, 2009).

Julie Leininger Pycior is a professor in the Department of History at Manhattan College in New York State. She has authored two books: *LBJ and Mexican Americans: The Paradox of Power* (Austin: University of Texas Press, 1997) and *Chicanos in South Bend: Some Historical Narratives* (Notre Dame, IN: Centro de Estudios Chicanos e Investigaciones Sociales, 1976). She has also edited *Bill Moyers, Moyers on America: A Journalist and His Times* (New York: New Press, 2004, reprinted in paperback, 2005). In addition, she has published several journal articles and has two book manuscripts in process.

Anthony Quiroz is a professor of history at Texas A&M University–Corpus Christi. He is past chair of the Department of Humanities at TAMUCC. He has published *Claiming Citizenship: Mexican Americans in Victoria, Texas* (College Station: Texas A&M University Press, 2005, reprinted in paperback, 2013. He is also the author of several book chapters and peer-reviewed journal articles.

Vicki L. Ruiz is Dean of the School of Humanities at the University of California, Irvine. A leading Chicana historian, she has served as president of the Organization of American Historians, president of the Berkshire Conference of Women's Historians, and president of the Pacific Coast Branch of the American Historical Association. She has written or coauthored ten books, three of which have won major awards.

Emilio Zamora is a professor in the Department of History at the University of Texas at Austin. He specializes in Mexican American history, Texas history, oral history, and transnational (US/Mexico) working-class history. Zamora has authored three books, coedited three anthologies, assisted in the production of a Texas history text, and written numerous articles. He has garnered three best book awards, a best article prize, and, in 2007–2008, a Fulbright García-Robles fellowship. Zamora's latest publications are *Claiming Rights and Writing Wrongs in Texas: Mexican Workers and Job Politics during World War II* (College Station: Texas A&M University Press, 2008) and (coedited with Maggie Rivas-Rodríguez) *Beyond the Latino World War II Hero: The Social and Political Legacy of a Generation* (Austin: University of Texas Press, 2009). He is a member of the board of the Labor and Working-Class History Association, a member of the advisory committee of the Voces Oral History Project (formerly the U.S. Latino and Latina WWII Oral History Project) at the University of Texas, a member of the advisory board of the Mexican American Cultural Center in Austin, and a member of the advisory board of the Recovering the U.S. Hispanic Literary Heritage Project, based at the University of Houston.

Index

Bolded page numbers indicate illustrations.

acculturation, 90, 96, 109, 115n20; Perales's process of, 96, 99, 103–6

ACGA. *See* Arizona Cotton Growers Association

ACLU. *See* American Civil Liberties Union

ACSSP. *See* American Council of Spanish Speaking People

AFL. *See* American Federation of Labor

AGIF. *See* American GI Forum

Alianza Hispano-Americana, the: civil rights advocacy, 292, 293; court cases and, 285, 286, 288–91; Estrada and, 18, 278, 279, 285–94

Allsup, Carl, 349; *The American G.I. Forum*, 263; on Héctor Pérez García, 16, 191–205

Alma Latina (LULAC publication), gender ideology in, 60

Alvarez, Rodolfo, on generational periodization in Mexican American history, 7–8

American citizenship. *See* Americanism; citizenship; class issues; identity

American Civil Liberties Union (ACLU), involvement in court cases, 287, 288, 291, 294

American Council of Spanish Speaking People (ACSSP), 39, 287, 333; and the desegregation movement in Arizona, 287–88; and Viva Kennedy clubs, 292

American Federation of Labor (AFL): and immigrant exclusion, 309–11; and Luisa Moreno, 146, 148, 154; in political campaigns, 327, 330, 334

American GI Forum (AGIF): California chapter, 200; against educational segregation, 196–97, 204, 219; and the El Paso hearings, 269; *The Forumeer* (monthly newsletter), 4; Forumeers, xiv, 193; and Gus García, 16, 175, 223, 224; and Héctor Pérez García, 192–96, 198–205, 206n23, 219; history of, xiii, 4, 193–196, 261–63; and immigrant laborers, 201–2, 204; inception of, 4, 16, 192, 193, 241; and the Longoria controversy, 175, 177, 194, 195; members, characteristics of, xiii, 9, 202; and *mestizaje*, 202; as "outside agitators," 194; participation in Operation Wetback, 201; and Vicente Ximenes, 18, 255–63, 265

FEPC. *See* Fair Employment Practices
Committee
Food, Tobacco, Agricultural, and Allied
Workers of America (FTA), 153–54. *See also*
United Cannery, Agricultural, Packing, and
Allied Workers of America (UCAPAWA)
FTA. *See* Food, Tobacco, Agricultural, and
Allied Workers of America

Galarza, Ernesto, **300**; early life of, 19, 302, 303;
education of, 302–7; and the El Paso hearings, 270; family of, 302–4, 314; labor activism
of, 19, 301, 304, 307–12, 314–16, 345; legacy of,
316; and the NFLU, 307–12; and the OEO, 313,
314; and the PAU, 305–7, 332; Pycior on, 19,
301–16; research of, 301, 303–6; as scholar-activist, 301–2, 311; Symposium, 316. *See also
works of by name*
Galarza, Ernesto, works of: *Barrio Boy*, 19,
102, 302; *Merchants of Labor*, 312; "Mexico
in the World War," 303; *Rimas Tontas*, 314;
*The Roman Catholic Church as a Factor in the
Political and Social History of Mexico*, 303;
Strangers in Our Fields, 311; *Thirty Poems*,
305
García, Gregorio "Greg," attorney, 285–89, 294;
"*Guerra al Prejucio Racial*" (with Estrada), 286
García, Gustavo "Gus" C., **208**, **276**; and alcoholism, 221–23; court cases, 17, 212–20; early
life, 210, 211; family, 210, 211, 220; education,
211; and Herrera, 211, 216, 219–23, 229, 230,
240–46; legacy of, 223–25; military service
of, 211; and Montemayor, 71; and Perales, 91,
108; Quiroz on, 16, 17, 209–25; work with
LULAC and AGIF, 16; Ximenes on, 223
García, Dr. Héctor Pérez, **190**; Allsup on, 16,
191–205; and the Civil Rights Acts of 1964
and 1965, 199; criticisms of, 170, 171, 200,
204; early life, 191; education, 191; family,
165, 191; as founder of the American GI
Forum, 16, 163, 175, 177, 192, 193, 196–98;
as "giant of the twentieth century," 16, 191,
205; and immigrant labor, 200–1; legacy of,
181–82, 203–205, 257, 273; and the Longoria
controversy, 16, 163, 167–71, 175–81, 194–95;
and LULAC, 196; military service of, 192;
and Lyndon B. Johnson, 198–200, 204; and
Operation Wetback (1954), 201; and Ximenes,
259–62, 264–70

García, Mario T.: on generational periodization, 8, 49n2; *Mexican Americans*, 8, 49n2,
59; other works, 11, 22n17; on the Mexican
American generation, 8, 11, 165–66
Garcia, Richard A.: on Perales, 14, 85–111; *Rise
of the Mexican American Middle Class*, 59
gender ideology, viii, 58, 61, 65, 72; challenging, 60–61, 69, 72; in LULAC publications,
60–62, 69. *See also* feminism; feminist(s);
Montemayor, Alice Dickerson
generation: Chicano (1960–1980), ix, 7, 14,
197, 199, 257 (*see also* Chicano movement;
Chicano studies); conquered (1848–1900), 7;
Hispanic (1980–present), viii, 7, 9, 197, 204,
347; immigrant (1900–1930), 7; Mexican
American (1930–1960), viii–x, xiv, 7–12, 14, 17,
18, 26, 39, 165, 191, 197, 203, 278, 328, 345–47.
See also generational model; generational
periodization
generational model, discussion of, viii–ix, 7–8,
39, 49n2, 346. *See also* generation; generational periodization
generational periodization, 7–8. *See also* generation; generational model
G.I. Bill of Rights (1945), 192
González Mireles, Jovita, **118**; career, 120;
Cotera on, 15, 119–38; creation of Spanish
education programs, 136, 137; and Dobie,
15, 125–34; early life, 119–24; education and
research, 124, 125, 129–32; family, 119–121,
134–37; as feminist, 136; prejudice against, 15,
129; and the Texas Folklore Society, 124–28,
132, 133. *See also works of by name*
González Mireles, Jovita, works of: "Among
my People," 130; "The Bullet-Swallower,"
130; *Caballero*, 135, 136, 138; contribution
to *Our Racial and Ethnic Minorities*, 133;
contribution to Spanish-language textbooks,
137; *Dew on the Thorn*, 131, 138; "Folklore of
the Texas-Mexican Vaquero," 128; folklore
publications, 125, 128–30, 132; memoirs, 119,
124, 136–38; "Shades of the Tenth Muse," 134;
"Social Life in Cameron, Starr and Zapata
Counties (1930)" (thesis), 129, 130; "Tales and
Songs of the Mexican Vaquero," 130
Great Depression, impact of, viii, 3, 4, 59, 66,
285, 325
Grounding of Modern Feminism, The (Cott), 57